FACING THE
SEA OF SAND

FACING THE SEA OF SAND

The SAHARA *and the* PEOPLES OF NORTHERN AFRICA

BARRY CUNLIFFE

OXFORD

UNIVERSITY PRESS

OXFORD
UNIVERSITY PRESS

Great Clarendon Street, Oxford, OX2 6DP
United Kingdom

Oxford University Press is a department of the University of Oxford.
It furthers the University's objective of excellence in research, scholarship,
and education by publishing worldwide. Oxford is a registered trade mark of
Oxford University Press in the UK and in certain other countries

© Barry Cunliffe 2023

The moral rights of the author have been asserted

First Edition published in 2023

Published in the United States of America by Oxford University Press
198 Madison Avenue, New York, NY 10016, United States of America

British Library Cataloguing in Publication Data
Data available
Library of Congress Control Number: 2022943247
ISBN 978–0–19–285888–7

Typeset by Sparks—www.sparkspublishing.com

Printed in Great Britain by
Bell & Bain Ltd., Glasgow

PREFACE

T HE Sahara is the greatest of the world's hot deserts, extending for a distance of 6,000 kilometres across Africa from the Atlantic Ocean to the Red Sea, creating a formidable barrier between the communities surrounding the Mediterranean and those who inhabited the rest of sub-Saharan Africa. For many scholars in the nineteenth century the desert was seen as an insuperable obstacle preventing the spread of the benefits of Western civilization. Admittedly the Nile created a corridor along which complex and creative societies flourished—Egyptians, Nubians, and others—and the Red Sea allowed traders from the Mediterranean to reach the Indian Ocean, benefiting African polities, like the kingdom of Axum, able to control essential ports on the eastern shore. But all this was consistent with the current belief that the cultural advances and inventions that formed the basis of civilization came from the Near East: the *ex oriente lux* hypothesis as it became known. People living in remote parts of the world didn't invent things: they simply benefited from the brilliance of others through the process of diffusion.

Overt diffusionism of this kind, still popular in some quarters into the early twentieth century, came under increasing attack as more was learnt of cultural development in different parts of the world through archaeological exploration. Yet it was a view of Africa still widely held well into the middle of the century. To some extent such a perception was understandable. Archaeological endeavour in sub-Saharan Africa had concentrated on the exciting issue of human origins and early Palaeolithic developments: there had been little effort spent on exploring the complexity of later sites.

All this was to change in the 1960s, when far more attention began to be focused on the study of settlements, especially in the Sahel—the zone of steppe and savannah lying beyond the southern edge of the Sahara—and in the desert itself. The new data that began to be published threw an entirely different light on questions of social complexity, state formation, and connectivity, allowing more subtle and sophisticated

narratives to be presented in the flurry of books on African archaeology published since the 1990s. Understandably these texts have focused on the African achievement and have tended to play down the contribution of the Mediterranean and the Near East. It was a valuable and necessary corrective, but it has created something of a new bias.

Any attempt to write a balanced account of the desert and its surrounding communities comes up against the problem of the disparity of the database. For the Mediterranean and the Near East, including Egypt, archaeological activity since the eighteenth century has produced a massive amount of detailed information about settlements, burials, religious sites, artefacts, and ecofacts. In addition to this, there is a rich historical record, in some instances going back nearly five thousand years. Greek, Phoenician, Carthaginian, and Roman sources provide a detailed picture of the impact of classical civilizations on North Africa, while later, Arab and other medieval texts become increasingly more informative. For sub-Saharan Africa the situation is very different. The tradition of research excavation had hardly begun by 1960, and thereafter, although there have been major advances in knowledge, the actual number of investigations has been minimal compared to the work undertaken in North Africa. Nor does the documentary record offer much compensation since it does not begin until the Arab traders started to take an interest in the region in the eighth century.

At the time of writing, political unrest throughout much of the Sahel is making archaeological work difficult and dangerous, and elsewhere in the Saharan region, in Libyan territory, the unstable situation has brought productive fieldwork programmes to a premature close. Since there is little prospect that any large-scale work will resume in the immediate future, the imbalance in the evidence base is likely to remain, at least for a while.

That said, work since the 1960s has enabled us to begin to appreciate the energy and complexity of the communities who lived around and within the desert, and to trace change over time. It has thrown new light on how they responded to changing environmental conditions as the desert margins shifted, and how, gradually, the links between neighbours grew to become a complex pattern of communication routes embracing the entire desert, binding north to south. So, in 1324, Mansa Musa and his entourage, with eighty camels, could set out with little concern across the desert from Mali to Cairo and on to Mecca, to return safely; and in 1591 a Moroccan force of three thousand infantry and fifteen hundred light cavalry, with six cannons, could cross the desert to confront the Songhai empire. Like the ocean, the sea of sand, far from being a barrier, became alive with movement.

This book, then, is about change, connectivity, and the compulsions that made humans challenge the desert. What it sets out to do is to show that Africa and Eurasia are one great landmass bound together by their shared history.

Questions of nomenclature inevitably arise when dealing with a complex area like Africa. Three points need clarification here. The indigenous peoples of much of the northern parts of Africa referred to themselves as Amazigh (pl. Imazighen) in the Tifinagh language, but in the literature they are usually called Berbers, a term used by the Arabs that was originally derived from the Greek *barbaroi*, meaning 'those who speak unintelligible languages'. We have chosen to use this more familiar name. 'Sudan' is another potentially confusing term. Nowadays we recognize it as the name of a nation state, but strictly it refers to the whole of the sub-Saharan Sahel, coming from the Arabic 'Bilad al-Sudan', meaning 'the land of the blacks'. When it is used as a geographical term in this sense, we will refer to 'the Sudan': the political entity will be called, simply, 'Sudan'. Finally, a distinction must be made between Mauritania, a modern state in West Africa, and Mauretania, the region of north-west Africa covering much of Morocco which became a Roman province.

B.C.
Oxford
September 2022

CONTENTS

1 The Desert, the Rivers, and the Oceans   1

2 The Long Beginning   37

3 Domesticating the Land, 6500–1000 BC   63

4 Creating Connectivities, 1000–140 BC   103

5 The Impact of Empire, 140 BC–AD 400   145

6 An End and a Beginning, AD 400–760   183

7 Emerging States, AD 760–1150   213

8 Widening Horizons, AD 1150–1400   255

9 Africa and the World, AD 1400–1600   293

10 Retrospect and Prospect   337

A Guide to Further Reading   355

Illustration Sources   385

Index   391

I

THE DESERT,
THE RIVERS, AND
THE OCEANS

H UMAN beings, like all living things, are at the mercy of the environment they
        choose to inhabit. But the environment is never still: it is constantly chang-
        ing, sometimes imperceptibly, sometimes with unsettling rapidity. The
underlying bedrock—the solid geology—provides a degree of stability. Its configura-
tion may create physical barriers or facilitate movement, it may offer mineral resources,
and under certain conditions it can become an aquifer storing life-sustaining water
beneath the surface. It also degrades into fertile soil as climate and plant life interact
with it. But the climate, too, is never still. Cyclic variations in the movement of the
earth drive changes, forcing regions of lush grassland to become deserts and then to
change back again.

   Human agency may also affect the environment. The management of large flocks
and herds can create soil erosion, exacerbating the onset of desertification, while
the development of a technology to capture water from the aquifers can transform
deserts into green and productive gardens and pastures. There are few places in the
world where the intricate dynamic between humans and their environment can be better understood than the northern part of the African continent, where the fearsome
Sahara desert dominates all.

1.1 The Sahara, so clearly seen from space, is the largest hot desert in the world. The image gives an immediate sense of the geography of northern Africa, with the rainforest belt to the south gradually giving way to woodland, savannah, and then steppe as the desert is approached. It also shows the desert reaching the Mediterranean except for the Maghrib, with the Atlas Mountains forming the backbone, the tip of Cyrenaica, and the Nile delta, zones where Mediterranean vegetation clings to the land.

Bedrock

Two hundred and fifty million years ago, in the Permian period, Africa, like all other parts of the world, belonged to a single landmass named Pangaea surrounded by the Ocean. But in the molten magma of the earth's core, constant currents put stresses on the solid surface crust, causing it to crack into large plates, some of which pulled apart from each other, allowing in the Ocean, while others collided, rucking up the edges to become mountain ranges. By sixty-five million years ago, the great landmass of Africa had torn free from what was to become the American continent, and other plates, later to become India, Australasia, and Antarctica, had broken away from its eastern side, Australia and Antarctica to flow south, while India, along with Africa, moved north, eventually colliding with Eurasia, leaving a narrow arm of the Ocean, called the Tethys Sea (now the Mediterranean), to separate North Africa and Europe.

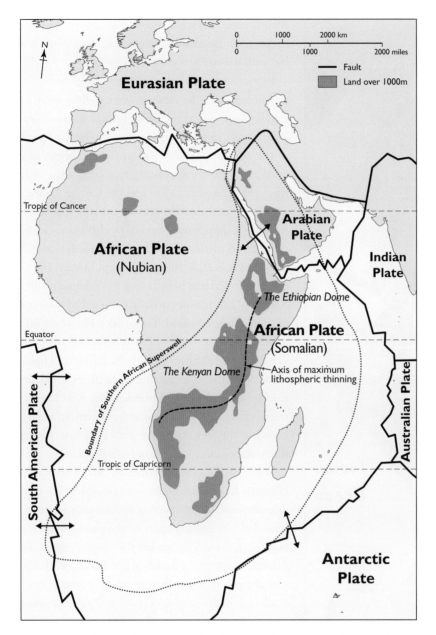

1.2 Africa began to take on its familiar shape when, in the mid Cretaceous period, the great landmass of Pangaea began to break up into plates. Pressure from the earth's core pushed up the hard crust (lithosphere), causing it to thin and crack. The African plate split into the Nubian and Somalian plates and pulled apart, the cracks creating the rift valleys.

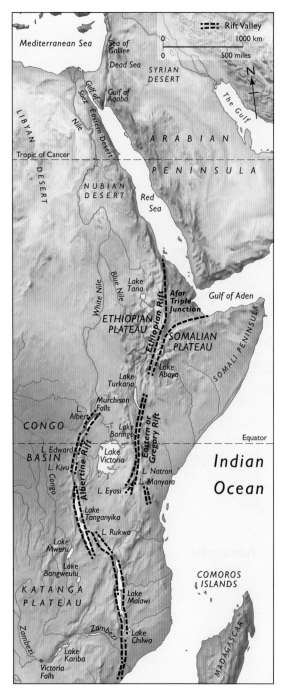

By this stage Africa had more or less achieved its present shape, with the island of Madagascar now broken away, but with the Arabian plate still attached.

In more recent geological times fragmentation has continued, with the Arabian plate pulling away, creating the Red Sea and the Gulf of Aden. Meanwhile, East Africa was experiencing new tensions as the upwelling of the viscous mantle of the earth's core began to push up the surface crust, creating two great areas of highland, the Ethiopian Dome and the Kenyan Dome. The stress was such that the crust eventually split, forming rift valleys, deep fissures flanked by cliff-like escarpments up to 1,000 metres high. There are three major fracture lines, the Albertine Rift, or Western branch, the Gregory Rift, or Eastern branch, and the Ethiopian Rift. The Albertine Rift is now partially occupied by a succession of sinuous lakes, Malawi, Tanganyika, Kiva, Edward, and Albert, while the Gregory Rift is home to Lake Turkana. The Ethiopian Rift tore through the Ethiopian Highlands to join with the wider parting of the plates, filled now by the Red Sea and the Gulf of Aden. The African rifts represent a fracture zone created as the eastern strip of Africa, known as the Somalian plate, pulls away from the rest of the continent, the African (or Nubian) plate.

Many of the characteristics of Africa that were to influence human behaviour were created by the tectonic movements that give structure to the continent. Its coasts, caused by the pulling apart of the plates, were, for the most part, sheer. This has left the country, especially the Atlantic coast, with a dearth of good ports, while the virtual absence of a continental shelf has meant that fish stocks are poor—a disincentive to the development of

1.3 The rift valleys run from southern Mozambique to the Red Sea, at the northern end joining the wide fissures created by the drifting apart of the African and Arabian plates. The Albertine Rift valley is, for the most part, filled with lakes.

1.4 The rift valleys are defined, for much of their length, by steep cliffs where the earth's crust has fractured and the plates have moved apart. The lowlands between provided congenial environments favourable to the evolution of humans, the wide corridors encouraging migration. The image is of the Great Rift Valley in Kenya.

sailing. The creation of a narrow protected passage, now the Red Sea and the Gulf of Aden, did, however, provide a convenient route for the maritime trade between the Mediterranean and the Indian Ocean which began to become more intense in the third century BC, and this encouraged the growth of ports along the African shore to the benefit of the communities commanding them. The Ethiopian Highlands had a rather different effect. Their elevation ensured heavy rainfall, and it was this that fed the Nile. The river, eroding the uplands as it flowed, generated a heavy load of sediment, which was deposited in the lower reaches of the valley as alluvium, so crucial for maintaining the fertility of the land. It was this upon which the prosperity of the Egyptian and Nubian states depended. The special microclimate of the highlands also supported a distinctive flora, including several plants that could be cultivated for food (p. 77 below).

The Ever-Changing Climate

When the German traveller Heinrich Barth made his epic journey across the Sahara to Timbuktu in 1850–4, he was astonished to discover scenes of humans and animals painted and carved on rock surfaces in remote regions of the desert. That the animals depicted were no longer to be found there posed a problem. So too did the authorship. He could not believe them to be the work of uncivilized tribesmen. 'No barbarian could have graven the lines with such astonishing firmness, and given to all the figures the light, natural shape which they exhibit.' The images, he suggested, were probably carved by Carthaginians, but that the animals the artists chose to represent could not possibly have existed in the prevailing desert conditions showed that the climate had once been far more congenial. This was the first indication that the Sahara had not always been a desert. Subsequent work has shown not only very many more images of the kind Barth discovered—so many that one observer has described the Sahara as the largest art gallery in the world—but has provided sound evidence to allow the many changes of climate experienced by North Africa to be carefully charted over the last twenty thousand years.

Climate change is a complex process caused by the interplay of many factors. In the 1920s the geophysicist Milutin Milanković suggested that the underlying drivers were shifts in the orbital parameters of the earth caused by the gravitational interaction of the earth with the moon and the larger planets. He identified three effects, precession of the equinoxes, obliquity, and eccentricity, each occurring in cycles of different periodicity. Of these, precession of the equinoxes is now known to be the prime cause of major changes in the climate experienced by the Sahara, creating a shift from

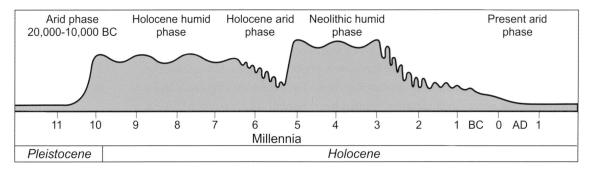

1.5 Changes in climate over the millennia had a dramatic effect on vegetation. Although the factors causing climate change were largely due to cyclic changes in the earth's orbit and inclination, they impacted on different areas in different ways. The diagram shows changes in humidity in the Fazzan from the end of the last ice age to the present day. For much of that time the climate, with its long humid phases, was far more suited to human occupation than it is now.

dry to wet over a span of twenty thousand years, after which the process goes into reverse. Two phases can be recognized, the one related to the wobble of the earth's axis of rotation, the other to the slow rotation of the earth's elliptical orbit round the sun. It is during this phase that the northern hemisphere is turned more directly towards the sun and absorbs more heat. Because of the lower thermal inertia of the land, the northern African landmass heats up more than the adjacent Atlantic Ocean, creating an area of low pressure. This draws in moist air from the Ocean, bringing summer monsoonal rains. During the winter the land cools, reversing the winds, returning the land to drier conditions. The greater the angle of the earth, and the more of the land-mass that is heated in summer, the further north the monsoonal rains penetrate. As the angle swings back, the process goes into reverse. Thus, precession of the equinoxes directly determines the extent of the greening or the desertification experienced by the Sahara over a twenty-thousand-year cycle.

The astronomical cycles that control the desert climate also drive the formation and thawing of the ice sheets over the northern part of the hemisphere, so there is a direct chronological relationship between the two phenomena. In the period when the ice sheets were at their greatest, during the Last Glacial Maximum, the Sahara desert was at its most extensive, but as the northern hemisphere began to warm and the ice melted, heralding the beginning of the Holocene period, so the desert became moister. This phase is known as the African Humid Period. The process began around 12,800 BC but was soon interrupted by the onset of a brief cold interlude known as the Younger Dryas period (10,900–9700 BC), triggering the expansion of the desert. Humidification quickly resumed and the Sahara became green again, the phase lasting until about 3000 BC when desertification began once more, by the end of the first millennium BC reaching a state comparable to that of the present day. Through the long humid period, from 9500 to 3000 BC, the climate of North Africa fluctuated, with several hot, dry episodes interrupting the predominant cool, damp norm. One, rather more persistent than the others, began about 6100 BC and lasted for almost a millennium. As we will see later, it had a significant effect on hunter-gatherer communities (pp. 63–5 below).

Charting the climatic fluctuations of the African Humid Period has challenged the ingenuity of scientists, leading to several quite separate studies being undertaken in different parts of the continent. One looked at changes in lake levels over the last twenty thousand years, the levels relating directly to precipitation. Another measured oxygen isotope concentrations in fossil foraminifera (single-cell organisms with shells) in ocean sediments accumulating in the river Niger outflow. Since the levels are directly related to salinity, and salinity is a factor of the volume of fresh water outflow, oxygen isotope levels are a proxy for rate of precipitation. In a third study, cores taken through the sediments which had accumulated in Lake Tanganyika enabled hydrogen isotopes from fossil leaf waxes to be measured: the higher the reading, the thicker the wax, representing a more arid climate. Finally, ocean cores taken off the west coast of Africa showed a variation in the thickness of the lenses of dust blown offshore from the Sahara, the variation reflecting the changing aridity of the desert. What is particularly satisfying about these varied studies is that the results are very closely comparable, providing a detailed and reliable picture of climate change over the last twenty thousand years.

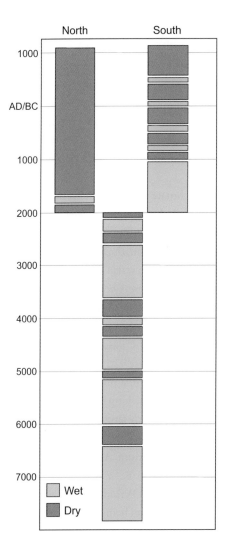

One of the surprising features which all these studies show is the suddenness of the onset of high humidity at the end of the Younger Dryas about 9700 BC. The transition lasted only a few centuries. At the end of the humid period, the change to desert conditions, beginning about 3000 BC, was also relatively rapid but was spread over a longer period of time and the many fluctuations were not exactly synchronous in all parts of the region. In the eastern Sahara, core sediments suggest a more gradual end to the humid period. There are also differences between patterns recorded to the north and south of the desert. In the north the land reverted rapidly to desert and remained so without alleviation. This could be because the area lay in the rain shadow of the Atlas Mountains and westerly airstreams off the Atlantic lost much of their moisture content on the western flanks of the range. In the south there was no impediment to the inflow of moist air from the ocean and the transition to desert was slower.

1.6 Even in comparatively small regions like the Western Sahara there were times when the effects of climate change differed from one subregion to another. The diagram shows that after 2000 BC the northern part of the Sahara remained continuously dry while the southern regions enjoyed episodes of more humid weather.

These changes in climate had a direct effect on human settlement and economy. One elegant study, focusing on settlements

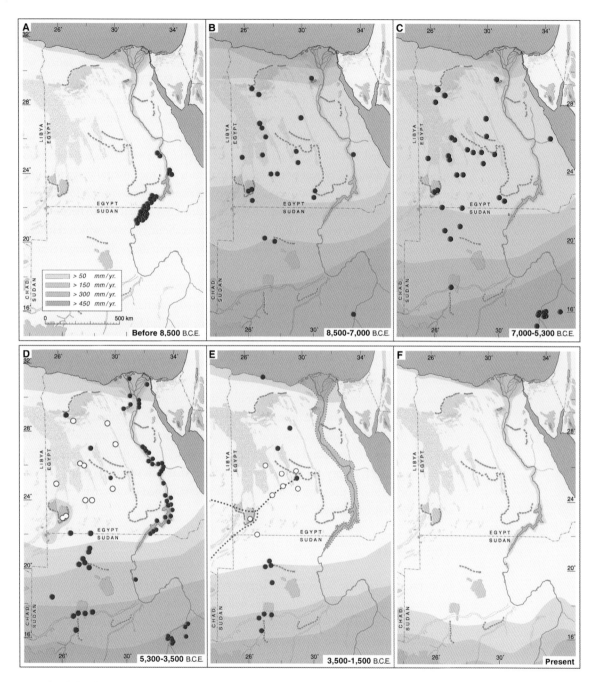

1.7 A detailed archaeological survey carried out in the eastern Sahara shows how climate change over five thousand years had a dramatic effect on where communities lived. The colours on the maps indicate rainfall zones measured in millimetres of rain per year.

9

in the eastern Sahara identified in the course of intensive fieldwork, shows this in a dramatic way. During the Last Glacial Maximum and the late stages of the Pleistocene, up to about 8500 BC, when extreme desert conditions prevailed, the eastern Sahara was totally devoid of settlement except for the valley of the Nile. With abrupt onset of the monsoon rains (8500–7000 BC) heralding the humid period, savannah spread widely across the area that had once been desert and hunter-gatherers followed, colonizing much of the region. As the humid optimum set in (7000–5300 BC), the density of settlement increased, but the higher rainfall meant that the Nile valley was too marshy for human habitation. The retreat of the monsoonal rains and the onset of desertification, beginning here about 5300 BC, saw a retreat of settlement southwards into areas still savannah and into the Nile valley, which had now dried out sufficiently to become habitable once more. The return to full desert conditions about 3500 BC, which restricted the community to the Nile valley, was one of the factors that drove the changes that led to the emergence of Egyptian civilization.

The long African Humid Period was of crucial significance in the development of North Africa. In the ninth millennium BC, it allowed communities of hunter-gatherers to spread wide throughout a vast region that for long had been a barren desert and to devise economic strategies suited to the environments they chose to inhabit. During this time, people learnt to domesticate plants and animals, and networks of communication became increasingly extensive. Then, around 5300 BC, desertification began to set in, and gradually, over the next two millennia, as the desert expanded, people were forced to move on to find environments where life could be sustained. Some moved north to the Mediterranean coast and the Atlas Mountains, others went south to the narrow corridor of steppe and savannah between the desert and the dense tropical forest, leaving, largely empty, the wide expanse of desert that now separated them. The rest of the story is about the ways in which people re-established connectivity across and around the desiccated waste.

The Desert

In its present state the Sahara is the largest hot desert in the world, a band of largely desolate, barren waste 1,800 kilometres wide, stretching for 6,000 kilometres across Africa from the Atlantic Ocean to the Red Sea. In Arabic *sahra*, meaning desert, was used as a proper noun for the first time by the Egyptian historian Ibn Abd al-Hakam in the ninth century AD.

For the most part the desert is of comparatively low relief, seldom above 1,000 metres, and is composed of rocky plateaux (hamada), stretching away in an endless monotony, some areas polished by the wind, others (regs) strewn with loose rock and

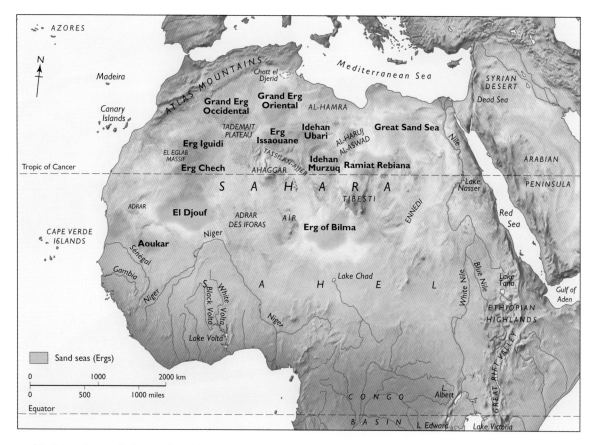

1.8 The Sahara desert is far from uniform. There are mountain ranges sufficiently high to attract precipitation and huge areas of sand sculpted into ever-changing dunes by the wind. Between, much of it is barren, rocky lowlands.

gravel. There are also vast seas of sand (ergs), which in places can be whipped by the wind into dunes 200 metres high. But within all this dun-coloured desolation arise ranges of spectacular mountains where rainfall is sufficient to allow plants and animals, including humans, to survive. The mountain massifs have very different characters. The Aïr Mountains of Niger are composed largely of granite, creating a plateau 500– 900 metres high with high domes rising to 1,800 metres. The Ahaggar Mountains of southern Algeria are composed of metamorphic rocks once penetrated by volcanoes. Subsequent erosion of the cones of soft ash has left the central plugs of lava standing gaunt in the austere landscape up to a height of 2,900 metres. Here rains are sufficient to support a relict wildlife including cheetahs and, until recently, West African croco- diles. In south-eastern Algeria the Tassili-n-Ajjer (Plateau of Rivers) is different again,

1.9 The ergs, or seas of sand, occur extensively within the Sahara and provide the classic image of the desert, but a far greater area is of rocky rubble or bare rock. The image is of the Erg Chebbi, Morocco.

1.10 (*Opposite top*) The Ennedi plateau, Chad, is one of the upland regions of the Sahara. It rises to about 1,500 metres and is composed largely of sandstone. High precipitation creates perennial springs like that feeding the Guelta d'Archei waterhole enjoyed by camels in the photograph.

1.11 (*Opposite bottom*) The Ahaggar Mountains are formed by ancient volcanoes, the ash cones of which have been eroded over time, leaving only the plugs of lava still standing proud. The high precipitation rate has allowed a relict fauna and flora from the earlier Holocene Humid Period to survive.

a sandstone upland rising to 2,100 metres dissected, as its name suggests, by river valleys. The highest of the Sahara's mountains are the Tibesti of northern Chad, rising to the peak of Emi Koussi at 3,445 metres. Much of the range is volcanic, with domes of lava and old craters, one 20 kilometres across, carved by deep canyons created by the intermittent rainfall.

These areas of upland, capturing what little moisture there is, are enclaves of life. Intermittent rain, falling mainly in August and September, creates rivers that flow for a while, to disappear in the desert, adding water to the aquifer beneath. It is sufficient to

green the landscape and to provide for human existence. But during the long African Humid Period things were very different. There was a richness of wildlife, providing first for hunter-gatherers and later for communities who had learnt to domesticate plants and animals. In the exuberance of being, they recorded their animals and their lives in the galleries of rock paintings and engravings that so astonished European travellers in the nineteenth and twentieth centuries.

The desert bears the scars of the former more humid periods: the wadi, where the rivers once flowed, and the dried-up lake basins. Some of the basins, especially those below present sea level, still receive rainwater, which, where the rock is impermeable, remains on the surface and is evaporated by the sun to create salt lakes. The largest of these is Chott el-Djerid in southern Tunisia, its name meaning 'Lagoon of the Land of Palms'. Here the saline marsh extends for over 7,000 square kilometres. Chott el-Djerid is only about 25 metres below sea level. Egypt's Qattara Depression is much larger and deeper—up to 133 metres below sea level—but the area of salt marsh within it is much less extensive. Elsewhere in the Sahara salt marshes were at one time more widespread, but with the rapid increase in desertification after 3000 BC they have gradually dried up, leaving thick deposits of salt—an extremely valuable commodity which was, and still is, widely traded.

The fourteenth-century traveller Ibn Battuta gives a vivid account of salt production at Taghaza, in the western Sahara, on the caravan route midway between Morocco and Timbuktu. It was, he tells us, an unattractive village, its buildings constructed of blocks of salt and roofed with camel skins. Nearby, slaves dug out salt in slabs and traders came up from the south to acquire it. 'The business done at Taghaza, for all its meanness, amounts to an enormous figure in terms of hundredweights of gold-dust.' At the town of Walata a load of salt was worth about an ounce of gold: by the time it reached Mali, it was valued at thirty or more times as much. They 'use salt as a medium of exchange just as elsewhere gold and silver are used: they cut it up into pieces and buy and sell with it'. The volume of salt on the move was considerable. In the nineteenth century, the salt mines at Bilma, between the Aïr and Tibesti mountains, employed between twenty and thirty thousand people a year to distribute salt throughout the region and to the more distant markets.

The Sahara desert is, by definition, an area of low rainfall. Such humidity as there is is brought in by two different systems. In the north a low-pressure system over the Mediterranean draws in moisture in winter from the Atlantic, while in the south the arrival of the Intertropical Convergence Zone—a continuous belt of low-pressure systems—coming from the south-west brings some cloud and rain. In the regions influenced by these systems, precipitation can reach between 100 and 250 millimetres a

1.12 Within the desert are salt lakes like the Chott el-Djerid, in Tunisia, shown here, where the mineral content of the water has been concentrated by evaporation, forming salt crusts. In parts of the desert, salt deposits formed millennia ago were, and still are, quarried to provide slabs of salt for trade.

year. Much of the central areas, however, seldom receives more than 20 millimetres, with some regions of the eastern Sahara having less than a millimetre. With lack of cloud cover allowing very high ground temperatures to develop, the evaporation rate is considerable. It is only really in the mountain regions, where sudden downpours can bring intermittent rivers briefly to life, that the rainwater can sink to the aquifers deep below the surface out of the sun's reach. The aquifers are expanses of porous rock holding water that has accumulated over hundreds of thousands of years. Many exist beneath the Sahara. The largest is the Nubian Sandstone Aquifer System, which underlies much of the eastern Sahara including most of Egypt, north-western Sudan, north-eastern Chad, and south-western Libya and is thought to contain 150,000 cubic kilometres of water. Another huge system, the Bas Saharan Basin, lies beneath much of Algeria, Tunisia, and parts of Morocco and Libya. These two vast aquifers feed many of the oases in the Sahara, the water being forced to the surface by pressure of the rocks above squeezing the saturated rocks deeper down. It was the oases that made it possible for networks of communication to thread through the desert.

Around the Desert

The desert is created, as we have seen, by the interplay of annual weather patterns. The dominant Intertropical Convergence Zone creates a low-pressure zone over the land, drawing in moist air from the Atlantic to fill it. The annual movement of this zone between 15–20° north and 8–16° south brings seasonal changes to the southern side of the desert. The northern side is affected by moist air flowing into the Mediterranean from the Atlantic. Together the systems control the zonation of vegetation flanking the desert to north and south.

South of the desert the changing zones of vegetation run south, more or less parallel with the latitude, as far as 8–6° north, where lies the edge of the dense rainforest filling the Congo basin and extending in a wide band along the Atlantic coast as far west as Sierra Leone, except for the Ghana-Bénin Gap, where woodland savannah reaches as far south as the Ocean. From the southern edge of the desert, formally recognized as the 150-millimetre isohyet (the line joining places of equal rainfall), to the edge of the equatorial rainforest, the vegetation grades from desert steppe to savannah with scrub and scattered trees and then to grassland savannah, a mixed grassland and woodland ecosystem where the trees are so spaced that there is no canopy closure. Gradually the tree cover increases through a forest–savannah mosaic before it gives way to rainforest proper. The wide band of steppe and savannah provides an open corridor stretching from the Atlantic coast to the Ethiopian Highlands. That part of the corridor that fringes the desert and forms a strip 1,000 kilometres wide is known as the Sahel, an Arabic word meaning 'the shore', reminding us that to the Arabs the desert was a sea. The Arabs also referred to the great plain south of the Sahara as 'Bilad al-Sudan', 'the land of the blacks'.

The northern edge of the desert corresponds with the 100-millimetre isohyet, which is roughly the northern limit of date palm cultivation. Beyond this lies a narrow band of desert steppe reaching the Mediterranean along much of its eastern length, but in Cyrenaica and in the west—the Maghrib—giving way to hilly, sometimes mountainous, land which enjoys a Mediterranean climate shared with much of southern Europe. The western Maghrib is dominated by the Atlas Mountains, rising to heights of over 3,000 metres, above which the Mediterranean vegetation gives way to steppe. The coastal zone of North Africa benefited not only from its moister climate but also from its maritime interface, which allowed its inhabitants to exploit the sea as a means of easy communication. As the various Mediterranean states rose to dominance, so

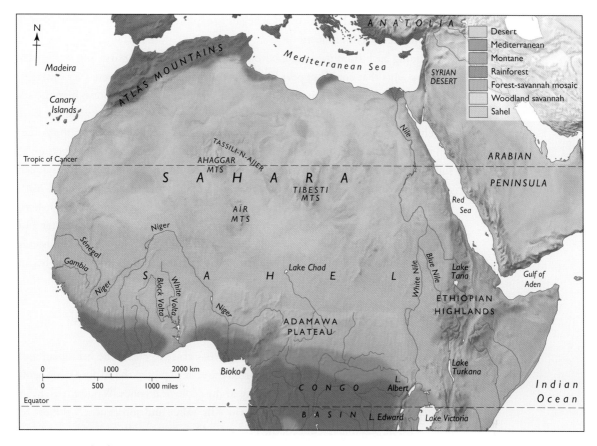

1.13 The zones of different vegetation covering the northern part of Africa run roughly east to west except where areas of uplands, like the Ethiopian Highlands and the Adamawa plateau in Cameroon, interrupt the symmetry. The map shows the situation today. When the climate changes, the boundaries of these zones move to the north or south.

North Africa was drawn into their orbit. From the sixteenth century, the whole region was known as Barbary, a word ultimately derived from Berber, the name the Greeks gave to the inhabitants of North Africa.

There remain the eastern and western limits of the Sahara to consider—zones where the desert faces the sea. Both are uncongenial, at best uninviting, desert steppe. The Red Sea coast is the more barren, seared by hot easterly winds blowing from the Arabian Desert. The Atlantic coastal zone is a little less hostile since it benefits from moist air from the Ocean. Although both of the maritime interfaces have ecozones where life could be supported, they played little part in human connectivity until trading ships from Ptolemaic Egypt began to use the Red Sea as a route to India in the third century BC and the Portuguese began to explore routes down the west coast of Africa in the fifteenth century.

Standing back from the detail, beyond the desert fringes to north and south were environments that could support human communities, but they were very different. The southern zone was contained between desert and equatorial forest: here the sea offered little useful connectivity. People could move easily within the zone but were largely cut off from the rest of the world. For the region north of the desert the potential was quite different. Here the long maritime interface facilitated the integration of the zone into a broad network of connectivity, including not only the Mediterranean and Europe but also the Near East and ultimately the Eurasian steppe and China. Inevitably the pace of cultural change for communities living along the northern fringe of the desert, bombarded by these disparate influences, was much faster and more intense than it was for those who lived to the south. Two very different systems emerged, and it was not until the latter part of the first millennium BC that they began to become aware of each other.

Distorting Factors

The tectonic pressures that pushed up the earth's crust to create the Ethiopian and Kenyan domes 75 million years ago distorted the eastern part of the African continent, interrupting the neat east–west regularity of the ecological zones. While the Kenyan Dome, fractured by the various arms of the Rift Valley and subsequently subject to heavy erosion, was much reduced, the Ethiopian Dome retained much of its integrity. It is the largest continuous mountain massif in Africa, reaching heights of 4,550 metres and seldom falling below 1,500 metres. The Great Rift Valley, which sliced through the middle of the dome, split it into three parts, one pulling away to become the mountainous region of what is now the south-western corner of the Arabian peninsula. Its former position, known as the Afar Triple Junction, though later filled with lavas and sediments, is still clearly visible in the relief of the region.

The Ethiopian Highlands, by virtue of their location close to the equator and in the path of the monsoon rains coming from the Indian Ocean, enjoy a mild, damp climate with a rainy season lasting from June until September, which creates a distinctive island of montane vegetation in the uplands above the surrounding steppe and savannah. Between 1,100 and 1,800 metres montane forest prevails, but higher up the vegetation gives way to grassland with pockets of woodland. It is a lush environment supporting a rich and varied fauna and flora highly attractive to human communities. The benign climate, combined with the fertile soil, allows a wide range of cereals, pulses, and other vegetables to be grown, in some areas producing two or three crops a year, while cattle, sheep, and goats thrive on the upland pastures. It was these natural benefits, and the fact that the Red Sea became a major trading route, that led to Ethiopia developing as a powerful state in the early first millennium AD.

The Great Rivers

Two great rivers, the Nile and the Niger, dominate the story of the Sahara. The Nile, claimed to be the longest river in the world, owes its existence to the tectonic movements that forced up the earth's crust, creating the Ethiopian and Kenyan domes. Both uplands have a downward tilt to the north, causing rain, which falls on them, to flow off in a northerly direction. In the Kenyan Dome the local rivers feed a huge shallow lake, Lake Victoria. The accumulated water cascades over the Ripon Falls on its northern side to become the White Nile. The second branch of the river, the Blue Nile, begins in Lake Tana, in the Ethiopian Highlands, and is joined along its course by other rivers draining from the plateau. The two branches of the Nile become one river at Khartoum.

The middle reaches of the Nile, between Khartoum and Aswan, cross a zone of tectonic uplift known as the Nubian Swell, where the basal sandstones have been penetrated by bands of harder igneous rocks.

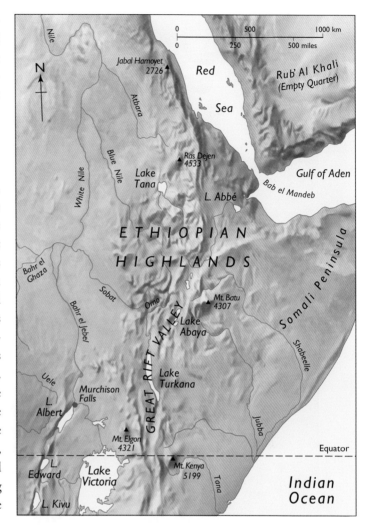

1.14 The Ethiopian Highlands, broken by the Eastern Rift, provide a variety of different environments, from dry savannah to lush montane vegetation, depending on altitude, allowing a range of different food plants to flourish. The region also commands routes, to the Sahel in the west and East Africa in the south, and has easy access to the Nile and the Red Sea.

This causes the river to make a massive S-bend, the changes in geology across which it flows creating rapids known as cataracts, of which there are six. Another tributary, the Atbara, also flowing from the Ethiopian Highlands, joins the main river between the Fifth and Sixth cataracts. From Aswan the Nile flows across the desert in a narrow valley as far as Cairo, where it begins to divide into many branches, creating the

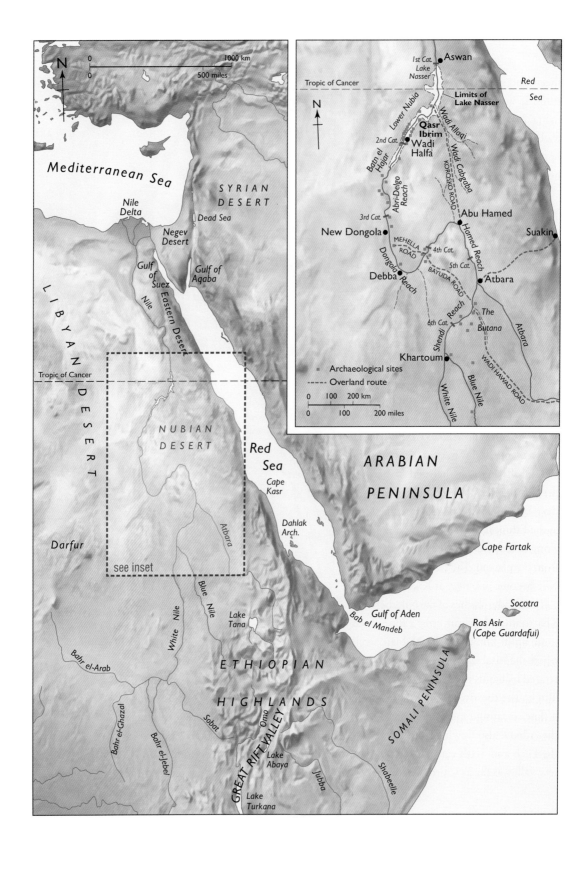

1.15 (*Opposite*) The middle Nile has for millennia served as a crucial link to the south, a route along which commodities such as wood, ivory, and slaves could be transported to Egypt and the Mediterranean. Its flanking deserts were also a source of gold. A series of overland routes complemented the river, bypassing some of the cataracts that made river transport difficult.

1.16 (*Right*) The stark contrast, evident today, between the lush vegetation along the Nile valley, the Faiyum Oasis and the delta, and the surrounding desert, has been a reality for millennia. The delta provided an interface between the Levant, the Mediterranean, and the long corridor of the Nile. It also provided a link between the Levant and the North African coast.

fan-shaped delta thrusting out into the Mediterranean.

The rate of flow of the river varies significantly throughout the year, rising rapidly in June, peaking in September, and subsiding in October. The greatly increased flow causes an annual inundation, which floods the low-lying land on either side of the river and brings with it a heavy load of silt to replenish the fertility of the soil. At Aswan the water might rise as much as 14 metres, the flood decreasing downstream to Cairo, where it is about half the magnitude. For the Egyptians living along the river, the annual inundation was essential to the continuation of life. The Greek historian Herodotus summed it up in his famous statement: 'Egypt is the gift of the Nile'. But he, like his contemporaries, was puzzled as to why the river should flood in summer, the hottest period, when other rivers throughout the world were at their lowest. The answer was that about 90 per cent of the water flowing in the Nile originated in the Ethiopian Highlands as a result of melting snow coinciding with heavy monsoonal rains in the summer period. The torrential flow eroded the soil, which was carried by the river as silt, the highlands contributing substantially to the river's load. By circuitous reasoning Herodotus arrived at more or less the correct answer.

The second great river of North Africa is the Niger. It rises only 300 kilometres from the Atlantic in the Guinea Highlands, flowing north-east, deep into Mali, to the edge of the Sahara before turning on a steep curve south-east, through the modern state of Niger and the forests of Nigeria before discharging into the Atlantic, where it has created a huge deltaic fan. The change of direction on the desert edge, known as the Niger Bend, provided a crucial route interchange where the caravans from the Sahara converged with riverine networks serving the forest zone to the south. Route nodes were places of innovation, and it was here that major trading towns like Timbuktu and Gao developed and became centres for population growth. But the Niger offered another benefit. From its headwaters in the Guinea Highlands the river passes through a zone of woody savannah and then open grassland savannah before entering the semi-arid grasslands of the Sahel. Here it divides into a multitude of branches, creating a huge area of fluvial wetlands, of some 400,000 hectares, known as the Inner Niger Delta—a palimpsest of watercourses, lakes, flood-plains, and marshes changing with the seasons and the progress of the Intertropical Convergence Zone. Monsoon rains falling on the Guinea Highlands bring floods during the wet season from July to September, turning the marshes into lakes and irrigating the land around. Some areas are flooded every year, others less often, while patches of higher land remain always above flood level. Throughout much of the year a hot, dry climate is maintained by winds from the Sahara. This combination of climate and seasonal flooding has created, in the Inner Niger Delta, a series of ecological niches highly favourable to an abundance of varied plant and animal life. It was here that human communities found that they could live in comparative ease, where populations could grow and complex societies could emerge: it was to become a focus, where the successive states which came to dominate West Africa in the first and second millennia AD were to flourish.

The parallels between the Nile and the Niger are evident. Both rivers owe their origins to monsoonal weather systems, which cause summer floods, creating ecological conditions highly beneficial to the development of complex societies, and both provided good communication routes with links to broader networks. Herodotus had heard a story of travellers who had trekked far across the Sahara and had eventually come upon a town where the people were 'black-complexioned'. 'A great river flowed by the town, running from west to east and containing crocodiles' (*Histories* 2.32). It sounds very much like the Niger. The explorers thought it was the upper reaches of the Nile. Herodotus accepted the identification and compared the course of this great river to that of the Danube, giving a pleasing symmetry to the geography of the world.

Compared to the Nile and the Niger, the other rivers of North Africa are of little significance. The Senegal, now forming the border between the modern states of Senegal and Mauritania, rises in the Guinea Highlands quite close to the source of the

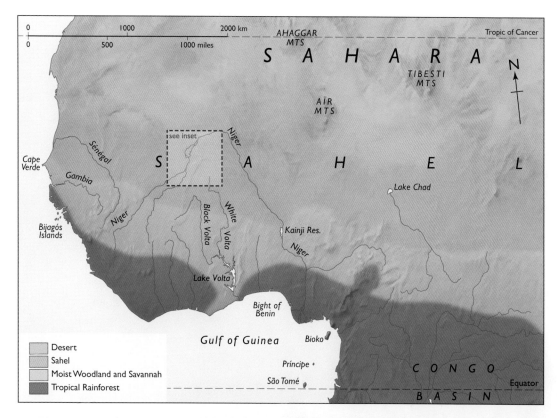

1.17 The river Niger makes a great sweep to the north, almost to the desert edge, before its southward journey, through the tropical forest zone to its delta and the sea. The northernmost stretch, the Niger Bend, provided a contact zone with the caravan routes crossing the desert. Before the bend is reached, there lies the Inner Niger Delta, a wide zone where the river splits into many courses criss-crossing a flooded deltaic area studded with lakes.

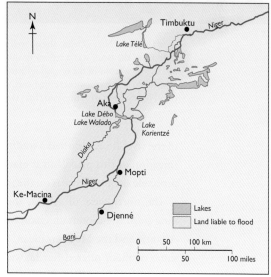

Niger and flows west to the Atlantic, providing a route between the Ocean and the Niger valley. It is possible that the Senegal was the river called Chretes in the account of a sea journey made by the Carthaginian explorer Hanno in the fifth century BC. Hanno came upon the river after sailing south for many days along the desert coast of Africa and described it as teeming with crocodiles and hippopotamuses. On an island in the estuary

  23

1.18 The Inner Niger Delta, always well provided with water and with annual floods bringing down silt to fertilize the land, was a region favourable to human occupation. Here communities began to settle and cultivate crops in the second millennium BC. By the latter part of the first millennium BC, some had established large permanent settlements, which continued to grow. The picture shows the confluence of the river Niger (right) with the Bani (left) close to the town of Mopti, Mali (left).

of the river he established a trading colony called Kernē. There can be no certain identification of this place, but if Hanno's great river is indeed the Senegal, then the most probable site for Kernē is on the island occupied now by part of the city of Saint-Louis.

The north-west of Africa, the Maghrib, is well supplied with short rivers running from the mountain chain of which the Atlas Mountains are a major part to the Atlantic and the Mediterranean. Of no particular significance as long-distance routes, some of them offered fertile, watered hinterlands. This was particularly true of the river Medjerda in Tunisia, its plains becoming a major supplier of cereals for Roman Italy. Others provided sheltered inlets suitable as harbours for coastal shipping.

Of Seas and Ocean

The seas and Ocean which confronted so much of North Africa have played contrasting roles in the development of the region. While the Mediterranean and that part of the Atlantic which flanks the coast of the Maghrib have, throughout time, encouraged intensive connectivity along the interface, the rest of the long Atlantic façade was largely neglected until the fifteenth century AD. The Red Sea is altogether different. It became a corridor of transit between the Mediterranean and southern Arabia and the Indian Ocean, only incidentally impacting on Africa. There are many reasons for these different responses.

In the case of the Mediterranean, the enclosed nature of the sea, its many peninsulas and islands, the currents, and the prevailing wind systems together combine to create marine microcosms, which are generally benign and facilitate movement. The main driver is the predominant current caused by the inflow of water from the Atlantic needed to replenish the enclosed sea, which evaporates at a much faster rate than its rivers can compensate. The current flows through the Strait of Gibraltar, eastwards along the coast of North Africa, swinging around at the eastern end and returning west. In places, the islands and peninsulas deflect the current to form gyratory systems. Added to this there are prevailing winds drawn in from the European landmass and from North Africa by low-pressure zones moving east along the Mediterranean basin. The combination of these factors makes all parts of the Mediterranean accessible to those sea travellers who have learnt to manage the winds and currents and have sufficient experience to plan their journeys to suit the seasons.

Some routes were more hazardous than others. Much of the North African coast from the Nile delta to Tunisia, with the exception of Cyrenaica, is generally low-lying and could only be seen by sailing close inshore, where a vessel would have been in danger from shoals and reefs. Such coasts were best avoided, and in consequence few harbours grew up. From Tunisia westwards the situation was much improved. The mountainous landscape of the Maghrib meant that ships' masters were able to keep land in sight from far out to sea, away from coastal risks, only approaching when they recognized landmarks signing the ports for which they were making. These constraints and opportunities were well understood by Phoenician sailors in the first millennium BC. To reach their trading colonies along the Atlantic coasts of Iberia and Morocco from their home ports on the coast of the Levant, they chose to sail westwards in the open sea, flanking Cyprus and Crete, to reach the safety of harbours established in Tunisia and on the western coasts of Sicily. From there they made for the Balearics and the coast of southern Iberia, which could be followed to the Strait of Gibraltar. The return journey was made using the North African current along the coast of the

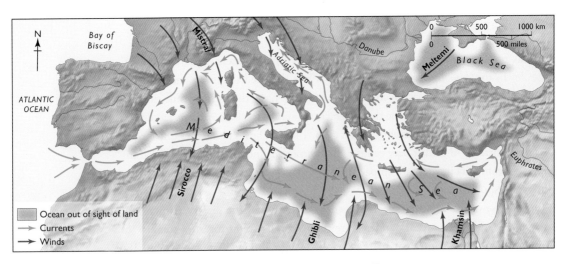

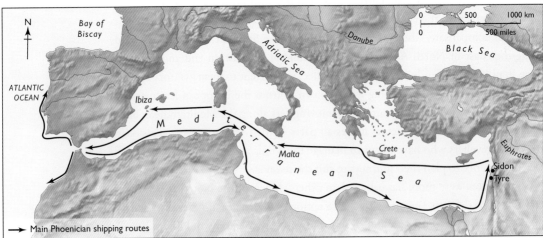

1.19 The Mediterranean provided a corridor along the north coast of Africa. The currents caused by the inflow of water from the Atlantic, together with winds blowing from Africa and Europe, created gyratory systems that made it possible to access most parts of the sea. The first people to sail regularly the length of the Mediterranean were the Phoenicians (lower map) who had begun their contacts with Iberia by the tenth century BC.

Maghrib, where they had established trading enclaves, taking on provisions at places like Carthage for the long haul home, using the open-sea routes where possible to avoid the dangers of the North African coast. Some ports did eventually develop on the Gulf of Syrtis and in Cyrenaica, but it was, for the most part, an inhospitable coast with few attractions. The Mediterranean was a sea that facilitated travel. In the sixth millennium BC, there is evidence of Neolithic farming communities moving westwards by boat as far as the Atlantic coast of Iberia. Thereafter, maritime exploration, colonization, and commerce proliferated and the peoples occupying the North African coast became caught up in the fast-moving changes that shaped Mediterranean history.

Compared to the vitality and variety of the Mediterranean, the Red Sea was a monotonous waterway, 2,300 kilometres long and averaging 300 kilometres wide, flanked for most of its length by unremitting desert. Since its currents were weak and variable, it was the winds that ruled. The system was simple. During the summer the north-west trade winds prevailed, funnelling down the corridor of the sea. In the autumn the system was reversed, with a south wind off the Indian Ocean blowing into the Gulf of Aden and driving the current north. A trader setting out from Suez in late spring would have had ample time to do business with the spice merchants of southern Arabia before returning home in the autumn. For a more adventurous ship's master setting out for India, the round journey could have taken as much as three years. By the Roman period, ports had been established along the African shore every 200 kilometres or so to enable supplies to be taken on board. At the northern end of the sea, places like Myos Hormos and Berenike facilitated trade with the Nile valley, but these ports, crucial though they were to the well-being of the Indian Ocean trading system, had little more than a local impact on the African continent. Further south, however, the port of Adulis, which served the kingdom of Aksum in the Ethiopian Highlands, enabled the state to benefit from its contact with the international trading network throughout much of the first millennium AD.

The Atlantic was an altogether different master, its prevailing pattern of winds and currents constraining the behaviour of the ocean-facing communities. On either side of the equator, gyratory wind systems prevail. In the northern hemisphere the dominant force is the north-east trades, which blow southwards down the coast of North Africa, veering westwards towards the Caribbean as they cross the Tropic of Cancer. In the southern hemisphere the equivalent system is the south-east trades, blowing northwards to hit and to veer round the coast of West Africa. The two systems meet in the Intertropical Convergence Zone, or doldrums, an area with little surface wind where sailing ships can become becalmed. In January the zone lies on either side of the equator, but by July, with the lessening of the wind pressure in the northern hemisphere, it moves north by about 5° of latitude. The ocean currents have much the same gyratory pattern, with the Canary Current and the North Equatorial Current flowing southwards down the coast of North Africa before sweeping westwards towards the Caribbean. In the southern hemisphere the South Equatorial Current runs northwards up the coast of South Africa and then across the Atlantic to America. A contrary current, the Guinea Current, flows from the west, inshore along the coast of West Africa, to the Bight of Bonny (by modern Cameroon). The overall result of all

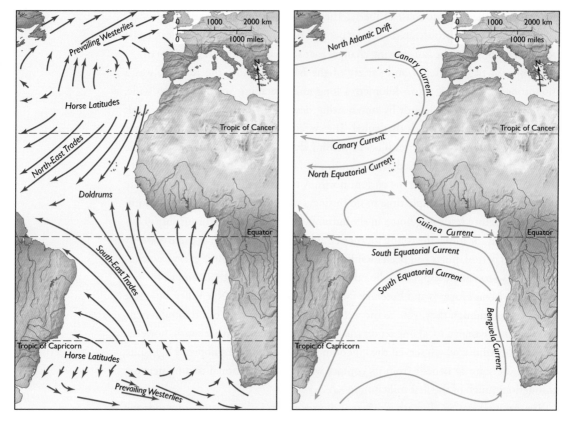

1.20 The Atlantic coast of Africa was difficult for sailors. The prevailing wind patterns (shown here in July), together with the currents, facilitated the journey south, but the return journey was far more problematical and would have needed much skill and effort to accomplish. It was not until the end of the fifteenth century that the route was fully mastered by sweeping westwards into the open ocean to make use of favourable winds.

this is that, by using the Canary Current and the Guinea Current, aided by the north-east trades for the first part of the journey, it was comparatively easy for a sailing ship to make its way southwards along the coast as far as Cameroon, though the last leg of the journey would have been hindered by the onshore south-east trades. Sailing northwards along the coast against the prevailing winds and currents was far more difficult but not impossible. It would have required making use of local currents and playing the winds by tacking manoeuvres or by vigorous rowing if the vessels were so equipped.

There is ample evidence to show that, by the middle of the first millennium BC, vessels were making regular trips along the coast of Morocco, probably as far as Cap Dra'a, where the Anti-Atlas Mountains approach the Ocean. If the *Periplus* of Hanno is to

 28

be believed (pp. 105–6 below), some adventurers travelled much further south, possibly as far as Cameroon, but such expeditions would have been rare. Until the beginning of the fifteenth century, the general wisdom was that it was impossible for a ship to pass south of Cape Bojador on the coast of the western Sahara, a few degrees south of the Canary Islands. It was the political imperative of finding a sea route to India and the East that drove the Portuguese, during the course of the fifteenth century, to push on south of the cape, eventually to round South Africa to reach the Indian Ocean (pp. 297–307 below). Rapidly changing ship design, including the introduction of the stern-mounted rudder and lateen-rigged sails, allowed vessels to sail close to the wind, making progress much easier. Even so, by the time that the India run was firmly established in the early sixteenth century, both outward and inward journeys were made by sweeping far out into the Atlantic to make best use of the wind systems, avoiding coastal waters altogether.

The long Atlantic coastline of Africa, from the Strait of Gibraltar to the Bight of Bonny, varied considerably in what it had to offer the sailor. The first stretch, south to Cap Dra'a, lay mostly within the Mediterranean climatic zone. Although offshore reefs made sailing hazardous, estuaries with good harbours and a copious offshore fish stock, especially tuna and sardines, attracted people to the sea, and in the first millennium BC people from the African mainland began to settle the Canary Islands. Further south the desert meets the Ocean, creating a desolate and uninviting prospect extending for 1,500 kilometres. Thereafter the vegetation of the mainland changes to savannah and then becomes more wooded until the rainforest is reached. Two rivers, Senegal and Gambia, provide access to the hinterland, though there is little evidence that the sea was much used. From Sierra Leone onwards to Cameroon, the long coastal zone is dominated by the equatorial forest. It is a region where longshore drift has created sand and shingle bars fringing the coast, encouraging the growth of impenetrable mangrove swamps in their lee, and rivers have built up marshy deltas like the huge delta of the Niger. The pounding of the onshore winds is another fact of life. Such conditions discouraged maritime activity. It was left to the Portuguese to establish trading ports at Cacheu and Elmina in the 1480s in their determination to exploit the local resources of gold, ivory, and slaves.

Enter Humans

For eight million years the geologically active area of East Africa nurtured the robust thread of primate evolution that led to the emergence of anatomically modern humans (*Homo sapiens*) 250,000–125,000 years ago. It was, as we have seen, an area subject to tectonic stress as pressure in the mantle pushed up the earth's crust to form the

Kenyan and Ethiopian domes and great rifts appeared as the Somalian plate began to pull away from the rest of the continent. The overall effect of these seismic events was to disrupt the predominantly east–west arrangement of the vegetational zones. The uplands, benefiting from the monsoonal weather systems coming in from the Indian Ocean, developed a montane environment surrounded, at lower altitudes, by a complex mixture of forest savannah, woodland savannah, and open, dry savannah. But all was not static. The cyclic climatic changes to which the world was subjected meant that the boundary between the forests and the grasslands was forever changing, often with some rapidity. Without being unduly deterministic, it is not unreasonable to suppose that it was these periods of rapid change that drove the rate of evolution.

The broad outline of human evolution has become clear over the last sixty years or so, but there are still many issues to be resolved, and new discoveries have, constantly, to be taken into account. Humans and their closest relatives, the African apes, began to diverge in East Africa between eight and five million years ago, with the gorillas branching off first and then the Panini (the chimpanzees and bonobos), leaving the Hominini as a distinct tribe from which the genus *Homo* eventually separated. The panins chose to live in the forest, while the hominins favoured the more open wooded savannah and bush, adapting to the environment by adopting a more upright posture, walking on hind legs. This freed the front limbs to become more dexterous, the digits developing to hold natural objects and use them as simple tools. The period between five and two million years ago saw a range of different hominins emerge. One was *Australopithecus*, a fully bipedal creature with legs shorter than a modern human and arms comparatively longer. The average height of a male was 1.5 metres and a female about a metre. Brain size was still small, 375–500 cubic centimetres compared to modern humans at 1,350 cubic centimetres. Several different gracile species have been identified, together with a more robust group, some of which are ascribed to a separate genus, *Paranthropus*. They had slightly larger brains and massive jaws with large molars for grinding coarse, fibrous food. Australopithecines spread across much of East Africa but had died out by a million years ago.

Sometime around 2.5 million years ago the first tools, made by modifying natural rocks, were created. They were very simple, comprising boulders from which flakes had been struck. The flakes, some of them with their edges retouched, were used as cutting tools, while the remaining cores were used for hammering and pounding. The development of simple tools represents a vital step in the history of humankind. The early assemblage of manipulated stone is referred to as the Oldowan industry, after the site of Olduvai Gorge in Tanzania, where it was first characterized. About 2.3 million years ago, there are indications in the fossil record of the hominins to suggest that significant changes were under way. Brain capacity increased, faces became flatter, and dentition was

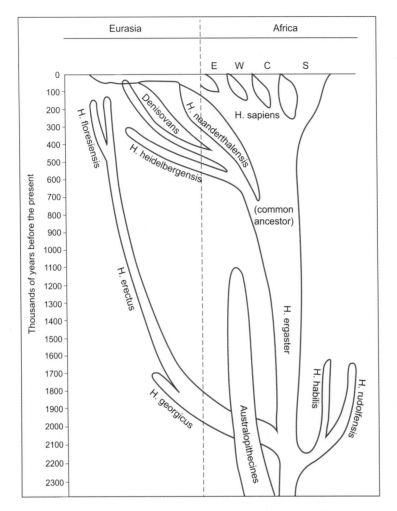

1.21 Although the evolution of modern humans is still imperfectly understood, sufficient is known to allow the main developments to be sketched. As the diagram shows, Africa was the centre where the hominins evolved. The full picture, if it can ever be completed, will show many more sub-branches. The letters E, W, C, and S refer to the east, west, centre, and south of Africa.

reduced in size. These are taken to be the signs of the emergence, from the more gracile australopithecines, of a new genus, *Homo*. It is conventional to refer to this creature as *Homo habilis*: the handy human responsible for making the tools. It is possible, however, that the diversity apparent in the fossil record at this time reflects more than one new genus and some palaeontologists prefer to ascribe the more robust forms of *Homo* to a separate species, *H. rudolfensis*.

The period 1.8–1.7 million years ago saw another phase of rapid development with the emergence of *H. ergaster*, a human with a more sturdy gait reflected in narrow hips, longer legs, and shorter arms. There is much diversification at this time, suggesting that different species were evolving side by side. *H. ergaster* was the first of the hominins to venture outside Africa. Remains have been found in Georgia dating to about 1.7 million years ago, the species spreading to the Far East not long after. Outside Africa the species is identified as *H. erectus*, though the Georgian remains have been separately classified as *H. georgicus*. The apparent avoidance of most of Europe by these first pioneers is explained by the fact that it was at this time in the grip of an ice age. The diaspora took with it the flake tool technology of the Oldowan tradition, while those remaining in Africa developed a new, more sophisticated style in which the stone core was chipped on two faces to create a regular pear-shaped tool with two sharp cutting edges—a technique referred to as the Acheulean hand axe tradition.

Evolution continued in Africa with the emergence of *H. heidelbergensis*, with a larger brain than *H. ergaster*, in the period after 780,000 years ago. By 600,000 they had spread to Europe, taking with them a developed Acheulean tradition, and it was in Europe that further evolution led to the emergence of *H. neanderthalensis*.

1.22 One of the oldest human-made tools, a hand axe from Olduvai Gorge, Tanzania, dates to one and a half million years ago. It is made from a core of stone from which flakes have been removed on both sides, creating two cutting edges. It belongs to the Acheulean tradition.

This is the simple version of the narrative. In reality the situation in Africa is likely to have been much more complex, showing a greater diversity, the different groups living in distinct ecological niches spread throughout the eastern and southern parts of the continent. It was from this rich gene pool that anatomically modern humans, *H. sapiens*, were to emerge sometime in the period 250,000–125,000 years ago. About 125,000–100,000 years ago, bands of *H. sapiens* began to move out of Africa, spreading first eastwards across Asia and later, by 46,000 years ago, into Europe to coexist for a while with the Neanderthals. Ten thousand years later, *H. sapiens* had become the only human species across the entire inhabited world.

New discoveries and further analysis will no doubt greatly enlarge our appreciation of the intricacies of the story, but the basic narrative is clear: it was in the geologically fractured region of East Africa, battered by seasonal monsoons and subject to long-term cyclic changes of climate, that humans evolved. They developed skills to make tools soon after 2.5 million years ago, and about 1.7 million years ago the first waves began to spread out of Africa, first to the East and later to Europe, but the successors of these first pioneers eventually died off, to be replaced by another human species, *H. sapiens*, who began their migration out of Africa about 125,000–100,000 years ago: their successors were to people the world.

Human Diversity

Throughout the long period of the evolution of the hominins, in what has been called the East African Garden of Eden, what stands out is the great physical diversity thrown up by the process of genetic mutation creating a wide variety of potential species to run the gauntlet of natural selection. In the still very incomplete fossil record, those we are most easily able to recognize are the successful variants who survived and rose to dominance, leaving the less well adapted to die out. As more fossils are discovered, it is becoming clear that throughout the four million years or so of hominin evolution many species were in existence at the same time, competing for resources and striving to adapt to the changing environment.

The *Homo sapiens* who began to evolve in East Africa around 250,000 years ago shared a large gene pool. Only a few of them moved out of Africa to begin to people Europe and Asia, carrying with them a more limited set of genes. A study of the DNA of *Homo sapiens* from around the world, both mitochondrial DNA, passed on along the female line, and Y-chromosome DNA, transmitted by males, shows that a far greater diversity exists in Africa, reflecting the fact that anatomically modern humans have existed in Africa for a lot longer than in the rest of the world. The physical diversity now apparent in the modern African population is, in part, due to the comparative isolation of the different regions, which has allowed natural genetic mutations to intensify certain beneficial physical characteristics.

The geographical constraints contributing to the development of physical differences among the African population are also a factor in language evolution. Four indigenous language groups are recognized: Afro-Asiatic, Nilo-Saharan, Niger–Congo, and Khoisan. Detailed studies of language have enabled the core areas where these language groups emerged to be defined: Afro-Asiatic in Ethiopia and the Red Sea coast, Nilo-Saharan in the valley of the White Nile, Niger–Congo in West Africa, and Khoisan in East Africa, now Kenya, Uganda, and Tanzania. The early modern distribution of these language groups reflects shifts in population spread over thousands of years, the most far-reaching being the expansion, beginning about 2000 BC, of Bantu-speaking farmers from Nigeria and Cameroon across most of southern Africa,

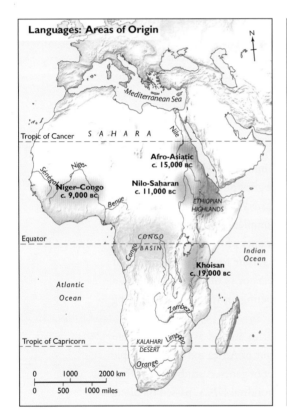
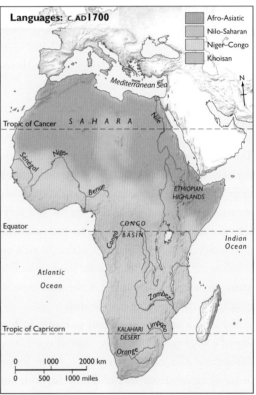

1.23 Four major language groups can be identified in Africa before the advent of Europeans. *Left*: The earliest known occurrences. *Right*: The situation *c.*AD 1700, by which time the Niger–Congo languages had spread with the movement of the Bantu, displacing Khoisan speakers, and Nilo-Saharan-speaking groups had extended along the Sahel corridor.

displacing the Khoisan-speaking herders and hunter-gatherers and driving them into the south-west corner of the continent.

Energetic attempts are being made to bring together the results of archaeological research, which reflects on material culture and behaviour, with studies of ancient DNA and linguistics to create a comprehensive and balanced narrative of the inter-play of humans and their environment over the last seventeen thousand years. These are early days and the data is fragmentary and uneven, but there are now areas of broad agreement that allow Africa's remarkable story to begin to be pieced together. What is already clear is that in Africa, probably more so than in any other region of the world, climate and climate change have played a dominant role in human history, and will continue to do so.

2

THE LONG BEGINNING

ANATOMICALLY modern humans emerged in East Africa 2–1.6 million years ago and spread, during a period of warm, humid weather 125,000–69,000 years ago, throughout the rest of the continent. From the time of these early pioneer movements until about 6000 BC, humans depended for their survival on hunting and gathering and were at the mercy of the natural environment to provide for them. But the environment was ever changing as the climate, dependent upon swings in the earth's orbit, veered from hot to cold over a cycle of about a hundred thousand years. Within this broad sweep there were other fluctuations caused by cyclic changes of lesser magnitude. In the intervals of cold, when the climate was arid, the Sahara became a desert, creating a massive barrier to human movement, forcing communities to develop in isolation from each other, whereas, during the warm and more humid periods, with vegetation flourishing, people could move over extensive territories and build up a greater connectivity. Frequent changes in the environment, sometimes over a short interval, meant that people had constantly to be on the move, or else had to modify their food-gathering strategies to cope with the new conditions.

While environment was a major factor in determining human development, demographic pressures also played a part. Humans, like all other animals, are genetically driven to reproduce, and so, if left without constraint, the population would expand exponentially. What prevented this from happening was the holding capacity of the environment: the number of people that the habitat could feed given the socio-economic strategies of the group. Over time an equilibrium was reached. If environmental conditions improved, raising the holding capacity and taking pressure off the community, the natural tendency would be for the population to begin to increase slowly at first and then more rapidly. Once the momentum was under way, it could quickly overshoot the new holding capacity, putting the community under stress and forcing change. Various responses were possible. To increase the food yield, the territory could be extended and new technologies could be introduced to drive productivity. Another way was to reduce the population by adopting practices of infanticide or senilicide, by imposing social constraints on conception and by encouraging migration. Intergroup tensions caused by pressure on resources could lead to heightened aggression and warfare, itself an effective way to reduce population.

The interaction of climate change and demographic pressures caused hunter-gatherer societies to change over time. They became more adept at exploiting the ecological niches in which they found themselves, learning new specialist skills and technologies. Group sizes tended to increase, and evidence for outright aggression between groups becomes more apparent. In the two hundred thousand years or so covered in this chapter, North African societies, driven to adapt to constantly changing environments, became increasingly sophisticated in their food-gathering methods, even to the extent of manipulating the wild plants and animals they had come to depend on. It was a small step from this to full domestication and settled farming.

Finding the Hunter-Gatherers

To create a narrative for the long hunter-gatherer period is not easy, particularly in a region like northern Africa, where the present climate and episodes of political instability make fieldwork difficult, but it is much to the credit of those who have ventured out that many hundreds of archaeological sites have been found and collections made of surface artefacts. Some of these sites have been examined by excavation, usually on a small scale, and dated using a range of scientific methods. A few have been subjected to more extensive excavation, allowing changes spanning long periods of time to be studied. Where possible these episodes of human occupation have been placed in their environmental context using animal bones, and more rarely plant remains, found stratified with the artefacts. This faunal and floral evidence—the ecofacts—reflects not only the climate and ecology of the territory over which the hunter-gatherer group ranged, but also their preferences for different foods and their skills in acquiring them. Since the communities tended to set up camps close to water, at oases, on riverbanks, and on lake shores, traces of occupation may sometimes be found stratified within naturally deposited layers of sediment. For long spans of time during the hunter-gatherer period, lakes, some of them very large, existed throughout the Sahara. Detailed analysis of the sediments which have accumulated in the lake basins has allowed episodes of human activity to be dated and correlated to changing patterns of climate.

The presence of hunter-gatherer communities is usually signalled in the field by a scatter of stone artefacts. This may be the only evidence available if stratified deposits are not encountered. The typology of the artefacts, and the technological skills embedded in their manufacture, can, however, provide evidence of the broad date range and the cultural affinities of the assemblage. A helpful generalization, proposed by the archaeologist J. G. D. Clark, was to divide the stone industries encountered in Africa and Eurasia into five modes marked by advances in technology. Mode 1 includes the simple flake tools of the Oldowan tradition. In Mode 2 are the more regularly controlled tools made by removing flakes from a core, the technique known as Acheulean. Mode 3 is characterized by tools made from prepared cores and flakes, some of which are turned into tanged points and scrapers. These types, characteristic of the African Middle Stone Age, have similarities to assemblages found throughout Europe, where they are referred to as Levallois-Mousterian. Mode 4 tools are based on long, parallel-sided blades struck from prismatic cores using punches. These are equivalent to the European Upper Palaeolithic. The final stage, Mode 5, involves the manufacture of microliths and backed blades which can be used as components of composite tools. In Europe they equate to the Epipalaeolithic and Mesolithic periods. The classification is, of course, a simplification, but it has the advantage of providing a broad framework, enabling the African sequence to be correlated with technological changes in Europe and Asia. It cannot, however, be used to create a universal chronology. In Africa changes from one mode to another took place at different times in different regions. In the densely forested region of West Africa, for example, simple core tools continued to be made until a few millennia ago and microliths and backed blades were never in use. The reason may well be that core tools, used as axes and hoes, were better adapted to a forest environment, where trees had to be cut down and edible roots dug up. Elsewhere, in the open Sahel, where hunting was the norm, arrows and spears using microliths to make the cutting edges and penetrating tips became the tools of choice.

Charting the Ever-Changing Landscape

We have seen (pp. 6–10) that cyclic alterations in the earth's axis have affected world climate and that this has had a dramatic effect on changing the environment of the

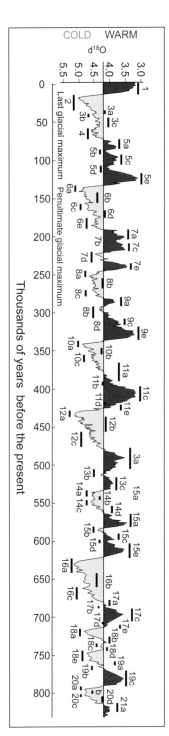

Sahara and the neighbouring regions. The most convenient way to give structure to these changes is to correlate them with marine sediments, sampled using deep-sea cores, which have accumulated on the sea bed. These sediments are made up largely of calcium carbonate derived from the shells of sea creatures. The oxygen, combined in the calcium carbonate, occurs as two different isotopes, ^{18}O and ^{16}O, the percentages of which are directly affected by sea temperature: the colder the conditions when the sea creatures were living, the higher is the ratio of ^{18}O. By establishing the isotope ratios at different depths in the cores and converting them to sea temperature at the time of deposition it has been possible to build up a sequence of Marine Isotope Stages (MIS) covering the last six million years.

The sequence vividly demonstrates the fluctuations of temperature, from extremely cold to extremely hot, that have occurred every hundred thousand years or so. Within this cycle lesser oscillations can be seen. Each is numbered, backwards from the present, to define a succession of stages. The period which concerns us in this chapter begins in a warm, humid period, MIS7, lasting from 250,000 to 184,000 BC. This is followed by a cold period, MIS6, from 184,000 to 126,000 BC. The next warm, humid period, MIS5, spans 126,000–69,000 BC. MIS4, a short period of cold from 69,000 to 57,000 BC, is followed by a brief warming, MIS3, 57,000–22,000 BC. After this, the temperature becomes very cold again during MIS2, 22,000–10,000 BC, before becoming rapidly warmer to MIS1, the phase in which we are today.

2.1 Deep marine sediments, composed of the remains of molluscs that had died and fallen to the sea floor, offer a way to measure changes in climate over hundreds of millennia. Deep-sea cores are taken and the ratios of oxygen isotopes measured at close intervals. Since the ratio is affected by the climate prevailing at the time, changes in ratios relate directly to climate change. In this way it is possible to build up a diagram of Marine Isotope Stages (MIS) reflecting palaeoclimate. The Marine Isotope Stages are numbered backwards from the present.

The Marine Isotope Stage system offers a broad chronology against which to consider human development in various parts of the world. It was during the cold, dry periods, MIS6, 4, and 2, that the Sahara became an arid desert essentially impassable, separating the populations of the northern coastal region from those of the Sahel in the south. But during the warmer, moister periods that intervened, when the desert became green, rivers flowed, and lakes, some of them of massive proportions, proliferated, the populations could expand and movements between north and south could resume.

Against this broad pattern of climate change there were many lesser oscillations, which will have affected human behaviour. Throughout the long warm period, MIS5, there were three peaks, 5a, c, and e, interspersed with more arid interludes, 5b and d. These fluctuations had a direct effect on the movement of *Homo sapiens* northwards out of Africa (p. 42 below). From about 28,000 BC, as the pace of human development increased, an understanding of the intricacies of climate change becomes more important. In the northern hemisphere, MIS2 corresponds with the Last Glacial Maximum, the period when the ice sheets were at their most extensive. The coldest phase lay between 22,000 and 17,000 BC. This was followed by a slightly warmer period, the Late Glacial Interstadial, with temperatures rising to almost as high as the present day until about 10,900 BC, when the temperature plummeted to a new cold interlude, the Younger Dryas, lasting to about 9700 BC. Thereafter the temperature rose very quickly, heralding the beginning of the Holocene, during which temperatures have approximated to those of the present day. We will return to the story of the Holocene changes in the next chapter.

The Spread of *Homo Sapiens*

East Africa, especially the Central Rift valley of Kenya and the Middle Awash valley in Ethiopia, was a region of temperate climate inhabited by a variety of terrestrial mammals and plants offering abundant food. For early humans it provided a welcome habitat, becoming a focus of behavioural innovation marked by a shift in tool-making technology from the standardized Acheulean assemblage characterized by the hand axe, to the more varied tool-kit of Mode 3 with its reliance on the Levallois prepared core and a range of specialist tools made from flakes. The Mode 3 industry, arising in East Africa around 280,000 years ago, marks the beginning of the African Middle Stone Age, which was to last in some areas to as late as fifty thousand years ago. The Acheulean tradition was not immediately replaced and in some regions was still evident about 160,000 years ago.

The Mode 3 technology of the Middle Stone Age is the product of *Homo sapiens*, and its distribution across Africa in a wide variety of ecozones—forests, savannah, semi-desert, and coast—reflects the agility of the species in adapting to new and varied environments. Inevitably, the need to adopt new food-gathering strategies, as the pioneer bands moved into less familiar territories, led to the appearance of specialized sets of tools.

Stone tools of the early phase of the Middle Stone Age have been found in the Sahara and along the coast of North Africa, implying that anatomically modern humans had reached the Mediterranean coast at least by 124,000 BC. This is confirmed by fossil remains found in the Maghrib. Recent redating of a human mandible found in the Moroccan cave of Jebel Irhoud suggests that *Homo sapiens* could have reached the region before 200,000 BC. Movement from East Africa across the Sahara would have been possible during the humid interglacial period between 340,000 and 200,000 years ago, when large lakes fed by river systems existed throughout the Sahara. A morphological study of a human skull from Jebel Irhoud showed that it had a continuous brow ridge, in contrast to later skulls, in which the brow ridge was interrupted. For this reason it is considered to represent an archaic version of *Homo sapiens*, one of the first humans to make the journey to the northern extremity of the continent. That morphologically similar skulls have been found in Israel, at Skhul and Qafzeh, shows that some of these archaic humans had begun to venture out of Africa.

For much of MIS6 (184,000–125,000 BC) the Sahara was an extremely cold and arid place hardly conducive to human occupation, but during MIS5 there were episodes of enhanced humidity around 122,000, 100,000, and 79,000 BC when hunter-gatherer groups may have been encouraged to explore the expanding grasslands. Then followed another arid period, MIS4 (69,000–55,000 BC), until about 22,000 BC, when humid conditions again returned.

There were, then, a number of times when conditions in the Sahara were favourable to humans, when lakes fed by rivers developed and the living was good. These were periods of population increase and times of enhanced mobility when migrating bands, finding the North African coastal zone already well populated, pushed on northwards across Sinai into the Levant. On present evidence it seems that the cold conditions of MIS5 (125,000–69,000 BC) were sufficient to deter movement out of Africa, but after about 50,000 BC a more benign climate encouraged communities who now had improved hunting equipment to venture north, eventually to colonize Europe and Asia. Those who remained in Africa continued to adapt to the varied environments in which they chose to live.

The Aterian Hunter-Gatherers

In North Africa the hunter-gatherer groups of the Middle Stone Age are generally referred to as Aterian, after the Algerian site of Bir el-Ater to the south of Tébessa. The main characteristic types of the Aterian assemblage are flake tools, some with well-defined tangs fashioned to facilitate hafting as projectile heads, others serving as scrapers. Bifacially worked leaf-shaped points are also a frequent component of the tool-kit. Geographically the Aterian is found across much of northern Africa, from the Mediterranean coast to the Sahel and from the Atlantic to Egypt's Western Desert. In the Nile valley it is hardly represented. Here the contemporary hunter-gatherer groups developed their own distinctive tool types, which showed much regional differentiation.

Users of Aterian tools were present in Africa for nearly a hundred thousand years. The earliest occurrences are found in Morocco dating to before 110,000 BC. They lasted until about 38,000 BC, when they began to disappear, though in some places the tradition continued until 18,000 BC. The earliest sites were established during the interglacial period, MIS5, when bands began to exploit a wide range of different environments, some of them sufficiently well endowed to allow communities to gain a livelihood from restricted territories, reducing their need for mobility. In such situations the tool-kits became more specialized to match the food-gathering methods appropriate to the particular ecozone. This led to the regional variation evident in Aterian assemblages. The onset of the cold, arid MIS4 (69,000–55,000 BC) drove communities out of the Sahara. At the rock shelter of Uan Tabu in the Tadrart Acacus in the south-west of Libya, a campsite where Aterian material had accumulated to a depth of a metre, abandonment came about 58,000 BC, by which time the desert had become too arid to sustain life. Further south, at Adrar Bous in the Aïr Mountains in northern Niger, occupation continued until about 43,000 BC, and at Haua Fteah, the much-frequented cave on the coast of Cyrenaica, Aterian hunters continued to shelter even later. Both Adrar Bous and Haua Fteah occupied environmentally favoured locations where the increasing aridity had much less effect.

Many regional studies show that the hunter-gatherer groups who spread throughout Africa during MIS5, and had managed to hold on in favoured regions as the climate became more arid at the beginning of MIS4, began to show significant cultural differences. While it is convenient to refer to them all as Aterian, stressing the similarities, this should not obscure the differences in the tool-kits, reflecting the way in which the individual groups readily responded to the changing demands of their environments. The Aterian and its related industries represent the spread of anatomically modern humans throughout Africa. They were inventive people with the mental

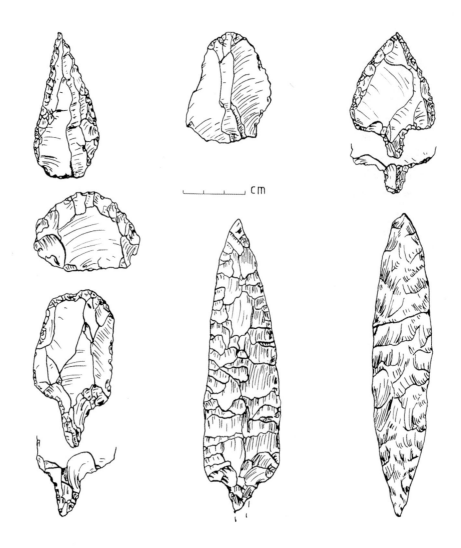

cm

2.2 Aterian tools of the African Middle Stone Age were made by striking large flakes of stone and then refining them to create a range of tools, some with tangs to facilitate hafting. This selection comes from various sites in North Africa.

agility to adapt and to survive, and they also began to display the acquisitive desires so typical of humans. This is demonstrated by the presence of red ochre pigment and of marine shells, perforated to make bead necklaces, found with their burials. Such rarities, used for personal adornment, were acquired through gift exchange, a process that helped maintain a degree of harmony between neighbours.

2.3 The cave of Haua Fteah, on the north coast of Cyrenaica, has been excavated on several occasions, producing evidence of a long series of occupation levels spanning the period from the Middle Stone Age to the Roman period. The photograph shows work in progress in 2012. The deep sequence of deposits, which is well dated, provides evidence of the succession of peoples who lived in, or passed through, the coastal zone.

The Later Hunter-Gatherers, 42,000–10,000 BC

A dramatic decrease in temperature, accompanied by the onset of more arid conditions about 42,000 BC, brought about widespread changes in the lives of hunter-gatherers in North Africa, marking the beginning of the archaeologically defined African Late Stone Age. It was a period of fluctuating climate. There were mild intervals between 37,000–34,000 BC and 26,000–23,000 BC before the onset of a cold, arid phase, coinciding with the height of the Late Glacial Maximum about 19,000–17,000 BC, with arid conditions continuing until 9700 BC. Throughout much of this long period, the Sahara was all but deserted, but the coastal zone of North Africa remained inhabited, as did the Nile corridor, which continued to provide links with East Africa.

The deeply stratified layers of occupation in the cave of Haua Fteah, on the coast of Cyrenaica, have provided a well-dated sequence spanning from the Middle Stone

Age to the Neolithic period. Following the Middle Stone Age deposit, with clear Aterian affinities, three distinct pre-Neolithic phases can be identified: Dabban (44,000/39,000–15,000/14,000 BC); Oranian (15,000/14,000–11,000/10,000 BC); and Capsian (10,600–5900 BC). Of these, the first two concern us here; the Capsian will be returned to later (p. 61).

The Dabban, named after the site of Hagfet ed-Dabba in Cyrenaica, is characterized by a blade assemblage, equivalent to Mode 4 industry, in which long blades were removed from prismatic cores with a punch and were blunted along one edge to make them easier to use. The assemblage also included flaked adze-like tools and, in later stages, grindstones for crushing grains and other plant foods. While it is possible that the Dabban blade industry evolved from the North African Aterian, similarities with developments in the Levant suggest that it may well have first appeared in the Near East and then been introduced into North Africa by hunters moving in from across Sinai. Another, though less likely, possibility is that the influences could have arrived from East Africa, where blade industries were evolving at this time. Contemporary sites are rare in North Africa, probably because, with the exception of favoured environments like Cyrenaica, climatic conditions were still too extreme in most regions to support hunting communities. At Jebel Gharbi, in Tripolitania, well inland, a site abandoned at the end of the Aterian period, about 38,000 BC, was not reoccupied again for another ten thousand years, by which time the climate had improved. The Dabban hunter-gatherers were well adapted to their environment. At Haua Fteah, where they continued to use the cave over a period of nearly twenty thousand years, the tool-kit underwent only minor modifications. Clearly, on this coastal upland region looking out to sea and enjoying a relatively stable Mediterranean climate, communities were free from the stresses that required constant adaptation.

Sometime about 15,000 BC there was a marked change at Haua Fteah when the Dabban came to an end and was replaced by a microlithic industry which used to be called the Eastern Oranian but is now generally known as the Iberomaurusian. The focus on microliths marks a significant technological departure from larger stone implements and their replacement with specialist tools constructed from small backed blades set in wooden hafts and held in place with resin. These composite tools could be made quickly and were easy to repair. Another advantage was that the small stone components could also be reused to make new tools. Iberomaurusian sites are widespread along the North African coast between Cyrenaica and Agadir on the Atlantic coastal region of Morocco. The earliest so far known are found in the Maghrib, where dates of 19,000 BC or a little earlier are recorded at the cave site of Taforalt, in eastern Morocco. The latest date so far known is 7000 BC, recorded for occupation in the Moroccan cave of Hattab II.

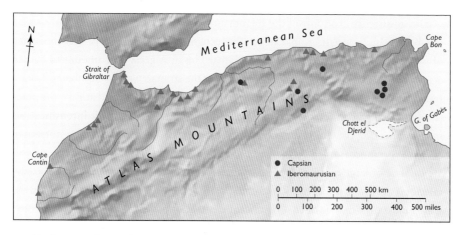

2.4 The hunter-gatherers who occupied the Maghrib in the period 26,000–6000 BC can be divided into two groups: the Iberomaurusian and the Capsian. The Capsian was later, and was more restricted in distribution.

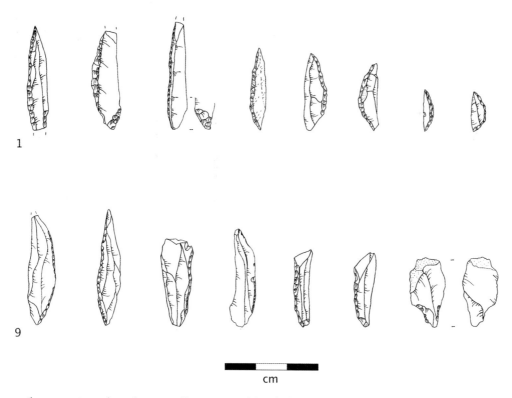

2.5 Iberomaurusian tools are characterized by stone microliths, which were set into wooden hafts to form composite tools.

The subsistence economy of the Iberomaurusian was based on hunting and gathering, but distinct specializations can now be recognized. At a number of sites the bones of wild Barbary sheep predominate. At Tamar Hat in Algeria they amount to 94 per cent of the animal bones present, suggesting that the animals were by now being herded rather than hunted. If so, this could be seen as a response to increased aridity, the practice later being abandoned when more humid conditions returned. Intensification in the collecting of wild plant foods, including grasses, acorns, and pine nuts, may also have been occasioned by the onset of more arid conditions. About 11,000 BC the appearance of large midden deposits suggests another change towards a more sedentary lifestyle. These middens often contain considerable quantities of edible molluscs, which must now have formed a significant element of the diet. It is probably no coincidence that it was about this time that large cemeteries, another sign of a more settled life, began to appear. At Grotte des Pigeons, Taforalt, a large number of interments were found towards the rear of the cave, one dating to 10,670 BC. What is of particular interest is that most of them display evidence of dental evulsion, the deliberate removal of healthy teeth during the life of the individual. At Taforalt and other Iberomaurusian cemeteries it was usually the top incisors that were removed, a process undergone by both males and females. Clearly the practice was intended to signify group identity and was probably one of the rites of passage that punctuated life at the time of either puberty or marriage. That the removal of incisors took place across the north-west of Africa throughout the Iberomaurusian period and into Neolithic times implies the maintenance of a strong cultural identity over a period of more than ten thousand years.

The question of the origin of the Iberomaurusian culture has been much debated. Some observers believe that the advanced microlithic technology was introduced from the Levant, but the early dates of around 20,000 BC for its first appearance at Taforalt have suggested to others that it may have developed in the Maghrib. More recently, however, the DNA of seven of the Taforalt skeletons has been analysed, showing that the community had a strong affinity with the Natufian hunter-gatherers of the Levant, implying close connections between the populations of the North African coastal zone and those of the Near East in the pre-Neolithic period. The simplest explanation is

2.6 (*Opposite top*) The Grotte des Pigeons, Taforalt, in Morocco, was used sporadically by hunter-gatherer groups from the Middle Stone Age to the Iberomaurusian period (*c.*83,000–10,500 BC). The cave became the cemetery of an Iberomaurusian community sometime in the thirteenth millennium BC. At least fifty burials have been recovered. The existence of the cemetery suggests that the community was now at least partially sedentary.

2.7 (*Opposite bottom*) Some of the individuals buried at the Grotte des Pigeons show evidence of dental evulsion, that is, the deliberate removal of healthy teeth, usually incisors, a practice widespread among the Iberomaurusians. This individual comes from the Hattab II Cave in north-west Morocco.

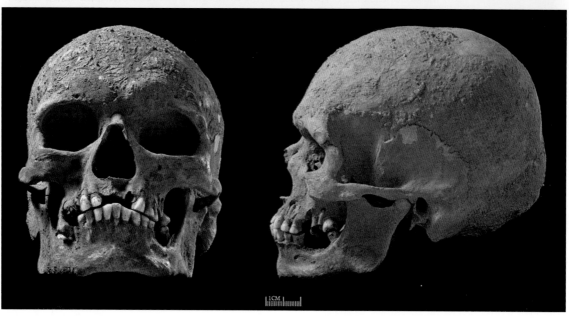

that there was an influx of a Natufian population into North Africa. This is supported by a study of the genetics of North African dogs, which show that they were descended from dogs first domesticated in the Near East. About a third of the genome of the present human population derives from sub-Saharan Africa, though whether from West Africa or East Africa is uncertain. It is the presence of a sub-Saharan component in the genome of the Taforalt population and its absence in the Natufian sample that argues against a population flow from the Maghrib to the Levant. While leaving many issues unresolved, the results of the DNA analysis are important in stressing the mobility of people around the southern and eastern sides of the Mediterranean, a mobility that could have had its roots in the Middle Stone Age.

The Nile valley was a very different world from the North African coastal zone, but the two were directly linked. Following the stone industries of the Middle Stone Age, it is possible to identify a blade industry broadly similar to the Dabban of Libya, named Khormusan after the site of Khor Musa. Following this, from about 23,000 BC, a number of quite restricted regional groups can be defined, initially using blade tools but after about 15,000 BC relying heavily on microliths. This regionalization implies a more sedentary existence with a greater reliance being placed on vegetable foods and on fishing, the communities benefiting from the presence of the lakes that had formed in the valley. While these changes in economic strategy, together with the enclosed nature of the Nile corridor, led to the formation of communities that were culturally distinct, similarities with the Iberomaurusian of the Maghrib show there must have been a degree of connectivity between the valley and the Mediterranean coastal zone.

The situation in the region immediately south of the Sahara is much less well known, but communities were making microlithic tools by 11,000 BC. The fact that the Sahara had been impassable for a long period of time leaves open the possibility that the microlithic technology might have been introduced from the east, from the middle Nile valley or East Africa. Human remains are rarely found in West Africa, but a well-preserved skull and a crushed skeleton dating to between 14,300 and 9700 BC were found at the rock shelter of Iwo Eleru in Nigeria. The skull displayed negroid characteristics. The fact that it was morphologically different from contemporary humans found in the Maghrib implies that the Sahara had for long been a real divide, allowing the Afro-Asiatic population of the north to evolve along different lines from the Niger–Congo population of West Africa.

2.8 (*Opposite*) This human skull, found at Iwo Eleru in western Nigeria and dated to the period 14,300–9700 BC, raises a number of questions. His sloping frontal vault and prominent continuous brow ridge are quite unlike the later population of the area and are more archaic than would be expected at this date. One suggestion is that he was a member of a relict population that had survived in West Africa but was entirely replaced at the beginning of the Holocene.

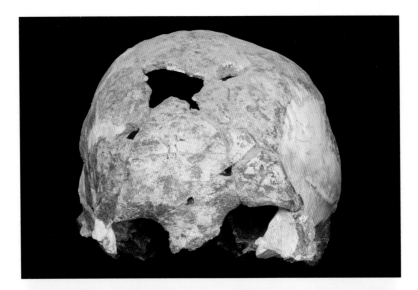

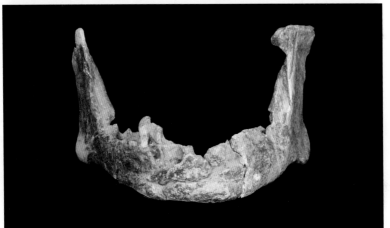

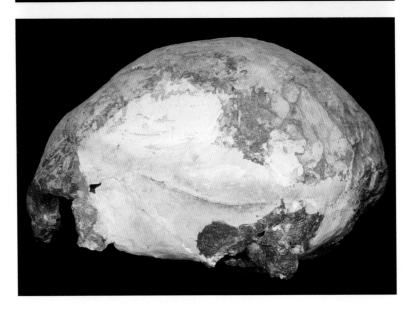

Standing back from the detail, for much of the period considered in this section, which lies within MIS3 and 2 (57,000–10,000 BC), the Sahara was an arid zone, hostile to human occupation. Although in times of climatic amelioration hunter-gatherer groups expanded into the northern and southern fringes, the desert still kept the two populations apart. Of the area to the south, sandwiched between the southern fringes of the desert and the northern edge of the equatorial forest, we know comparatively little. For the northern zone, between the northern extremity of the desert and the Mediterranean Sea and the Atlantic Ocean, the evidence is much richer. The Mediterranean, at this stage, formed a barrier separating Africa from Europe, but east–west communication, extending to the Levant and deep into the Nile valley, created a degree of connectivity reflected in both material culture and the genetic structure of the population. In favoured areas of this broad northern zone, the Maghrib, Cyrenaica, and the Nile valley, communities became increasingly less mobile, focusing their attention now on exploiting local resources, be it Barbary sheep or Nile perch. As the population grew, so too did the sense of community and social identity.

The Greening of the Desert, 10,000–6000 BC

In the northern hemisphere the Last Ice Age began to move to a close about 12,700 BC, when there was a sudden rise in temperature, heralding the Bølling–Allerød Interstadial, a warm, moist interlude. Then, about 10,900 BC, the temperature suddenly plummeted again, marking the onset of the Younger Dryas, with temperatures falling to even lower levels than during the Last Glacial Maximum. The Younger Dryas was brief, coming to a sudden end about 9700 BC, when temperatures rose rapidly once more to give rise to a climate much like that of the present day. This moment is taken to mark the beginning of the Holocene, the era of consistently warm weather in which we now live.

The main driver for this change of climate was the cyclic shift in the earth's orbit, but this also triggered more regional changes. In Africa the West African monsoons began to increase in strength, forcing the Intertropical Convergence Zone to move north. In July it had been about 8° north; now it had moved to 28° north, greatly increasing rainfall over the Sahara, encouraging the growth of vegetation. This set in motion an intensifying feedback cycle: vegetation absorbs more sunlight, which increases the energy of the monsoon, bringing more rain. The overall result was that the boundaries of the vegetation in all zones moved north. The rainforest spread inland from the West African coast, the savannah moved into what had been the tropical steppe, while the steppe spread into the area that was previously desert. Meanwhile, in the north, new airstreams drawn into the Mediterranean caused Mediterranean vegetation to spread

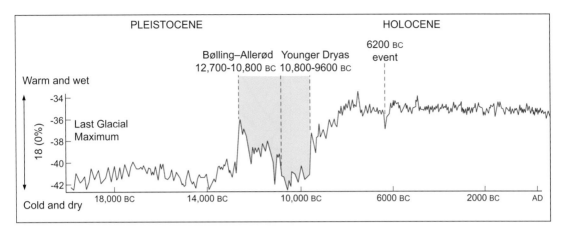

2.9 Using the deep-sea cores (Figure 2.1 above) it is possible to trace changes in temperature, in detail, since the end of the last ice age. The plot clearly shows the sudden cold period of the Younger Dryas (10,800–9600 BC) and the brief downturn in temperature about 6200 BC.

south across the northern part of the desert, driving the subtropical steppe in front of it to move even further south to meet the northern advance of the tropical steppe. The result was that the vast area that had been arid desert was now blanketed in steppe and savannah with lusher Mediterranean vegetation to the north. In the central regions of the Sahara, plants now flourished which before had only been found 400–600 kilometres to the south.

Although the shift in rainfall patterns had been very rapid, it took many centuries for the new zones of vegetation to become established. By this time perennial rivers were flowing from the mountain ranges of the Sahara and low-lying areas had become lakes. Some, like Mega-Chad (now much reduced as Lake Chad), Megafazzan in Libya, the Chotts Megalake in Tunisia and northern Algeria, and the Ahnet-Mouydr Megalake in southern Algeria, reached very considerable proportions. Mega-Chad was the largest, at 1,000 by 6,000 kilometres, owing its size to the volume of water flowing into it from the Ahaggar, Aïr, and Tibesti mountains. It was approximately the size of the Caspian Sea. The mountain ranges, together with the lakes, rivers, and their great alluvial fans, created environmental micro regions within the Sahara. Another formative factor was the westerly wind, which blew in from the Atlantic bringing additional moisture to the western parts of the desert. The effect did not reach as far as the central and eastern regions, which remained much drier, and in places like the Libyan Sand Sea, desert conditions still prevailed.

Between the forests clustering around the lakes and rivers and the arid zones, much of the Sahara was a patchwork of steppe and grass savannah with shrubs, interspersed

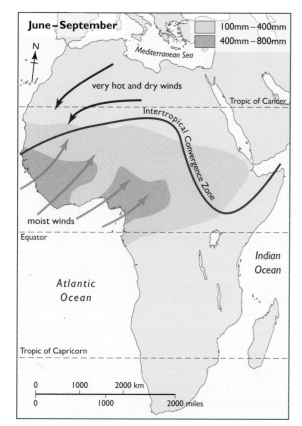

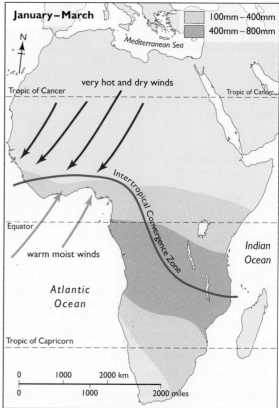

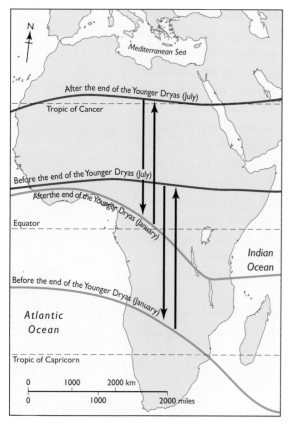

2.10 (*Above and left*) The weather systems affecting northern Africa are complex, but one controlling factor is the strength of the winds at different times of the year, which determine the position of the Intertropical Convergence Zone (which, over the ocean, creates the doldrums). The top two maps show conditions today. Between June and September the ITCZ is in the north, allowing the moist winds of the Atlantic to reach into the Sahel. From January to March the ITCZ moves south, concentrating precipitation in the southern part of Africa, where it is augmented by moist wind from the Indian Ocean. The lower map shows the position of the ITCZ before the beginning of the Younger Dryas cold phase, *c.*10,800 BC, and before its end, *c.*9600 BC.

2.11 (*Opposite*) Changes in the position of the Intertropical Convergence Zone directly affect vegetation. The two maps show the situation at the time of the greatest humidity, *c.*6500 BC, and when the humidity was much reduced, *c.*4500 BC.

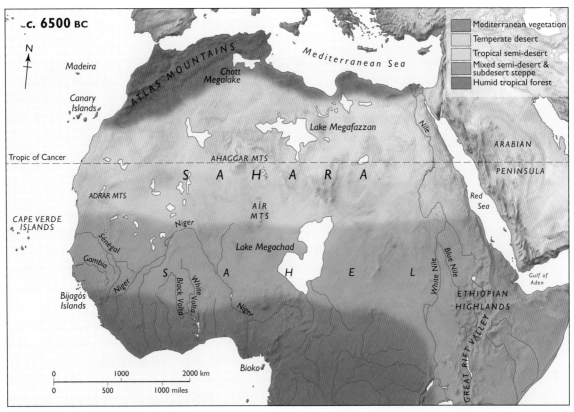

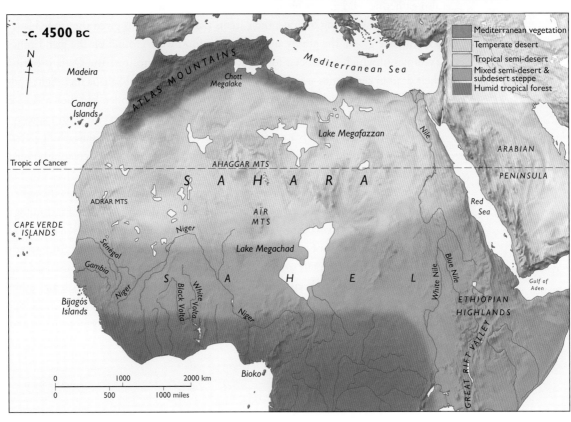

with areas of thicker tree cover. These varied ecozones provided habitats for a rich fauna. Antelopes, gazelles, hartebeest, elephants, giraffes, and hippopotamuses were easy game, while the rivers and lakes offered fish and edible molluscs. The Nile valley was home to water buffaloes, warthogs, wildebeest, and zebra. The Sahara, which had been so forbidding, had now become a rich and inviting environment for hunter-gatherers.

Settling the Desert

The sudden and dramatic change in the climate in the century or so after 9700 BC heralds what has been called the African Humid Period. It was to last until about 3000 BC, when a gradual reversion to more arid conditions set in. During the African Humid Period the population grew and communities spread out across the vast territory that had once been uninhabitable, developing increasingly sophisticated strategies to ensure a constant supply of food.

In favoured areas like the Nile valley, hunter-gatherers were becoming increasingly sedentary even before the onset of the African Humid Period, attracted by the copious stocks of fish provided by the river and the lakes that had formed in the valley. In the middle Nile valley, in the period 13,000–9000 BC, communities named after the site of Qadan were fishing and hunting large animals, including wild cattle. They were also gathering wild grasses using sickles made with microlithic blades set in wooden hafts. Constant cutting of grass, their stems rich in silica, has given the stone blades a distinctive gloss. The grains and wild plant food were ground on the grindstones examples of which have been found at many of the campsites. The Qadans buried their dead in cemeteries—another sign of sedentism. At Jebel Sahaba fifty-eight bodies were found, nearly half of whom, irrespective of age or gender, had died a violent death, evidenced by stone missile tips embedded in their bodies and slash marks on their bones. The cemetery is a reminder that a sedentary way of life, unleashing population growth, would inevitably lead to competition for rare resources, creating conflict between groups.

From 11,000 BC hunter-gatherers spread gradually from the Nile valley, the Sahel, and the North African coastal zone into the greening desert. All used a technology based on microliths to make tools and weapons, and all adopted methods to maximize food resources. Stands of wild grasses useful as food could be kept free from weeds and protected from animals to increase yield, while docile animals like Barbary sheep could be offered food to keep them near at hand, safe from predators. Fish and other aquatic resources, even hippopotamuses, presented a ready source of food, encouraging hunting groups to stay close to lakes and rivers. An assured food source of fish and

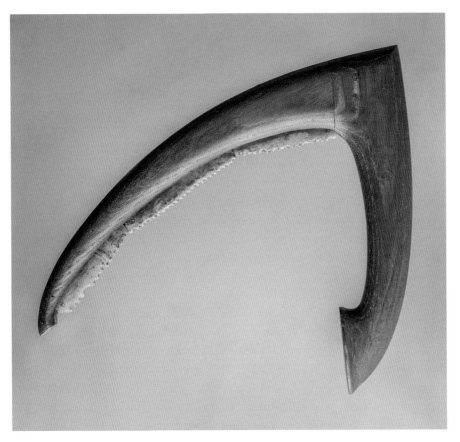

2.12 One of the flint blades of a composite sickle. From Merimde Beni Salama in the western Nile delta region of Egypt dating to the Neolithic period. The replica, from the Museo Egizio, Turin, shows how the blades were hafted.

wild grasses reduced the need for the group to range over wide areas, and this, and the need to store food surpluses, led to increased sedentism. Once a more static mode of substance was in place, other consequences followed. Population numbers rose, partly as a result of a more assured food supply and partly as a response to reduced mobility. In mobile hunter-gatherer groups there was usually a three- to five-year gap between births. In more sedentary societies the frequency of births increased. One result of population growth, as we have seen, was intergroup tension, but this, and other detrimental consequences, could be alleviated by encouraging a sector of the group to move away from the home base to find new territories to exploit. A more settled way of life, requiring food to be stored, led to other social changes. Systems of storage (delayed consumption) meant that those controlling the surpluses could arrange for a tithe to be used in cycles of gift exchange, enhancing social bonds between neighbouring groups. Surpluses could also be used in commercial transactions, creating mechanisms for status differentials to emerge. In other words, the stage was now set for societies to become more complex.

Technology developed to serve the socio-economic changes now under way. In addition to the composite tools made of microliths and grindstones for treating plant foods, bone harpoons with barbs down one side are now frequently found. Harpoons of this kind were mainly used for fishing but could also be useful in bringing down small game. But perhaps the most surprising innovation was the manufacture of pottery, a procedure that saw the transformation of malleable clay into a physically different material by the use of fire: it was a major technological advance. Pottery was made and used in West Africa from as early as 9000 BC, well before the technique had appeared in the Near East. By 6000 BC it had spread to the Nile valley. Two basic types were made: open bowls suitable for cooking, and closed forms with a narrow neck, which could be used for storing water. Ostrich eggs were already used as water containers, but pots had the advantage that the water seeping through the fabric evaporated on the outside, keeping the water inside cool. At Ounjougou, in Mali, where the earliest pots, dating to 9400 BC, were found, the community spent much time collecting the grains of wild grasses that grew throughout the territory. The availability of pottery meant that the seeds could be boiled, creating a palatable form of porridge. The facility to boil food was a significant new advance. Pottery vessels were also items of value and much effort was put into decorating them, usually involving the use of a comb to impress patterns all over the outer surface before they were fired. Each community would have used their own favoured designs. In this way pottery became a symbol of group identity.

Another technological advance was boatbuilding, a skill essential to communities whose livelihood depended in large measure on fishing. The only tangible evidence

2.13 Bone harpoons of the Neolithic period (fourth millennium BC) from the middle Nile. Harpoons were used for both hunting and fishing. The largest is 70 centimetres in length.

2.14 The earliest pottery was made in West Africa c.9000 BC. These examples, from Nabta Playa, Egypt, date to 7000–6100 BC. The wavy-line decoration, characteristic of pottery of this period, extends over a wide area.

 59

so far available is a log boat found at Dufuna, in north-east Nigeria. The vessel, 8.4 metres long, carved from a tree of black African mahogany, is dated 6500–6000 BC. It was an accomplished piece of work, implying that log boat construction was already a long-established skill by the time that the Dufuna boat was hewn from the trunk.

The increasingly sedentary nature of life of some communities is demonstrated by the thick deposits of debris which accumulated at the hunter-gatherer settlements. At the rock shelter of Uan Tabu, in the Tadrart Acacus highlands of south-west Libya, a substantial layer of domestic waste was found containing pottery and tools of stone, bone, and wood. It had accumulated in the period 6800–6400 BC and clearly implies constant use of the shelter over a long period of time. In the same region, excavations at Ti-n-Torha exposed the remains of ten huts built against a rock face. The associated occupation levels, beginning about 7000 BC, show that the community depended on Barbary sheep, gazelles, and hares, as well as fish and birds and a range of wild grasses, all available within easy reach of the home base.

In the Sahel, communities living on the edge of the Inner Niger Delta used the aquatic environment to fish, collect molluscs, and hunt hippopotamuses, turtles, and crocodiles, while exploiting the terrestrial environment for rhinoceros, warthog, equids, and antelope. With such a range of resources to choose from, life was good.

Although the archaeological evidence for the occupation of the Sahara after 9700 BC is rich, the processes by which the colonization of so vast an area took place are little

2.15 Although fishing played an important part in the economy, evidence for boats is sparse. The most spectacular is this dugout canoe found in waterlogged conditions at Dufuna, Damaturu, in northern Nigeria. It is 8.4 metres long and dates to 6500–6000 BC.

understood. However, the Sahel probably featured large in this. The people exploiting this area show a strong similarity to those living in the Upper Nile region, and it may well be that groups of hunter-gatherers from the Nile spread westwards along the Sahel corridor, from where some moved north into the steppe that occupied much of what is now the Sahara. There could also have been movements from the west, from the wooded savannah of Mali, from where, on present showing, the earliest pottery making was taking place. At any event, by 6000 BC the vast region covered by the wooded savannah, the grassland savannah, and the steppe, that is the region between the northern edge of the equatorial forest and the centre of the present Sahara, was now the preserve of hunter-gatherers, many of them favouring aquatic environments, using a similar range of microlith-tipped tools, bone harpoons, and pottery decorated with wavy lines. But the apparent cultural unity is deceptive. The many varied ecozones called for different responses from the communities attempting to exploit them, while the expanses of empty land between created a patchwork effect. Such social links as there were between neighbouring groups were managed by cycles of gift exchange.

Language was a unifying factor. Most probably spoke a language belonging to the Nilo-Saharan group, except for those in the west, where the Niger–Congo languages were spoken.

The northern half of the Sahara was different. Here the predominant stone industry is referred to as Capsian and is known throughout Algeria, Tunisia, and Libya. It was a long-lived tradition developing from the Iberomaurusian, the early phase of which, referred to as Typical Capsian, is relevant to this chapter. At the cave site of Haua Fteah it is dated to 10,600–5900 BC. Hunting continued much as before, relying on a range of animals including aurochs and hartebeest. Hares were also hunted, and large quantities of land snails were collected for food, their shells being deposited in middens forming sizeable mounds. The Capsian originated in the coastal region, but, with the amelioration of the climate, expanded south as steppe vegetation gradually extended across what had been desert. The Capsian hunter-gatherers, like their predecessors, spoke Afro-Asiatic languages.

The sudden improvement in the climate around 9700 BC meant that, within a thousand years or so, hunter-gatherers had been able to move into regions that had only a short time before been desert. They had learnt to manipulate the wild fauna and flora with such success that they were able to settle into more sedentary modes of existence. Already wild grasses were being nurtured and collected, and Barbary sheep herded. It would not be long before the first steps were taken towards the domestication of crops and animals.

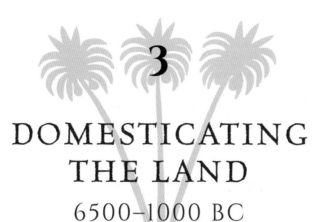

3

DOMESTICATING
THE LAND
6500–1000 BC

B Y 6000 BC hunter-gatherer communities had roamed the Sahara for nearly
three thousand years using their specialist skills to extract a living from the variety of different environments in which they found themselves. Although there
were minor fluctuations in climate requiring a degree of mobility, the broad-spectrum
foraging now being practised had a resilience. If one food source failed, another could
be exploited to compensate. The relative stability that prevailed over long periods of
time allowed people to grow familiar with the behaviour of the plants and animals on
which they depended and to begin to manipulate them. Wild Barbary sheep could be
loosely herded, fodder could be gathered and laid out to attract herbivores to congregate, making them easy prey, and selected stands of wild grass, chosen because they did
not readily shed their seeds, could be protected. This growing symbiosis with the natural world was a first step towards domestication.

The Holocene Humid Period, which had begun quite suddenly with the arrival
of the Atlantic monsoons about 9700 BC and had converted the desert into a green
and welcoming land within a millennium, remained reasonably stable until around
6200 BC, when a new phase of aridity set in, lasting for several hundred years. The
event seems to have been triggered by the release into the Atlantic of huge quantities
of cold water following the collapse of an ice dam in northern America. It was of such
magnitude that it affected Europe and South-West Asia and can be recognized in the
Holocene temperature record of the Fazzan in North Africa. What effect it had on the

3.1 Barbary sheep lived wild in northern Africa and at first were hunted, but there is evidence to suggest that some of the more sedentary hunter-gatherer communities loosely managed flocks, protecting them from predators and providing fodder, making it easier to capture and kill a beast or two when meat was needed.

hunter-gatherer communities of the Sahara is difficult to discern, but at the very least it must have rendered some of the more marginal foraging territories untenable, creating social stresses requiring readjustment. It may be no coincidence that it was at just this time that some North African communities began to adopt domesticated animals and cultivated crops spreading from the Near East. The main crops, wheat and barley, could flourish only in certain areas, like the Nile delta and valley, where the climate was suitable, but domesticated animals, sheep and goats, followed by cattle a little later, began to be widely adopted throughout North Africa, providing foraging groups with an assured food source. Wherever suitable water supplies existed, hunting began to give way to pastoralism.

About 5300 BC the monsoonal rains that had sustained the green Sahara began to retreat southwards. This led to the aridification of the eastern Sahara, while the western

part of the desert, still benefiting from moisture brought in by the westerly winds blowing across the Atlantic, retained its humidity for some time to come, and it was not until about 3000 BC that full desert conditions began to engulf the entire region once more. The increase in aridity was rapid, and by about 2000 BC much of the Sahara was no longer inhabitable. Some of the pastoralists moved north into the Maghrib and the Mediterranean coastal zone, while others migrated south into the steppe and savannah, a zone where wild plants suitable for cultivation were already gathered by the indigenous hunter-gatherers. In the mêlée of readjustment that ensued, some of these native grasses were brought into cultivation and systems of agropastoralism developed, leading to a full sedentary way of life.

In the Nile valley, where the river and its annual flood created a zone of comparative stability suitable for the growth of wheat and barley, Near Eastern crops and domesticated animals were rapidly adopted and the population began to expand, augmented by pastoralists forced to migrate to the valley from the desert by the deteriorating climate. With population growth came the appearance of increasingly complex societies and soon the emergence of states. By the end of the second millennium, Egypt and the early kingdom of Kush were flourishing.

In the long corridor of the Sahel, south of the Sahara, a region less constricted than the Nile valley and therefore less overpopulated, there was little pressure on people to coalesce and form more complex societies, but larger groupings and a degree of specialization between communities can begin to be recognized, especially in the Inner Niger Delta region and on the shores of Lake Chad.

By the end of the second millennium, the Sahara had become a significant barrier, a hostile desert confronting the communities of the Sahel, the Nile valley, and the North African coast. By now events in the Mediterranean, notably raiding by the Sea People, were beginning to impact on Africa. In the next millennium the sea was to become a significant force for change in the continent.

The Beginnings of Pastoralism

Pastoralists have a distinctive way of life. They depend largely on the products of their domesticated animals to sustain the community and therefore it is the needs of their livestock that determine patterns of mobility and settlement. People might augment their diet by hunting and by gathering wild plants, but there is little, if any, reliance on cultivated crops. It used to be argued that pastoralism was a specialist strategy that had emerged from broad-based farming regimes involving crop cultivation, but the evidence from Africa shows that this was not always the case. Here the broad-spectrum foragers, who had worked the land for millennia, simply adopted domesticated sheep, goats, and cattle while continuing to rely on wild plants for their carbohydrates. The advantage of domesticated livestock was that they provided an assured food source in times of stress. They could be killed and eaten if necessary, but in normal times it was their milk, and, in the case of cattle, also their blood, that contributed to the diet. The milk was of particular importance since it provided fat, lacking in hunted prey but so necessary for sustained health, while blood was a source of salt.

The questions that arise, then, are when, where, and by what processes did domesticates first appear in Africa? The issue has been dominated by a long-running debate, which began in the 1980s, surrounding claims that African cattle (*Bos taurus*) were descended from stock first domesticated in the Western Desert of Egypt. The argument hinged on the interpretation of cattle bones found at Bir Kiseiba in contexts dated to 7500 BC, and at Nabta Playa a little later, about 6800 BC. The excavators argued that they were domesticated on the basis of the morphology of the bones, and that the absence of other large animals, such as hartebeest and addax, from the midden deposits showed that the local conditions must have been too harsh for large herbivores to exist unless, as in the case of cattle, they were supported by humans supplying them with water and fodder. The counter-arguments put forward were that the bones of the supposed domesticated cattle showed no significant difference from those of wild aurochs, and that the environment could have supported large animals, the absence of hartebeest and addax being the result of selection by hunters who simply preferred to catch cattle.

There the argument rested until DNA analysis offered the possibility of independent assessment. The first results tended to suggest that African cattle had, indeed, been domesticated in Africa, but recent, more extensive, studies show conclusively that there was only one domestication event, which took place in the middle Euphrates valley between 8600 and 8200 BC, and it was therefore from the Near East that domesticated cattle were introduced to Africa. The study also showed that some hybridization took place between the incoming domesticated cows and African wild aurochs.

Sheep and goats present a more straightforward picture. They were domesticated in south-east Anatolia in the second half of the ninth millennium BC, broadly the same time that cattle were being domesticated in Mesopotamia. By about 6500 BC, the three domesticates were being husbanded by communities in the southern Levant and along the east side of the Arabian peninsula, and it was from one or both of these regions that domesticated livestock were introduced into north-east Africa.

There are at present too few dated assemblages to give much precision to the timing and route of the introductions, but the broad picture is now reasonably clear. The arrival of sheep and goats (where the species cannot be distinguished they are referred

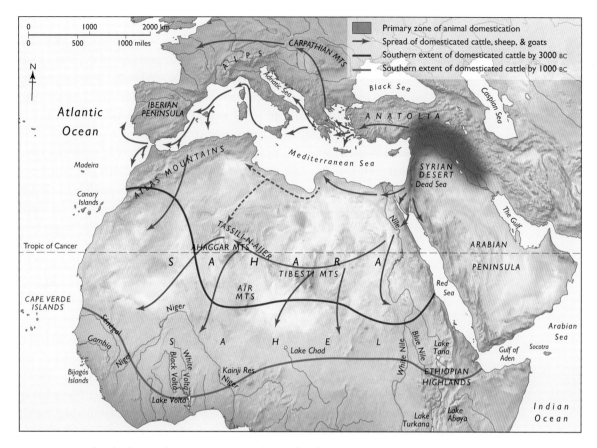

3.2 Domesticated cattle, sheep, and goats were introduced into Africa from the Near East, beginning in the sixth millennium BC. Two routes were used, one from the Levant to Egypt, the other via Anatolia and Greece to the Mediterranean and then on to Iberia and the Maghrib. Some of the incoming domesticated cattle interbred with wild African cattle.

to as caprines) appears to have preceded that of cattle by a few centuries. In Sodmein Cave on the Red Sea coast low numbers of caprines were found in contexts dating to before 6000 BC. In the oasis settlements in the Western Desert of Egypt, they first appear about 5900 BC, while in Lower Egypt, in the Faiyum, and in the cave of Haua Fteah in Cyrenaica, they are first attested about 5450 BC. At first sight this evidence might suggest that sheep and goats were introduced into Africa first across the Red Sea and only later reached the delta and the Mediterranean coast. There would be nothing surprising in this. Contact between the Red Sea and the Western Desert at this time is shown by the presence of cowrie shells at sites in the desert oases. It should, however, be remembered that many early sites may lie deeply buried beneath the silt of the delta and new discoveries may yet change our understanding. It might be safer, therefore, on present showing, to allow that from around 6000 BC domesticated sheep and goats may have been introduced into north-east Africa by several routes, some across the Red Sea, others by land to the delta, from where they spread down the Nile valley to the Sudan and along the north coast to Cyrenaica, with a more widespread diffusion to other parts of northern Africa occurring after 5200 BC.

The spread of cattle seems, on present evidence, to have followed that of sheep and goats several centuries later. At Nabta Playa and Bir Kiseiba the first domestic cattle appear after 5700 BC and are attested about the same time further south in the Sudan at El-Barga, near Kerma. In Lower Egypt, in the Faiyum, the earliest cattle are dated to 5200 BC. Cattle herding spread through the central Sahara and to the Maghrib in the fifth and fourth millennia, but it was not until the second millennium, in response to the growing aridification of the Sahara, that cattle herders moved south into West Africa (p. 79 below). If there was, indeed, a real time lag between the introduction of caprines and cattle into Africa, it could be explained by supposing that the management of domesticated sheep and goats was easier for the African hunter-gatherer groups to take on. Some of them were already herding wild Barbary sheep, so it was not a big step. Once the principle of livestock management had been mastered, the more demanding task of caring for herds of cattle, which needed to be taken to water daily, could be contemplated. Pastoralists would soon have learnt to accommodate to the constraints of so vast and varied a region. Those with easy access to water would have favoured cattle, while in the drier regions sheep and goats were easier to manage. Some will still have devoted time to hunting and fishing, and most will still have collected wild grasses and other plants to supplement the diet. Pastoralism has many faces.

What drove the spread of domesticated animals into Africa is a matter of debate, but one distinct possibility, as we have suggested above (p. 63), is the sudden onset of the cold, dry period around 6200 BC, which was to have an effect on the Near East and North Africa for between two and four centuries. The sudden change in climate may have encouraged farming communities to move south from the Levant to the well-watered Nile delta region, and local hunter-gatherers may have seen in the flocks and herds another way to extend the food supply in times when foraging had become more difficult. At any event, in the space of a few hundred years, the inhabitants of large swaths of North Africa had begun to make the transition from foraging to pastoralism.

For herders, cattle took on a totemic importance, expressed in different ways in different societies. The most common practice was the ritual burial of articulated or

3.3 In the sixth millennium, the sedentary communities of Nabta Playa in the Western Desert of Egypt created ritual monuments, built of large standing stones, associated with burials of oxen. Claims have been made that alignments within the stone circle relate to solar and stellar phenomena.

disarticulated remains of cattle in pits, sometimes associated with simple stone monuments. At Nabta Playa more complex rituals were evident. Here a megalithic monument was built comprising a stone alignment leading to a stone circle 4 metres in diameter. Nearby were two mounds covered with stone slabs and beneath one of them was a chamber containing the skeleton of a long-horned bull. It is tempting to see this as evidence of a bull cult of the kind practised later in Egypt appearing here as early as the fifth millennium.

Another way in which animals were monumentalized was through depiction. The Sahara is famous for its rock art—engravings and paintings of animals and humans—found in many of the highland regions. Though notoriously difficult to date, the representations have been grouped into five major styles spanning the nine thousand years or so BC when the region was sufficiently humid to support a rich animal life.

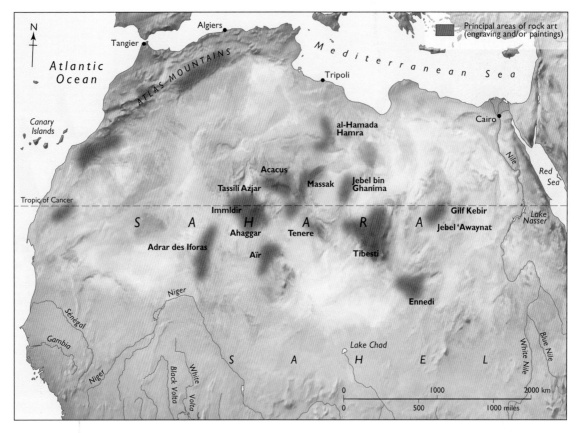

3.4 (*Above*) The communities living in the Sahara used rock surfaces to depict, by engraving or in paint, the animals they encountered. Many date from the African Humid Period and reflect the fauna that was hunted. Others, showing pastoral scenes, are later. Later still are the depictions of chariots pulled by horses, and of camels.

3.5 (*Opposite top*) The earliest period of rock art, known as the Bubalus Period (10,000–4000 BC), depicts wild animals now extinct in the region. The engraving of an elephant shown here comes from the Wadi Mathendous in the Fazzan region of south-west Libya.

3.6 (*Opposite bottom*) The Pastoral Period (5200–1000 BC) is characterized by domesticated animals, often with their herders. This example was found in the Tassili-n-Ajjer, Algeria.

The earlier images may relate to the hunter-gatherer period, but it is clear that many of them were composed during the long period of pastoralism from about 5500 to 1500 BC or later, since they illustrate scenes of herd management with human figures looking after long-horned cattle, the artists taking the trouble to depict breed variations. Scenes include the herding of cattle, milking, and even riding. The horse makes an appearance, but not until about 1500 BC.

The Spread of Near Eastern Cereal Crops

The introduction of domesticated animals to Africa from the Near East was accompanied by the spread of cultivated plants: various types of wheat, barley, lentils, chickpeas, and flax. But unlike the animals, which could thrive in many different environments, the crops were less tolerant, requiring winter rainfall or irrigation and a cool growing season. This restricted the initial spread to the coastal zone of North Africa, Egypt, Nubia, Eritrea, and northern Ethiopia. There were two routes by which transmission was made: the land or coastal route from the southern Levant to the Nile delta region, and a maritime route from Anatolia and Greece, through the central Mediterranean, to the Maghrib.

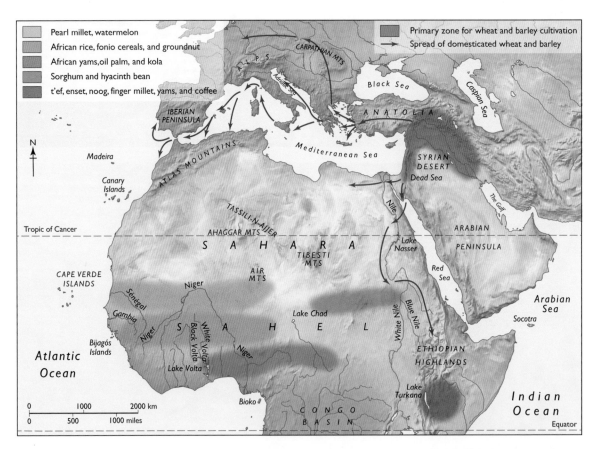

3.7 Domesticated wheat and barley were introduced into Africa from the Near East. They could only survive in environments where the moisture levels were high and they could ripen before the heat became too intense. In the sub-Saharan region a number of native plants were brought into cultivation.

3.8 Villages of farmers became widespread in the Faiyum Oasis in the sixth and fifth millennia. These sedentary communities produced surplus grain, which was stored in pits, often basket-lined. In the example shown here a sickle—a wooden shaft with inset flint blades—remains in position where it was found on the floor of the pit.

The Nile delta and the Faiyum Oasis provided a congenial environment for domesticated animals and plants to thrive. Along the edge of the Faiyum Oasis, farming settlements were well in evidence by about 5450 BC. Caprines, cattle, and pigs were reared, and six-row barley, emmer wheat, and probably flax were grown. The grain was being stored in basket-lined pits found in clusters, suggesting the cooperative effort of a reasonably sized community. Though mixed farming was now well established, fishing remained an important part of the economy. The limited life of many of the Faiyum settlements suggests that a degree of mobility was still practised. Settlement in the delta seems to have been more stable. At Merimde Beni Salama, on the western edge of the delta, a permanent farming settlement had been established by 5000 BC. It covered some 18 hectares and was composed of mud-brick houses arranged along narrow streets. Some had hearths and storage jars set in the floors, as well as clay-lined storage baskets. The permanence of the community is shown by the fact that, over the millennium or so of occupation, episodes of demolition and rebuilding led to the creation of a mound 2.5 metres high. The economic base of the settlement was mixed farming, much like that of the Faiyum, with fishing and hunting continuing to make a contribution, and cattle becoming more numerous over time.

The introduction of mixed farming to the delta region by 5450 BC represents a sudden cultural break and is likely to have been associated with the movement of people from the southern Levant, though on what scale it is difficult to say. Sites yet to be discovered, deep in the mud of the delta, could well take the story back a few centuries and show that the cultural change was less sudden than it at present appears to be.

The delta and the Faiyum were favoured regions, not only for the beneficial climate and the abundance of water, but because of their position commanding a number of routes: the land route from the Levant across Sinai; the coastal route westwards along the Mediterranean littoral; the Nile valley, offering access deep into Africa; and the two seas, the Mediterranean and the Red Sea, giving unlimited scope for those with a knowledge of sailing. The discovery in the delta and the Faiyum of seashells from both seas and diorite cosmetic palettes and green feldspar beads from Nubia demonstrates the extent of the exchange networks now in operation.

We have seen something of the spread of domestic animals southwards along the Nile valley. Seeds of cultivated crops and the knowledge of how to grow them soon followed. In Upper Egypt farming communities known as the Badarian culture became well established during the fifth millennium. Besides the all-important fishing, they herded caprines and cattle and grew wheat, barley, lentils, and tubers. Further south, in Nubia, the same animals and crops were taken up by the indigenous population, known rather unimaginatively as A Group, by the fourth millennium, and barley was being grown in the Western Desert about 5000 BC. When cereal growing reached Eritrea and Ethiopia is less clear, but barley, horse-beans, and chickpeas were in evidence in the first millennium BC, and in all probability the suite of Near Eastern crops had been introduced a millennium or so before.

3.9 (Opposite) Sedentary communities with assured food supplies had time for creative activities. At El-Badari on the upper Nile, in the latter part of the fifth millennium, someone had the leisure to carve this figurine from a piece of ivory.

The Mediterranean Contribution

The appearance of cereal growing in coastal North Africa raises a number of interesting questions. In theory it would have been quite possible for domesticated crops and animals of Near Eastern origin to have spread from the Nile delta westwards along the coast to the Maghrib, where they were well in evidence. But little is known of the desert zone between the Nile and Tunisia. However, the key sequence from the cave of Haua Fteah in Cyrenaica shows that pottery first appeared between 5400 and 4900, with the herding of sheep and goats coming later. Both are incorporated in the indigenous Capsian foraging regime, but no evidence for cereal cultivation is found until the Roman period. Herding may have been introduced from the delta, but the apparent absence of the full farming package is in stark contrast to the Maghrib, where mixed farming was being practised as early as 5800 BC. The simplest explanation would be to suppose that the Maghrib received its domesticated crops and animals from the eastern Mediterranean by sea.

There is now ample evidence from the Mediterranean to show that, during the first half of the sixth millennium, farming communities were journeying by boat from Greece and the Balkans and setting up coastal enclaves around the shores of Italy, southern France, and eastern and southern Spain intent on colonizing new territories. Some braved the Strait of Gibraltar and established settlements on the Atlantic coast of Portugal by 5500 BC. As part of this maritime enterprise, farming settlements were also set up on the North African coast. Three clusters have been recognized: one on the Atlantic coast of Morocco, one focusing on the Tangier peninsula, and one on the coast of eastern Morocco just west of Melilla. The colonists brought with them the full Near Eastern farming package: domesticated cattle, sheep, goats, and pigs, together with wheat, barley, and pulses. Another introduction was of a distinctive range of pottery known as Impressed Ware, or Cardial Ware if the impressed decoration was made using the seashell *Cardium*. Where there is good stratigraphic evidence, it can be shown that sheep and goats were introduced first, with cattle and pigs arriving a little later. The date for the earliest farming settlement in Morocco centres around 5800 BC. The process of settlement, known as enclave colonization, was, no doubt, complex, with groups of pioneers setting out every generation or so, hopping along the coast to find new land. Pottery styles suggest that those who settled in the Tangier region came from Catalonia and Andalusia. This is supported by a study of the DNA of early farmers in Morocco, which confirms that the population has a strong Iberian component.

The introduction of Near Eastern domesticated animals and cultivated crops into Africa, both by the overland route to the Nile delta and by the maritime route to the

Maghrib, took place in the first half of the sixth millennium. After the initial contacts, which probably spanned several centuries, elements of the new system were taken up by the indigenous foraging groups and selectively integrated into their way of life. As always, climate imposed constraints. While sheep, goats, and cattle spread across the Sahara, crops were restricted by rainfall to the North African coast and to the Nile valley and the Ethiopian Highlands, where the necessary environmental conditions prevailed. Geography was once more limiting human agency.

Africa's Own Contribution

The great swath of sub-Saharan Africa, from the Atlantic to the Red Sea north of the forest zone, provided a varied array of mostly grassland environments where plants suitable for cultivation thrived. Five distinct regions can be identified, each with its own offering of potential food plants. In the west, the West African Sahel, stretching from the Atlantic coast across the Niger Bend nearly as far as Lake Chad, is the home of pearl millet (*Pennisetum glaucum*) and watermelon. Immediately to the south lie the West African grassy woodlands, where African rice (*Oryza glaberrima*), fonio cereals, cow-pea, and groundnut are to be found. To the south again, but extending further to the east, is the forest margin home of African yams, oil palms, and kola. East of Lake Chad, and spreading to the valley of the Upper Nile, lie the east Sudanic grasslands, where the prominent crop plants are sorghum (*Sorghum bicolor*) and hyacinth bean. The fifth zone is the Ethiopian Highlands, encompassing a number of ecological zones supporting a range of domesticates including t'ef (a cereal grain), oilseed noog (niger seed), peas, ensete (a relative of the banana), finger millet (*Eleusine coracana*), east African yams, and coffee. There was certainly no lack of plants to be cultivated. The question is, when did the cultivation of the individual crops begin?

It must be admitted that the evidence is, at present, sparse, and where reliable dates for cultivated crops have been obtained, there is no reason to assume that they are the earliest examples of cultivation. One way to augment the African evidence is to take into account data from India, where crops native to Africa, where they must first have been cultivated, have been found in dated contexts. Cultivated pearl millet, cow-peas, hyacinth beans, sorghum, and finger millet have all been found on Indian sites from the first half of the second millennium BC, implying that they must all have been cultivated in Africa before that time (p. 83 below).

In the West African Sahel, cultivated pearl millet has been found in the Tilemsi valley, in Mali, in contexts dating to about 2400 BC and on other sites in the region dating to 1700 BC. In the West African grassy woodlands, cow-pea is known from 1700 BC and the baobab tree by 1000 BC, but the other local crops have not been noted

3.10 Sorghum (*Sorghum bicolor*) grew wild in the eastern Sahel and was being collected by hunter-gatherers in quantity. It was probably in this region that it was first cultivated in the third or second millennium. There is little physical difference between the wild and the cultivated varieties.

before the mid first millennium BC. In the forest margin, oil palm was being exploited by as early as 4000 BC but intensively only from about 1700 BC. The main crop in the east Sudanic grasslands was sorghum, but it is difficult to distinguish between the wild and cultivated varieties. It was certainly being extensively collected in the Western Desert of Egypt and the Sudan as early as 7000 BC. In the Ethiopian Highlands there is no evidence of crop domestication before the mid first millennium BC, but the discovery of cultivated finger millet in India by 1000 BC offers an indication of how old its cultivation in Ethiopia may be.

The incomplete data so far available makes it difficult to offer confident generalizations about the origin of plant cultivation in Africa, but it is clear that pearl millet was being grown in the west in the third millennium BC and sorghum and finger millet were under cultivation in the east at least by the second millennium. Further work may push these dates back much earlier. It remains now to consider the context in which the sub-Saharan communities became farmers. Once more the changing climate was the driver.

The Climate Again

At the height of the African Humid Period, around 5000 BC, we have seen that pastoralists, dependent on their herds of cattle, had spread widely throughout the Sahara. It was an ideal environment for them. The precipitation level, while sufficient to provide the water which the cattle needed daily, was not high enough to attract the tsetse fly (*Glossina* species), which carried trypanosomiasis, the sleeping sickness so devastating especially to cattle. Over much of the western and central Sahara the climate remained reasonably stable until about 3200 BC, when a southerly movement of the Intertropical Convergence Zone caused the environmental zones to begin to shift to the south, disrupting human settlement patterns. Over the next thousand years or so, as the Sahara became more arid, pastoralists were forced to migrate southwards. This was made possible because the 500–750-millimetre isohyet, which marked the northern limit that tsetse fly could survive, also moved to the south, opening up new lands for the cattle herders to exploit. That they took advantage of this is shown by the number of sites producing cattle remains dating to the second millennium found in a broad band through southern Mauritania, Mali, Niger, and Chad. These pastoralists had moved into lands long occupied by hunter-gatherers, the two communities gradually integrating. It was here that wild crops, traditionally collected by the foragers, were brought into cultivation and a new agro-pastoral way of life began to take root. The increase of population caused by the influx of pastoralists seems to have driven the foragers to take up cultivation.

The establishment of settled farming communities in the Sahel and the Sahel–Sahara border was at first restricted to core regions where there was adequate pasture for animals and sufficient water for the cultivation of pearl millet. Such favoured regions were found in the foothills of the Tichitt–Walata–Néma escarpment in southeast Mauritania, the Inner Niger Delta, and around the shores of Lake Chad in northeast Nigeria. In all three regions there is evidence of a stable agro-pastoral economy, population growth, and the advance of social complexity.

Along the 200-kilometre Tichitt escarpment, a land blessed with many small lakes, nucleated settlements of stone-built houses began to appear in the period between 1900 and 1500 BC. The settlements vary in size from small hamlets 2 hectares in extent to a massive agglomeration of 80 hectares, suggesting that a social hierarchy may have

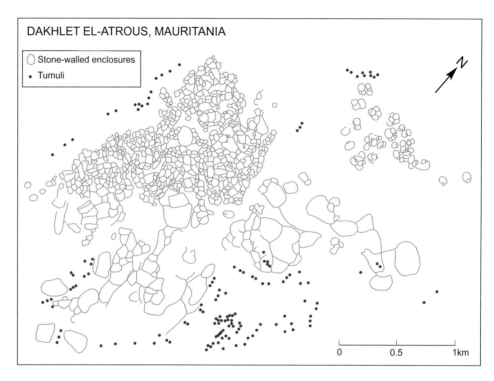

DAKHLET EL-ATROUS, MAURITANIA

○ Stone-walled enclosures
• Tumuli

0   0.5   1km

3.11 The Dhar Tichitt ridge in Mauritania, overlooking a fertile, well-watered landscape, was a favoured place to congregate for farmers relying on sheep, cattle, and cultivated pearl millet. Many settlements are known; the largest, Dakhlet el-Atrous, shown here, covered some 93 hectares. It was composed of stone-walled enclosures beyond which the burial mounds (tumuli) were located.

been evolving. What is of particular interest is that different settlements specialized in manufacturing craft products, like grindstones or beads, which were traded to neighbouring sites. Increasing aridity about 1000 BC began to bring the development to an end.

In the Inner Niger Delta the story was different. When the area became inhabitable early in the second millennium, the first communities to arrive had neither crops nor domestic animals but relied on fishing, hunting, and gathering. In the middle of the second millennium, agro-pastoralists from the north, some possibly from the Tichitt escarpment, moved in but appear to have coexisted for some time with the indigenous population.

The situation further east, in the Gajiganna region near Lake Chad, is different again. The settlement began, as the level of the lake receded, with the arrival of pastoralists in the early second millennium. Gradually the population increased until, by about 1500 BC, permanent villages of mud-brick houses were being built, some of

3.12 The stone-built enclosures of Dhar Tichitt were used for settlement, and for corralling livestock.

them sufficiently long-lived to account for the accumulation of 2 metres of stratified deposits. At what stage cultivated crops were introduced is unclear, but pearl millet is attested as early as 1200 BC. It was about this time that similar changes were happening further south in central Nigeria, leading to a development known as the Nok culture (pp. 120–2 below).

The three examples hint at the complex processes that saw the establishment of agro-pastoral communities in the Sahel as the mobility, initiated by the onset of desert conditions, drove pastoralists south from the Sahara. The mêlée of different groups, indigenous and immigrant, quickly adapted to the environments in which they found themselves, many of them choosing to rely on the drought-resistant pearl millet as a staple crop to support their increasingly sedentary way of life. As the agro-pastoral strategies became established, so populations began to grow and social systems became more complex.

The southern edge of the savannah gives way to the West African grassy wood-lands and then, further south, to the forest margin. Little is known of the early stages of cultivation in this region. It may be that some indigenous plants, like fonio cereals, cow-peas, and groundnuts, were cultivated as early as the second millennium, before domesticated pearl millet spread to the region, but only the baobab tree is attested before 1000 BC. In the forest margin the early cultivation of the staples, oil palm, African yams, and kola, remains to be studied.

In the eastern Sahara and Sahel, east of Lake Chad, the retreat of the monsoonal winds caused aridification to begin about 5000 BC, earlier than in the west. This drove groups of cattle-herding pastoralists east to the Nile valley, where they encountered a sedentary population cultivating cereals introduced from the Near East. The Badarian culture, which arose in the Upper Nile at this time, reflects the impact of the incoming cattle herders, not least in the adoption of cattle sacrifice, which from now on became a significant part of Egyptian ritual behaviour. The escalating desiccation of the Sahara after 3000 BC forced the remaining cattle herders to move south into the Sahel of the Sudan, the zone where sorghum and hyacinth bean grew and were exploited in their wild form by indigenous foragers. It may have been the influx of the pastoralists from the north that led to the cultivation of these plants in the third or second millennium.

The Ethiopian Highlands, by virtue of their many different environmental niches, nurtured a wide range of native plants suitable for cultivation. The region also had a cli-mate conducive to the reception of Near Eastern crops. By the end of the second mil-lennium, wheat, barley, lentils, and flax had been established and the local finger millet was also being grown. Little is known of the effects on the region of the changing cli-mate after 3000 BC, but it is unlikely that the highlands would have avoided the impact of displaced pastoralists.

The evidence for the early appearance of agriculture in sub-Saharan Africa may at present be sparse and ill-focused, but taken together a broad picture emerges. The changing climate leading to the aridification of the Sahara drove pastoral groups south into the land occupied by hunter-gatherers and east to the Nile valley, where cereal growing was already well established. The processes of integration were complex. In the restricted, but lush, Nile valley the productivity of the land and the fast-growing popu-lation forced the rapid rise of complex states dependent on livestock and Near Eastern cereals, a change given greater impetus by the intensification of trade with the Near Eastern states. In the south the integration led to the emergence of new agro-pastoral societies based on animal husbandry and the cultivation of local plants. Here the rela-tively unbounded nature of the environment and the lack of long-distance trade net-works meant that, although the communities grew and became more socially complex, the development of states was delayed until trade networks across the desert began to expand in the late first millennium BC and early first millennium AD.

The Indian Ocean Interface

The Ethiopian Highlands was a favoured region. Not only was it a complex of congenial environments nourishing a rich fauna and flora, but it was a major route node. It commanded routes from the north, along the Nile and Red Sea, from the south by way of the rift valleys and from the west along the Sahel corridor. It also lay at the end of a sea route leading, via the Gulf of Aden and the coast of southern Arabia, to India. In the third millennium, the Indus valley saw the emergence of an urban culture named after the town of Harappa which flourished in the period 2600–1700 BC. The Harappan cities were trading extensively with the Mesopotamian states by means of coastal traffic using the Persian Gulf and it was probably at this time that ships ventured along the coast of southern Arabia to Yemen, where plants producing incense were grown. In this way contact with Africa grew—Africa was only 35 kilometres away, across the Bab el-Mandeb. The discovery in Yemen of Ethiopian obsidian, a black, glassy volcanic rock, shows that local trading contacts existed at this time.

The full extent of trade between Ethiopia and India is still to be demonstrated, but it is known that food featured large. Sorghum, pearl millet, and cow-pea, crops first cultivated in the African Sahel, and finger millet, a product of Ethiopia, have all been found in India in contexts dating to about 1700 BC (p. 77 above). The establishment of these African crops in India implies that quantities of seed was transported, presumably for both food and cultivation. In reverse, broomcorn millet (*Panicum miliaceum*), ultimately a Chinese cultivate, recorded in India and Yemen in contexts dating to 2000 BC, was transmitted to Africa to take root in Nubia about 1700 BC. Another introduction from the East was zebu cattle (*Bos indicus*)—a hump-backed breed first domesticated in India. It was introduced to East Africa about 2000 BC. No doubt many other commodities were carried between India and Africa in the third and second millennia. Some hint of the range is given by the black peppercorn found in the nostril of the pharaoh Rameses II (*c*.1200 BC). Peppercorns were a luxury product traded from the south of India.

The Atlantic Interface

We have seen that in the first half of the sixth millennium BC farming communities moving by sea were establishing themselves along the Mediterranean coasts of France

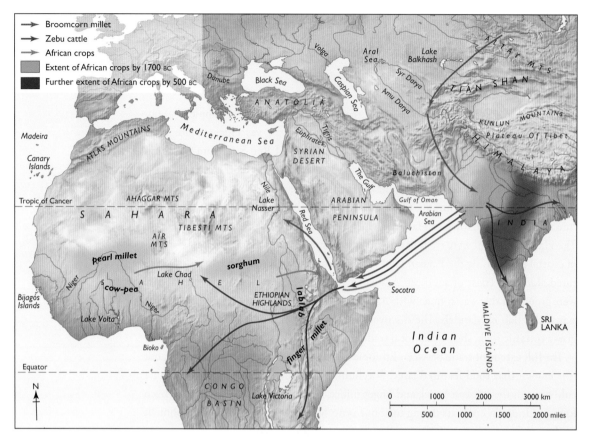

3.13 The Indian Ocean provided a corridor of communication along the Arabian coast, between the complex societies of the Indus valley and East Africa. There was much interchange between the two continents in the second millennium. African crops, such as pearl millet, finger millet, cow-pea, and sorghum, were exported to the Indus valley, while broomcorn millet (*Panicum miliaceum*) and zebu cattle were introduced into East Africa.

and Spain, with some sailing through the Strait of Gibraltar to settle on the Atlantic coast of Portugal. As part of that general movement, groups bringing with them their domesticated animals and seed grain set up enclaves at several points on the coast of Morocco (pp. 76–7 above). By the second half of the sixth millennium, farming had become well established in Morocco. Given the sailing capabilities of the pioneer farmers it is likely that the coastal communities of Iberia and North Africa would have remained in contact. Little is known of this until the end of the fourth or beginning of the third millennium, when ivory from the African elephant *Loxodonta africana*, then roaming wild on the foothills of the Atlas Mountains and the extensive grasslands of the Maghrib, was exported in some quantity to the estuaries of the Guadalquivir and Tagus to meet the demands of the local Iberian elite. There is no indication of what goods were offered to the Africans in reciprocation.

In the third millennium, connectivity intensified. By now a distinctive assemblage of pottery typified by Maritime Bell Beakers, well-made red-fired vessels with impressed herringbone decoration, was being manufactured in the Tagus region. Beakers of this kind have been found in Africa, on the Tangier peninsula, and on the Atlantic coast in the region of Rabat, with others finding their way inland, some reaching the Algerian steppe. Bronze missile points, known as Palmela points, and other bronze weapons were also now being exported to North Africa, with concentrations along the Atlantic coast as far south as Casablanca. Some are found inland near Fez and in western Algeria south of Oran. Until the end of the third millennium much of the contact between Africa and Iberia seems to have been by way of the Atlantic coast. During this time the farming communities living along the Mediterranean coast of Iberia received their supplies of ivory from eastern Mediterranean merchants who were able to acquire tusks of Asian elephants (*Elephas maximus*), but from the late third and early second millennium this is replaced by African ivory. It was at this time that flat axes, halberds, and daggers made of bronze in the workshops of Iberia during the time of the Argaric culture were exported to North Africa. Though few actual examples have been found, these types are well represented in rock art engravings in the Atlas Mountains.

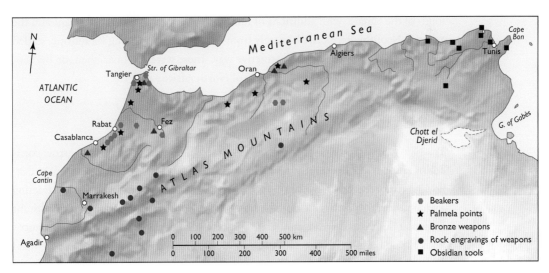

3.14 In the third and second millennia, the communities of the Maghrib were exchanging commodities with Europe. Bronze weapons and Beaker pottery from Iberia and obsidian from the central Mediterranean islands found their way to Africa, while ivory and ostrich eggshells were traded to Iberia.

 85

The evidence, then, is clear. Throughout the third millennium and well into the second, maritime networks bound the western Maghrib and southern Iberia and contacts intensified over time. For the Iberians it was ivory and ostrich eggshells for making jewellery that were the attraction. Gold may also have been traded, but there is no positive evidence of this. In return, the Africans received striking Beaker pottery and a range of bronze tools and weapons. These are the items we can recognize in the archaeological record. Many other commodities would also have exchanged hands: animal skins, textiles, exotic feathers, and the like, items that must have excited the elites on both sides of the sea as they waited eagerly for the trading ships to arrive.

Less is known about the networks connecting the eastern Maghrib, but at the end of the sixth millennium obsidian from the island of Pantelleria, between Tunisia and Sicily, was being transported to Tunisia, and later, in the fifth millennium, the prolific quarries on Lipari, off the north coast of Sicily, were supplying a more extensive region including eastern Algeria. The networks linking the eastern Maghrib to Sicily and Italy probably continued to operate during the following millennia, but there is little direct archaeological evidence of this.

For the inhabitants of the Maghrib, from the sixth millennium onwards, the Mediterranean and its Atlantic extension became an essential part of their world, the more so after the end of the fourth millennium, when the desert behind them became increasingly arid and hostile to movement. In their contained world, the people, whose genetic mix was based on the first Palaeolithic population to reach the area from the south of the Sahara, with additions of hunter-gatherer genes from the Levant and the genes of Neolithic farmers, ultimately from the Near East, arriving via Europe, settled down to develop in their own distinctive way. These were the Imazighen, or Berbers, who came to feature large in the history of North Africa.

The Precocious Nile

The Nile valley is, by any standards, a remarkable phenomenon: a long, narrow corridor of unusual fertility tightly defined and protected by interminable desert. The fast-flowing river teems with fish and is supported by a band of lush vegetation, attracting a wide variety of animals including humans. The monsoon rains falling on the distant Ethiopian Highlands create annual floods, refertilizing the flanking lands with nutritious silt and adding to the ever-growing delta. There could hardly be a more ideal ecological niche for life to flourish. Added to this is the power of the river itself, facilitating rapid movement and enabling heavy loads to be transported. The natural flow carries vessels from south to north, while the prevailing wind blows in the opposite direction, powering vessels with sails to make headway against the flow as far south as the great S-bend in the middle reaches of the river, where cataracts interrupt progress. Here overland portages replaced the river. When the Greek historian Herodotus wrote that Egypt was the gift of the Nile, he was recognizing the basic truth that, without the remarkable life-giving power of the water and the silt load that it carried, the civilizations that arose along its valley would not have been possible.

For hunter-gatherers the Nile was a paradise, providing fish in plenty, game animals, birds, and stands of wild grasses. But, after the onset of the African Humid Period, about 8500 BC, the valley became dank, marshy, and unhealthy, losing its attraction, while the desert became more hospitable, drawing communities away. The retreat of the monsoonal rains after 5300 BC began to reverse the trend, with hunter-gatherer groups returning to the river, driven from the surrounding lands by increasing aridity. By this time, domesticated animals and cultivated cereals were beginning to spread from the Levant to the delta region and then down-river, to be taken up by the local foragers, those in the desert fringes adopting domesticated cattle to become pastoralists while those occupying the valley itself took up crop growing, the mild climate and ample water favouring the growth of cereals. Around 3500 BC, as the aridity became intense and oases dried up, the pastoralists living in the desert fringes were driven to the valley, bringing with them the specialist skill of cattle herding and a belief system in which cattle held a central place (pp. 68–9 above).

The unusual fertility of the valley suited the cultivation of wheat and barley. The floods occurred in late summer. By autumn, when the water had receded, leaving the ground moist with its coat of fresh silt, it was time to sow the crop, which could then grow through the warm Egyptian winter and be ready for harvest in the spring before the temperature became too hot. In a good year the yield would have far exceeded the subsistence needs of the population, but the knowledge that floods could fail, bringing famine, meant that the storage of surpluses became an essential safeguard. Such a system, requiring cooperation and coordination, led inevitably to the creation of a complex social hierarchy. People were tasked to oversee the collection of tithes and the storage and distribution of the surplus, while the corvée labour needed to clear the canals so that water reached the widest possible area had to be arranged and overseen. Better organization, extending the holding capacity of the land, encouraged a growth of population which was further bolstered by the influx of pastoralists moving into the valley. The pressures and tensions caused by a high population density, even though the land could support the number of people, were contained by an increasingly complex social system requiring laws, lawgivers, and the authority to manage compliance.

The valley environment was claustrophobic. Constrained by the desert, the only direction of movement was up or down the river, and for this boatbuilding was essential. The earliest boats were constructed from bundles of reeds, a skill that no doubt dated back to the time of the earliest hunter-gatherer communities. By the fifth millennium, the inhabitants of Merimde, in the delta, were using oars, as shown by clay models. The use of planks to build hulls was under way in Upper Egypt by early in the fourth millennium, and the first sails are attested in the same region by 3400–3300 BC. By this stage technology had mastered the river. The only problem was the accessibility of suitable timber, and for this the most convenient source was the northern Levant, which produced the famous cedars of Lebanon.

The need for raw materials like timber encouraged the growth of networks of exchange and eventually led to campaigns of conquest. The Eastern Desert and the Red Sea hills were particularly rich in copper and lead, as well as desirable building stone like porphyry and granite, and gemstones such as jasper, emerald, and amethyst. Extensive deposits of gold were found in Nubia, and from the south came ivory and ebony. As society became more complex and hierarchies evolved, so the demand for raw materials grew. By acquiring these goods and controlling their distribution the elite could demonstrate their power. Personal display was a way of exercising superior status, but there was the danger that the more the trading expeditions were successful, the lower became the value of the goods acquired. One effective way to counter this was to remove valued items from circulation by the social requirement that they be buried with the dead. Conspicuous consumption of this kind not only kept the value of the rare commodity high, but, when seen to be done, it greatly enhanced the status of the lineage whose departed were so honoured. The danger inherent in such a system was that expectation grew and each elite burial had to be made more elaborate than the last. Failure to manage this led to loss of status, which could cause political instability. Another of the outward and visible signs of power was monumental architecture in the form of palaces, tombs, and temples. Their construction reflected the ability to access fine building stone, architects, and other specialists and mass labour. Since all required an underpinning of food in considerable surplus, it was in the interest of the elite to control, and to continue to increase, production.

The system, when working, was one of unstable equilibrium. It could easily be upset. Successive failures of the annual flood could undermine production, the supply of raw materials could decrease as sources became depleted or inaccessible, ambition might overstretch capacity, external enemies might invade or faith leaders falter. Complex states are fragile edifices.

The Rise of Pharaonic Egypt

The rich archaeological record of Egypt, so avidly researched for more than three centuries, together with the wealth of hieroglyphic texts that survive, have enabled a

detailed historical narrative of Egyptian civilization to be devised. In the conventional scheme the history of Egypt is divided into a Predynastic period (4500–3000 BC) and a Pharaonic period, the earlier part of which is divided into six major episodes, Early Dynastic (3000–2686 BC), Old Kingdom (2686–2160 BC), First Intermediate period (2160–2055 BC), Middle Kingdom (2055–1650 BC), Second Intermediate period (1650–1550 BC), and New Kingdom (1550–1069 BC). The scheme provides a convenient framework for considering the development of the early state.

The Predynastic period saw the emergence of small, independent villages clustering along the Nile, their well-being relying on agricultural production. Plank-built sailing ships were in use, and limited trade in gold, silver, and copper was under way. Bronze working, a skill probably learnt from the Near East, was being practised by the middle of the fourth millennium. It was in Upper Egypt, where the Nile was at its most constricted over a distance of 300 kilometres, that social complexity first becomes apparent. As the population increased and trade intensified, some of the villages began to grow rapidly, and three of them, Naqada, Hierakonpolis, and This, rose to become regional centres. Hierakonpolis was not far from the goldfields in the Eastern Desert, and the Nile at this point was only 250 kilometres from rich sources of copper and stone to be had in the Red Sea Hills.

Throughout the fourth millennium, the three towns developed as focuses of craft production as well as becoming administrative and cult centres, and towards the end of the millennium they were united under the leadership of a single king. The rise of the ruling elite can be traced in the burial-grounds of Abydos. In the period 4000–3500 BC the tombs were still largely undifferentiated, but thereafter elaborate and well-furnished tombs begin to appear, until about 3200 BC, when the tombs of the kings of Dynasty 0 and Dynasty 1 (3200–2890 BC) can be identified. In one of the multi-room tombs, dating to about 3200 BC, four hundred jars of Palestinian origin, possibly originally containing wine, were found. The tomb also yielded 150 labels inscribed with hieroglyphs—the earliest so far known—their presence reminding us that the movement of goods in such quantity required an efficient accounting system. The extent of the trading networks is vividly displayed by Tomb 11 at Locality 6 in Hierakonpolis. The tomb had been looted, but sufficient remained to show that its occupant had been adorned with beads of carnelian, garnet, turquoise, faience, gold, and silver, accompanied by items of lapis lazuli, ivory, obsidian, and crystal. Access to luxury goods coming from as far afield as Anatolia and Afghanistan was now an essential mark of status.

The far-flung routes that sustained the elite of Upper Egypt were heavily dependent on the Nile. Downstream, to the north, the delta could be reached in about two weeks. Here traders had access to the produce of the Levant, the cedar wood so essential for

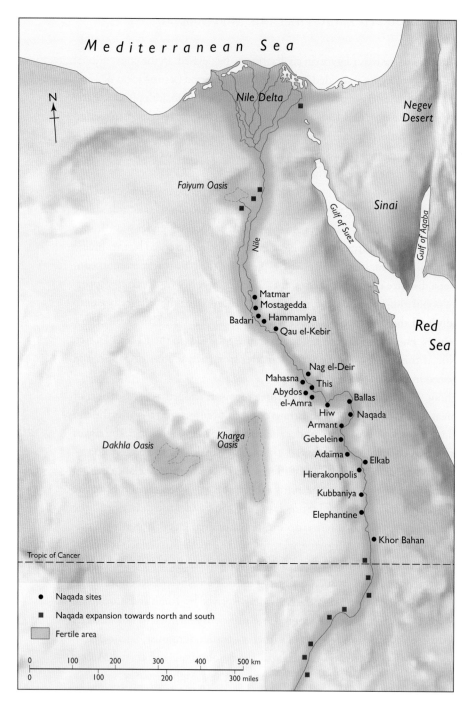

3.15 The Nile valley, the delta, and the oases in the Western Desert provided food in plenty for the burgeoning population of Egypt. The Eastern Desert offered other resources like copper and gold, while the river and the Red Sea facilitated the supply of more exotic commodities from the south. In the fourth millennium, the polity dominating the upper Nile, named after the site of Naqada, expanded their influence north to the delta and south to Nubia.

boatbuilding and the oils and fragrances used in burial rituals. At Abydos the entrance passage of the tomb of Sekhem-khet (r. 2648–2640 BC) had been so doused in aromatic oils that the scent still pervaded the tomb when it was opened five thousand years later. Nor should we forget the huge consignment of Palestin-ian wine supplied to an earlier king at Aby-dos. It was through the Levantine traders that links were forged with Mesopotamia and its even more extensive networks. Travelling south from Upper Egypt, upstream beyond the First Cataract, Lower Nubia could be reached, whence came gold, ivory, ebony, and incense. By 3000 BC the kings of Upper Egypt had learnt much of the world beyond their borders. Nurtured by the river and pro-tected by the desert, they commanded the commodities passing between Africa and the states of the Levant and Mesopotamia. When the ambition of the rulers, under-pinned by the strength of the agricultural base, led inevitably to territorial expan-sion, the obvious direction of advance was downstream to the delta, through which so much of the international trade was articulated.

3.16 Navigating the Nile was crucial to maintain state authority and to manage commerce. The development of the sail made it possible to use the powerful north wind to make easy progress up-river, against the flow. The jar, from Naqada, shows a river craft with a fore-mounted square-rigged sail. It dates from about 3100 BC.

The unification of Egypt between the First Cataract and the delta around 3000 BC involved the aggressive takeover of many polities strung out along the 1,000 kilometres or so of the river. The process is nicely symbolized on the famous Narmer Palette, found at Hierakonpolis, showing the king striking a submissive foe, a triumphant procession, and rows of decapitated ene-mies. Once the lower Nile had been conquered, the changed political reality demanded the establishment of a new administrative centre close to where the Nile split into the many channels of the delta. It was here that Memphis was founded, the centre from

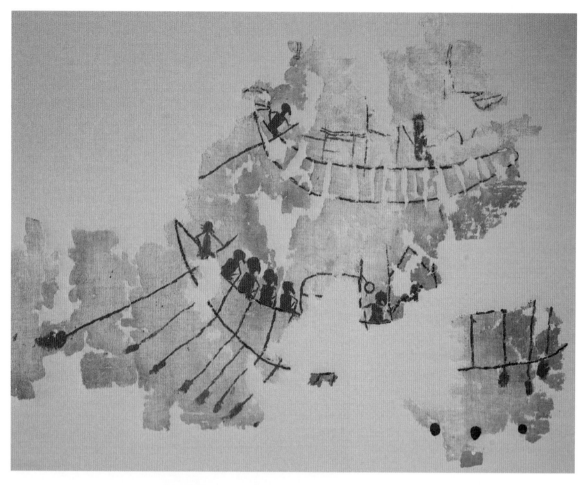

3.17 When the wind conditions were not right, or greater speed was needed, rowers could be used, like those shown here in action in this painting on a piece of linen from El-Gebelein in Upper Egypt dating to the fourth millennium BC.

which the god-king presided. From the outset the high officials were buried close to Memphis, at Saqqara, the elaboration of their tombs showing their growing power. At first the kings still chose to be buried in the royal cemetery at Abydos, but from the time of the Third Dynasty (2686–2613 BC) the bodies of royalty were buried at Saqqara.

With the unification of Egypt, attention turned to the south, to Lower Nubia, the source of gold and the route through which so many exotic commodities passed. A military expedition was mounted and the river annexed as far as the Second Cataract, where a fort was built at Buhen, bringing Lower Nubia under direct Egyptian control.

3.18 Tomb U-j of Dynasty 00 (c.3200 BC) at Abydos in Upper Egypt was a multi-roomed structure. One of the rooms was packed with a large number of Palestinian storage jars once containing wine or oil. The find reflects the intensity of the trade between the Levant and Egypt at this time.

About the same time, a military force annexed much of northern Sinai and a border post was established at Ein Besor in southern Palestine.

The Old Kingdom came to an end in 2160 BC. The period that followed, known as the First Intermediate period (2160–2055 BC), was, according to the surviving texts, a time of great upheaval, notable in the archaeological record for the total absence of monumental architecture. Why, after eight hundred years of strong central rule, the state should have collapsed is unclear, but there were probably many contributory causes. This was a time of intense aridification, coinciding with a succession of low Nile floods, which brought famine. Added to this, the state had become so complex that the administration now consumed an increasing percentage of the gross annual product. The growing power of officials, not least the provincial governors, further diminished the prestige of the king. Under these many pressures the unified state became

3.19 The Narmer Palette, dating to *c.*3000 BC, was found at Hierakonpolis. On one side it depicts King Narmer, wearing the White Crown of Upper Egypt, about to strike a subservient foe. The other side shows the king wearing the Red Crown of Lower Egypt, accompanied by his officials and standard bearers, on their way to inspect the decapitated bodies of his enemies. The message is that Narmer, by his strength and power, had brought Upper and Lower Egypt under his sole authority.

unsustainable and collapsed. After an interlude of devolution, Egypt was reunited by the dynasty that had maintained control of Thebes, instituting the Middle Kingdom (2055–1650 BC).

To explore the vicissitudes experienced by the Egyptian state is beyond the scope of this book, but certain developments of general relevance to our broad themes can be briefly mentioned. Unified government lasted for four centuries until the state fragmented again. During the Second Intermediate period that followed (1650–1550 BC), Upper Egypt continued to be ruled from Thebes, while the whole of Lower Egypt, from El-Amarna to the coast, came under the control of the Hyksos, an elite from the Levant who arrived in the wake of an influx of population already settled in the delta. At the same time Lower Nubia was lost to Egypt. The Hyksos rulers opened Lower Egypt to influences from the Levant, bronze-working technology became widespread, and new weapon sets were introduced, including scale armour, the composite bow, and the two-wheeled chariot pulled by a pair of horses.

About 1550 BC the pharaoh Ahmose came to power in Thebes and expelled the Hyksos from Lower Egypt, once more unifying the country. During the period that followed, known as the New Kingdom (1550–1069 BC), Egypt grew to be more powerful than ever. Realizing that the country was under constant threat from the Near Eastern states, the Egyptian leaders took the initiative by conquering the Levant and inland regions as far as the banks of the Euphrates. Meanwhile, in the south, the whole of Nubia was conquered as far as the Fifth Cataract, giving Egypt control of the Nubian goldfields. By the fifteenth century, then, Egypt had created an empire bounded only by the desert and the sea.

But it was not to last. Hittite pressure on the Levant eventually put an end to Egyptian domination here, while the delta was threatened by the mysterious Sea People—stateless marauders who probably came from Asia Minor and caused widespread disruption in the eastern Mediterranean between 1220 and 1180 BC. The desert people in Libya also got caught up in this episode of turmoil. The first we hear of the unrest is about 1220 BC, when the pharaoh, Merneptah, had to face a concerted attack

3.20 A relief on the wall of the Great Temple at Medinet Habu, Egypt, vividly depicts the attack of the Sea People on the Nile delta being repelled by Rameses III (1184–1153 BC). The attackers are coming under fire from Egyptian archers.

in the Western Desert from Libyans and their allies, 'northerners coming from all lands'. The incident is described in an inscription from Karnak, which makes clear that this was no ordinary raid. The Libyan king brought his family, treasure, and livestock with him, clearly intent on settling in the delta. The force was defeated and many thousands were killed, leaving the Egyptians in awe of the quantity of spoils taken: gold, silver, weapons, furniture, cattle, and goats. The Libyans presumably came from the coastal region, where they would have been in contact with the Sea People. Another Libyan raid on the delta is recorded in 1189 BC. Other attacks followed involving a variety of foreign foe culminating in a great sea battle in 1186 BC at which the pharaoh, Rameses III, was triumphant. The turbulence affected the whole of the eastern Mediterranean. Although the Egyptians seem to have fought off the attacks and the attempted invasions, the old power structures were collapsing and the trading networks were in disarray. The centralized state began to fall apart once more. As Egyptian control of Nubia was lost about 1070, the New Kingdom collapsed to give way to the Third Intermediate period (1069–664 BC).

In its two-thousand-year history the Egyptian state grew from a collection of villages scattered along the Nile in Upper Egypt to an empire with highly distinctive social and religious systems, art, architecture, and writing. A constant feature recurring throughout its fluctuating fortunes was that the original Upper Egyptian core, blessed by ample resources and protected by its remote desert location, was able to reassert itself after every downturn of fortune. By the end of the second millennium BC, the world of which Egypt was a part was changing both politically and economically. The most far-reaching change was that the seaways were beginning to capture the trading networks, undermining the control that the Nile had once exercised. Although the Nile valley continued to play a significant part in African history, the energy that had created Africa's first state was now waning.

Kerma and the First Kingdom of Kush

To the Egyptians, the land immediately to the south of the First Cataract was known as the land of Wawat and beyond that lay Kush, occupying Nubia. Through this territory flowed the Nile, making its great S-bend up to the confluence of the Blue Nile and White Nile. To this point the river was bounded by desert, but beyond, to the south, the desert gave way to steppe—the beginning of a very different world. Up-river from the First Cataract, near Aswan, there were five other cataracts to be negotiated before the confluence of the two Niles was reached. This hindrance was exacerbated by the fact that the predominantly north wind, which aided sailing up-river, was of little use on the river's great reverse curves. It was for this reason that overland portages across

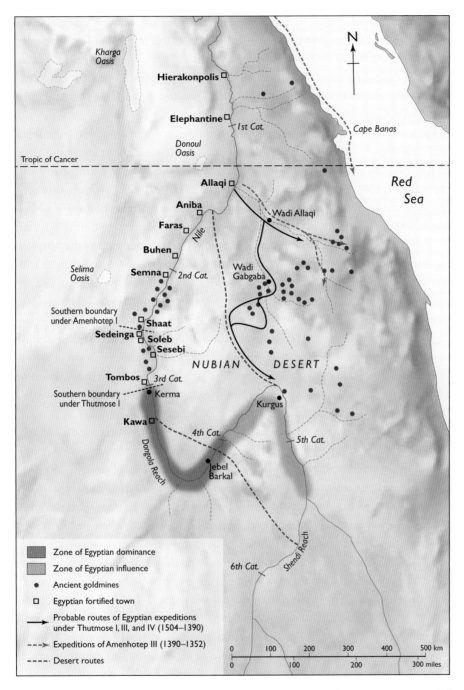

3.21 Egypt made several attempts to bring Nubia under control in the period 1500–1350 BC. Control of the goldfields in the Eastern Desert provided a strong incentive.

the desert came into being, with the added advantage of considerably shortening the journey. The fertility of the valley and the high water table in times of flood provided ample good arable and pasture to support the growing population, but it was concentrated on three stretches of river, Lower Nubia up to the Second Cataract, the Dongola Reach between the Third and Fourth Cataracts, and the Shendi Reach on either side of the Sixth Cataract.

For a thousand years, from the mid third millennium to the mid second millennium, the region was dominated by the city of Kerma, situated just above the Third Cataract on the Dongola Reach, which became the centre of a powerful state growing rich on trade between Africa and Egypt. The advance of the Egyptians above the Second Cataract in the period 1950–1850 BC, and the construction of a massive fortress to guard the new frontier, brought Egypt to within 250 kilometres of Kerma, but after the Egyptian withdrawal, Kerma extended its power, taking over some of the Egyptian infrastructure, both fortifications and personnel. The state now controlled 1,300 kilometres of the river as far upstream as the Fourth Cataract. Its enhanced status as a significant player in the power game is evident in a communication from the Hyksos king, now in control of the delta, to the king of Kush inviting the Kushites to invade Upper Egypt, a request with which they were pleased to comply. Later, with the reunification of Egypt, the Egyptians turned their attention once more to Kush. The town of Sai was taken about 1530 BC, and at a battle fought at the Third Cataract, the pharaoh Thutmose I (1504–1492 BC) is said to have killed a Kushite king and to have quickly advanced to the Fifth Cataract, bringing an end to the first kingdom of Kush.

Over the thousand years or so of its life, Kerma had grown to become a substantial city, creating deposits up to 12 metres thick. It was defended by a wall of mud-brick with projecting towers fronted by a wide ditch. The city was dominated by a centrally placed religious building constructed of timber-laced mud-brick. There was also a royal palace with extensive store rooms, administrative buildings, and quarters set aside for industrial production including bronze working and pottery manufacture. In the nearby cemetery, the earliest graves were simple pits containing the body, along with pottery vessels and sacrificed sheep and goats. But over time the burial ritual became more elaborate until, by the mid second millennium, royal tombs can be identified, complex constructions built of mud-brick, some vaulted and painted. The dead kings were now accompanied by sacrificed humans, in one case four hundred individuals, and the burial structures were covered by massive mounds up to 90 metres in diameter. The elite now exercised their power through their command of resources and demonstrated that power through monumental funerary structures.

The first kingdom of Kush was, like Egypt, a product of the Nile. It owed its existence to the fertility of the valley, but its real strength lay in its gold resources and in its

3.22 The town of Kerma, on the middle Nile, was dominated by a huge three-storey structure built of mud-brick known as the Western Deffufa. It was probably constructed in the early second millennium BC and served as a religious focus.

geographical position on the interface of two other worlds, the steppe, which formed the great corridor of the Sahel stretching westwards, and the fabled land of Punt, now modern Eritrea, where the Ethiopian Highlands meet the Red Sea. From the Sahel came the cattle, which featured large in the ritual of the state. Punt was the source of a range of exotic goods in great demand in Egypt, the Levant, and beyond. Kerma acquired these goods by trade, probably through middlemen in the Gash delta, an inland delta where the river Gash, rising in the Ethiopian Highlands, was dissipated in the desert. Here the discovery of quantities of pottery made in Kerma, dating to 2300–1700 BC, indicates the presence of traders.

The Egyptians were aware of the richness of Punt, and to outflank the Kushites, who commanded the river route and no doubt added a percentage to the price of goods in transit, sent a number of expeditions direct to Punt by sea between 2500 and 1100 BC. The best known is that dispatched by Queen Hatshepsut (1473–1458 BC) and recorded on reliefs carved in the mortuary temple of Deir el-Bahri. The expedition of five ships carrying marines was received by the king and queen of Punt, depicted with their attendants. On another scene a native village is shown with domed, reed-built huts

3.23 The Land of Punt is depicted on a painted relief in the mortuary temple of Hatshepsut at Deir el-Bahri (she died in 1458 BC). In the centre is a conical reed-built hut raised on a platform reached by a ladder, set in a grove of myrrh and palm trees.

raised above ground on poles set in a grove of palms and myrrh trees. Another part of the relief shows an Egyptian. A hieroglyphic inscription explains the scene:

> The loading of the cargo boat with great marvels of the Land of Punt, with all the good woods of the divine land … with ebony, with pure ivory, with pure gold from the land of Amu … resin, antimony, with apes, monkeys, hounds with skins of leopards of the south, with the inhabitants of the country and their children. Never was brought such things to any king, since the world was.

Eritrea was well placed to provide the exotic goods that Egypt so much desired to help maintain its elaborate prestige goods system. Ebony and incense grew there, and on the opposite shore of the Red Sea the coast of Arabia was also a major source of incense, while ivory, animal skins, and live wild animals could be acquired from further south, in East Africa, by way of the Rift Valley corridor. The mention of 'inhabitants of the country and their children' suggests that the king of Punt was not averse to selling his excess of population into slavery. And it may have been through Punt that the African crops from the Sahel were passed on to traders working the route between the Gulf of Aden and India, the same network along which broomcorn millet and zebu cattle reached Africa (p. 83 above).

How frequent were the sea-bound expeditions to Punt is difficult to say, but at least eight voyages are recorded between 2500 and 1100 BC and there may have been many others. Nor were the inhabitants of Punt afraid to send trips of their own along the Red Sea. A painting in the tomb of Min at Thebes depicts rafts fitted with cross-rigged sails and steering oars carrying cargo en route to one of the Egyptian Red Sea ports. The sea route between Punt and Egypt offered an alternative to the Nile route passing through the kingdom of Kush. The relative balance of trade between the two may have had an effect on the fortunes of Kerma, but in all probability the weight of demand for the exotic produce of Africa and the Arabian coast was so great that both routes could have thrived. Kerma also had its resources of gold in the surrounding desert to sustain the stability of the state.

Standing Back

The detail may be complex, but the broad story of the period 6500–1000 BC is clear. Across the long interface which Africa shares with Eurasia, from Morocco to the Gulf of Aden, domesticated livestock and cultivated grain began to be introduced to the continent before 6000 BC and were quickly taken up in all the ecological niches which would support them. This initial spread of farming techniques from the Near East may well have been set in motion by the sudden dry, cold interlude beginning about 6200 BC, forcing communities to move out of their homelands to seek new lands, their arrival stimulating the indigenous population to adopt new methods of food production. The African environment limited the spread of Near Eastern cereals, but not domesticated livestock. Cattle, sheep, and goats were quickly adopted by the hunter-gatherers of the Sahara region, then a green land with sufficient water and grassland to make pastoralism a viable way of life.

When, eventually, desiccation set in after 3000 BC, pastoral communities were driven east to the Nile valley, there to merge with farmers already well entrenched, and south into the Sahel, where they settled among the indigenous hunter-gatherers and began to cultivate a variety of plants native to the Sahel and the forest edge. While these processes were under way, in the long Nile corridor, hemmed in by the desert, population pressures led to the emergence of increasingly complex societies whose desire for exotic commodities stimulated trading networks which, on the one hand, linked Africa closer to Eurasia, and on the other, created a new connectivity binding the disparate communities of the whole of northern Africa. Once again, climatic change can be seen to be one of the dominant forces, perhaps the prime mover, setting in motion far-reaching economic and social change.

4

CREATING CONNECTIVITIES
1000–140 BC

B
Y the beginning of the first millennium BC the desertification of the Sahara was well under way and over the next thousand years the desert was to continue to get drier. But the process was not even. In the north there was no let-up, but in the south short, slightly more humid episodes intervened. Elevation was also a factor. The more mountainous regions continued to attract precipitation sufficient to support human groups. But overall, as the oases in the depressions began to dry out, much of the desert became a hostile environment. Some water sources, however, remained in the desert regions where the aquifer was close to the surface, providing for those who wished to live around them or travel from one to another. In the more benign environments to the north and south of the desert and along the Nile, communities flourished and developed greater levels of complexity. In the Maghrib, occupied by the Berbers, two regional kingdoms began to emerge, Mauretania in the west and Numidia in the east, and both were to play a significant part in Mediterranean history. In the south, in the Sahel, several centres of power developed the characteristics of small states, while in the Nile valley, the existing states of Egypt and Kush maintained their prominence, though Egypt came under the dominance of successive foreign powers.

While the indigenous African polities continued to develop under their own energies, events in the Mediterranean were beginning to make an impact. The Phoenicians, whose home lay on the coast of the Levant, had begun to establish trading posts at the western end of the Mediterranean and along the Atlantic coasts of Iberia and Africa in the early centuries of the first millennium, while in the seventh century the Greeks established colonies in Cyrenaica and set up a trading enclave in the Nile delta. Some centuries later, in 149 BC, the Romans took the first step in what would eventually lead to the annexation of the whole of the North African zone. The growing consumer demands of the Mediterranean states inevitably affected Africa, invigorating long-established trade routes and encouraging new ones to be set up. It was now that the networks in the Sahara, which had developed to serve local needs, began to carry increasing volumes of goods over longer distances, creating a new connectivity.

Travellers' Tales

The literate communities who came into contact with Africa had many tales to tell. There is no lack of anecdote: the debate lies in what credence should we place on them. Take, for example, the story of the circumnavigation of Africa by Phoenician sailors, recorded by the Greek historian Herodotus in the fifth century BC. He says that they were commissioned, about 600 BC, by the Egyptian pharaoh Nekau II, to sail from the Red Sea around the coast of Africa and return to the Mediterranean:

> and so they sailed into the southern ocean [the Indian Ocean]. When autumn came they went ashore wherever they might happen to be, and having sown a tract of land with grain, waited until it was fit to cut. Having reaped it, they set sail again.
>
> (*Histories* 4.42)

Eventually, three years after setting out, they sailed through the Strait of Gibraltar into the familiar Mediterranean. Herodotus adds a tantalizing detail: 'they declared that in sailing round Libya [Africa] they had the sun on their right hand'. He offers no comment on the veracity of the report of the circumnavigation but said he did not believe the story about the sun. Had he understood that the world was a sphere with an equator he would have realized that in the southern hemisphere, when passing westwards around the southern tip of the continent, the sun would, indeed, have been on the right hand. While this does give credence to the Phoenician claim to have completed the circumnavigation, it cannot be taken as proof.

Another story about Phoenician, or rather, Carthaginian, coastal exploration is contained in the *Periplus of Hanno*, an intriguing document but one notoriously difficult to interpret. What survives is a ninth-century AD manuscript written in Greek which claims to be a copy of an account of a voyage made by Hanno along the West African coast 'beyond the Pillars of Hercules' which 'he dedicated in the sanctuary of

Baal'. The style of the Greek, which was copied in the late manuscript, is early, suggesting that the original Greek document had probably been written in the fifth or fourth centuries BC, its author having translated it from a Punic source, either a document or an inscription kept in the temple in Carthage, not long after the original was composed about 500 BC. The translation was probably recopied on a number of occasions, allowing scribal errors to creep in. Added to this, some parts of the original seem to have been omitted. Given that the text is corrupt and incomplete, it is not surprising that even the volume of scholarly ingenuity that has been lavished on its interpretation, and on the identification of the places named, has left many problems unresolved.

That said, there is much to be gleaned from the text. Hanno faced two tasks. His first was 'to found cities for the Phoenicians' along the Atlantic coast of North Africa. The second was to explore the coast beyond the southern limit of settlement. It may be that there were two separate expeditions conflated into the single account. To accomplish the first we are told that he had a fleet of sixty penteconters (fifty-oared ships) carrying thirty thousand colonists, provisions, and equipment—numbers that are surely inflated. The colonizing phase of the journey ended before they reached the river Lixos, 'a large river which flows from Libya [Africa]. Along it the Lixitai nomads grazed their cattle. Among them we remained for some time making friends. Behind them, higher up live inhospitable Ethiopians [black Africans] in a land infested with wild animals and divided by high mountains.' The identification of the Lixos is uncertain but the best fit would be Oued Dra'a, which marks the divide between the Maghrib, dominated by the Atlas Mountains, and the Sahara desert. Taking on board interpreters from among the Lixitai, Hanno continued south, following the barren desert shore. The text says that this part of the journey took two days, but some scholars prefer to amend that to nine (*theta* instead of *beta*) to allow for a journey of 1,600 kilometres. After the desert they founded a trading colony called Kernē, on an island which seems to have been close to the estuary of a great river called the Chretes. Sailing along the river, they encountered 'savages wearing wild animal hides', who threw rocks at them. They then found a second river, 'great, wide and swarming with crocodiles and hippopotamuses'. The geography is difficult to make sense of, but one plausible suggestion is that the river Chretes is the Senegal and Kernē is an island in its estuary, with the second river being the Gambia.

From there the journey proceeded along the coast, the explorers observing many wonders. The land was occupied by black Africans, 'who fled from us' and spoke a language incomprehensible to the Lixitai. How far the expedition followed the coast is unclear. Some commentators suggest as far as Sierra Leone; others, impressed by the description of a volcano called the Chariot of the Gods, suggest that they were in sight of Mount Cameroon before the decision was made to turn back. That they sailed some

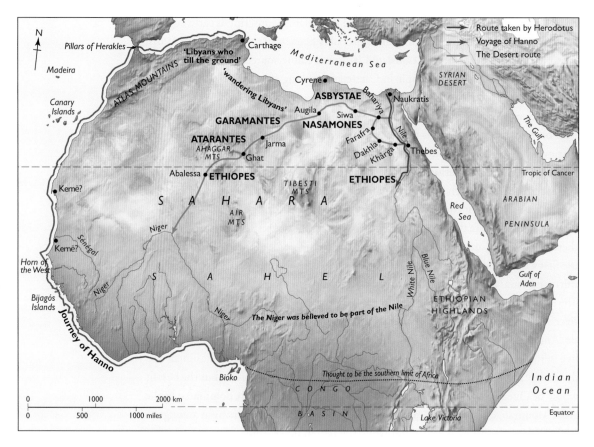

4.1 By the fifth century BC, Africa was beginning to be known by the Greeks and Phoenicians. The Carthaginian Hanno had travelled by sea around the west coast of Africa, possibly as far as Cameroon, and *c*.450 Herodotus had travelled down the Nile to the First Cataract. He had a reasonable knowledge of the Libyan tribes of the north between the Nile and Tunisia and also knew of the route from Egypt westwards across the desert to a great east-flowing river, probably the Niger, which he thought must be the upper reaches of the Nile.

way along the forested coast of West Africa is not in doubt. It may be that the original intention was to circumnavigate the continent but exhaustion, fear, or loss of confidence on finding that the coast suddenly turned south, perhaps all three, conspired to persuade Hanno to return the way he had come.

By any standards it is a remarkable story. Although some have argued that it was a fabrication, there is sufficient evidence to suggest that the journey took place. The principal argument of the detractors is that contrary winds would have made the return journey impossible. This is not so. Although the voyage would have been difficult, it could have been managed by a skilled ship's master.

Hanno was not the only explorer to be drawn to the Atlantic coast of Africa. About the same time Euthymenes, a Greek from Massalia (Marseille), made an Atlantic voyage. Details are lacking, but he too came upon a massive river crawling with crocodiles and hippopotamuses which may have been the Senegal. Another explorer was the Persian Sataspes, who was sent to circumnavigate Africa by Xerxes in lieu of a death sentence passed for a crime he had committed. He journeyed as far as the land of a 'dwarfish race who wore a dress made from the palm tree' and who herded cattle and lived in towns. There can be no certainty about how far he got, but he was at sea for some months before he gave up and returned home, expecting, perhaps, to be pardoned, only to be impaled for his previous misdemeanours.

Herodotus provides one further story about the Atlantic, which he had learnt from Carthaginian traders. Somewhere along the African coast there was a favoured beach where they went to trade with the natives. On arrival they would lay out their trade goods in an orderly fashion along the strand and would then retire to their vessels and send up a smoke signal:

> The natives would see the smoke and come down to the shore, and, laying out to view so much gold as they think to be the value of the wares, withdraw to a distance. The Carthaginians then come ashore to look. If they think the gold enough, they take it and leave. But if it does not seem sufficient, they go back on board the ship and wait patiently. Then the others approach and add to their gold, till the Carthaginians are satisfied. Neither party deals unfairly by the other, for they themselves never touch the gold until it comes up to the value of their goods, nor do the natives ever carry off the goods until the gold is carried off.
>
> (*Histories* 4.196)

Where these acts of 'silent trade' took place is uncertain, but it is likely to have been south of the coastal zone settled by the Carthaginians, thus beyond Agadir, and quite probably somewhere to the south of the Sahara. This is the first indication we have that West African gold was an item of trade by the fifth century BC.

Our final travellers' tale is about the Sahara desert and, again, is recounted by Herodotus (*Histories* 2.32–6). It concerns a group of young men from the tribe of the Nasamones, living on the Libyan coast, who, with nothing better to do, decided to explore the desert. Equipped with ample supplies of food and water, they travelled roughly south through the inhabited region until they reached the 'region of wild animals', and from there they went into the desert, where 'all is fearfully sandy and waterless and destitute of life'. After many days crossing the desert, they came to a plain with fruit trees, but while picking the fruit they were attacked by 'small men of less than moderate height', who led them through swamps to a town where 'everyone was of

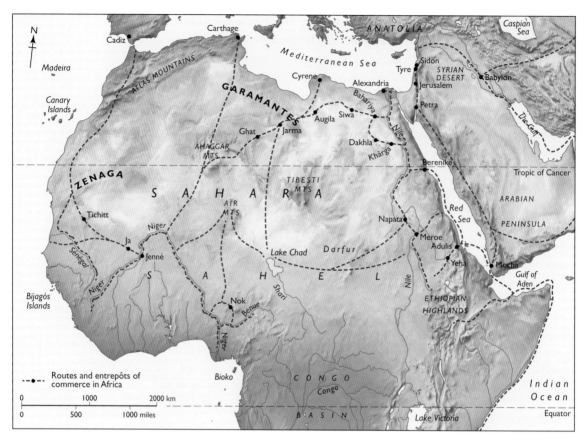

4.2 In the first millennium BC, the desert was crossed by a number of caravan routes, which linked the North African coast to the Sahel. As the Mediterranean states developed their consumer markets, and the demand for exotic goods became greater, so the intensity of traffic on the desert routes increased.

the size of their captors and black in colour.... A great river ran past the town, flowing from west towards the rising sun and in it were seen crocodiles.' Eventually the adventurers made it back to tell their tale. How far, and in which direction, they travelled has been much debated. Some suggest that the destination was the Lake Chad region, but most favour the suggestion that they had reached the river Niger, probably at the Niger Bend, where the river nudges the desert. Herodotus has more to say about the desert (pp. 122–4 below).

These travellers' tales may be frustrating in their lack of geographical detail, but they offer unique glimpses of the sub-Saharan world at the moment when the networks of connectivity were beginning to be created. They also reflect on the curiosity of the classical writers about the larger world beyond their own. The exploits of the young

Nasamones are a reminder that travel and exploration may be motivated by a curiosity and desire to acquire knowledge as much as by a compulsion to get access to rare raw materials.

Lands to the North of the Desert

The northern coastal region of Africa, from the Nile delta to the Atlantic, divides into two natural regions, the long desert zone from the delta to the Gulf of Gabès, relieved only by the fertile Cyrenaican plateau, and the Maghrib with the Atlas Mountains forming its backbone. As we have seen, these two very different environments determined the social and economic development of the resident communities as early as the hunter-gatherer period (pp. 43–8 above). The difference was very apparent to Herodotus writing in the fifth century BC. He identifies the divide as Lake Tritonis, now Chott el-Djerid, which, at the time, drained into the Gulf of Gabès. To the east were 'the tribes of wandering Libyans' who lived in the coastal region. Behind them, to the south, was the 'wild beast tract' and beyond that 'the ridge of sand'. To the west of Lake Tritonis lived the 'Libyans who till the ground and live in houses'. The divide he makes is between mobile pastoralists and sedentary farmers.

Herodotus knew far more about the 'wandering Libyans' than about the farmers, his information presumably coming from the Egyptians and the Greek settlers in Cyrenaica. These were the Libyans who had attacked the delta in the last centuries of the second millennium BC and who were depicted in all their finery in Egyptian wall paintings. He is able to list twelve different tribes, enlivening his descriptions with colourful anecdotes about dress, hairstyle, and behaviour. There is little about the economy, but the Nasamones, we are told, led something of a transhumant life:

> In summer they leave their flocks and herds on the sea shore and go up the country to a place called Augila [the oasis of Awjila] where they gather dates from the palms, which in these parts grow thickly and are of great size, all of them being of the fruit-bearing kind.
>
> (*Histories* 4.172)

They also collected locusts, which were dried, crushed, and sprinkled on their milk. The mode of transport of these wandering Libyans is hardly mentioned, but the Asbystae, who lived inland from Cyrenaica, used the chariot, a practice which Herodotus thought they had copied from the Greek colonists.

In this eastern stretch of North Africa, the Cyrenaican plateau stands out from the surrounding arid region. It is a fertile, well-watered land with a pleasant Mediterranean climate, geographically part of the Aegean world, the same distance from Crete as is

4.3 The Libyan tribes living in the coastal zone west of the Nile came into close contact with Egypt, first as raiders and later as settlers. They appear in Egyptian art distinguished by their dress, as here in a painting in the tomb of Seti I (c.1279), where they are shown with elaborate long cloaks, feathered headdresses, and tattoos on their arms and legs.

Athens. It is little wonder that the Greeks living on the overcrowded island of Thera (modern Santorini) decided to establish a colony there. The first settlers chose the off-shore island of Plataea, and from its relative safety built up friendly relations with the natives on the nearby mainland, after two years relocating to Aziris on the mainland coast. A few years later, about 630 BC, encouraged by the advice of their neighbours, they moved inland and founded the city of Cyrene in the fertile heart of the high pla-teau. By the middle of the sixth century, other colonies were being set up around the coast. The relationship between Greek settlers and indigenous Libyans was entirely symbiotic. Both communities flourished from the trading relationship that developed, and the Greek lifestyle began to be adopted by the natives. As Herodotus put it, the Asbystae who lived inland from the colonies 'ape the manners of the Cyrenaeans'. But that said, the Greek presence was a tiny enclave in a vast region of nomads.

Of the Maghrib Herodotus knew comparatively little except that this was a land of sedentary agriculturists, a more wooded territory where lions, elephants, and bears roamed. Three tribes were mentioned by name and he was aware that horse-drawn chariots were in use, but beyond that his information ran out. Culturally the Maghrib divided in two: an eastern part comprising Tunisia and eastern Algeria and a west-ern part including western Algeria and the whole of Morocco. Originally made up of many different kingdoms, by the third century BC the polities were beginning to coalesce into three larger kingdoms: the Massyli and Masaesyli in the east, which soon became Numidia, and the Mauri in the west, who became the leaders of Mauretania. The emergence of these larger polities owed much to the tensions and opportunities thrust on them by the colonial powers as Carthage engaged in its life-and-death struggle with Rome. As significant players on the Mediterranean stage they began to act like Hellenistic states.

But we must go back a little in time to see how this all came about. At the end of the second millennium BC, after the chaos caused by the Sea People in the eastern Mediterranean, several port cities on the coast of the Levant, collectively referred to as Phoenicia, began to develop long-distance trading links with the western Mediterranean and in particular with the metal-rich area of south-west Iberia known as Tartessos. Historical sources claim that around 1100 BC the Phoenician entrepreneurs established three trading ports: Utica on the estuary of the Medjerda in Tunisia; Gadir, now Cadiz, on an island off the Atlantic coast of Spain; and Lixos on the Atlantic coast of Morocco near Larache. While there is as yet no positive archaeological evidence of a Phoenician presence at this date, early foundations are quite possible. Phoenician settlers were well established at Huelva in south-west Spain in the tenth century, and several trading centres along the Atlantic coast of Iberia are known to have been functioning by the ninth century. The base at Utica was well chosen. With Motya at the western extremity of Sicily it controlled the vital sea passage between the east and west Mediterranean and would have been an important port of call on the return journey to Phoenicia using the east-driving winds and currents along the north coast of Africa. Utica, however, failed. Sited on the delta of the Medjerda, it was constantly under the threat of being silted up, and for this reason a new port city, Carthage, was established on a nearby bay at the end of the ninth century BC, a date given by tradition and confirmed by archaeology. Carthage was founded by Phoenicians from Tyre in Lebanon, and for more than two centuries maintained close ties with its mother city. All this time it functioned as a trading enclave with little land of its own, its livelihood dependent on the throughput of goods and on providing services for the constant flow of passing ships. An annual fee was paid to the Libyans for the limited surrounding land worked by its citizens. The benefit for the Africans was that Carthage provided a market for their agricultural surpluses, which they could exchange for an inexhaustible supply of luxury goods.

All this changed after 574 BC, when the Babylonian king Nebuchadnezzar appropriated Tyre and the rest of Phoenicia. From that moment on, the link with Lebanon was cut and Carthage assumed the role of leader of the Phoenicians in the west. The

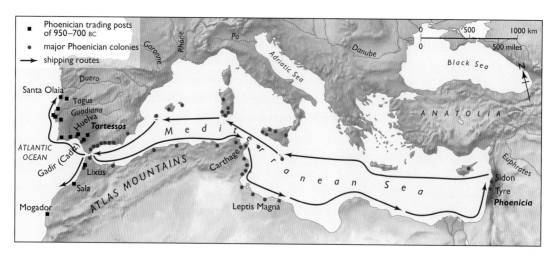

4.4 As early as the tenth century, the Phoenicians from the Levant were making regular sea journeys the length of the Mediterranean and out through the Strait of Gibraltar to the Atlantic to trade for metals with the Tartessans in south-western Iberia. By the seventh century, they had established trading enclaves along the Atlantic coast from Mogador, off the coast of Morocco, to the river Mondego in Portugal. Their return journey along the coast of North Africa was facilitated by a number of coastal ports.

city expanded, acquiring more territory to feed its growing population, and began an expansionist policy to wrest control from the Greeks who had settled in the central Mediterranean. In 510 BC Carthage took over the Greek city of Oea (Tripoli) on the Gulf of Syrtis. Later they were to threaten the Greek cities on Sicily, resulting in the First Punic War (264–241 BC), which saw the Romans, who had joined on the side of the Greeks, emerge triumphant. For the next hundred years, hostility between the two powers dominated Mediterranean history. The Second Punic War (218–201 BC) was fought in Iberia and later Tunisia, where the Romans won the decisive battle of Zama in 202 BC. The Third Punic War (149–146 BC) was Rome's *coup de grâce*. Carthage was besieged and destroyed, and Rome had taken another step towards Mediterranean domination.

The vicissitudes of the power struggle, fascinating though they are, cannot be dealt with here. What is relevant is what they tell us about African society at this time. During the Second Punic War two tribes in the eastern Maghrib, the area known as Numidia, were drawn into the conflict on opposing sides: the Massyli, under King Gaia, were allied with Carthage, while the Masaesyli, led by King Syphax, fought on the side of Rome. World events were providing a stage on which intertribal rivalries could be played out. But it was a febrile time when loyalties could quickly change.

4.5 Carthage, in modern Tunisia, founded in the ninth century BC, became a focal point in the Phoenician and Carthaginian network controlling the central Mediterranean. The city was dominated by a circular military harbour and a rectangular commercial harbour, which are still evident today.

In 206 BC the Massyli, now led by Gaia's son Masinissa, decided to go over to the Romans, against whom he had fought in Spain. Meanwhile, Syphax joined the Carthaginian cause. Towards the end of the war Syphax, defeated in a battle with the Romans, retired to his capital, Cirta (Constantine), on the Algerian coast. Masinissa and the Romans followed, and he was captured and handed over to the Roman general Scipio. Thereupon Masinissa married Syphax's wife, Sophonisba, a somewhat rash act which aroused the suspicions of Scipio, who demanded that she be paraded in his triumph in Rome. To resolve the impending indignity Masinissa sent his new wife poison, which she obligingly took. The next year, at the battle of Zama, Masinissa was able to demonstrate his loyalty to Rome by his brilliance in leading six thousand Numidian and three thousand Roman cavalry in two decisive charges against the Carthaginians. As a reward he was given Syphax's kingdom, thus becoming king of united Numidia, extending from the western boundaries of Algeria to Tripolitania.

Carthage was now confronted by the Numidians on land and the Romans at sea. The rest of the story is briefly told. For the next fifty years, Masinissa extended his power, eventually, in 149 BC, provoking the Carthaginians to war. The Romans took advantage of the opportunity and intervened, and in 146 BC Carthage was destroyed. Masinissa, who had died at the age of 90 two years earlier, was succeeded by Micipsa, one of his forty-four sons, who was to rule Numidia for thirty years.

The sheer opportunism shown by those caught up in these events was typical of the time. Masinissa was behaving like a Hellenistic monarch. During his long reign and that of his son, ninety years in all, Numidia had become a powerful state, yet without the institutions of the state. Its strength lay in two things: its farming villages, controlled by simple links of kinship, which provided the grain exported to Greece and Rome, and its famous cavalry, an extra-tribal organization which owed its allegiance to the king. 'The kings', says Strabo, 'are much occupied with horse breeding, thus 100,000 foals in a year have been counted.' Given such systems, there was no need for the complex, and potentially treacherous, infrastructure of state bureaucracy. Yet some level of state organization is implied by the development of an alphabet by the fourth century BC. Nor was Numidia without its monumental architecture, as the tombs of the Numidian elite demonstrate. The great stone-built tumulus at Medracen in the Aurès Mountains, quite possibly the tomb of Masinissa's father, Gaia, may well have been modelled on that of Alexander the Great at Alexandria. The Numidians have been characterized by some observers as a barbarian people emulating Hellenistic kingdoms, yet they had created a state system, and a very successful one, constructed in an African mode.

South of the Sahara

Unlike the people living north of the desert, about whom we learn a lot from contemporary literary sources, the communities of the Sahel are without a voice, their own or other observers', leaving us to have to rely on sparse archaeological evidence. Sufficient is available, however, to show that significant changes were under way, continuing processes set in motion in the second millennium as pastoralists, driven out of the Sahara by desertification, settled among the foragers of the Sahel and began to cultivate crops. Along the Tichitt escarpment, the complex pattern of settlements which had begun

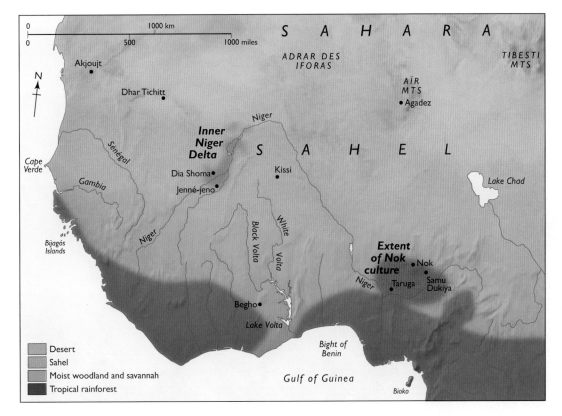

4.6 In West Africa, south of the Sahara, the different environmental zones provided opportunities for sedentary communities to develop, while the Niger offered a major route of communication. Before the Niger Bend is reached, the river braids, creating an extensive area of well-watered land, the Inner Niger Delta. Here permanent settlements began to grow, developing a degree of complexity. The area of moist woodland savannah in Central Nigeria saw the extension of iron production and the emergence of an accomplished art style represented by terracotta figures referred to as the Nok culture.

about 1900 BC continued until about 400 BC, by which time it had begun to fade out, weakened by the gradual onset of drier conditions. Meanwhile, in the middle Niger region, large settlements were beginning to appear. At Dia Shoma, in Mali, the occupation area extended to 19 hectares during the first phase of settlement, dating to 800–400 BC. Its occupants were agriculturists running flocks and herds and growing rice. Similarities in pottery styles suggest that the settlers may have come from the Tichitt region. The same is true of Kolima Sud Est in the Méma region, where the settlement reached 11 hectares in extent.

The most thoroughly studied of the middle Niger tell sites is Jenné-jeno in the Inner Niger Delta. Here occupation began about 250 BC, and by the end of the first

4.7 The Inner Niger Delta, Mali, marked by its lush vegetation. The course of the river Niger and the Niger Bend can be clearly seen.

4.8 The settlement of Jenné-jeno, on an island (centre) on the eastern edge of the Inner Niger Delta, began to develop *c.*250 BC. As it grew over the centuries, satellite settlements developed around it. The photograph was taken at high-water mark following the summer rainy season. Crops such as African rice grown on the fertile floodplain played an important part in trade.

millennium AD the tell had grown to considerable proportions, some 33 hectares, with an estimated population of 26,000 living within a kilometre of the centre. The early village, dating to 250 BC–AD 50, was only 7 hectares in extent, but it was already the dominant site within a cluster of smaller settlements scattered closely around. The economy which sustained them was based on running animals on the flooded and dry-season pastures, and on rice growing, but the cluster of settlements also occupied an important route node between the savannah highlands to the south-east, where there were good sources of iron ore, and the Sahara to the north, from where copper and salt were to be had. An added advantage was that it lay on a navigable river, which allowed goods, including surplus food, to be transported with ease. Further east, on the west side of Lake Chad, extensive nuclear settlements began to develop around the middle of the first millennium.

Taken together, the evidence, especially that from the middle Niger, shows that a sedentary lifestyle, leading to population growth, was creating large settlement complexes with central focuses surrounded by smaller agglomerations within which certain craft specializations were beginning to appear. There was, however, no evidence of an emerging elite in the form of rich burials, nor of any attempt to intensify subsistence strategies, which might have been expected had a strong social hierarchy existed. All this is very different from the development of kingdoms in North Africa and the complex state systems in the Nile valley. It suggests that the social integration so evident in the settlement pattern was maintained by other means, perhaps through the sharing of expertise in production and occult powers, leading to a heterarchical organization rather than a hierarchy. One reason for the development of this kind of social system could be that long-distance trade in rare commodities had not yet begun in the region, and without access to desirable exotics there was little incentive to generate and control surpluses. All this was to change by the end of the first millennium BC. These are fascinating issues with much to offer our understanding of human social behaviour, but more evidence will be needed for the implications to be better understood.

The nature of the beginning of metalworking in sub-Saharan Africa is another issue difficult at present to resolve, the outstanding question being whether the techniques of copper and iron extraction were introduced from outside Africa or whether they were developed independently in the sub-Saharan region. There can be little doubt that knowledge of the processes of copper working was transmitted to the Nile valley from the Near East. Copper artefacts were circulating in Nubia as early as 4000 BC, and there is evidence of copper smelting in Egypt during the Old Kingdom (2868–2160 BC) and in Kerma between 2300 and 1600 BC. At broadly the same time, copper and bronze tools of the kind developed in Iberia were circulating widely in the Maghrib.

Early copper working is known in two areas in the western Sahara, at Akjoujt in Mauritania, 180 kilometres inland from the Atlantic coast, and at Agadez in the Aïr Mountains of Niger. At Akjoujt, in the Grotte aux Chauves-Souris, malachite was being mined and smelted in the period 850–300 BC, and a range of implements and ornaments—arrows, spearheads, axes, chisels, awls, bracelets, earrings, and beads—were being made and circulated within the region. General similarities to types found

4.9 (*Opposite*) Iron smelting was introduced into the upper Nile valley and to the Carthage region from the Near East between 900 and 600 BC, and from those two points of entry the technology spread to Nubia and to much of the Maghrib. Iron working is also attested in four locations south of the Sahara in the period 900–600 BC. While it is possible that the technology was transmitted to the south from the Maghrib, a strong argument could be made for iron working being independently developed in the southern centres.

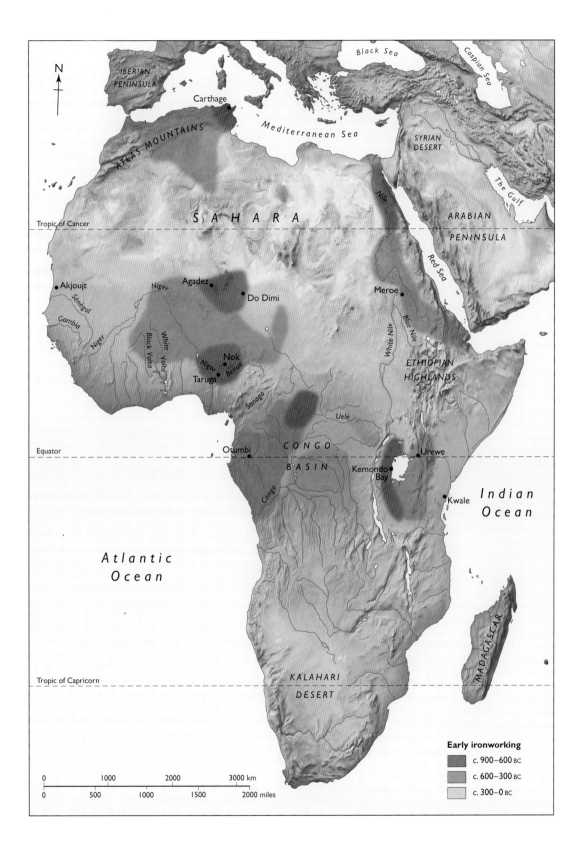

N

IBERIAN
PENINSULA

Black Sea

Caspian Sea

Carthage

Mediterranean Sea

SYRIAN
DESERT

ARABIAN

ATLAS MOUNTAINS

S A H A R A

Nile

The Gulf

Tropic of Cancer

PENINSULA

Red Sea

Akjoujt

Niger

Agadez

Do Dimi

Meroe

Sénégal

Gambia

Niger

Black Volta

White Volta

Niger

Nok

Benue

White Nile

Blue Nile

ETHIOPIAN
HIGHLANDS

Taruga

Sanaga

Uele

Equator

Otumbi

C O N G O

B A S I N

Kemondo
Bay

Urewe

Congo

Kwale

Indian
Ocean

Atlantic
Ocean

MADAGASCAR

Tropic of Capricorn

K A L A H A R I

D E S E R T

Early ironworking

c. 900–600 BC

c. 600–300 BC

c. 300–0 BC

0   1000   2000   3000 km

0   500   1000   1500   2000 miles

in the Maghrib suggest that it may have been a Phoenician-inspired enterprise. Agadez is more remote. It was originally argued that copper working began here about 1700 BC, but the early dates have been dismissed as being doubtful. The earliest uncontested evidence suggests the activity to date to sometime between 900 and 300 BC. The question of whether this was an indigenous development or one inspired by contact with the Phoenician world or with the Nile valley remains unresolved. The simplest explanation of the evidence so far available is that knowledge of the technology was introduced from the Mediterranean world by way of the cross-desert caravan routes.

The introduction of iron working presents a similar set of problems. Early claims for evidence of smelting as early as the third and second millennia are now considered unreliable. The earliest generally accepted dates show that iron working had spread through Niger, Nigeria, Cameroon, Gabon, and Congo by about 800–700 BC, but, unlike copper working, iron smelting was widely practised, and by an early date African iron workers had developed a sophisticated type of smelting furnace with a pit to tap slag. While it remains possible that iron working was introduced to the south from Phoenician colonies in North Africa or possibly by way of Egypt, this novel technology and the rapid spread of iron production through the sub-Saharan region is a powerful argument in favour of independent invention in Africa.

Faces in the Savannah

The southern and western slopes of the Jos plateau in central Nigeria, which lies within the zone of moist woodland savannah between the tropical forest and the grassy savannah, was densely occupied in the first millennium BC. Sedentary occupation began as early as the mid second millennium, when pastoralists moved south from the Sahara region, as desertification intensified, and settled among the indigenous population, taking up the cultivation of pearl millet and cow-pea. Cattle, sheep, and goats were, no doubt, important to the economy, but the soil of the region is too acid for bones to be preserved. A degree of cultural continuity spanning about 1500–1 BC can be recognized, one expression of which lies in the existence of highly distinctive, carefully modelled figures, usually human in form, made in terracotta. These figures define what has been called the Nok culture and were produced in great numbers in the period 900–300 BC. They are accomplished creations, usually half or three-quarters life-size, often displaying elaborate hairstyles, stylized yet capturing human individuality. Both males and females are depicted wearing arm- and neck rings and loincloths, and sometimes hats. Each one is different, suggesting that they are more likely to represent real ancestors rather than generalized gods. Where found in archaeological contexts, they are inevitably broken

4.10 The originality of the Nok master craft workers is evident in these two examples, dating to the period 900–300 BC, recovered from recent excavations. (*a*) is from Pangwari E, Nigeria (310 mm high); (*b*) is from Daji Gwana 1, Nigeria (730 mm high).

or fragmentary, either discarded in occupation deposits or buried as collections in small pits, the latter probably representing ritual deposition, marking the end of the 'life' of the statue.

The middle phase of the Nok culture (900–300 BC) sees the development of iron smelting on a large scale. Terracottas associated with pit furnaces have been found at Taruga and Samun Dakiya dating to 500–300 BC. It may well be that the production of iron in sufficient quantity for trade provided the surplus needed to support the skilled specialists who made the figures. Analysis of the clay used suggests that manufacture took place in only one or two centres. There is little evidence of long-distance exchange except for beads of chalcedony, jasper, and carnelian found buried with the dead. The implication is that the Nok communities remained relatively isolated in their benign savannah environment.

The People of the Desert

The long period of desiccation that began about 3000 BC rendered vast areas of the Sahara uninhabitable and, as we have seen, drove large numbers of herders out of what had been their traditional pastures. But the desertification was not total. In places where the aquifer was close to the surface, oases fed by fresh water could provide sustenance for small communities of pastoralists and for travellers. The remnants of some lakes still survived, and in some upland areas, like Aïr, Ahaggar, Tibesti, and Tassili, precipitation was sufficient to support resident populations. But at best these were isolated communities, separated by vast tracts of rocky or sandy desert. With the climate now reasonably stable, the first millennium BC was a time when these desert communities began to develop networks which linked them to each other and to the agro-pastoralists to the north and south, and it was along these networks that commodities began to flow in increasing quantity.

To begin to understand the desert routes we must turn to Herodotus once more, to his account of North Africa. Having described the coastal pastoralists (pp. 109–11 above), he goes on to tell us that

> Further inland is that Libyan country which is haunted by wild animals and beyond that a ridge of sand reaching from Egyptian Thebes to the Pillars of Herakles. Along this ridge, at intervals of about ten days' journey, there are heaps of great lumps of salt in hillocks: on top of every hillock a fountain of cold, sweet water shoots up. Men dwell around it who are the last inhabitants of Libya before the desert.
>
> (*Histories* 4.181)

His cognitive geography is straightforward: a coastal zone of pastoral tribes, a wild beast zone, a ridge of sand, and then the desert, which he describes as a country 'waste and waterless, without animal life, or rain or wooded growth'. It is a reasonably accurate generalization for the northern part of Egypt and Libya, his waterless waste being the huge Libyan erg—the sea of sand. The oases which he describes, surrounded by their crusts of salts formed by evaporation, were spaced at about ten-day intervals. This is the maximum time that a caravan could travel without taking a period of several days for rest and recuperation. At a rate of travel of 45–50 kilometres a day, the spacing of these major resting places would have been about 500 kilometres apart. Between them there may have been other oases suitable for an overnight stop.

Herodotus names the major stops along the sand ridge. This is invaluable, but not without its problems. The first stop on the way was the oasis of Siwa, which occupied the western extremity of the great Qattara Depression. The oasis, deep in the desert, 250 kilometres from the Mediterranean coast and 560 kilometres east of the Nile, was famous throughout the ancient world as the home of the oracle of the god Ammon. Its inhabitants were called Ammonites. Herodotus starts the journey from Thebes, on the Nile, but it would have taken considerably longer than ten days to reach Siwa. More likely the journey began down-river and led first to the oasis of Bahariya. Even so, from here it would have taken fourteen days to get from there to Siwa. From Siwa the next stop was Augila (modern Awjila), a distance of 460 kilometres, which could have been accomplished in ten days. 'This is the place to which the Nasamones travel to harvest

4.11 The Siwa Oasis lies in the Western Desert, 550 kilometres from Cairo, between the Great Sand Sea and the Qattara Depression. It was an important resting place on the caravan route running east to west across the desert and was famous as the home of the oracle of the god Ammon.

dates' (p. 109 above). After another ten days' trek was an oasis with a great many fertile date palms in the territory of the Garamantes, 'a mighty tribe who spread earth over the salt and cultivate it'. They drove four-horse chariots to chase 'Ethiopians [black Africans] who live in caves and feed on lizards and serpents'—a reference, perhaps, to slave raiding. We will return to the Garamantes later (pp. 128–31). It was possible to get from here to the coast, to the land of the Lotus-Eaters who lived by the Gulf of Gabès, in thirty days, but the main caravan route continued to the south-west, to the land of the Atarantians. Identification is uncertain, but the stop was probably made at the oasis of Ghat, having covered a distance of 440 kilometres. The next oasis was among the Atlantes, an African tribe living close to a very high mountain, which the locals called the Pillar of Heaven. Most likely this stop was made in the Ahaggar, per-haps at Abalessa, at the foot of the highest peak in the Sahara, rising to 2,918 metres. Beyond the Atlantes, Herodotus admits, 'my knowledge fails', though he had heard of a salt mine and of people who built their houses from blocks of salt. In later times a route is known to have continued from Abalessa to the Niger Bend, a distance of 900 kilometres, two ten-day treks.

It is interesting to recall the journey of exploration made by the young Nasamones who probably reached the Niger Bend (pp. 107–8 above). They would have set out from Augila and taken a route much like that described by Herodotus. They were probably following well-used tracks known to locals, but it may well have been their journey that opened up the route and made it known to the enterprising Garamantes. A further speculation is worth considering. Their journey was probably undertaken about 500 BC, just at the time when the Phoenicians and others were exploring the Atlantic coastal routes, discovering, for the first time, West African gold. Could it have been rumours of the riches to be had in the far west that inspired the young men to take to the desert tracks which brought them as far as the Niger Bend? This cara-van trail became much frequented. In the medieval period, it provided the most con-venient route between Timbuktu and Cairo: the first stage of the pilgrimage route to Mecca. The journey, of some 4,100 kilometres, took eighty-two days, a rate of about 50 kilometres a day. The many other caravan tracks through the desert in regular use in the Middle Ages had their origin in the distant past. It was in the middle of the first millennium BC that they began to join up to become a network that allowed people and goods to cross the desert, linking south to north and east to west.

What cargoes were on the move at this early date is a matter of speculation. Later we know that gold and salt featured large, the desert salt providing a dietary essen-tial for the agriculturists of the Sahel, while West African gold was much in demand in the Mediterranean world. That gold is referred to in Herodotus' description of the 'silent trade' is sufficient to demonstrate its importance as early as the fifth century BC.

4.12 Gold coins were first minted in the Greek city of Cyrene *c.*435 BC, possibly using West African gold, but mostly Cyrene used silver until the end of the fourth century, when gold coinage appeared more regularly. This example is dated 323–305 BC.

Another commodity was slaves, hinted at by the Garamantian raids on tribesmen to the south, living in the Tibesti Mountains. Nor should we forget the importance of dried dates from the northern oases, or the local distribution of copper from sources in Mauretania and the Aïr Mountains. While there is little evidence of long-distance trade in the archaeological record at this time, it may be relevant that the Greek colony of Cyrene began minting its first gold coins about 435 BC. Quite possibly they were using West African gold. Other tantalizing hints include a glass eye bead found at Nin-Bèrè in the Sèno Plain, south of the Niger Bend. It is of Phoenician origin and dates to the fourth or third century BC. Another bead, of cobalt-blue glass, dating to the third–first century BC, was found at Jenné-jeno. Direct evidence of trade is, at present, slight but is likely to increase with further excavation.

How the desert caravans were organized at this time is unknown. Much has been made of the depictions of horse-drawn chariots found in rock art throughout the desert region. Chariots were first introduced to Africa by the Hyksos from the Levant (1650–1550 BC), and the tradition may have spread from there. It was certainly well established by the mid first millennium, according to Herodotus. But these light two-wheeled vehicles would have been of limited use in desert transport. They could carry very little other than the driver and would have got bogged down in sandy regions. Useful in raids, they were also a vehicle for elite display, and it is in this way, being

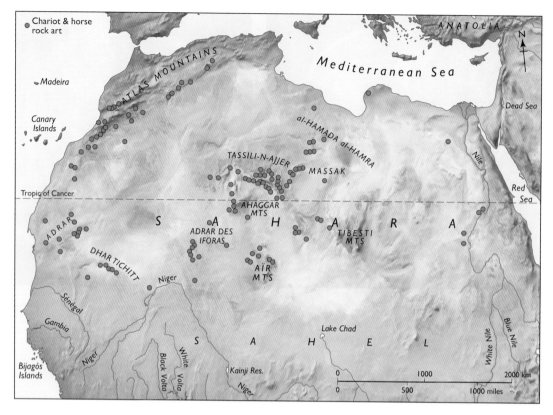

4.13 Among the images found on rock surfaces throughout the Sahara are scenes of two-wheeled chariots, pulled by horses, being driven furiously across the desert. Such a mode of transport is unlikely to have been used to carry goods. A more probable explanation is that chariot driving was a means of elite display. The images date to the second half of the first millennium BC.

furiously driven, that they are usually depicted. That said, horses did play an important part in the life of people living north of the desert, as the famous Numidian cavalry shows, and could well have been used in desert transport. So, too, could the donkey (*Equus asinus*). Domesticated donkeys bred from the Nubian and another, unknown, wild ass were known in Upper Egypt by 3000 BC. As a beast of burden they probably played an important part in the transport of goods along the caravan routes.

When the camel (*Camelus dromedarius*) came into regular use in the desert is still to be defined. Camels were domesticated in the Arabian peninsula by the second millennium and are attested in Africa at Qasr Ibrim in Nubia as early as the ninth century BC. By the seventh century, they were being used for military purposes in Egypt. Camels were used for traction, pulling carts and ploughs, by the Romans in North Africa, and by AD 400 they had reached Senegal. The evidence is patchy but would

4.14 A spirited rendering of a chariot and its rider from Adrar Tekemberet, Immidir, Algeria, probably of later first millennium BC date.

4.15 Camels, which were more frequently used in the Sahara as the first millennium BC progressed, could carry considerable loads and greatly facilitated the growth of caravan traffic. This rock engraving was found in the Tassili-n-Ajjer, Algeria.

 127

allow that camels were widely used in caravan trains in the Sahara by the later first millennium BC. They are frequently depicted on rock art, but the images are undated.

Our knowledge of the opening up of the desert routes to regular traffic and exchange is still rudimentary, and it will require a great deal more archaeological work before the picture becomes clearer, but taking the scraps of evidence together it would seem that the sixth–fifth centuries BC was the crucial time when the long-established regional networks began to see increasing traffic, with people and goods now moving over greater distances. But desert travel could be hazardous. Herodotus tells the story of fifty thousand Persian troops who set out from Thebes to the Siwa Oasis, there 'to enslave the Ammonians and to burn the god's oracle'. They got as far as the first oasis stop at El-Kharga and after a rest began on the next stage of the journey but were overwhelmed by a violent sandstorm and were never seen again (*Histories* 3.26). The desert was not a place for the inexperienced, especially those intent on attacking a god.

The Garamantes

The Garamantes, who occupied the Fazzan, were described by Herodotus as an 'exceeding great nation'. They lived south of the coastal pastoralists but were, themselves, cultivators. Their territory sat astride the east–west caravan route we have been considering and commanded two major north–south routes between the Sahel and the Mediterranean. This centrality, at a communications nexus, accounts for the remarkable development of the kingdom between 900 BC and AD 700. In the second half of the first millennium BC they had begun to assume the characteristics of a state, and during the first half of the first millennium AD they had become powerful enough to hold their own against the Roman world (pp. 169–72 below). One of the strengths of the Garamantes lay in their ability to access water, stored in the aquifer, by means of a system of foggaras. The method entailed choosing sloping ground and, upslope, sinking a shaft down to the water-bearing stratum. From the base of the shaft a tunnel was then dug to function as an underground aqueduct, channelling the water to a point, downslope, where the tunnel broke through the surface, allowing the water to flow into holding tanks. Additional shafts were dug along the line of the underground aqueduct to provide access for maintenance. From the holding tanks water could be channelled to irrigate the land below. It was a highly effective system that allowed large tracts of land to be brought under cultivation. Originating in the East, in Iran or Arabia, the technology had been introduced into Egypt by the second half of the first millennium BC and was being used by the Garamantes by the end of the millennium.

With assured supplies of water a wide range of crops could be grown. By 500–400 BC emmer, six-row barley, bread wheat, date palms, figs, and grapes were flourishing,

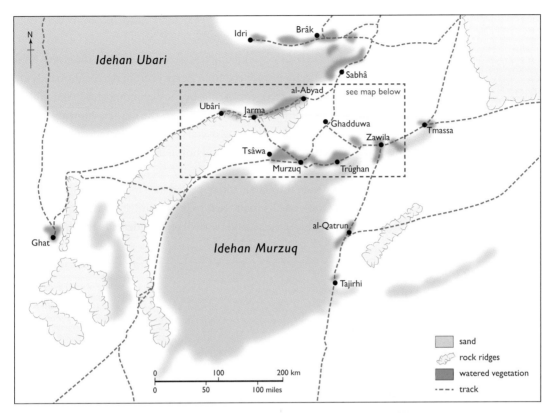

4.16 The Garamantes occupied a crucial route node in the Fazzan, in Libya, between two seas of sand, the Idehan Ubari and the Idehan Murzuq, where water was close to the surface. By tapping groundwater, using the foggara system, they were able to bring large tracts of land into cultivation, allowing the population to grow.

and pigs, sheep or goats, cattle, horses, and donkeys were reared. It was the classic Near Eastern package of domesticates introduced from Egypt or from the Maghrib or both. At first no native African crops were grown, but by the beginning of the first millennium AD sorghum and pearl millet had been added to the output, allowing double cropping to be practised, greatly increasing overall yield. The introduction of these crops to the north shows that sustained links had now been established with sub-Saharan Africa.

It is conventional to divide the Garamantian period into four phases: Early (900–500 BC), Proto-Urban (500–1 BC), Classic (AD 1–400), and Late (AD 400–700). The first two phases concern us here; the second two will be considered in the next chapter

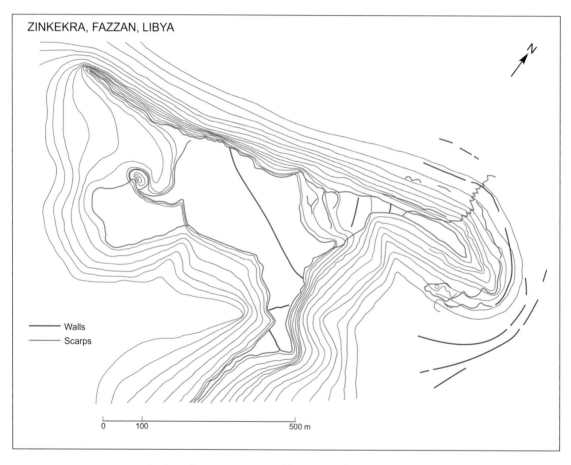

ZINKEKRA, FAZZAN, LIBYA

—— Walls
—— Scarps

0   100   500 m

4.17 In the Early Garamantian period (900–500 BC) strongly defended hill-forts dominated the ridges. One of the most thoroughly studied is Zinkekra. Multiple defences protected the hilltop settlement. Cemeteries developed on the lower slopes.

(pp. 169–72). Much of the evidence available comes from an in-depth study of Wadi al-Ajal, where the earliest settlements are sited along the edge of an escarpment and are fortified. The largest, Zinkekra, was occupied until around 500–400 BC. Its abandonment roughly coincides with the beginning of a new settlement in the centre of the valley below at Jarma (ancient Garama), a settlement that grew to become the principal urban focus of the kingdom. The shift of location marks the beginning of the second, Proto-Urban, phase. In the early layers of Garama, the discovery of Greek black glazed pottery of the fifth and fourth century BC, and the first appearance of sub-Saharan crops about the same time, shows that the Garamantes were now trading widely across Africa from the Mediterranean to the Sahel. The expeditions to the south, to collect slaves, which Herodotus mentions, may have been motivated by the need for labour to construct and maintain the foggaras and work the extensive fields, but any surplus would have found a ready market in the Greek cities of Cyrenaica, along with cereals, probably their main export.

Many factors combined to make the Garamantes a highly successful state. The adoption of cultivated crops and of the foggara system, making large-scale cultivation possible, allowed them to produce food in surplus. This sustained a growth in population which led to the development of a more complex social system, but it was their location, commanding one of the most important route nodes in the Sahara, central to so many far-flung markets, that set them on the path to becoming a powerful and prosperous people able to maintain their independence in the face of Rome.

Egypt, 1069–30 BC

Perhaps the most remarkable thing about Egypt's last thousand years was that, in spite of being under the rule of foreign kings—Libyans, Nubians, Assyrians, Persians, and Macedonians—the highly distinctive culture that had been honed over the previous millennia was maintained, and at times enhanced, by the new leaders, who showed respect, even nostalgia, for the greatness the country had once enjoyed. The Egypt of the Third Intermediate period (1069–664 BC), the Late period (664–332 BC), and the Ptolemaic period (332–30 BC) may well have been different from the golden age of the past, but it was still, unmistakably, Egypt.

The Third Intermediate period was a time when centralized government gave way to political fragmentation. At one time, about 730 BC, there were two kings in the delta and two in the rest of the valley. There were inevitable conflicts, but a level of stability was maintained. Military power was now replacing that of the administrators, and with the loss of Nubia, Egypt was becoming inward-looking, consumed by its own problems.

The Libyans of Cyrenaica and the Western Desert had now emerged as a new force. During the troubles with the Sea People, 1220–1180 BC, towards the later stages of the New Kingdom, bands of Libyans had moved into the delta. At first they were successfully repelled (p. 96 above), but pressure grew and the raids turned into a large-scale migration. The principal tribes mentioned were the Meshwesh and the Libu. Over time many settled in the oases, the western delta, and in the Nile valley between Memphis and Herakleopolis. Each group of immigrants was governed by its own tribal leaders, who gradually assumed control of the state. For about four centuries, Lower Egypt was ruled by Libyans. Tribesmen also served in the army. In 925 an Egyptian expedition against Israel and Judah involving twelve hundred chariots included detachments of Libyans and Nubians.

While the Libyans were assuming power in the north, the Kushites in Nubia were regrouping under new leaders, following the Egyptian withdrawal, and in the second half of the eighth century they were strong enough to mount successive attacks on Egypt, eventually setting themselves up as rulers of both Upper and Lower Egypt. Once in power the Kushite overlords began to interfere with political events in Palestine, bringing them into conflict with Assyrian interests, provoking retaliation, which, in 667 BC, resulted in the Assyrian invasion of Egypt. Three years later, the Assyrians reached and sacked Thebes. With the Kushite domination at an end, and with Egypt now ruled by Assyrian vassals, the Saite dynasty, whose power base lay in the delta, a semblance of peace returned.

Sometime in the mid to late seventh century a trading enclave organized by the Greek city of Miletus was set up in the delta, at Naukratis, near the capital, Sais, on the Canopic branch of the river, 70 kilometres inland from the port of Thonis-Herakleion. It provided Egypt with a direct link to the Greek trading network, which now dominated the eastern Mediterranean. In 570 BC it was formally recognized by the Egyptian state as the channel for all Greek trade. As such it became a cosmopolitan place attracting merchants from many Greek cities as well as Phoenicians, and began to open up the delta to broader Mediterranean influences.

The fate of Egypt was now inextricably linked to the power struggles being played out in the Near East which saw the growth of Persian might following the accession of Cyrus the Great in 559 BC. With Egypt strengthening its links to the Greek world, confrontation with Persia became inevitable. In 525 BC the Persians invaded, and apart from a brief period of independence from 404 to 343 BC, Egypt was to remain under Persian rule until 332 BC. During this time, Egyptian culture flourished. The Persian state was tolerant, indeed respectful, of the various ethnic groups making up its vast empire, so long as tribute continued to flow into the Persian capital, Persepolis. The most effective way to ensure the productivity of the empire was to encourage the governors of the occupied territories to invest in a strong sense of cultural continuity to maintain the identity of the subject population. Even so, the geographical isolation of Egypt meant that revolt was an ever-present temptation for those with ambition.

The long-drawn-out conflict between the Persians and the Greeks culminated in Alexander the Great's triumphant rampage through the Persian empire, which began in 334 BC. In two great battles, at Issos in north-west Syria in 333 BC and Gaugamela on the Tigris in 331 BC, he defeated the armies of Darius III and went on to campaign through the rest of the empire. He entered Egypt in 332 BC, and at the temple of Ptah at Memphis he was crowned, thus assuming the position of pharaoh. He also visited the oracle of Ammon at Siwa, further establishing his credibility as a supplicant to Egyptian cultural traditions. By instituting the construction of a new port city, Alexandria, he was making a clear statement that Egypt was now part of the Mediterranean world. Alexander's death in Babylon in 323 BC heralded a period of unrest. His Macedonian generals jostled for power and eventually, in 305 BC, Ptolemy Lagides, who had been governor of Egypt, set himself up as the country's king, founding a dynasty that was to rule Egypt until 30 BC, when the country was integrated into the Roman empire.

Under the Ptolemys, Alexandria became the capital, a city famed for its opulent palaces. Strabo, writing at the end of the first century BC, was impressed: 'the city has the most beautiful public enclosures and palaces that cover a fourth or third of its entire area'. It soon became a world-famous cultural centre, its great library a home for international scholars like Eratosthenes of Cyrene (c.285–194 BC), who served as its librarian. But, like many international ports, Alexandria soon became overpopulated, sheltering a multicultural mix, fractious and easily stirred to violence. On the death of Ptolemy IV in 205 BC, trouble erupted and his minister Agathokles and his associates were handed over to the braying mob. Polybius describes the final scene:

> some began to bite them, others to stab them, others to gouge out their eyes. As soon as any of them fell, the body was torn limb from limb until they had mutilated them all: for the savagery of the Egyptians is truly appalling when their passions are aroused.
>
> (Polybius 15.33)

For all its cultural achievements, the Ptolemaic period was one of decline. As the authority of the royal household weakened, old rivalries surfaced, creating endemic social discord that the rule of law could no longer contain. The greatness of Egypt was at an end.

Nubia and the Kingdoms of Kush

The first state to emerge in Nubia, based on the city of Kerma, was brought to an end when the Egyptians invaded Nubia in the sixteenth century BC and annexed the territory as a province of Egypt, a situation that was to last until the end of the New Kingdom about 1069 BC. Their eventual withdrawal left Kush to develop once again in relative isolation. The first centre of power to emerge developed in the Napata region, in the fertile Dongola Reach of the Nile between the Third and Fourth cataracts. It commanded the main crossing of the desert road, which provided the overland portage cutting across the great bends of the river. The earliest royal cemetery in the region, dating to the ninth century, was at El-Kurru, but the royal burial-ground later moved to nearby Sanam. About 300 BC the focus of power shifted from Napata to Meroe on the Shendi Reach between the Fifth and Sixth Cataract, where the desert road again crossed the river on its journey to the south. Meroe was to remain the centre of power in Nubia until the fourth century AD.

The revival of the kingdom of Kush, following the withdrawal of the Egyptians, took some time, but by about 760 BC the Kushites had begun to show their new-found strength, advancing down-river and capturing Thebes, where they established a new capital, before going on to take control of the rest of Egypt. Their brief ascendancy was cut short by the arrival of the Assyrians. Later, in 593 BC, an Egyptian army invaded Nubia, defeating the Kushites near the Third Cataract, but the victory does not seem to have been followed up. Nubia was invaded again, this time by the Persians, in 525 BC, and later the Macedonian dynasty took an interest in the country, pushing up-river from the First Cataract to take control of the route to Wadi el-Allaqi with its prolific goldmines. Thereafter the frontier region remained in flux.

The Kushites had a reputation for being good fighting men, especially with the bow. A detachment who fought with the Persian army under Xerxes in the fifth century was described with evident fascination by Herodotus. Referring to them as Ethiopians, the name used for black Africans, he says that they were

> clothed in panthers' and lions' skins, and carried long bows, not less than four cubits in length, made of palm trees, and on them they placed short arrows made of cane; instead of iron, they were tipped with a stone, which was made sharp ... Besides this they had javelins, and at the tip was an antelope's horn, made sharp like a lance: they also had knotted clubs. When they were going into battle they smeared one half of their body with chalk, and the other half with red ochre.
>
> (*Histories* 7.69)

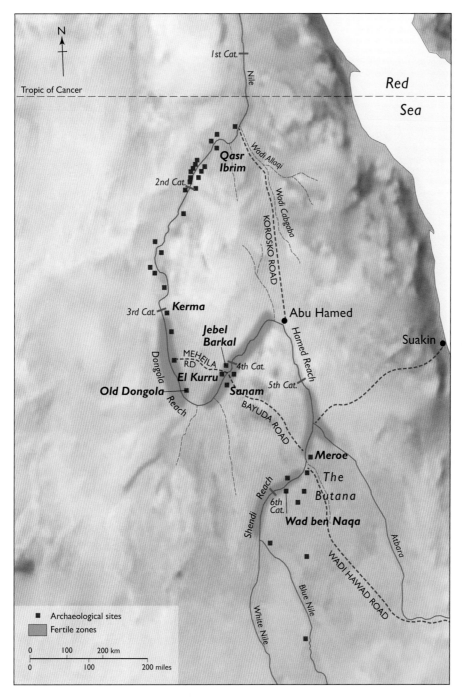

N

1st Cat.

Tropic of Cancer

Red

Sea

Nile

Wadi Allaqi

Qasr
Ibrim

2nd Cat.

Wadi Cabgaba

KOROSKO ROAD

3rd Cat.   **Kerma**

**Jebel
Barkal**

Abu Hamed

Suakin

Hamed Reach

MEHEILA
RD   4th Cat.

El Kurru

Old Dongola   **Sanam**

5th Cat.

Dongola Reach

BAYUDA ROAD

Meroe

Shendi Reach

The
Butana

6th
Cat.

Wad ben Naqa

Atbara

WADI HAWAD ROAD

Blue Nile

White Nile

■ Archaeological sites

Fertile zones

0   100   200 km

0   100   200 miles

4.18 The middle Nile became the focus of the kingdom of Kush, whose rulers are known from the ninth century BC to the fourth century AD. The river and the desert roads facilitated the transport of commodities between East Africa and Egypt, while the fertile stretches of land along the river and the goldfields in the Eastern Desert provided the wealth and stability on which successive regimes were based.

135

4.19 The kingdom of Kush was famous for the skill of its archers, shown here on a relief from the mortuary temple of Hatshepsut at Deir el-Bahri, Egypt, dating to *c*.1470 BC.

The power of the kingdom of Kush and the ability of its rulers to build elaborate monuments to themselves and the gods did not depend on the productive capacity of their land. Unlike the Egyptians, for whom the flood-plain and delta of the Nile and the well-watered western oases offered the prospect of generating considerable food surpluses, the productive land of the Kushites was far more limited in extent. Between the First and Third Cataract the river ran in a very narrow flood-plain. Upstream from that, the riverside alluvium and low-lying basins of the Dongola and Shendi reaches offered some, but limited, land for crop growing and animal husbandry, while to the south of Meroe lay the rainlands of the savannah upon which the state largely depended. The most productive region was the western Butana, the lands between the Upper Nile and its tributary the Atbara, where three large wadis drain into the Shendi Reach. Here the land was dotted with small temples associated with *hafir*s, large communal water tanks, around which clustered small settlements. The temples and *hafir*s, provided by the state, must have been a constant reminder to everyone of the ritual power of the king over the all-important water supply. In these lands sorghum and bar-ley were grown and sheep, goats, and cattle grazed. Yet the ability to produce a surplus was limited. What tithes were raised were appropriated by the monarchy and used to support the court, the priesthood, and the other non-productive members of society.

The real strength of the Kushite kingdom depended upon its dominance over trade and its ability to control its people, which gave it the power to raid and to make war. Aggressive forays harvested a range of commodities to enhance further the power of the state. It was a simple feedback mechanism. So long as the monarchy could manipu-late a reliable, and preferably growing, supply of prestige goods, the state would remain strong.

The king's control of commodities is nicely demonstrated by the contents of two palace store-rooms. At Wad Ben Naqa, on the Shendi Reach, large numbers of stor-age jars were found together with quantities of raw ivory and blocks of wood, prob-ably ebony, while the palace stores at Jebel Barkal yielded the sealings for pots, baskets, sacks, and wooden chests, reflecting the bureaucracy of acquisition. The Kushite kings, by tribute, exchange, and raiding, were able to accumulate a wide range of exotic goods, including gold, ivory, ebony, wild animals, animal skins, ostrich eggs, and feath-ers, which could be used for exchange for Egyptian and Mediterranean products such as wine, oil, metal goods, jewellery, glass-ware, faience, furniture, and pottery. These items were then distributed to the clients of the kings, and, by them, redistributed fur-ther down the hierarchy. That the kingdom was to survive for more than a thousand years, until about AD 400, is a reflection of the remarkable hold that successive kings exercised over the flow of commodities.

The kings of Kush built a powerful state that, from time to time, became a player on the world stage. When the Persian king Cambyses was in Egypt in 525–521 BC, he paid tribute to the king by sending a purple robe, a gold chain for the neck, armlets, an alabaster box of myrrh, and a cask of palm wine. This gift, acknowledging the king's exalted status, sounds very much like the gesture made to open diplomatic relations. Herodotus, who reported the event, could not resist adding an anthropological obser-vation. The recipients, he said, were 'the tallest and handsomest men in the world', and for their king they chose the tallest and strongest (*Histories* 3.20–1). By the reign of Darius I (521–486), the Kushites were sending a tribute to the Persian king every three years: 'Two choenices [2.3 litres or more] of virgin gold, two hundred logs of ebony, five Ethiopian boys, and twenty elephants' tusks' (*Histories* 3.97). Kushites, along with ambassadors from other subservient states, are depicted on the relief carved on the wall of the Apadana, the great audience hall in the Persian capital of Persepolis. They are shown bearing gifts for the king, a jar (perhaps of gold dust), elephant tusks, and an animal like an okapi.

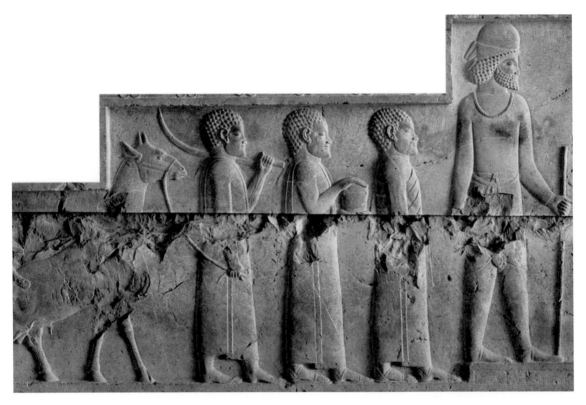

4.20 Kush became a supplicant state within the Persian empire. On a relief decorating the Apadana, the great hall in the centre of the Persian capital of Persepolis, three Kushite ambassadors are shown bringing gifts for the Persian king.

While there can be no doubt about the power and sustainability of the Kushite state, it was a system very unlike those of the Mediterranean and Near East. Their land had a low productive capacity, which probably accounted for the absence of an elaborate administrative structure. What was important was the hegemony they exercised over disparate regions stretching far into the savannah, giving them assured access to rare raw materials. As such it was comparable to other states of the Sahel. What was remarkable was its longevity.

Ethiopia and the Red Sea

The Sahel meets the Red Sea on a front some 500 kilometres broad, close to where the Ethiopian Highlands approach the sea. In terms of modern political geography this region is now Eritrea and the Tigray province of Ethiopia. To the north and south lie

4.22 Much in demand in the Hellenistic world were elephants for use in war. Elephants from East Africa were brought by boat to the Egyptian Red Sea ports. The model, showing a war elephant in action, comes from Nubia.

Nile at Koptos. The journey from Myos Hormos, across the Eastern Desert, was 200 kilometres. That from Berenike was almost twice as long, but Berenike had the advantage that it was 300 kilometres further south, which meant that by ending the sea journey there, and taking the longer route across the desert, the traveller avoided the long sea journey up the Red Sea and the difficulty of having to sail contrary to the northerly winds and navigate the shallow coastal reefs, conditions that made this part of the voyage so tedious.

The port of call, where the African goods were taken on board, was Adulis, on the Eritrean coast, but little is known of its first-millennium BC form. The commodities passing through the port to be loaded onto the Ptolemaic ships would have been the ones we are now familiar with: ivory, ebony, incense, spices, and slaves. But demand for another item, elephants, was now on the increase as supplies from North Africa began to be depleted. The elephant played an important role in Hellenistic warfare, and East Africa now became the main source of supply. The transport of wild elephants by sea between Adulis and the northern ports must have been a demanding occupation for the sailors, and traumatic for the beasts. The skull of one young elephant who did not survive the journey was found buried at Berenike.

The bustle of shipping along the Red Sea and Gulf of Aden, to and from India, is vividly presented in the *Periplus of the Erythraean Sea*, a document composed in the mid first century AD for the benefit of ships' masters, providing details of the sailing conditions and the layout of ports, and listing the goods available along the route. The anonymous compiler says that he relied heavily on information gathered by a sailor named Hippalus. But Hippalus was only one of many who sailed these seas whose knowledge was acquired first-hand and passed on from generation to generation. The *Periplus* would have been the culmination of experience of many going back deep into the first millennium BC.

Nine Hundred Years of Change

In the last millennium BC, each of the natural regions of northern Africa developed at its own pace, many in comparative isolation. In the Nile valley, where states were already well established, they continued to flourish under changing authorities. In Nubia the successive kingdoms of Kush developed largely without outside interference, forming a central hub between the Sahel, the Ethiopian Highlands, and the Nile valley. It was an African state in origin and appearance. Egypt, on the other hand, distinctive though its culture was, was drawn increasingly into the Near Eastern and Mediterranean worlds by its successive Assyrian, Persian, and Macedonian overlords. By the end of the millennium, Egypt had become little more than the productive hinterland of Alexandria, itself a Mediterranean city.

The Maghrib followed a different trajectory. It was, culturally, an island, isolated by sea and by sand, in which powerful kingdoms emerged loosely linked to the outside world by a façade of coastal colonies set up by Phoenician and Carthaginian traders. Only later was it drawn into their battles for control of the western Mediterranean.

Confronting these two large regional complexes, the Nile and the Maghrib, was the desert, now at its most arid and yet still with pockets of life clinging to the oases, the remaining lakes, and the uplands, where precipitation was still sufficient to sustain life. And to the south lay the great corridor of the Sahel, of steppe and savannah where agriculturists were fast developing complex societies linked by regional distribution networks. This was a separate world, at least for a while.

Sometime in the sixth century BC, the network of routes, fingering into the desert from north and south, began to join up, and people started to embark on journeys of exploration, the Phoenicians and Carthaginians developing a maritime route along the Atlantic coast while the more adventurous tribes on the northern fringe of the Sahara began to probe routes deep into the desert. Whatever their motivation—simple curiosity, search for prowess, or a desire to acquire rare commodities—cross-desert networks were soon established and regular trade began to flow. One of the desert tribes, the Garamantes of the Fazzan, by virtue of its central position on the north–south and east–west routes, became powerful and soon developed an agricultural strategy dependent on a sophisticated water management system. As trade intensified, so the Garamantes acquired the attributes of a state. By the first century BC, the Sahara was criss-crossed by caravan routes still largely serving the regional needs of local communities. In the centuries to follow, the consumer demands of the Mediterranean world would begin to play a more dominant role.

5

THE IMPACT OF EMPIRE
140 BC–AD 400

For 850 years, from 146 BC, when the Roman armies sacked and destroyed Carthage, until AD 698, when the Arab armies repeated the act, Rome had a presence in Africa. During that time the Roman world had extended its dominance over a huge tract of land, from the deserts of North Africa and Arabia to the forests of the North European Plain. Its centre became a massive consumer of materials and manpower drawn in from the provinces and from beyond its frontiers, and when the unstable equilibrium of this system began to falter, and centralized power started to break down, rapid decline set in, exacerbated by a fall in birth rate within the frontiers and a population build-up without. Like all empires, the trajectory of the Roman empire can be divided into three stages: construction and expansion, comparative stability and prosperity, and decline. All three stages generated massive energies, which affected, in different ways, not only the conquered territories but also lands beyond the frontiers. When Rome annexed a part of North Africa, it was inevitable that the rest of Africa, too, would feel the impact both of the initial conquest and of the reverberations which followed long afterwards.

In this chapter, we will consider the situation in the whole of northern Africa during the first two phases of empire, the conquest and the consolidation, beginning with the destruction of Carthaginian power at the end of the Third Punic War (149–146 BC) and ending with the integration of Mauretania into the empire in AD 43 and the long peace and prosperity which followed, lasting well into the fourth century AD. During this time, a significant percentage of the population of northern Africa lived under the rule of Rome, many becoming citizens; a few even became emperors.

The Creation of Roman Africa

The belief that Rome acquired her empire in self-defence contains an element of truth. In the case of its conflict with Carthage it was clear to all that the two states, who both depended on the sea for their livelihood and were divided only by a narrow strait, could not coexist for long. And so, when Carthage, provoked by the Numidian king Masinissa, attacked Numidian interests, Rome eagerly embraced the opportunity to obliterate her rival once and for all. The destruction of Carthage, followed by the ritual act of sowing the site of the old city with salt, brought Carthaginian power to an end, thus satisfying Rome's immediate aims. At this stage territorial aggrandizement was not a pressing issue. The land once owned by Carthage, defined by a ditched boundary running from Thabraca (Tabarka) on the north coast to the Gulf of Gabès, became the Roman province of Africa. No attempt was made to appropriate Numidian territory, which remained free as a client kingdom under the protection of Rome, ruled by Masinissa's son Micipsa. It was not long before Roman merchants set themselves up in Micipsa's capital, Cirta, to develop regular trading relations with the African population and to grow rich on the profits. Further west, the kingdom of Mauretania retained its freedom under its king, Bocchus. To the south of the two kingdoms, in the pre-desert zone, lived the Gaetuli, who, according to the geographer Strabo, occupied scattered settlements, some of them large enough to be called towns (*oppida*). This implies that they were dependent upon a sedentary economy based on crop growing, but the probability is that they also practised some kind of transhumance, with animals being taken up to mountain pastures when the steppe became too hot and dry in the summer.

The period of peace and prosperity ended with Micipsa's death in 118 BC. Succession often posed problems in the North African kingdoms because, instead of primogeniture, with the kingdom passing automatically to the king's eldest son, the right of kingship could be given to the eldest of the family or be divided between the sons of the previous king. Such a system could create tensions, often developing into outright conflict. So it was in 118 BC, when the kingdom was divided between the two sons of Micipsa, Hiempsal and Adherbal. The potential instability of the arrangement encouraged his illegitimate nephew Jugurtha, a skilled soldier who had served in the Roman army in Spain and had many supporters in Rome, to make a bid for power. Having dispatched one cousin, he chased the other to Cirta, where, in the ensuing carnage,

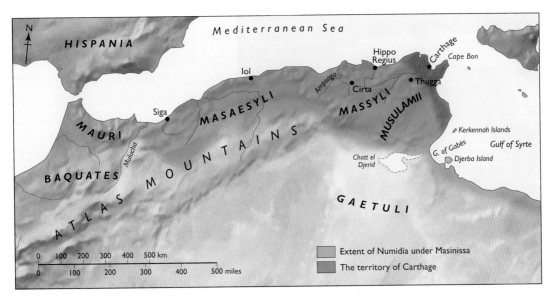

5.1 The tribes of the Maghrib at the end of the reign of Masinissa (238–148 BC).

Roman merchants were killed. Until this point Rome had stayed out of the affray, but with the death of its citizens it was forced to act and in 111 BC the senate declared war on Jugurtha. The campaign was successful and Jugurtha was driven out of Numidia, but, having moved south to the territory of the Gaetuli, he managed to sustain a level of guerrilla resistance. At first he enjoyed the support of his father-in-law, Bocchus of Mauretania, but Bocchus eventually tired of the situation and in 106 BC handed Jugurtha to the Romans. Two years later, having first been paraded in the triumph to celebrate the victory of his Roman opponent, Marius, he was ceremonially killed.

The Jugurthine war was an unedifying episode, which showed the fractured and self-seeking nature of the native elites and the vicious opportunism of the Roman army commanders. Bocchus' treachery in handing over Jugurtha is matched by Marius' ruthlessness in slaying all the male inhabitants of Cirta and selling the women and children into slavery. Six years of warfare left Numidia in a ravaged state, yet still the Roman senate was reluctant to absorb it all into the empire, though it did appropriate the fertile coastal strip of Tripolitania. In the settlement to follow, Bocchus was given the western part of the country, and what remained of Numidia was allowed to pass to Jugurtha's brother Gauda, to be ruled successively by himself, his son Hiempsal II, and his grandson Juba.

5.2 Juba I (85–46 BC), king of Numidia 60–46 BC.

The fate of Numidia now became caught up in the civil wars that dominated the last decades of the Roman Republic as ambitious members of the Roman elite fought for supremacy. One of the contenders, the outstanding military commander Gnaeus Pompeius, served as governor of Africa. During this time Pompey had been a supporter of Juba's father, Hiempsal II, and when Juba (r. 60–46 BC) succeeded to the kingdom, the new king continued the family's alliance with Pompey's cause even after Pompey's assassination in Egypt in 48 BC at the instigation of his rival Julius Caesar. A year before, Caesar had sent troops to Africa to take control of the province of Africa and of Numidia. The conflict lasted for three years and ended with Juba's defeat at Thapsus, followed by his death. In the aftermath Numidia was divided: lands in the west were passed to King Bocchus II; the territories around the old capital of Cirta were given to a mercenary, Sittus, and settled by veteran soldiers to form a small client kingdom; and the rest of Numidia became the province of Africa Nova. Carthage was refounded, and a colony of veterans was established. Later, in 27 BC, under the emperor Augustus, the two provinces were united as Africa Proconsularis, with a single legion, the Third Augusta, based at Ammaedara (modern Haïdra) to ensure order.

Large areas of Numidia, together with the territory once held by Carthage, comprised fertile farmland and enjoyed an equable climate. As a result it was densely occupied with a sedentary population. Mauretania to the west was mountainous and more sparsely settled. The coastal region was occupied by the Mauri, while the Middle Atlas was the home of other tribes, among whom the Baquates were the most prominent. The Romans showed little interest in the sprawling and difficult country, being content to leave it in the hands of its own leaders so long as they remained friendly to Rome. It was no surprise that the Mauretanian king Bocchus I felt it expedient to hand over Jugurtha to the Romans, and in the later conflict between Juba I and the forces of Caesar, his successor, Bocchus II, was rewarded for his support of Caesar's cause with a further gift of Numidian territory. With Rome now heavily entrenched in North Africa, Bocchus II recognized that Rome was in North Africa to stay and willed his kingdom of Mauretania to Octavian (later to become the emperor Augustus). When Bocchus died in 33 BC, Mauretania was regarded as a convenient place to settle colonies of veteran soldiers, but taking over such a large and not particularly productive territory as a province was an unattractive prospect at a time when Augustus was trying to consolidate the disparate parts of the Roman empire, still in trauma after a long period of civil war. His solution was to establish it as a client kingdom and in 25 BC it was placed under the rule of the Numidian king Juba II, whose father had died after his defeat by Caesar in 46 BC. The young Juba had been taken to Rome and brought up in the household of Julius Caesar, and later Octavian, and educated as a Roman. Later

5.3 Juba II (c.48 BC–AD 23), king of Numidia 30–25 BC, and of Mauretania 25 BC–AD 23.

he fought alongside Octavian at the battle of Actium in 31 BC. In Rome he had met and married another royal offspring, Cleopatra Selene II, who, like him, was being brought up in comfortable exile. She was the daughter of Mark Antony (Octavian's rival at Actium) and Cleopatra VII, the last of the Ptolemaic rulers of Egypt. It must have seemed to Augustus fitting that the thoroughly Romanized successors of the Numidian and Egyptian royal families should be put in charge of Mauretania.

The decision was a success. A new capital was built on the coast at Iol Caesarea (Cherchel) and became a centre of Hellenistic culture, with little evident trace of its African heritage. Juba spent much of his time in research and writing, sponsoring

5.4 The Medracen, in the Aurès Mountains of Algeria, is the mausoleum of a Numidian king dating to the third century BC. The inspiration for its architecture comes from the tombs of Hellenistic rulers in the East, reflecting their cultural aspirations.

biological expeditions and, according to Pliny, sending explorers to the Canary Islands. Mauretania became a prosperous kingdom and, apart from a minor revolt of border tribes, the Gaetuli and Musulamii, in AD 3–6, remained in peace throughout Juba's forty-eight-year reign, a staunch ally and profitable trading partner for Rome.

To the east of Numidia, where the gulfs of Gabès and Syrtis bite deep into the coast of Africa, the desert comes close to the sea. The principal attraction of the region was the three towns of Sabratha, Oea, and Leptis Magna, which gave the name Tripolitania to the coastal strip. The towns served as collection centres for local agrarian produce, mainly grain and olive oil, and also for goods brought in from the south by way of the caravan routes crossing the desert. The region was taken into the Roman orbit following the destruction of Carthage in 146 BC. Later, in 92 BC, Rome acquired Cyrenaica and its five cities as a bequest from the king of Egypt, and in 74 BC the territory was organized as a separate province. Later, in 20 BC, it was united administratively with the island of Crete.

Egypt also passed under Roman control with little trouble. The authority of the Ptolemys had been in decline for some while and the people had become increasingly fractious. Drawn into the struggles of the Roman civil wars, the last of the Ptolemys, Cleopatra VII, sided with Mark Antony. Her death, following Antony's defeat at the battle of Actium in 31 BC, left Egypt open to the triumphant Octavian, who, the next year, entered the country, recording the event, on an inscription listing his achievements, with the modest one-liner 'I added Egypt to the empire of the Roman people'.

For the Egyptians it meant little change. They were now ruled by a vice-regal governor (prefect), who was directly responsible to the emperor, and three legions were deployed to keep order from their bases at Nikopolis, near Alexandria, Babylon (Cairo), and Thebes. The stability that the new regime brought was a welcome contrast to the turbulent times under the last of the Ptolemys.

In little over a century, from the destruction of Carthage in 146 BC to the acquisition of Egypt in 30 BC, Rome had established its control over the entire coastal region of North Africa and the Nile valley down to the First Cataract. Most of it was administered directly as provinces, while the western extremity, Mauretania, was left in the safe hands of a client king. North Africa had now become, irretrievably, part of the Mediterranean world. The old North African states were no more. Numidia had gone,

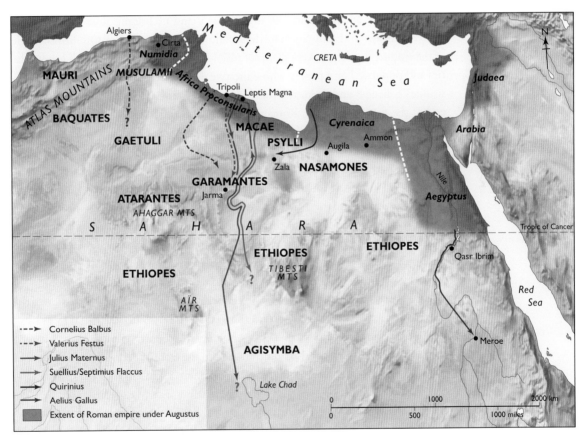

5.5 During the reign of the emperor Augustus (27 BC–AD 14), Egypt and much of North Africa became part of the Roman empire, but the lure of the desert encouraged a number of expeditions to be mounted to explore the south during the first century AD. The central position of the Garamantes meant that they were sometimes involved as intermediaries.

and Mauretania, while in name a kingdom, was ruled by a man steeped in the culture of the Graeco-Roman world. But the population remained African, and in the mountains and along the vast pre-desert interface, many tribes, among them the Baquates, Musulamii, Gaetuli, Garamantes, and Nasamones, maintained their traditional ways and loyalties and were a constant reminder to the provincial administration that their authority quickly ran out as the desert was approached.

Exploring the Desert Fringes

The boundaries of the empire were liminal places and as such were fraught with danger, yet for those seeking glory they offered opportunity. On the northern edge of the empire, Julius Caesar bridged the Rhine to probe the dense German forests, and crossed the Ocean to explore the mysterious island of Britain. Both exploits were treated with awe and admiration by those following events at home. On the other side of the empire, the deserts were places of instability, bereft of easily defensible boundaries and populated by a people whose lifestyle demanded mobility. They offered irresistible challenges and, from the time of Caesar's victory at Thapsus in 46 BC to the end of the first century AD, Romans engaged with the people of the desert fringes, drawn in by episodes of local discontent and by an innate curiosity to learn more of this alien world.

The first attempt to penetrate the desert came in 26–25 BC when the prefect of Egypt, Aelius Gallus, led an abortive expedition into the Arabian desert. Taking advantage of the army's disarray, the Kushites of the middle Nile advanced into Egypt in 24 BC with their own army of thirty thousand. They sacked Aswan and, at Philae, destroyed the imperial statues which the Romans had set up a few years before. Among the trophies they carried off was the bronze head of Augustus, which was eventually found by archaeologists in Meroe. In retaliation, the new prefect, Gaius Petronius, led an expedition deep into the kingdom of Meroe, but, on receiving the submission of the queen, withdrew, leaving a garrison at Primis (Qasr Ibrim). Since the threat from Kush was limited and the economic benefit of holding the country minimal, it was judged that no further investment should be made, and the frontier was soon moved further north to Hiera Sykaminos (Maharraqa), 80 kilometres south of the First Cataract.

The next recorded engagement with desert tribes was an expedition led by Cornelius Balbus against the Garamantes in 20 BC. Balbus set off from Sabratha, on the coast of Tripolitania, making for the oasis of Cidamus (Ghadames) and then struck out south-east across the desert to Garama (Jarma), the Garamantian capital, receiving its submission before returning, via Wadi al-Ajal, to the coast. In the same year he made another incursion into the desert, probably starting from the vicinity of Algiers and travelling south through the mountains. For his achievements he was awarded a triumph: as Pliny reminds us, the first foreigner to be so honoured (Balbus was from Gades in Spain). It may have been about this time that another expedition, led by P. Sulpicius Quirinius, governor of Crete and Cyrene from 21 to 15 BC, was being mounted against the Marmaridae, south of the Cyrenaican plateau. He also encountered the Garamantes, probably somewhere around Zala, on the eastern limit of their territory. If the campaign did indeed take place while Quirinius was governor, it might have been part of an effort, coordinated with Balbus, to assess the extent and strength of the Garamantes with a view to conquest. In the event the possibility was never followed up.

Border troubles flared up at the end of the century when, in 3 BC, a Roman proconsul was killed in Tripolitania by the Nasamones, and in AD 3 the Gaetuli, who occupied the southern slopes of the Aurès Mountains, rose in revolt. It was serious enough to require the attention of the proconsul, Cossus Cornelius Lentulus, who took three years to bring the rebels to heel. The cause of the uprising is not recorded, but it is most likely to have resulted from friction over land rights.

5.6 In 24 BC the Kushites raided Roman Egypt. One of the trophies they brought back was a greater than life-size bronze head of the emperor Augustus which had once adorned one of the towns in the north. It was buried beneath the steps of the temple at Meroe, where it was found in 1910.

The Gaetuli practised transhumance, which involved the seasonal movement of livestock between pastures. Such a lifestyle was difficult for the Roman administration to contend with, especially when trying to register land rights for purposes of taxation. The problem was to recur a decade later. Whether or not the Garamantes played a significant role in either of these incidents it is difficult to say. As sedentary agriculturists dependent on commanding trade, their interests lay in maintaining stability.

A more serious uprising broke out in AD 17. The tribe involved were the Musulamii, possibly a division of the Gaetuli, who objected to the construction of a military road across the eastern Aurès. The road cut through their transhumance routes and was, in all probability, built to enable some kind of control or surveillance of the migrating tribesmen. The rebellion was led by Tacfarinas, who had once served in the Numidian cavalry, and soon grew to include Mauretanians under their leader, Mazippa. It was an effective operation, relying on guerrilla tactics. At one stage Tacfarinas petitioned the emperor Tiberius for land for his people, but was refused. The insurgency continued for six years and was given a new impetus when, in AD 23, Juba II died, leaving his kingdom to his son Ptolemy—young, inexperienced, and highly unpopular among his people. Disgruntled Mauretanians flocked to Tacfarinas, and now the Garamantes joined in, if in a rather half-hearted way, sending lightly armoured troops and acting as receivers of Tacfarinas' plunder. For the Romans the situation had taken a serious turn: the rebels were intent on expelling the occupiers from Africa. The next year, AD 24, the new proconsul, Dolabella, instilled a renewed sense of urgency and, compelling Ptolemy to play an active part, led a surprise attack on the rebels' camp at Auzia. The historian Tacitus completes the story: 'The enemy were taken unawares. They had no weapons, order, or plan and were dragged to death or captivity like sheep.' Tacfarinas died while resisting capture. In the aftermath the Garamantes took the precautionary step of sending a deputation to Rome to sue for peace.

The rebellion had lasted for seven years and had involved many of the tribes of North Africa both inside and outside Roman-controlled territory. If it had demonstrated anything, it was that Rome was here to stay. Ptolemy, rewarded for his reluctant support, remained in power in Mauretania until he was murdered in AD 40 on the orders of the new emperor, his cousin Caligula. Ptolemy had no heir, so a legate was installed responsible to the emperor. This prompted a revolt among many of the Moorish tribes, but it was quickly subdued and in AD 44 Mauretania was finally incorporated into the empire as two separate provinces: Mauretania Tingitana, with its capital, Tingis (Tangier); and Mauretania Caesariensis, with its capital, Iol Caesarea. During the campaign the governor, Suetonius Paulinus, had led a force through the Atlas Mountains and into the desert beyond, eventually, after ten days, turning back, his troops suffering from thirst and heatstroke. Why he made such an effort is unclear. There is unlikely to have been much military advantage to be gained, but curiosity had been satisfied and the boundary of the world probed. With the incorporation of Mauretania into the empire, Roman territorial ambitions in Africa were at an end, at least for the time being. The empire had reached the limit of its ecological niche, the desert edge, but what lay beyond continued to excite the imagination.

Nero was the first to take up the challenge by sponsoring an expedition up the Nile in the AD 60s. There are two accounts, which differ, suggesting that there may have been two separate expeditions. The account by Pliny is short, saying that little was accomplished but adding that it was in preparation for an invasion of Ethiopia which Nero planned to make. The second, more informative account is by Seneca, Nero's tutor:

> I myself have heard two centurions whom Emperor Nero had sent to investigate the source of the Nile tell how they accomplished a long journey for which the king of Ethiopia [Meroe] provided them with an escort and commended them to the next near-est king, by which means they penetrated far beyond his realm.
>
> (*Naturales Quaestiones* 6.8.3)

He goes on to describe 'tremendous marshes' that were so entangled that there was no way through, where the explorers saw 'two rocks from which tumbled the vast might of the river'. It is quite possible that the entangled marsh was the Sudd, on the White Nile, 1,000 kilometres south of Meroe, but there is no great waterfall anywhere near. It could be that the story was conflated and that they reached much further south, as far as Uganda, but it is more likely that the waterfall was an invention to provide a suitable end to the story, allowing them to claim to have accomplished their mission. Whatever the truth, it was a spirited attempt. But why was Nero so interested? Was he really con-templating an invasion deep into Ethiopia? Was he interested in finding another route to the Indian Ocean to bypass the pirate-infested Red Sea, as one recent writer has sug-gested? Or was it simply innate curiosity? At any event, two centurions was a modest investment, suggesting no great commitment.

A little later, attention turned to the land of the Garamantes and to what lay beyond. The Garamantes had negotiated a treaty with Rome in the aftermath of the rebellion of Tacfarinas. The conditions seem to have been honoured until AD 69, when the Garamantes began to interfere in the squabble between the coastal cities of Oea and Leptis Magna. Offering their support for Oea, they pillaged the land of Leptis Magna and put the city under siege. Rome's response was to send an army under the command of Valerius Festus, which rapidly restored order, recovering most of the booty. Terms were set and peace was re-established. There matters rested for fifteen years when a revolt by a neighbouring tribe, the Nasamones, had to be put down by the governor, Suellius Flaccus.

It was probably the same man who, in AD 87, decided to lead an expedition to the south. The initial stage of his journey took him to Garama, the Garamantian capital, from where he travelled south for three months, probably reaching as far as the Tibesti Mountains. There is no suggestion that the Garamantes were other than helpful, and he returned safely. It may well have been the report of this journey that encouraged another traveller, Julius Maternus, to follow a similar route about AD 90. He began his journey in Leptis Magna and made straight for Garama, arriving thirty days later. There he met the king of the Garamantes, who invited him to join an expedition to the land of the black Africans, quite possibly a slave-raiding trip. After travelling for four months and fourteen days, the party reached the country of the Agisymba, where they saw a large lake with rhinoceros. The lake was most likely Lake Chad. Who Maternus was and what motivated him to embark on the journey remains unknown, but the most likely explanation is that his goal was to assess the commercial prospects of the south. That he, and Flaccus before him, could travel safely through Garamantian territory is a measure of the strength of the treaty negotiated by Festus in AD 70 and the fact that the Garamantes, living beyond the Roman frontier, were beginning to profit from their location as middlemen in the rapidly growing trade between the desert and the Mediterranean world.

Africa within the Empire

By the beginning of the first century AD, large numbers of Africans were living within the Roman frontier—the various Berber peoples of North Africa and the Egyptians of the delta and the Nile valley—and for centuries to come they were to experience the relative peace that Roman rule imposed. The energies once spent in tribal conflicts could now be invested in more productive activities, but this was not to say that life was better for everyone. The evils of capitalism were ever present: commercial exploitation, nepotism, massive disparities in wealth, and the miseries of slavery. But Rome did not itself impose all this anew: it merely condoned and exacerbated systems of inequality deeply rooted in indigenous society. The prime interest of the Roman administrators was to extract taxes from the provinces to support the vast infrastructure that underpinned the state. The most effective way of doing this was to leave customary property relations in place as far as possible and to build an administrative structure, based in cities, to extract the prescribed tithe. Roman Africa was highly productive, particularly Numidia and Egypt, and was relied on to provide grain to feed the urban masses in Rome and later in Constantinople as well. In Caesar's time, Africa Nova generated nearly 50,000 tons of grain a year. Within a century the yield had increased tenfold. Tripolitania, and to a lesser extent Numidia, also produced huge volumes of olive oil.

All this contributed to the wealth of North Africa and is reflected in the growth of cities, of which the country could boast about six hundred.

Many benefited from the burgeoning prosperity. There were, of course, some foreign speculators buying up property as investments, but by far the largest percentage of the population was of Berber ancestry. One such was an unnamed man whose third-century tombstone was found at Mactar in Tunisia. With a quiet pride he records his life story:

> I was born of poor parents: my father had neither an income nor his own house. From the day of my birth I always cultivated my field; neither my land nor I ever had any rest as the season ripened the crop. When the harvest gangs arrived to hire themselves out in the countryside round Cirta, capital of Numidia, or in the plains of the mountain of Jupiter, I was the first to harvest my field. Then, having left my neighbourhood, for twelve years I reaped the harvest of another man, under the fiery sun; for eleven years I was chief of a harvest gang and scythed the corn in the fields of Numidia. Thanks to my labours, and being content with very little, I finally became master of a house and a property: today I live at ease. I have even achieved honours: I was called on to sit on the senate of my city, and, though once a modest peasant, I became a censor. I have watched my children and my grandchildren grow up around me; my life has been occupied, peaceful, and honoured by all.

The harvester of Mactar was one of the fortunate ones: few peasants could have recorded such an advancement. Yet the opportunities were there. The playwright Terrence began life as a Berber slave but was taken to Rome, freed, and his education paid for by his one-time owner. The writer Apuleius also boasted of his African ancestry, describing himself as 'half Numidian, half Gaetulian'. He had a more privileged upbringing. His father was a member of the urban elite in Madouros on the coast of Algeria, where he served as a *duumvir* (magistrate). When he died, Apuleius, who had been educated in Carthage, used his legacy to go to Athens to study. These were the lucky ones who, through patronage or birth, could succeed in the Roman system. At the other end of the scale were the Egyptian slaves who spent their working lives under the scorching sun in the quarries of Mount Porphyrites in the Eastern Desert, hacking out blocks of stone so that emperors could have their images recorded for posterity. Disproportions in wealth had long been a feature of Berber and Egyptian society. Yet while they were accentuated by the Roman system, there were ample opportunities for advancement for those with the ability or ambition to take them.

There are many hints in surviving inscriptions that Roman administrators dealt creatively with the native people who came within the sphere of their authority. In some cases, land was assigned to tribal groups. In other areas, councils of tribal elders (*seniores*) were recognized, and in even more remote regions, in the Atlas Mountains, altars recording meetings and peace treaties between Roman governors and the local tribe, the Baquates, suggest an even looser form of association. What is clear is that there, in these more out-of-the-way regions, elements of the old tribal system were allowed to continue by pragmatic administrators who recognized that in tradition lay stability.

The major towns, particularly those founded or refounded during the Roman period, followed the classical model, but in some, traces of their native origins can still be seen. A fine example is Thugga (Roman, Dougga), which occupies a hill slope overlooking the rich cornfields of the Oued Khalled, 40 kilometres south-west of Carthage. It was founded in the sixth century BC and continued as a provincial town under the Romans. There are the usual Roman buildings, a forum, a market, a theatre, temples, and baths, but what is most striking is that, instead of streets carefully set out in a grid system so characteristic of Roman urban planning, the buildings have been fitted into a network of winding lanes inherited from its Numidian origins. Of the early buildings there is little to be seen, but beneath the Roman forum lay a temple built and dedicated to Masinissa in the tenth year of Micipsa's reign (139 BC). Also of the second century BC is a spectacular Libyco-Punic mausoleum designed for a member of the Numidian elite. The influence of Carthage on the town is reflected

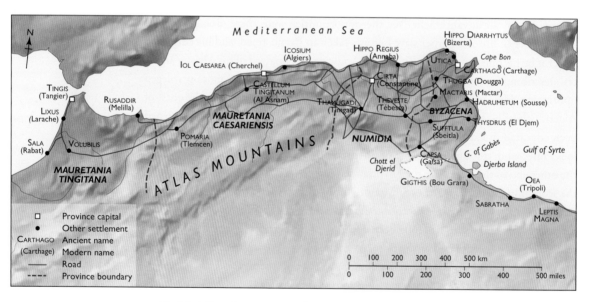

5.7 The Maghrib in the Roman period saw the development of a large number of towns and of a road system to service them. The map shows how slight was the Roman impact on the western Maghrib.

5.8 Under the Romans the small town of Dougga, in Tunisia, grew, and many grand public buildings were added, but the winding streets of the old Numidian settlement still dominate.

by temples originally dedicated to the Punic deities Baal Hammon and Tanit. Later rebuilt in Roman style, they were rededicated to Saturn and Caelestis. In Thugga we can glimpse a small, sophisticated Numidian town developing within the Punic sphere but still making its native heritage apparent even after the impact of Rome.

While North Africa was quickly assimilated into the Roman world, Egypt remained a place apart regarded with awe and suspicion, a place to be kept at arm's length. Romans of senatorial rank and leading equestrians were forbidden to enter the country without the permission of the emperor, and native Egyptians were excluded from senior ranks in the administration. The country was governed by a prefect, who was directly responsible to the emperor. Behind these elaborate precautions lay the fear that the country, well protected by its geography, abundantly productive, and with an excitable population, could easily be stirred to rebellion. It was for this reason that three legions were deployed within easy reach of the major cities to ensure control,

5.9 (*Opposite top*) The town of Dougga began life as a Numidian settlement. On the edge of the town stands a mausoleum built for a member of the Numidian elite in the second century BC. It owes much to the Punic style, popular in funerary architecture. The original structure was found in a ruined state and was further damaged when an inscription was removed, but it was reconstructed in 1908–10.

5.10 (*Opposite bottom*) Under Roman rule the economy of North Africa flourished and large estates were created by the elite. This mosaic floor from Carthage shows a country estate probably belonging to the owner of the town house in which the mosaic was laid.

5.11 (*Above*) Timgad, the Roman city of Colonia Marciana Ulpia Traiana Thamugadi, in the Aurès Mountains of Algeria, was founded by the emperor Trajan *c.* AD 100 as a colony for military veterans. Its rigorous chequerboard layout, so typically Roman, contrasts with the rambling plan of Dougga, which was influenced by the earlier native settlement.

with detachments sent to garrison forts along the roads in the Eastern Desert serving the vital Red Sea ports. Egypt was a special place with its own long-established deities, its deeply revered monuments, and its adherence to traditional mortuary rites like mummification. So long as the dispersed army was able to keep the country secure, allowing Egyptian grain to flow to Rome and protecting the trade goods in transit, this alien, other, place was best left to itself.

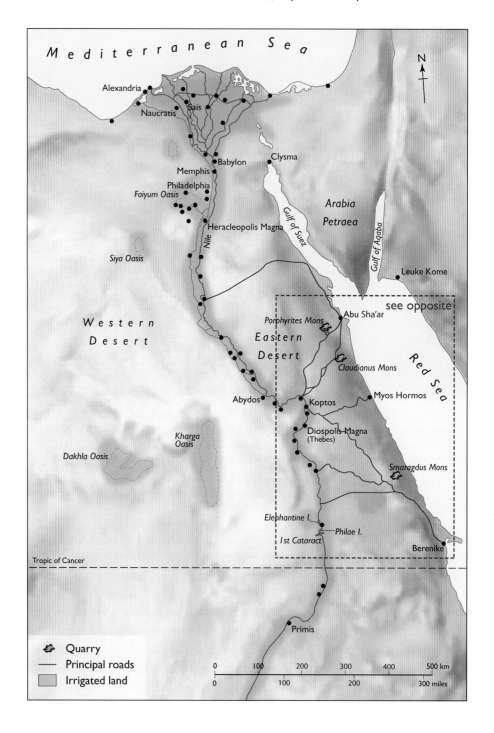

Mediterranean Sea

Alexandria
Naucratis
Sais
Babylon
Clysma
Memphis
Philadelphia
Faiyum Oasis
Heracleopolis Magna
Siya Oasis

Arabia Petraea

Gulf of Suez
Gulf A Aqaba

Leuke Kome

see opposite

Western Desert

Eastern Desert

Porphyrites Mons
Abu Sha'ar

Claudianus Mons

Red Sea

Abydos
Koptos
Myos Hormos

Kharga Oasis

Dakhla Oasis

Diospolis Magna
(Thebes)

Smaragdus Mons

Elephantine I.
Philae I.
1st Cataract

Berenike

Tropic of Cancer

Primis

Quarry
Principal roads
Irrigated land

0	100	200	300	400	500 km

0	100	200	300 miles

Nile

162

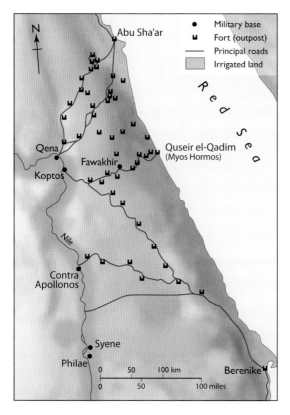

5.12 (*Opposite and left*) Under Roman rule Egypt became a major supplier of grain for Rome and a conduit of trade with India. The importance attached to Red Sea trade is shown by the number of garrisons established along the roads in the Eastern Desert to protect the movement of goods arriving at the Red Sea ports of Berenike and Myos Hormos. Quarries were opened in the desert to provide fine stone for monumental buildings.

The Mediterranean coast of Africa was now lined with burgeoning ports, from Tingis (Tangier) to Alexandria, through which the products of Africa and the East flooded into the Roman consumer markets. The largest was Alexandria. In the first century BC, Diodorus Siculus estimated its population to be three hundred thousand free residents, suggesting a total population, including slaves, of about half a million. Carthage came next at between one and two hundred thousand, then Leptis Magna at just under a hundred thousand. The size of the population reflected the volume of goods passing through. Carthage dealt mainly with the produce of Numidia, grain, oil, and fruit, Leptis Magna with the trade in Tripolitanian olive oil and more exotic products from the heart of Africa, while Alexandria, in addition to being the transhipment port for Egyptian grain, handled all the trade goods from Arabia and India as well as commodities from East Africa passing through Meroe and along the Nile. The quantity of produce flowing annually through the ports on the African interface was considerable. The drawing out of this resource through and from Africa cannot have failed to have a dramatic effect on African communities living beyond the frontier.

163

The States Without: Meroe, Aksum, and Beyond

The border skirmishes between Rome and the Kushites on the Nile, initiated by the Kushite attack on Aswan in 24 BC, were quickly resolved (p. 152 above), and the frontier was finally established at Hiera Sykaminos, where it remained until AD 298 when the emperor Diocletian withdrew Roman forces to Aswan, leaving the Kushites to fill the vacuum. For three centuries, relations between Roman Egypt and the kingdom of Meroe remained friendly and trade between them continued. The Red Sea route was now beginning to eclipse the Nile, but even so Meroe remained prosperous until the beginning of the fourth century.

The decline that followed is not easy to analyse, but its reality is evident in the abandonment of the practice of marking royal burials with pyramids. What seems to have happened is that, with the slackening of trade with Egypt, the kings of Meroe, now experiencing increasing poverty, lost their authority, and political fragmentation set in. The collapse of centralized government led to the emergence of new centres of power, but they were not strong enough to prevent incursions from the neighbouring state of Aksum and the desert tribes who had begun to move in like predators around a weakened beast. Some hint of the confusions of the time is offered by an inscription set up at Aksum by the Aksumite king Aezana which records a successful campaign against the Noba, who were occupying land and towns once within the kingdom of Meroe. The Noba were a desert tribe who had lived in the Western Desert since the third century BC. The discovery of two Aksumite inscriptions at Meroe, one carved on a throne, suggests that the town had now passed into Aksumite control. By the mid fourth century, the temples were in disrepair, and a mass grave, postdating the destruction of one of the temples, had been dug to accommodate the dismembered remains of thirty men, women, and children. These were troubled times.

The fourth and fifth centuries saw rapid change within the old kingdom of Meroe. New polities emerged from the ruins of the old as desert tribes, benefiting from greater mobility arising from increased use of the camel, sought new land along the river. By the mid sixth century, three new kingdoms had emerged: Nobadia, Makuria, and Alodia. While they were deeply rooted in the Kushite past, the progressive adoption of Christianity marked a significant change.

The rise of the state of Aksum was largely due to the development of Red Sea shipping routes during the Roman period. Located at the northern end of the Ethiopian Highlands, it commanded the important route node linking East Africa to the Red Sea and had within its territory the harbour town of Adulis, a favoured port of call where ships could restock before the long haul north to Berenike and Myos Hormos. An added advantage of its position was its proximity to the Somali coast and to Yemen,

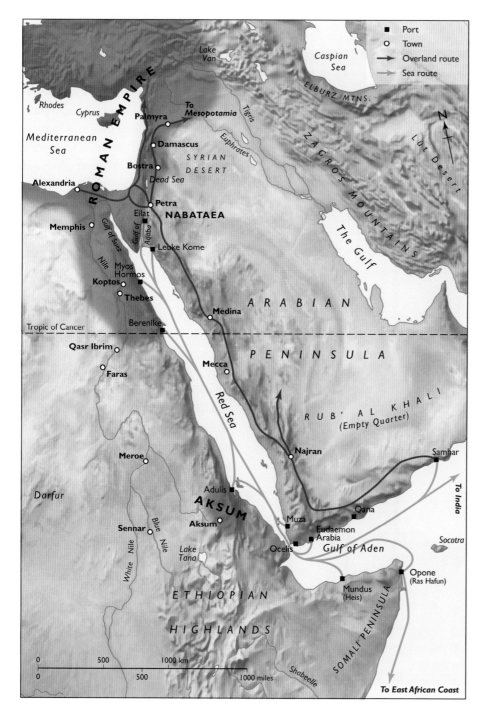

5.13 During the Roman period the kingdom of Aksum developed as a strong polity dominating the trade routes. The Red Sea trade was now augmented by the growing importance of overland trade along the western edge of the Arabian desert, using Petra as a focus for onward distribution.

5.14 In Aksum massive monolithic stelae were erected to commemorate the burial places of the elite. The largest still standing, known as the Obelisk of Aksum, is 24 metres high and weighs 160 tonnes. It dates from the fourth century AD. The doors and windows carved on the faces are all false.

where the much-valued frankincense and myrrh grew in profusion. Between the first and fourth centuries AD, Aksum developed rapidly, its commercial importance as a trading state being shown by its coinage. By the late third century, it was issuing three denominations, in copper, silver, and gold. The gold coins, designed for international exchange, were inscribed in Greek to give them wide acceptability. The most important of Aksum's exports were ivory and tortoiseshell, for which, in return, it received a wide range of Mediterranean luxuries: fine metalwork, gems, glass, and wine.

By the fourth century, Aksum, the capital, was a loose agglomeration of buildings, including royal tombs marked by tall stelae carved to represent multi-storey buildings. They were designed to impress. The largest weighed 517 tonnes and, had it ever been erected, would have stood to a height of 33 metres. The adoption of Christianity by the elite about AD 340 brought such ostentation to an end, and by the late sixth century the royal tombs were identified by more modest funerary chapels.

The Aksumites had expansionist tendencies. We have seen that in the fourth century there is some evidence to suggest an incursion into the Nile valley to appropriate part of the fragmenting kingdom of Meroe. About the same time, they seem to have established control over part of southern Arabia. It was in this moment of rapid change in the early sixth century that a much firmer hold was taken on Yemen (pp. 184–5 below). As long as consumer demand from the Mediterranean world held, be it Roman or Byzantine, Aksum could flourish.

By the time that the *Periplus of the Erythraean Sea* was composed, in the middle of the first century AD, sailors from the Red Sea had rounded Cape Guardafui—the tip of the Horn of Africa—and were exploring the east coast of Africa at least as far south as present-day Dar es Salaam on the coast of Tanzania. While still in the Gulf of Aden, before reaching Cape Guardafui, ships' masters could have chosen to stop at Mundu or Damo on the incense coast of Somalia, and once round the cape they would have made for the landing place of Opone (modern Ras Hafun). It was described as a market that 'produces cinnamon ... as well as the better sort of slaves, which were brought to Egypt in increasing numbers, and much tortoiseshell of much better quality than elsewhere'. Among the commodities carried from the Egyptian Red Sea ports for barter were wheat, rice, ghee, sesame oil, cotton cloth, and honey. Excavations at the beach camp at Opone, where the exchanges took place, have yielded pottery from Egypt, the Persian Gulf, and India, reflecting the extent of the trading network. The *Periplus* goes on to list the landing places along the coast of Azania (East Africa) between Opone and Rhapta. Rhapta has not positively been identified but is thought to lie in the Rufiji delta, 120 kilometres south of Dar es Salaam. This would make the length of coast visited about 2,000 kilometres. Rhapta was clearly a place of some significance. The *Periplus* calls it a port of trade ('here there is much ivory and tortoiseshell'), while the geographer Ptolemy, writing in the mid second century, refers to it as a 'metropolis'. The locations in between were not significant trading ports but places to stop over during the journey. An island is mentioned, possibly Zanzibar, flat and wooded, with many rivers where the natives used sewn boats and dugouts for fishing and capturing tortoises. And all along the coast were 'men of great stature who are pirates' ruled by chiefs. It is difficult to judge the intensity of the trade with Azania, and lack of success so far in identifying the beach markets means that archaeology has little yet to offer.

Ptolemy's *Geographia*, compiled in the second century but with later additions up to AD 400, has a few other observations to add. His information on East Africa comes from a number of sources: men like the merchant Marinus of Tyre, Theophilus, 'who voyaged to Azania', and a certain Diogenes, 'who was one of those who were accustomed to sail to India'. Diogenes appears to have learnt, either by personal observation or, more likely, from local natives, of 'lakes from which the Nile flows'. Ptolemy gives coordinates of two lakes, which, he says, were fed by streams flowing from the 'Mountains of the Moon'. It is tempting to believe that Diogenes' informants had some knowledge of the great lakes, like Lake Victoria and Lake Turkana. The tales they told of them to the foreign sailors encountered on the coast were adopted by the geographers of the day and were to inspire later generations of explorers.

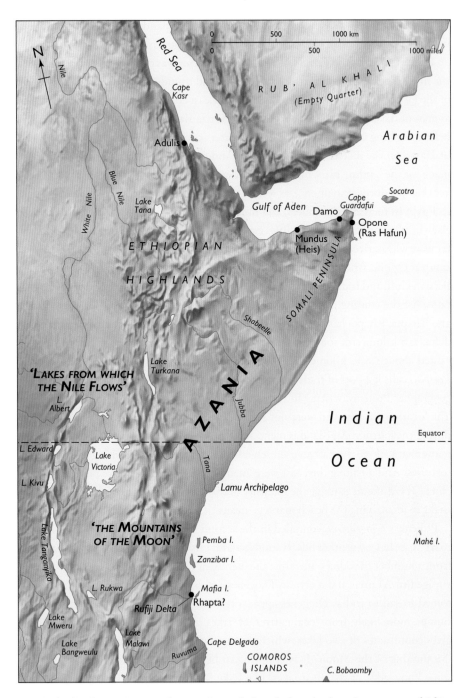

5.15 By the fourth century AD, trading expeditions had reached south, along the east coast of Africa probably as far south as the Rufiji delta in Tanzania.

The Garamantes Again

The Garamantes occupied strings of oases dominating a complex of desert routes in the area now known as the Fazzan, to the south of the Roman province of Tripolitania. From this favoured position they could profit by articulating trade between the desert tribes and the Roman cities and could mount predatory attacks on Roman-held territory if they so wished. In the first half of the first century AD, relations with the Romans were ambiguous, but from AD 70 the state settled into its role as a trading hub, taking advantage of its position to embrace, selectively, aspects of Roman life.

In the Classic Garamantian period, covering the first to the fourth centuries AD, Garama emerged as the capital and was adorned with stone-built public buildings and temples. It lay in the centre of Wadi al-Ajal, and was one of several large settlements strung out in front of the main escarpment in a landscape densely packed with villages and hamlets. At its most extensive the territory of the Garamantes covered about a quarter of a million square kilometres and incorporated a hundred or so villages with a total population estimated to be in the order of fifty to a hundred thousand. Such a

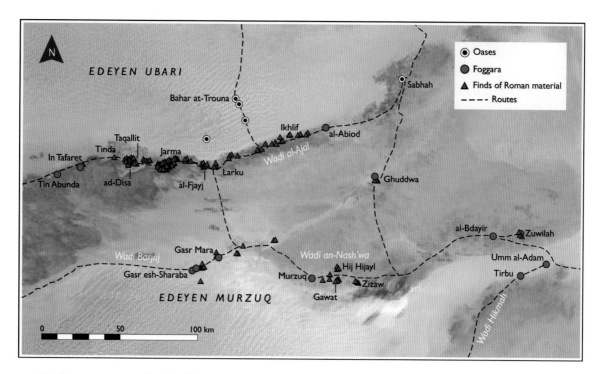

5.16 The Garamantes remained on friendly terms with the Roman world, and the desert-edge settlements flourished. The foggara system of irrigation ensured a high level of food production.

large sedentary population could be accommodated only if there was an efficient system of food production. The foggaras, by now well developed, irrigated extensive field systems in the wadi bottoms, while the introduction of sorghum and pearl millet from the Sahel, alongside wheat and barley, greatly extended productivity. Date palms added significantly to the food supply. Surpluses in all of these crops, and in horses and camels bred locally, could be exported both to the port towns of the Mediterranean coast and to the dispersed communities of the Sahara.

Craft skills in working iron, copper, ivory, ostrich eggs, and semi-precious stones like carnelian and amazonite, and making fabrics and leather goods, were practised in the villages and farms to provide for local needs and to be used for trade. The significance of slaves to the economy is less clear. Slaves procured in the south would have been employed in some number in the dangerous work involved in constructing and maintaining the foggaras, and in working the fields. Some may have been traded to the Mediterranean, but the Roman preference for African children as slaves could have been accommodated by trading the offspring of slaves working in Garamantian territory. Wild animals for the circus were also valuable commodities. Some could have been hunted locally, while others would have been acquired from the south. The other desirable product was gold, which may have been procured from West Africa in the form of gold dust to be passed on to the Roman market in its unworked state.

The Garamantes, then, were ideally situated to manipulate the supply of manpower and raw materials flowing to the Roman world in the same way as the Kushites supplied Egypt. They would have acquired the commodities through raid and tribute as well as through regular trade, the systems being controlled by the elite. Little is known of the organization of the hierarchy, but kings are mentioned in the few available texts, and cemeteries reflect social disparity, the more elaborate tombs—pyramid tombs, large stepped tombs, and mausoleums—being located close to the centre of power at Garama. The grave goods from the elite tombs favour exotic materials imported from the Roman world: wine, a range of drinking vessels including glass beakers in abundance, oil, oil lamps, and a variety of jewellery. In other words, status was displayed by one's ability to acquire the outward and visible signs of civilized life from the alien world beyond.

By the third century, there are signs of social change beginning to take hold. Stronger, more fort-like structures (*qsurs*) were being built in the centres of many of the villages. There is also evidence that water was becoming increasingly scarce as the water table began to drop, causing the foggara system to be constantly modified. The insecurity which this generated could well have been the cause of the rash of fortifications, reflecting a weakening of centralized power. These internal factors are likely to have exacerbated, if not been the direct cause of, the decline in trade evident in the fourth century.

5.17 Among the varied commodities acquired from the south were wild animals for use in spectacles in the amphitheatre. The mosaic from Zliten, Libya, shows such a scene, with bound captives being attacked by leopards.

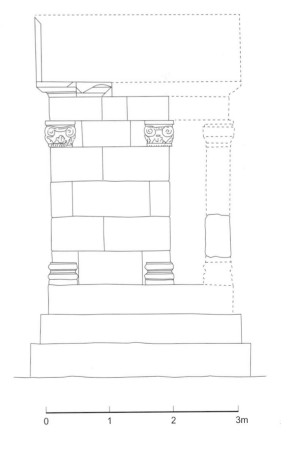

5.18 The Garamantes acquired Roman goods through trade and selectively adopted Roman building styles. An example of this is the Watwat mausoleum, constructed in classical mode. The false columns at the corners were provided with composite capitals in contrasting Ionic and Corinthian orders.

0   1   2   3m

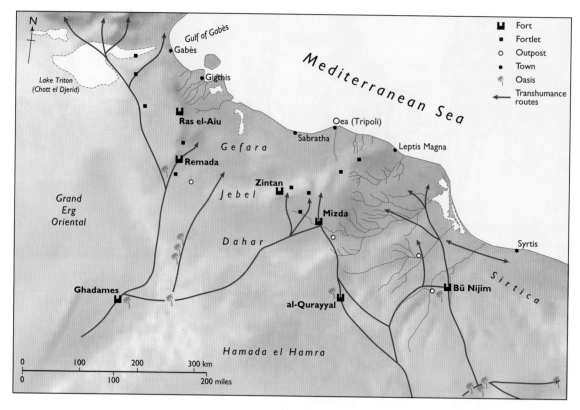

5.19 By the third century BC, Rome was beginning to take a more defensive stance in Tripolitania, erecting a string of forts and fortlets to protect the coastal strip from the tribes of the interior.

As early as the third century there are signs of trouble from the desert tribes, who now began to threaten the coastal towns. The Garamantes are not specifically mentioned and may, themselves, have suffered attacks from the desert nomads. In response to the troubles, the emperor Septimius Severus built a screen of forts and fortlets to guard the approaches to the coastal zone with the purpose of keeping a careful eye on tribal movements. Several times patrols encountered Garamantes, but they seem to have been innocent traders bringing barley to sell to the troops garrisoned at the forts. The fact that these records were kept at all implies a heightened vigilance.

The World beyond the Desert

The absence of any written accounts for the Sahel in the pre-Islamic period means that we have to rely entirely on archaeological evidence to reconstruct a history of the first

half of the first millennium AD. The task is not helped by the fact that archaeological activity has been limited, and statistically reliable evidence is sparse in the extreme. That said, several sites which have been subjected to high-quality excavation provide an indication of the complex processes under way. A key site is Jenné-jeno, on the edge of the Inner Niger Delta in Mali, where, as we have seen (pp. 116–17 above), a nucleated settlement began to develop about 250 BC. By AD 400 it had expanded considerably from its original 7 hectares, reflecting a population growth made possible by having a stable economy heavily reliant on the production of rice. The community was able to articulate local and regional trade in commodities like iron, which was being worked on the site, and salt coming from the desert. The discovery of a bead which may have originated in India hints at the broader network of which the settlement was a part. Jenné-jeno is but one site in the middle Niger region where the density of occupation intensifies during the first millennium AD. The main concentrations focus on the Méma, the Macina, and the Lakes region of the Inner Niger Delta, and it may have been in one of these areas that West Africa's first empire, Ghana, arose (p. 209 below).

Another region of precocious development was the Niger Bend, where later the Songhai empire was to build its centre of power. Fieldwork at Kissi, in Burkina Faso, has brought to light a cluster of settlement mounds and cemeteries extending over some 400 hectares, in date spanning from the end of the first millennium BC to the thirteenth century AD. Excavation of the early levels dating to the first half of the first millennium AD have produced items of copper alloy that may have come from Carthage, a glass bead from the Middle East, cowrie shells (*Cypraea moneta*) from the Indian Ocean, and woollen fabrics. The fabrics could have been made locally, but the absence of spinning and weaving equipment on the site suggests that they are more likely to have arrived as trade goods.

The third region, where complex, long-lived settlements are known, is around the shores of Lake Chad, the land of the Agisymba, visited by Julius Maternus in the first century AD. It was in this region that the empire of Kanem was to emerge by the ninth century.

The three centres of social complexity, the Inner Niger Delta, the Niger Bend, and Lake Chad, that were to become empires in the later first millennium AD, all benefited from trading systems which had begun to link communities on both sides of the Sahara in the first four centuries AD. The local and regional networks, already in existence, were now being built into more extensive international systems. Those communities who commanded the supply of rare resources were discovering that there was a fast-growing market for them. This underpinned their stability while opening the way for societies' leaders to exercise even greater control.

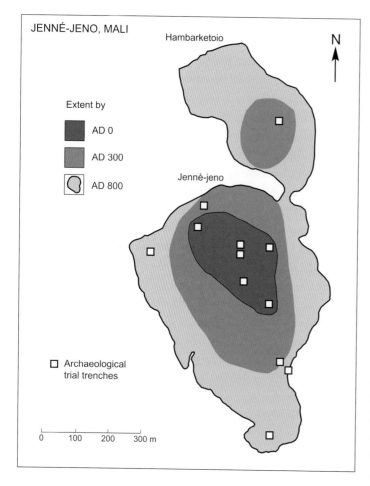

JENNÉ-JENO, MALI

Hambarketoio

N

Extent by

AD 0

AD 300

AD 800

Jenné-jeno

Archaeological
trial trenches

0   100   200   300 m

5.20 (*Left*) The settlement of Jenné-jeno, on the edge of the Inner Niger Delta in Mali, established in the third century BC, continued to grow in the first millennium AD.

5.21 (*Opposite*) Settlements in the Sahel like Jenné-jeno served as centres of exchange between the productive woodland and forest belt of the south and the traders who used the caravan routes to ship commodities across the desert to Roman North Africa.

Commodities on the Move

Our knowledge of trade is based entirely on items mentioned in classical texts and on artefacts found in archaeological contexts. It is an imperfect record, partial and extremely difficult to quantify, but what is certain is that during the period when Rome dominated the Mediterranean, the sheer volume and value of goods on the move was colossal. One small example will help make the point. Accounts kept on an Egyptian papyrus record that a single cargo brought from Muziris in India to Alexandria, made up of aromatic plants, ivory, and textiles, was valued at 131 talents. That sum would have been sufficient to purchase 1,000 hectares of the best farmland in Egypt. And that was only one vessel in the flotillas of ships that every year made the Indian Ocean passage. Many vessels put into Adulis, benefiting Aksum, while the kingdom of Meroe was able to sustain itself by articulating the trade between East Africa and Egypt. There can be little doubt that in the first four centuries AD the eastern network, involving the Red Sea and the Nile valley, saw a huge throughput of goods. The African states facilitating this flow benefited greatly.

But what of the central and western Saharan networks? Along the whole of the Roman frontier there will have been trickle trade involving short-range exchanges: goods passing into and out of the empire handled by local tribesmen and Roman traders in the frontier zone. A customs tariff found at Zarai, in Numidia, gives a good idea of the kinds of goods involved in this level of exchange. Wine, garum (fish sauce), and

 174

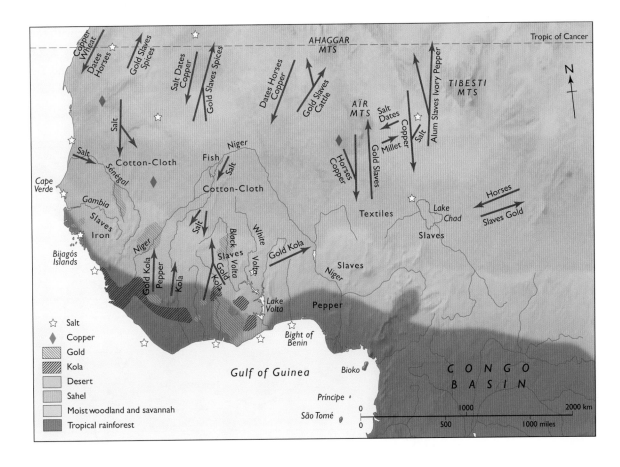

purple dyed fabrics were being traded for slaves, horses, cattle, sheep, and pigs—items difficult to identify as trade goods in the archaeological record. Such exchanges would have taken place at informal markets outside the forts along the frontier zone. The goods offered by the tribesmen were all produced by their own pastoral activities, augmented, perhaps, by a little raiding.

In the Fazzan the situation was more complex. Here, the sedentary Garamantes were able to command the trans-Saharan routes to and from Lake Chad in the south and the Niger Bend in the west. Garamantian middlemen transhipped these goods to the Roman towns of Tripolitania together with their own surplus produce: grain, horses and other animals, dates, cotton fabrics, carnelian gemstones, and natron, a salt used as a flux in glass making. In return, Mediterranean goods flooded in in large quantities absorbed into the social system to benefit most levels of Garamantian society. The relative value of trans-Saharan goods to locally produced commodities is difficult to judge, but in all probability the produce generated in the Fazzan greatly outweighed the value of the items in transit. How and where the exchange with the Roman world took place is unknown, but the main markets were most likely at the Roman-controlled oases of Ghadames, Zintan, al-Qurayyat al-Gharbiya, and Bu Njem—the places chosen to be most strongly fortified by the Romans in the early third century.

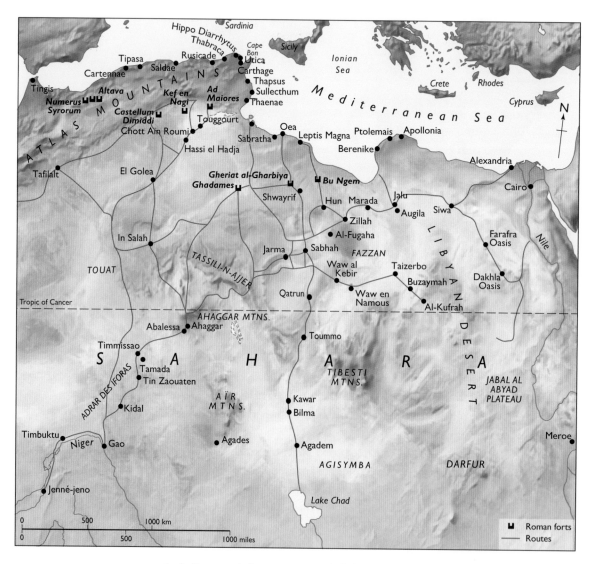

5.22 In the Roman period, two major routes linked to the south, one with the river Niger, the other with the Lake Chad region. The Garamantes benefited from their control of the Fazzan, where many of the routes converged.

We have left unresolved the question of what products may have been traded to the Garamantes from the rest of Africa. The only one that can be identified archaeologically is amazonite, a cloudy blue stone used to make beads. It comes from Eghei Zuma in the northern Tibesti, the land of the Tebu. These were the cave dwellers mentioned by Herodotus against whom the Garamantes mounted raids to acquire slaves. Beads of amazonite and carnelian have been found on various sites in the Inner Niger Delta and the Niger Bend region, reflecting connectivity across the central Sahara. It was from these southern regions that the slaves, so crucial to Garamantian society, must have come.

The scale of the slave trade between Africa and the Roman world is difficult to judge, but an order of magnitude can be offered. It is estimated that the slave population of the Roman world in the second century AD was between five and ten million, requiring between a quarter and half a million replacements a year to sustain the level. Many of the number will have been born to slave mothers, but even so in the order of fifty thousand to two hundred thousand would have had to be acquired from outside the empire every year. Since black slaves were always in a minority in the Roman world, sub-Saharan Africa will have contributed only a small percentage to this number. In the medieval period, three to five thousand slaves a year were transported to the markets in Europe and the Near East. A figure in this range, or perhaps a little higher, would probably be in the right order for the Roman period. Of these some will have come, via Meroe and Aksum, ultimately from East Africa and the eastern Sahel. The annual movement of slaves from the western and central Sahara is unlikely, therefore, to have been great, but would still have been at a significant level, in the order of several thousands.

The other commodity of international value was gold. The possibility of gold from West Africa reaching the Mediterranean world in the middle of the first millennium BC has already been considered (pp. 124–5 above), but there is no positive evidence to suggest that gold was regularly traded thereafter. However, that the gold coins were first produced by the Alexandrian mint in AD 296 and the Carthaginian mint in AD 298 implies that a significant quantity of gold was becoming available at the end of the third century. Most likely it was African gold, a contention given added support by the fact that, of the measures still used for gold dust in North Africa as late as the nineteenth century, one equated to the weight of the Roman gold coin the *solidus*, the other to the Roman ounce. The absence of evidence for gold working in West Africa at this time, and the rarity of gold in archaeological contexts in the Sahara, cannot be taken to imply that trade in gold was insignificant, but as to its volume and reliability of supply we know nothing. Nor is it clear which route was preferred, that through the

Fazzan or the more westerly route through the Touat oases. These are matters for further research.

The Peoples of the Desert

In considering the movement of goods it is all too easy to forget the carriers involved and the problems they faced in transport. Scattered through the hyper-arid Sahara were small sedentary communities whose survival depended on exchange and trade. Since trade relies on the transport provided by nomadic pastoralists, and pastoralists were dependent on food produced in the settlements, the sedentary and nomadic communities necessarily developed a symbiotic relationship. Pastoralists moving through their customary networks from one pasture to another to feed their animals carried dates to exchange for grain and had the capacity to carry trade goods for others. In such a simple system the interdependence and collaboration so crucial to survival is managed through an infrastructure of regional agreements based on kin linkages and tribal alliances.

Regional systems of this kind, probably already in operation in the second millennium, were self-sustaining, but as more complex sedentary states began to form to the north and south of the desert, demand for, and supplies of, commodities increased. The result was that the volume of goods on the move increased, as did the distances over which they were transported. This does not necessarily mean that the nomadic carriers embarked on longer journeys. Most probably continued to work within traditional networks, where kinship relations and customary agreements provided the security to caravans on the move. It was at oases on the borders of their territories that goods destined for international transit changed carriers. What might be viewed as trans-Saharan trade began as a series of overlapping systems of intra-desert exchanges.

The demands of the Mediterranean consumer market drove increased levels of Saharan trade, but without the social and physical networks that facilitated mobility within the desert and the capacity of the sub-Saharan communities to support the system, it could never have developed to the extent that it did. One crucial element in all this was the animal power that made it all possible. Horses and donkeys could carry loads, but their upkeep was demanding, and on long hauls between oases they could not survive. Far better was the one-humped camel (*Camelus dromedarius*), which could go without water for ten to fifteen days and could exist on rough forage. It was designed for desert conditions. To conserve water it could adjust its body temperature, so reducing its rate of perspiration. Its single hump carried 30 kilograms of fat that could be metabolized when required, while its ability to close its nostrils and protect its eyes with bushy eyebrows and double eyelashes meant that it could withstand sandstorms. Its soft, splayed feet were well designed for travel across sand, but some breeds had tougher feet more suited to gravel and broken rock. There were differences, too, in their tolerance for salty vegetation. Such variations meant that breeds could be chosen to suit the particular terrain in which they had to work.

Camels were first domesticated in Arabia, but surprisingly little is known about their spread across Africa (pp. 126–8 above). The fact that a Roman general could expect the inhabitants of Leptis Magna to provide him with four thousand in the late fourth century suggests that they were not in short supply. In all probability camels had begun to be used in the Sahara in the early first millennium BC, and had become the regular beast of burden on the Saharan routes by the first century AD.

Archaeology has comparatively little to say about the peoples of the Sahara at this time, but one tantalizing discovery offers some insights. At the oasis of Abalessa,

5.23 Camels energized the cross-desert trade. This humble example, dating to the first–third centuries AD, comes from Egypt.

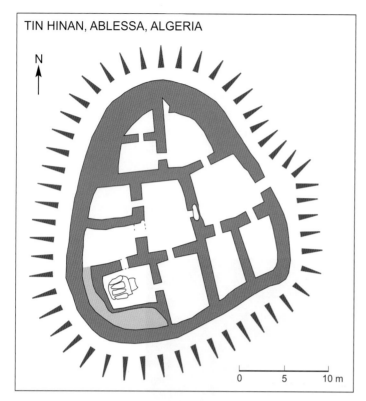

TIN HINAN, ABLESSA, ALGERIA

0   5   10 m

5.24 A rich burial, identified as that of Queen Tin Hinan, was found laid in the back room of a strongly fortified house built on top of a steep-sided rocky outcrop on the western edge of the Ahaggar Mountains. She was accompanied by Roman grave goods of the fourth and early fifth century.

on the western edge of the Ahaggar in southern Algeria, there is an oval mound known locally as the tomb of Queen Tin Hinan. When excavated it proved to be a natural rock outcrop with a large fortified house built on top. The house, which had been turned into a tomb, was defended by a strong outer wall, dry-built of stone, protecting ten rooms arranged around a courtyard. In one of the rooms was found the body of an unusually tall woman, aged about 40, lying on a carved wooden couch decorated with red leather. On her right arm were eight bead bracelets of silver and on her left arm, seven bracelets of gold. Around her neck she wore a gold pendant and a necklace made of many stone beads including carnelian and amazonite. There were other stone beads as well as beads of silver and antimony scattered around. Other offerings included baskets of grain and dates, and wooden bowls possibly once holding milk. Roman glass and a coin suggest a date in the fourth or early fifth century. Elsewhere in the building a Roman lamp of the third century was found. Around the building were a number of other burials, reflecting the sanctity of the place.

The legend attached to the site is that it is the tomb of Tin Hinan, a lady who had arrived long ago from the land of the Berbers to the north riding a fine white camel attended by another woman and a number of slaves. They carried with them loads of millet and dates. She was accepted as queen by the local Tuareg, and her daughter and the two daughters of her attendant became the leaders of Tuareg tribes. While the legend is fascinating in its many implications, the tangible archaeological evidence gives a remarkable insight into the access that members of the desert elites had to exotic goods circulating through the trading networks.

The Beginning of the End

By the late third century, while Aksum flourished, the two other African states, of Meroe and the Garamantes, showed signs of stress caused by multiple factors. In the case of the Garamantes, the progressive drop in water table led to internal tensions, resulting in a fragmentation of authority. It may also have destabilized their nomadic neighbours, adding to the uncertainties of the time and encouraging raids, which led to the fortification of villages and the construction of mud-brick forts. Scarcity of water may also have been a factor, causing a greater mobility among the desert neighbours of Meroe, whose raids on the kingdom contributed to the growing weakness that allowed Aksum to make predatory advances. Added to all this was the economic disruption now experienced by the Roman world and the effect this had on the demand for goods. In the territory of the Garamantes there was a noticeable fall in the volume of Mediterranean imports, implying a diminution of trade in the fourth century. The stability that had characterized the first three centuries AD was now fast coming to an end.

The pastoralists occupying the desert fringes had always found the rigidity of the Roman frontier difficult to accept, particularly if their traditional pastures lay partially within the land claimed by the empire. The first of the troubles to be recorded were in Mauretania Caesariensis in the middle of the third century when the Bavares, who lived in the mountains within the province and to the south-west in the Hodna basin, rebelled against Roman authority. The initial skirmishes lasted from AD 253 to 259 but escalated when the Bavares were joined by the Quinquegentiani and the Fraxinenses. The revolt was suppressed in AD 263, but troubles simmered and erupted again at the end of the century.

The desert tribes now presented a threat along much of the frontier. In Tripolitania matters came to a head in AD 363 when Leptis Magna was pillaged by the Austuriani, who were related to the Nasamones, and raids continued until they were defeated by a Roman force in AD 367. But olive plantations and vineyards had been destroyed, and the coastal cities never really recovered in the face of the sporadic raids that continued for the next forty years.

The Roman empire was now suffering from barbarian raids along all its frontiers. Many of the marauding tribes were highly mobile. Eighty years after the pillage of Leptis Magna, North Africa was in the hands of Vandals, barbarians who had swept down from beyond the northern extremities of the empire, through Iberia and across the strait, attracted by the richness of North Africa.

6

AN END AND
A BEGINNING
AD 400–760

S INCE the middle of the first millennium BC the Mediterranean world had had
an increasing impact on the northern parts of Africa. Now, a thousand years
on, with the impending collapse of the Roman system, it was to be caught up
in a wave of near-continuous political upheaval lasting for two and a half centuries.
The narrative moves rapidly and the cast is overcrowded with forceful characters. To
understand what is happening in Africa a broad outline of events must be given before
we can begin to explore the way in which African societies, maintaining their deeply
rooted continuities, responded to the fast-changing situation.

Changing Elites: A Quick Sketch

The end of the third century AD was a traumatic time for Rome. In the East the almost
constant and costly war with the Persians, now the Sasanian empire, dragged on, while
along the entire north European frontier pressure from the barbarians grew, peri-
odically erupting into raids thrusting deep into the empire, the more devastating of
the incursions reaching as far south as northern Iberia, central Italy, and the Aegean.
Roman confidence was deeply shaken, the birth rate declined, the economy began to
collapse, and would-be contenders for leadership fought with each other for the dubi-
ous honour of leading Rome back to greatness. When it seemed that the entire edifice

was about to shatter, the system threw up a saviour. In 284 the Praetorian Guard chose an Illyrian soldier, Diocletian, to become emperor.

It was an inspired choice. Diocletian's reforms were far-reaching and effective. At the core lay his realization that the empire was too large for one man to govern and the solution was to divide it into two parts: a western empire, Latin-speaking, adhering to its traditional gods, and an eastern empire, Greek-speaking, with a growing interest in the new religion of Christianity. To formalize the divide and to provide a stable administrative underpinning, each half was to be ruled by an Augustus supported by a Caesar acting as second in command. After a fixed term of office the Augusti were to step down, the Caesars taking their places. This was the Tetrarchy, the rule of four. To support the new structure a wide-ranging series of reforms were put in place to stabilize the economy.

The succession worked well at the beginning, with Diocletian and his co-Augustus, Maximian, retiring at the end of their term of office, but it was too idealistic for the turbulent times and soon broke down. It had, however, given some respite, and out of the confusion of conflicting rivalries emerged Constantine, a man with the strength and ability to bring the vast empire into some kind of, albeit brief, equilibrium. Realizing that the innovative centre of the empire had shifted to the east, in 330 Constantine chose the city of Byzantium, commanding the Bosporus, to become the empire's new capital: New Rome, Constantinople. And so power shifted, the west slowly declining while the east, soon to become known as the Byzantine empire, grew in power, with Constantinople serving as its capital for the next thousand years.

In the west the comparative peace enjoyed during the first half of the fourth century began to fragment as barbarian raids from the north intensified. By the beginning of the fifth century, confederations of Germanic tribes, together with migrants from the Eurasian steppe, broke through the frontiers to carve out territories for themselves from the carcass of the old empire. One of these confederate hordes, led by Vandals, crossed the Rhine frontier in 406 and made their way south to Iberia. It was from there, in 429, that they mounted a successful invasion of North Africa.

By the time that the last of the western Roman emperors was deposed in 476, much of the old empire of the west had been divided up into kingdoms ruled by men of German descent. In the east, however, the Byzantine control remained strong, in the Balkans, Asia Minor, Syria, the Levant, Egypt, and Cyrenaica, and the belief remained that, eventually, the west would be recovered. So it was that, when the empire had regained its strength under the emperor Justinian (r. 527–65), a Byzantine army, at huge cost and effort, set about the task with some degree of success. Italy, southern Spain, and North Africa were clawed back into the empire.

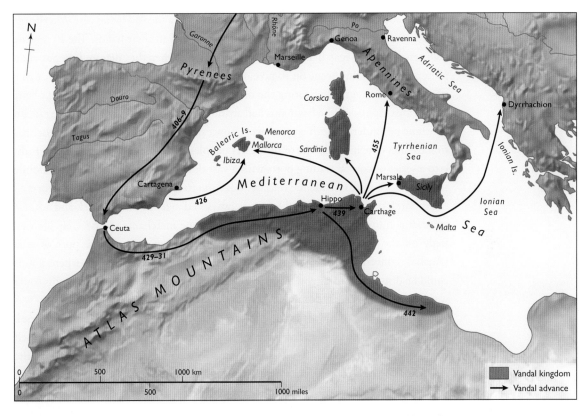

6.1 The Vandals, along with another Germanic tribe, the Suebi, and the Alans, whose homeland lay to the east of the Black Sea, crossed the Rhine in 406 and made for Iberia. The Suebi settled in the peninsula, but in 429 the Vandals crossed to Africa and took over much of the infrastructure of the Roman state.

In the east the Byzantines faced an altogether different enemy, the Sasanians (Persians). Rivalry between the Romans and Persians went back deep into history. They confronted each other across the deserts of Mesopotamia, Syria, and Arabia, and this ill-defined buffer zone provided a convenient theatre where generals and emperors from each side could demonstrate their prowess. In 570, provoked by Aksumite expansion into southern Arabia, which had the approval of Byzantium, the Sasanians sent a military unit, supported by a naval detachment, to Yemen to establish a presence and to impose some control over shipping using the Red Sea and the Gulf of Aden. This offered a real threat to the interests of Byzantine merchants trading with East Africa and India. Tension built up, but the situation remained stable until 602 when the Sasanians, judging the Byzantines to be too distracted by internal troubles, began a spectacular western advance, overrunning Syria and moving into Asia Minor. By 618 they had advanced to the Nile delta, taking Alexandria the following year. After three further years of campaigning, the whole of Egypt was in their hands. The Byzantine counter-offensive began in 622 and culminated in 627 when they defeated the Sasanian army at Nineveh and went on to take other strategic sites in Mesopotamia. In 630 a peace treaty was agreed restoring the old frontiers. Egypt was once more part of the Byzantine empire and the Sasanians had abandoned Yemen, allowing Red Sea trade to continue unhindered. Both empires were now exhausted, with little energy or inclination to intervene in the affairs of the desert peoples who separated them. Arabia, hitherto a series of coastal trading ports with a vast desert hinterland occupied by mobile tribesmen in a state of endemic warfare, was soon to spring into world prominence.

Seaborne trade along the Red Sea was always in danger of pirate attack and adverse weather conditions. It was for this reason that some merchants came to rely increasingly on the overland caravan route along the Arabian coast to the port of Aila (Aqaba), conveniently located at the north end of the Red Sea, from where goods could be dispatched to Egypt, Syria, and the Mediterranean. Halfway along this route was the town of Mecca, dominated by several powerful families whose business was trade. Born to one of those families, in 570, was Muhammad, who, in early life, took part in the family business. Later, having married a rich widow, he devoted himself to study and meditation. He was accustomed to spending long periods alone in the desert, and on one such he had a vision which inspired him to believe that he had been chosen by God to be a prophet to the Arabs. The revelations he received were eventually written down to become the Koran. In 622, finding that his teaching had become dangerously unpopular among traditionalists in his home town, he and his followers fled to the desert town of Medina, which thereafter became the centre of the new religion, Islam ('surrender [to God]'). Those who accepted it became Muslims ('surrendered ones'). It was the God-given task of Muslims to fight unbelievers.

The death of Muhammad in 632 left the question of succession unresolved—an issue that has continued to divide Muslims ever since—but after much debate Abu Bakr, a friend and follower of Muhammad, was appointed caliph to lead the Muslim community. Exercising considerable skill, he brought the dissension and intertribal warfare to a temporary end. His successor, Umar ibn al-Khattab (r. 634–44), had to face the unenviable task of keeping the militant tribesmen gainfully employed. Muhammad had made it clear that Muslims should not fight each other; unbelievers, however, were fair game. And so began the Arab conquest as armies of ardent young men set out to take the faith of Islam to the limits of the world. By 715 they had reached the Pamir Mountains in the east and the Atlantic Ocean in the west. Of the Old World, the Sasanian empire had fallen and only the core of the Byzantine empire and some of the Christian states of Europe still held out.

The momentous power struggles of the period 400–800 could not fail to impact upon Africa. Regions that had been under Roman domination passed first under the control of Vandals or the Sasanians, and, later, were largely recovered by the Byzantines, only to be lost, finally, to the Arabs. How the indigenous peoples of North Africa developed, responding to the foreign influences that impacted on them, we will examine in the following pages.

The Vandals in Africa

The Vandals were Germans who had crossed the frozen Rhine together with their allies the Alans and the Suebi in 406 and had advanced through Gaul, crossing the Pyrenees to settle briefly in southern Spain, in the fertile province of Baetica, where they took over the flourishing Mediterranean ports. Here they quickly learnt the value of ships and the sea, not only to protect themselves from the remnants of the Roman navy but as a force to be used for raiding and conquest. By 426, within only a generation of crossing the Rhine, they were attacking the Balearic Islands and later raiding the north coast of Africa, there learning at first hand of the richness of the farmland and the wealth of the villa estates and cities. So attractive was the continent that the decision was soon made to embark on one further migratory move and to settle in North Africa. In 429, under their leader, Geiseric, a large invasion force set out for their new home. The historian Procopius records that this was done in eighty units, each of a thousand people, surely an exaggeration. It is more likely that the force was in the order of fifteen to twenty thousand.

Progress along the North African coast was rapid. The next year they besieged the city of Hippo Regius (Annaba, in present-day Algeria). It was a long-drawn-out affair lasting more than a year but ended when the Vandals pulled back, allowing the exhausted inhabitants to leave: Hippo Regius became the Vandals' first capital. The town's most famous citizen, the elderly bishop Augustine, died during the siege. When it became clear that the Vandals intended to remain in Africa, the Romans bowed to the inevitable and in 435 negotiated a treaty making over much of Numidia and parts of Mauretania to the invaders. It was very much in Rome's interest to be on good terms with the Vandals because Rome's very existence depended on ensuring a constant supply of North African grain now that much of the grain from Egypt was being channelled through Alexandria to Constantinople.

The treaty was honoured for a few years, but in 439 Geiseric decided to march on Carthage, which he captured with little difficulty. Carthage was of great strategic significance and, once it was under his control, it was possible for the Vandal navy to acquire the Balearic Islands, Corsica, Sardinia, and Sicily, making the west Mediterranean a

Vandal sea. Rome was all but helpless. As one contemporary bewailed, 'the very soul of the Republic was destroyed by the capture of Africa'. A new peace treaty, drawn up in 442, confirmed the new status quo and also gave the Vandals control of Tripolitania. But it was not to last. Unable to resist the ultimate goal, the Vandals attacked and captured Rome, encouraged by a letter from the emperor's wife begging Geiseric to rescue her and her daughters, who were threatened by palace intrigues. At a crucial meeting held on 2 June 455 between Geiseric and Pope Leo the Great, the Vandals agreed not to destroy the city or kill its citizens but to be satisfied with all the plunder they were able to carry away.

North Africa was seen by the Vandals as a place to settle and to lead a good life, using it as a base from which to build a maritime empire in the western Mediterranean. It was simply a case of appropriating the profitable estates and maintaining the existing administrative structure to ensure efficient government. The one point of tension was religion. The Vandals subscribed to the Arian branch of Christianity and were opposed to the Roman version popular in North Africa. This resulted in the replacement of the Roman priesthood with Arian appointees. Apart from the anger and disruption caused by this, and by the confiscation of estates, life continued largely unchanged. Latin remained the common language, the absence of German loanwords showing that the impact of Germanic culture on the country was minimal. Procopius looks back, with nostalgia and no little envy, on an elite more Roman than the Romans of his day:

> The Vandals, since the time when they gained possession of Libya, used to indulge in baths, all of them, every day, and enjoyed a table abounding in all things, the sweetest and the best that earth and sea provide. And they generally wore gold and clothed themselves in garments [of silk] and passed their time dressed thus, in theatres and hippodromes and in other pleasurable pursuits, above all in hunting ... And most of them lived in parks, which were well supplied with water and trees; and they had great numbers of banquets, and all manner of sexual pleasures were in vogue among them.
>
> (*The Secret History*)

Outside the heartlands of North Africa held by the Vandals, the Berber tribes were left largely to themselves. Much of Mauretania was beyond Vandal control and thus, still, nominally under the authority of the Byzantines. These tribal areas were useful in providing mercenaries willing, indeed eager, to serve in the Vandal armies. Such men would have fought under their own commanders. The force that plundered Rome in 455, and shared the booty, included large numbers of Moors. Employment with the Vandal army brought wealth and experience. The return of these battle-hardened troops to their home territories in the mountains and the pre-desert gave a new strength and confidence to the tribal leaders, fuelling their ambition.

6.2 In North Africa the change of leadership altered little. This mosaic of the late fifth or early sixth century shows a prosperous Vandal landowner leaving his villa, a reminder that the Roman style of life continued uninterrupted.

6.3 The Vandals were Arian Christians. The Chapel of the Martyrs at Thabraca, Tunisia, housed many tombs, the lids of which were decorated with mosaics. This example, commemorating a woman named Valentia and dating to the sixth century, shows a three-aisled basilican church.

After the death of Geiseric in 477 trouble broke out with the Berber tribes in the border areas. Mauretania Caesariensis was taken over by a king, mentioned in an inscription of 508 as 'King of the Moors and Romans'. Another inscription from the Aurès Mountains refers to a king who 'never broke faith with the Romans'. Both were claiming authority from their Roman past. As members of the Berber elite, their ancestors may have served as officials when Rome ruled. Other polities are also mentioned. There was a prince of Hodna in the mountains south of Sitifis (Sétif) and a tribal principality led by Antalas in the mountainous plain around Thala within Vandal-held territory. Antalas was to lead his tribesmen against the Vandal king Hilderic in the early sixth century, winning a significant victory. It all speaks of a regrouping and resurgence of power centres based on old tribal loyalties.

The desert tribes also posed a constant threat. One nomadic tribe, the Leuathae (also known as Laguatan), occupying the territory between Syrtis and the oasis of Augila (Awjila) in Tripolitania, who had been involved in the raids of 363, remained a serious threat throughout the Vandal period. They took control of much of the jebel and were not pushed back to Syrtis until a successful campaign was launched by the Byzantines in the middle of the sixth century.

Another desert tribe living in southern Tunisia was also causing trouble. Procopius describes, with evident fascination, the preparations made by the nomads led by Cabaon in the face of a Vandal attack. Cabaon placed his camels, turned sideways in a circle as protection for the camp, making his line fronting the enemy about twelve camels deep. Then he placed the children and the women and all those unfit to fight together with their possessions in the middle, while he commanded the mass of his fighting men to stand between the legs of the animals, covering themselves with their shields. Confronted with this, the Vandals were at a loss to know how to proceed. They were horsemen armed with spears and swords, and their horses refused to charge the camels. The Berbers, meanwhile, hurled volleys of javelins at them, bringing down great numbers of attackers and their horses. Totally dispirited, the Vandals fled.

The resurgence of Berber power after the death of Geiseric was facilitated by a weakened and divided Vandal rule. Tribal loyalties remained strong, even in areas that were heavily Romanized, and with the lessening of central control following the Vandal invasion, the more remote of the Berber tribes living in the mountains and pre-desert region began to strengthen their sense of identity, finding local causes to give them a new purpose. Berber tribalism had always been present; now it was becoming overt once more.

The Berber elite are difficult to trace historically and archaeologically, but one spectacular demonstration of their existence are the *djeddar*s: monumental tombs found

6.4 Throughout the Roman and Vandal period, native Berber-style burial monuments continued to be built in some parts of the country. At Frenda, south of Tahert, Algeria, there is a cemetery containing thirteen monuments, known as *djeddars*. They are thought to date from the fourth to the seventh century.

in the mountainous Frenda region of Algeria south of Tahert. In all, thirteen tombs have been identified, divided between two hilltop cemeteries. In form they are stepped pyramids covering elaborate funeral chambers, some with external chapels and altars, and are clearly in the tradition of royal tombs going back to the third century BC. The mausoleums date from the fourth to possibly as late as the seventh century, but none can, with certainty, be ascribed to a particular king. What little iconography survives shows that some, at least, of the occupants were Christian, while roughly carved panels of men on horseback hunting lions and ostriches echo the noble iconography of the past.

The Byzantine Reconquest

In 468 the eastern and western empires launched a massive attack with the aim of ousting the Vandals from North Africa, but the expedition came to grief in a fierce naval battle fought off the Cap Bon peninsula on the approach to Carthage. There matters rested until 533, when the emperor, Justinian, dispatched a force under Count Belisarius to retake North Africa. This time it was a success. Carthage fell to the Byzantine army and the next year the capture of Hippo Regius brought Vandal rule to an end. The Vandals had been present in Africa for little over a hundred years, but the Byzantine conquest was hardly a re-establishment of the old order. North Africa was Latin-speaking and adhered to the Catholic Church of St Augustine or the Arian doctrine favoured by the Vandals; the new Byzantine administration was deeply Greek in character. It was a very different regime. More to the point, the new masters found themselves confronted by increasingly active Berber opposition from both within and without, requiring a massive investment in new fortifications to keep the countryside secure. The towns, too, were given new defensive walls or citadels to shelter the population in times of danger. The investment in money and manpower was huge. The defensive wall constructed around the central buildings in the town of Tébessa is estimated to have required the equivalent of eight hundred men working for two years. It is just one of hundreds of fortifications.

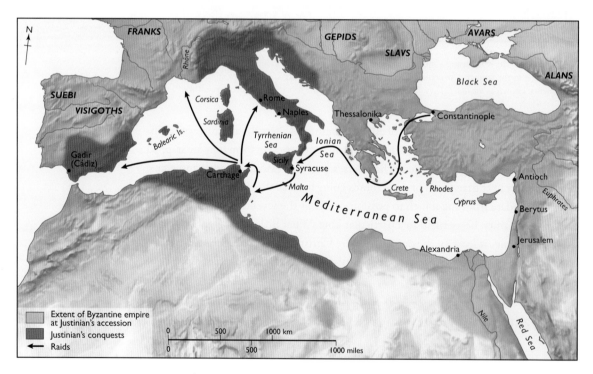

6.5 In 533 the Byzantine emperor Justinian sent Count Belisarius to reconquer the old Roman West. He accomplished much of his mission, but at vast expense, greatly weakening the Byzantine empire.

6.6 The legacy of the Byzantine occupation of North Africa was a large number of forts built to protect the towns and countryside. Ksar Lemsa in Tunisia exemplifies the foreboding which many must have felt at the time.

Life in the old province was now very different. Under Vandal rule the productivity of North Africa and the proceeds of raiding in the Mediterranean had remained in the country, creating a high level of prosperity. Under the Byzantines any surplus left after the huge cost of the defensive works was taken to Constantinople to support the city and the administration of the empire. Whereas before, the Berber elite living within the frontier shared in the general prosperity, and the leaders of the wilder tribes living in the mountains and desert could be kept happy with pensions and honours, now there was widespread discontent focused particularly in Mauretania, the Aurès Mountains, Byzacena (southern Numidia), and the Tripolitanian desert fringe. Added to all this, the febrile politics of the Byzantine world spilled over into North Africa. In the power struggles now gripping the Byzantine leadership the Berber leaders were to play an increasingly influential role, often using allegiance with a particular Byzantine faction to enhance their prestige in their own tribal squabbles. The century of Byzantine rule was anything but peaceful.

To follow the unedifying events in detail is not necessary here since they are bound up with Byzantine politics, but one incident will give a flavour of the times. In 543 Sergius, commander of Tripolitania, allowed his troops to plunder one of the desert-edge tribes, the Laguatan, and when a deputation of eighty elders went to Leptis Magna to complain, all but one were killed. Insurrection followed involving the tribes of Tripolitania and Byzacena. The unrest dragged on for years, exacerbated by disarray among the Byzantine hierarchy, one observer bewailing that 'mouldering Africa perished in flames'. Some semblance of order was, at last, re-established in 548 and fifteen years of comparative peace followed. But in 563 the murder of the Berber leader Cutzinas, who had been an ally of the regime, by the Byzantine governor led to renewed rebellion, with the Moors joining in. An army sent from Constantinople was defeated and three generals killed. There was another uprising in 587, and in 595–6 Berber rebels made a concerted attack on Carthage, but by the turn of the century an uneasy peace had been established.

The century of Byzantine rule in North Africa had been a turbulent time. For the Berbers it provided conditions for the different tribes to reaffirm their identities by fighting for their traditional lands. New confederacies were formed and old friendships, and rivalries, were renewed. It was, in many ways, a reversion to the situation 750 years earlier, before the Romans had set foot on the continent. The Berbers were once more an effective fighting force and ready to face the next onslaught of foreigners.

The Eastern Front

Until 630, when Byzantines and Sasanians concluded their peace treaty, the Sasanian empire had posed a potential threat to the interests of African communities. The most direct was the invasion of Egypt in 618, after which, for ten years, the country had been under Persian domination. But the Sasanians had already shown a close interest in the Red Sea trade, which, they well understood, provided a significant underpinning to the Byzantine economy. If they were to control the Gulf of Aden—the approach to the Red Sea—they would be able to do serious damage to their old enemy. The other power with an interest in all this was the kingdom of Aksum, which drew much of its wealth from Red Sea trade. Thus, when riots broke out in cities on the Arabian coasts between Christians and Jews, the Aksumites decided to intervene by sending in troops. They were supported by detachments sent by the Byzantines, whose interests also lay in preventing a Sasanian build-up on the Arabian shore. The Arab leaders, however, had other ideas and appealed to the Sasanians for help. It was the opportunity the Sasanians had been waiting for, and in 570 they sent in a land force supported by a naval detachment to take the principal city, Sana'a. Various attempts to oust them led, in 598, to the Sasanian decision to take firmer control by annexing southern Arabia, where they were to remain for thirty years. It was not until the Byzantine victories over the Sasanians in Mesopotamia in 628 that they withdrew from Yemen. By this time the Arabs were becoming a significant force in their own right.

The Aksumite kingdom was now in decline, partly because of overextension in its involvement in Arabia and partly because the overland caravan route along the coast of Arabia to Aila (Aqaba) was beginning to compete with the sea trade upon which their prosperity had depended. Another cause of decline seems to have been overpopulation putting a strain on local resources. Eventually Aksum ceased to be the capital, and the minting of its gold coinage, used for international trade, came to an end. The community now began to turn in on itself as the Arabs grew in strength and took command of the Red Sea.

The Arab conquest of Egypt in 639–46 brought the Egyptian Red Sea ports under Arab control. Later, further ports were developed to the south at Aydhab and Badi, bringing much of the west coast of the Red Sea, as far south as the modern border between Sudan and Eritrea, into the Arab domain. Beyond that, the Nubian state of Alodia (pp. 201–4 below) maintained some access to the sea, providing a route between Christian Nubia and the Indian Ocean network.

The Arab Conquest of North Africa: First Incursions

Following the death of Muhammad in 632, the first caliph, Abu Bakr, united the Arabian peninsula, bringing its population to Islam. The second caliph, Umar ibn al-Khattab (r. 634–44), presided over a spectacular advance as Arab armies exploded out of the peninsula, reaching the Iranian plateau in the east and Tripolitania in the west. Before he died, he instructed his followers that the western advance had gone far enough and they were to leave 'the distant and treacherous west alone'.

The fall of Egypt had been rapid. It began when the Arab army, flushed with success in Syria and Palestine, was led by its ambitious commander into Egypt, ignoring explicit instructions not to do so. They captured the town of Farama, on the eastern edge of the delta, in January 640 before marching to the Byzantine fortress of Babylon, on the Nile, which they besieged. As the siege proceeded, they allowed themselves a spring diversion, raiding the prosperous and undefended Faiyum. In June reinforcements arrived from Medina and the siege intensified, forcing the Byzantine commander to lead his troops out into battle. The Arabs were met at nearby Heliopolis, the Byzantine forces suffering defeat and retiring back to Babylon. Negotiations followed,

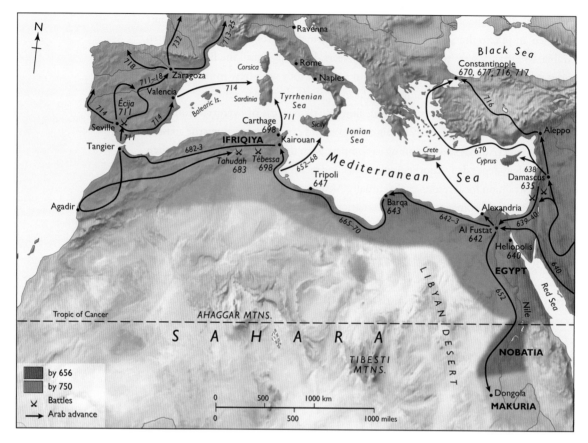

6.7 The Arab conquest of North Africa began in 639 and within a century the whole region was under Arab control.

and arrangements were completed for the Byzantines to withdraw, but the emperor refused to ratify the terms and the siege continued until March 641, when the Arabs scaled the walls and new terms were hastily agreed. On 9 April the Byzantine defenders were permitted to march away. Alexandria still held out but, realizing that Egypt was lost, the Byzantine commander agreed terms, which guaranteed Christians the right to continue to worship in their churches and allowed the army a year to organize their departure. On 29 September 642 the last of the Byzantine forces left Egypt and the Arab army entered Alexandria.

The advance along the north coast continued with dispatch and Cyrenaica was soon occupied. The next year the Arabs had reached Tripolitania, destroying Sabratha, besieging Tripoli, and raiding the eastern Fazzan. It was at this stage that Umar, concerned that the army's lines of communication were overextended, and who had never really approved of the army entering Egypt in the first place, issued his order to halt.

But the wealth of the Maghrib was too tempting and the next caliph, Uthman, authorized the governor of Egypt to mount further exploratory raids on the west. Meanwhile, the Byzantines in North Africa had been preparing for the onslaught. The exarch (governor) Gregory had proclaimed his independence from Constantinople to provide himself with freedom to act. He established his capital at Sufetula (Sbeilta)—a good position to meet an attack from the east—and gathered a large force of Berber supporters. The Arab attack, when it came in 647, was devastating. Gregory was killed and the survivors retreated, leaving southern Byzacena at the mercy of the Arabs. The invaders, however, were content with the massive bribe they had extracted, and returned to Egypt. The wealth of North Africa was now apparent and the way was open. But distractions in the heart of the Arab world, leading to civil war (the first *fit-nah*) and the emergence of the Umayyad dynasty based in Damascus, deflected attention from North Africa, leaving it in peace for the next fifteen years. During this time, Byzantine authority was partly re-established, but much of the south of the country was now in the hands of the Berber chiefs. Both waited nervously for the next onslaught.

The Arabs Arrive to Stay

Our knowledge of the conquest comes largely from Arab texts written several centuries after the event. They are inevitably selective, focusing on grand deeds and heroic figures, presented to reflect the moral standards of the compilers, embroidered with wisdoms far from the realities of the times they chose to depict. We are dealing with legends, yet the bare narrative they tell, shorn of the more exuberant flourishes, is probably largely correct.

When the turmoil of the first *fitnah* had subsided with the establishment of the Umayyad dynasty in 661, the advance into the Maghrib could begin. A series of exploratory raids, mounted from the Arab forward base in Tripolitania, soon showed how Africa had changed: Byzantine power was in rapid decline, while the influence of the individual Berber kings was growing. It was a new situation that required new tactics. So it was that when Uqba ibn Nafi set out for Byzantine Africa about 670, his first act was to establish a base at Kairouan, in eastern Tunisia, strategically sited between the coastal plain and the highlands to the north and west. It was a garrison city (*misr*), an army base around which Berber allies could congregate to fraternize and to learn the benefits of Islam. An alliance with the Berber king Kusayla (Kasila), whose kingdom

6.8 Kairouan in Tunisia was founded as a fortress city by the Arab general Uqba ibn Nafi in 670. The town is dominated by the Great Mosque, which was built in the ninth century when Kairouan became the capital of the Aghlabid emirate. The mosque became a major centre of learning.

of Djedar probably lay in Mauretania, ensured the security of the position, and it was about this time that Kusayla took the sensible step of converting to Islam. The next decade was one of stasis, with the heavily fortified territory of the Byzantines in the north confronting the Berber tribes in the south and the Arab armies in the east. Meanwhile, Uqba was consolidating his position in Tripolitania. Between 661 and 664 he was suppressing a revolt led by desert tribes, and in 666–7 he moved against the oasis town of Waddan and from there raided south into the Fazzan, attacking Jarma (Garama) and Ghadames.

The equilibrium in the Maghrib was finally disrupted when Uqba returned to the front in 681, now clearly intent on military conquest. Kusayla was imprisoned, leaving Uqba free to embark on a spectacular 2,000-kilometre dash to the west, fighting off native opposition as he made his way to the Atlantic, where, according to the legend, he rode his horse into the Ocean, with sword in hand, proclaiming, 'God is the most great! If my way was not hindered by this sea I would ride on to the unknown kingdoms of the west, preaching the unity of God, and putting to the sword the rebellious people who worship other gods but him.' It is a vivid image which one almost wishes to be true. The campaign was ill-judged since it alienated all the Berber tribes along his greatly overextended line of advance. While he was away, Kusayla had managed to escape and was now organizing the Berber resistance in alliance with the Byzantine forces. Uqba began his return in 683 but was ambushed at Tahudah and he and his force annihilated, leaving the triumphant Kusayla to take Kairouan and push the Arabs back into Tripolitania. It was, however, a brief victory: in 686 a punitive expedition sent out from Egypt defeated Kusayla in battle, the king dying in the action.

Nearly a decade passed before the Arabs turned again in force to the Maghrib. The new initiative was led by Hasan ibn al-Nu'man, who, in 695, made straight for Carthage, which he captured with little difficulty. He then went on to engage with a Berber force from the Aurès Mountains led by a charismatic female, Kahina, who had the reputation of being a prophetess. Meanwhile, the Byzantines managed to regroup and retake Carthage, forcing Hasan to retreat to Cyrenaica. It was a brief respite, and in 698 he returned in strength to capture and destroy Carthage, replacing it with the new town of Tunis, built on the lagoon nearby. Kairouan now became the capital of the Arab province of Ifriqiya.

The next stage of the conquest was led by Hasan's successor, Musa ibn Nusayr, who arrived as governor in 705. The ninth-century historian Ibn Abd al-Hakam summarizes what then happened:

> He raided westwards as far as Tangier, pursuing the fleeing Berbers, whom he killed or captured until they surrendered and obeyed the governor he appointed over them. Tangier and its region he left in charge of his *mawla* [client], Tariq, at the head of seventeen thousand Arabs and twelve thousand Berbers, ordering the Arabs to teach the Berbers the Koran and instruct them in the faith.
>
> (*The Conquest of Egypt, North Africa, and Spain*)

Tangier had been taken in 710 and the next year Tariq led his force into Spain to begin the conquest of the Visigothic kingdom. His name is now commemorated in Jebel Tariq, Gibraltar, his first foothold in Europe.

In the years to follow, Pomaria (Tlemcen), on the route to Tangier, served as the headquarters of a campaign, mounted in the 730s, which led to the conquest of the Sus, the desert border south of the Atlas. The whole of North Africa as far west as Agadir on the Atlantic coast of Morocco was now in Arab hands.

Accommodation and Revolt

It was the Arab presence that helped to mould the Berbers as a people. In popular legend the prophetess Kahina was said to have foreseen the eventual victory of the Arabs and that her sons would join the Arab armies, a retrospective myth, perhaps, explaining the eagerness with which many Berbers flocked to the Arab side. Fighting alongside a triumphant army was a way to gain plunder and reputation. Tariq was a Berber from the region of Djerid, in southern Tunisia, who had been a prisoner of war before being freed and given a command of his own. His decision to lead his force into Spain was the act of a Berber commander pandering to the demands of his followers, who expected him to provide opportunities to raid and plunder. Until the foundation of the garrison city of Kairouan, the Berbers were generally opposed to the Arab advance, but the presence of the garrison began to introduce the local population to the teachings of Islam. Uqba's exploits in the early 680s had been vehemently opposed by the Berbers, but Hasan's success at the end of the century showed that the Arab presence was a reality to be accepted, and that, in working with them to dismember the remnants of the old Byzantine order, there were opportunities to be had.

The Latin-speaking population were allowed to follow their religion, but if they chose to do so, they had to pay a poll tax to the Arab state. Most of the Berbers, on the other hand, were considered to be pagans and, once conquered, were forced to make their *islam* (submission) to the Arabs. This put them into a position of bondage, but the advantage was that they were now Muslims, a status that brought with it considerable benefits. As the career of Tariq showed, even a one-time captive could flourish if he was a believer. Subject status could be tolerated so long as the rewards of campaigning in Spain continued, but with the conquest over, about 740, the disadvantages came more sharply into focus. This applied not only in North Africa but to subject peoples throughout the caliphate. The disparity in status between Muslim Arabs and native peoples who had become Muslims was now causing widespread disquiet and was feeding into the growing discontent with the Umayyad caliphs ruling from Damascus.

Many regarded the Arab elite as having strayed from the strict teachings of Muhammad and longed for a return to the old ways. Out of this discontent grew the Kharijite movement, which began in Iraq and quickly spread. The Kharijites were levellers who abhorred the ostentation of the leaders and recognized no difference between

Muslims of different ethnicity. Anyone, they believed, suitably learned and devout, could become caliph. Their aim was to create a theocratic republic. There was, they proclaimed, 'no ruler but God'.

The movement quickly took root in the fertile soil of North Africa, where the Arab elite were treating the Berber Muslims like captives, demanding they give up their daughters to be sold into slavery and taking a tithe of their livestock. Finally, in 740, after years of discontent, a revolt broke out in Tangier and spread rapidly across North Africa to Kairouan. The Arab force which tried to contain the rebels was wiped out. The next year an army 27,000-strong was sent, but met fierce resistance in the mountains south of Tangier. A new force arriving two years later reached Kairouan. Here they were besieged, but eventually broke out to defeat the Berbers after a ferocious battle. The momentum of the rebellion had begun to falter, but a further revolt in 755 led to the capture and destruction of Kairouan, which remained unoccupied for six years. Ten years later rebellion flared up again, but was violently put down. This was a time of discontent throughout the Arab world. In 750 the Umayyads were ousted and replaced by the Abbasid caliphate, but the change of regime had little effect and by the 770s the unity of the Muslim world had fragmented. Spain was now an independent state under an Umayyad ruler, and in North Africa a number of independent Kharijite polities had emerged in the wake of the Berber revolt.

The Polities of the Middle Nile

The old kingdom of Meroe stretching along the middle Nile was in a state of collapse by the middle of the fourth century. The most likely cause was a decline in the Nile trade as activity along the Red Sea route increased, weakening the power of the centralizing authority that had maintained the unity of Meroe. The kingdom disintegrated into a series of regional cultures, which, by the sixth century, had re-formed into three states: Nobadia in Lower Nubia with its centres at Qasr Ibrim and Faras, Makuria on the Dongola Reach with Old Dongola as its capital, and Alodia in eastern Sudan, its capital at Soba on the Blue Nile up-river from Khartoum.

Sometime in the early seventh century, Nobadia was annexed by Makuria. Both polities had maintained close relations with Byzantine Egypt, and in the 530s, to strengthen the ties, the Byzantines had mounted a campaign to convert them to Christianity. One mission, sent in 543, persuaded the Nobadians to accept the Coptic Church, while about the same time or a little later, the Makurian elite embraced the Chalcedonian doctrine, linking it closely to Constantinople. In 580, at the request of the Alodian king, the Nobadian bishop sent a priest to baptize his people into the Coptic Church. Thereafter the middle Nile states maintained their strong Christian

6.9 Qasr Ibrim occupied a clifftop location overlooking the Nile in Lower Nubia, now reduced to an island in the lake created by the building of the Aswan Dam. The site was occupied from the second millennium BC. It was strongly fortified by the Romans at the time of Augustus but the military withdrew about 100 AD, leaving the settlement to continue. Christianity was introduced in the sixth century. The Christian cathedral which now dominates the site was probably built in the eighth century.

culture, even though they were cut off from the rest of the Christian world by the surrounding Muslims.

The Arab conquest of Egypt was followed up, in 641–2, by a military expedition to Makuria, but it was soundly beaten and forced to retire. Ten years later, a more successful Arab advance was mounted, getting as far as Dongola, which was besieged. The town managed to hold out, helped by the Makurian archers, whose skill so impressed the Arabs. Eventually a deal was struck, known as the treaty of Baqt, bringing hostilities to an end. Its terms were far-reaching. Makuria would provide 380 good-quality slaves to Egypt, and in return there would be free trade between the polities, the Nubians receiving wheat and textiles. The free movement of citizens was guaranteed, but fugitives would be extradited and the Makurians were responsible for maintaining a mosque for visitors and resident Muslims.

6.10 Christianity spread throughout Nubia after the sixth century. Many churches and monasteries were built, some of the monasteries growing to considerable proportions. The monastery of El-Ghazali, Sudan, illustrated here, was founded in the seventh century and modified and extended on a number of occasions until the thirteenth century.

The agreement drew a line at further Muslim expansion to the south, thus protecting Nubian Christianity, a concession thought to be highly inappropriate by some Islamic theologians at the time. The most remarkable thing about the treaty was that, apart from a few minor breaches, it was to govern relations between Egypt and Nubia for seven hundred years. One of the breaches is said to have involved a Makurian raid on the Egyptian capital, Fustat, in 747 in response to the imprisonment of the Coptic patriarch. He was subsequently released. Yet the treaty held, and over the next two centuries Makuria was to remain a bulwark of Christianity.

The kingdom of Alodia to the south was specifically exempt from the treaty of Baqt, though it maintained friendly relations with Makuria. Its great strength lay in its location. As the centre of trade routes from north to south and from east to west, it was able to acquire goods from Ethiopia, the Sahel, and the Red Sea for onward exchange with the Makurians, receiving in return commodities from Egypt. They were the true middlemen without whom the rest of Nubia would not have been able to flourish. It was in Alodia that the growing number of black slaves required by the Muslim world were gathered for their long journey north.

Geography had endowed Nubia with many favours: it was reasonably fertile, productive, and, above all, very well connected. More to the point, the treaty of Baqt had guaranteed exceptional security. Given these benefits, the two African states of Makuria and Alodia were able to develop in peace in their relative isolation for centuries to come.

The Communities of the Western Sahel

For the sedentary agriculturists living in the western Sahel, the four hundred years from 400 to 800 were a period of consolidation and growth. This is particularly apparent in Mali, in the Inner Niger Delta, in the regions of Méma, Macina, and the Lakes, where the evidence is at its clearest. Climate may have played a part in their growth. The dry period which characterized the formative centuries

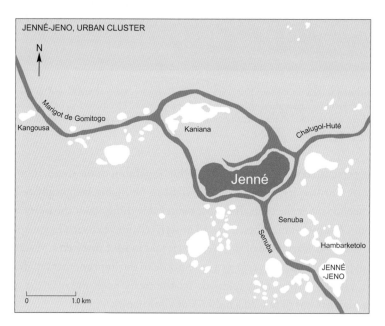

6.11 (*Above and opposite*) The settlement of Jenné-jeno continued to develop until the end of the ninth century. It was surrounded by a number of smaller settlements, which spread along the river. A wide range of productive activities was carried out by the extended community, the smaller settlements specializing in only one or two.

from 300 BC to AD 300 gave way to a wetter period, when it is estimated that, over the next three centuries, precipitation rose significantly to about a fifth higher than the average between 1930 and 1960. The overall effect would have been to allow agrarian productivity to increase and the population to grow. This is evident at Jenné-jeno, where, in period III (400–900), the main settlement grew from 25 to 33 hectares and was now protected by a substantial wall. By its final period, 800–900, the main urban nucleus was surrounded by sixty-nine satellite settlements lying within a radius of 4 kilometres. Not all were necessarily occupied at the same time, but if they were, the total settlement area would have been about 190 hectares. Estimating population is notoriously difficult, but the excavators suggest between 7,000 and 13,000 for Jenné-jeno and between 15,000 and 27,000 if the main settlement and the satellite settlements within a kilometre are included. If the urban nucleus and all the satellites were occupied at the same time, the total population could have reached 42,000.

Jenné-jeno is the most thoroughly researched settlement complex in the middle Niger region, but work at other settlements supports the idea of a rapid growth of population in the middle centuries of the first millennium AD. In the Méma region tell complexes like Akumbu reached their greatest extent about 700, while the largest, Toladié, with radiocarbon dates of between 430 and 670, approached 76 hectares in extent. In the Lakes region, the tell known as KNT2, 9 metres high, was occupied

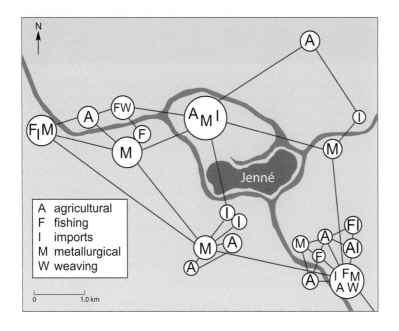

6.12 The city of Gao, in Mali, is situated on the Niger, from which position it could command the river as a highway of communication. Several trans-Saharan routes terminated at Gao, making it a significant route node from the eighth century. As the image shows, the desert comes to the edge of the river, which here flows in a wide floodplain.

between 250 and 800. Other major settlements include Gao, on the middle Niger, occupying a crucial position where the route along the river is crossed by the overland route from the Sirba goldfield in the south to the Mediterranean coastal cities. Two settlements, Gao Saney and Gao Ancien, both founded by local fishermen, have been examined. The earliest phases are not well understood but both appear to have begun by 700: thereafter the rate of growth was rapid, Gao Saney reaching 35 hectares with an accumulation 6–7 metres deep. The site of Kissi, to the south (p. 173 above), continued to flourish, possibly as part of the same trade network attracting Berber merchants from the north. Imported textiles found here, and at the sites of Iwelen and Mammanet in the Niger valley, date from the eighth century.

The social systems which allowed these large agglomerations of population to emerge are not easy to reconstruct from the archaeological evidence. These sites are not cities in the classical sense of the nucleated Near Eastern city, tightly controlled by a secular or theocratic elite, but they are, nonetheless, urban communities functioning within a cooperative structure. An analysis of the satellite mounds around Jenné-jeno suggests that their inhabitants performed a series of specialized activities—agriculture, fishing, metallurgy, and weaving—and at some, imported goods and symbolic items were found indicative of resident specialists. But not all of these activities were in evidence at all sites. Generally, at the smaller mounds only one activity—agriculture, fishing, or metallurgy—was practised. If this really means that selective productive activity was restricted to individual locations, then perhaps we are seeing a heterarchical system reflecting cooperative communities of dispersed specialists working together in harmony without the need for centralized decision making. In such a system, skilled people like metalworkers, able to transform one material to another, might acquire a reputation for having supernatural powers. The farmers, too, by being in communication with the seasons, might be seen to have special powers. Thus, each activity group would develop a distinct identity. It required the cooperation of all to provide for the physical and spiritual needs of the broader community.

From its inception in the last centuries BC, Jenné-jeno was dependent on trade. It had ample supplies of agrarian products and fish to offer, but was devoid of metals and stone, which had to be imported. Iron ore and, later, iron blooms (crude iron) came from at least 75 kilometres away. The wood to make charcoal for smelting and forging had also to come from some distance, as did the sandstone to make grindstones, rubbers for fine grinding, and hammers. Copper came from even further away. The nearest ore was to be found at Gaoua in Burkina Faso, a distance of 350 kilometres. Sources at Akjoujt in Mauritania and Agadez in the Aïr Mountains were even more distant. To provide these essentials, the traditional trading networks that had served the settlement since its foundation must have continued to function, linking to other dendritic networks, allowing exotics like glass and stone beads to arrive in the middle Niger region (p. 173 above). In the middle centuries of the first millennium AD, the volume and range of the imports increased, now including beads made of basalt, granite, and quartzite from the Sahara, and, no doubt, Saharan salt so essential for the health of the population. It is likely that gold from the southern goldfields was also being carried north in greater quantities, and perhaps also slaves, but salt, gold, and slaves in transit leave little archaeological trace. Something of the extent of the trading network is, however, illustrated by the appearance, from the sixth century, of distinctive pottery bowls with three or four feet, which are found on a number of sites in the middle Niger region extending into Mauritania, Guinea, and Burkina Faso. Traded for their intrinsic value or for their contents, their widespread distribution gives a good idea of the extent and vitality of the networks now serving, and giving a degree of coherence to, the western Sahel.

The absence of elite burials and religious monuments in the region of Jenné-jeno would give support to the suggestion that the community was arranged on a heter-archical basis, but the appearance of monumental structures in other regions implies that more hierarchical systems existed at the time. In the Lakes region, at Tondidarou on Lake Tagadji, is a complex of megalithic alignments and two funerary monuments 80 and 150 metres in diameter, a sure indication that some in society were able to exert massive coercive power. The larger of the mounds dates from between the seventh and ninth century. Other clusters of funerary monuments are known, though where dates are available, they tend to be a century or two later. At best, then, the evidence we have at present suggests that, in certain areas, elites may have begun to emerge by the seventh or eighth century.

The megalithic structures and burial mounds found at Tondidarou are comparable to a group found near Koumbi Saleh in Mauritania and others between the rivers Senegal and Gambia dating to the latter part of the first millennium AD. All are likely

6.13 Tondidarou, 150 kilometres south-west of Timbuktu in Mali, is named after a forest of megaliths which once stood here (Songhai: *tondi* 'rock', *daru* 'standing'). The monument is seen here in a photograph from 1931–2, just before a number of the more impressive stones were removed and sent to museums in Dakar and Paris. The monument is dated to between the third and the eighth centuries.

to be the burials of the newly emerging elite, establishing their claim to land. In this phenomenon we may be seeing the early stages in the development of polities, some of which came together to become the kingdoms of Takrur and Ghana (Wagadu in the Mande language), the earliest of the West African states. Ghana is first mentioned by the Arab geographer al-Fazari, writing at the end of the eighth century. He refers to it as 'a land of gold'. In a later source, the *Tarikh* of al-Yaqubi, Ghana is described as the westernmost of several Sahelian kingdoms, others being Kaw Kaw, and Kanem in the Lake Chad region. Ghana probably came into being early in the eighth century as a confederation of polities brought together under the authority of an over-king. There has been much debate about its exact location and extent, but the archaeological evidence points strongly to the middle Niger as being the centre of its power, allowing that it probably stretched some distance to the west. Ghana was to feature large in the gold trade that developed with the Muslim north in the following centuries (pp. 234–41 below).

Of the other kingdoms mentioned in the *Tarikh*, Kaw Kaw was centred on Gao, with Kissi serving as another important population centre within its territory. As we have seen, Gao occupied a crucial position on the Niger where the caravan routes from the North African coast joined the river network. One of the settlements that grew up on the desert road leading to Ghadames and then to the Mediterranean was Tadmekka (Essouk), which was probably already a significant centre by the eighth century.

Kanem, the third kingdom described by al-Yaqubi, was, he tells us, composed of three vassal kingdoms brought together under one supreme ruler. He was unimpressed: 'their dwellings are huts made of reeds and they have no towns'. Archaeology has little more to add.

The coming together of several polities under one ruler is the process we have seen to fit the archaeological evidence best for the beginning of the kingdom of Ghana. A similar process could lie behind the emergence of Kaw

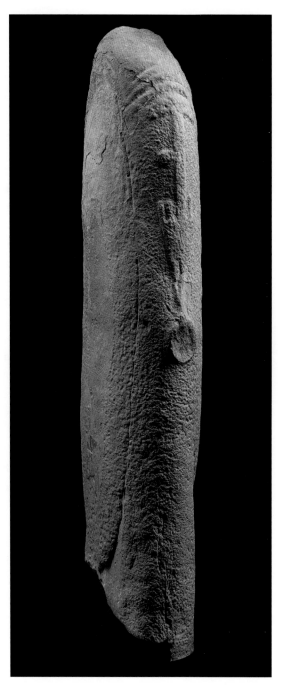

6.14 One of the decorated megaliths from Tondidarou, now in Paris.

Kaw. This crystallizing out of larger political entities may well have been exacerbated by the intensification of trade from the middle of the first millennium AD. The foundation of Tadmekka and the expansion of the kingdom of Kanem northwards along the trade routes leading to the Fazzan are reflections of the growing importance of the lines of communication across the desert.

The Desert Communities

The viability of trans-Saharan trade depended entirely on there being people in the desert capable of transporting goods and willing to do so. Such people were pastoralists living symbiotically with the sedentary communities occupying the oases and other favoured environments (pp. 178–9 above). The most extensive of these groups were the Tuareg, who occupied the heart of the Sahara from western Libya and southern Algeria to Mali, Burkina Faso, Niger, and northern Nigeria. Their language, Tamashek, is a Berber language, a branch of Afro-Asiatic, and comparison of the physical characteristics of modern Tuareg with the skeletal remains of the Garamantes shows there to be close similarities, suggesting that they originated in North Africa. Tradition also supports a northern origin. The legend of Tin Hinan (pp. 179–80 above) presents the tall princess and her attendant coming from the north as the founders of the tribes of the Ahaggar. Further support comes from the name Tuareg, which means 'people of the Fazzan'. Taken together the evidence is sufficient to suggest that the various tribes who make up the Tuareg were Berber pastoralists who penetrated the desert from the north. The nature, timing, and cause of the movement are difficult to untangle, but the female in the tomb of Tin Hinan shows that the Berbers had reached the Ahaggar by the late fourth or early fifth century. One possible cause for the movement south is that increased precipitation in the period 300–700, which will have improved grazing within the desert, may have encouraged pastoralists to migrate over time. If, as the evidence now suggests, trade was intensifying in the second half of the first millennium AD, encouraged by the demands both of the remnant North African classical states and of the developing polities of the Sahel, the combination of factors would have been sufficient to draw Berber pastoralists into the desert to adapt to a mobile lifestyle predicated on the well-being of their livestock and the movement of goods. The success of that adaptation is evident in the fact that there are today three million Tuareg still following their traditional way of life.

The western Sahara was also penetrated by Berber tribes who moved south from the Atlas Mountains and the desert fringes. These were the Sanhaja, who worked the western routes to Bilad al-Sudan ('land of the blacks'). There is little to be said of their migration to the south, but at Sijilmasa, in the Tafilalt Oasis in the desert south of the

Atlas Mountains, evidence of temporary occupation has been discovered dating to the fourth to the sixth centuries, and by the eighth century the oasis was being used on a seasonal basis. The importance of the site as a base for trading expeditions to the south led to the foundation of a permanent town by Kharijites from Kairouan, traditionally in 758. Thereafter, Sijilmasa became a focal point on the caravan route, which brought salt from the desert and gold from Ghana (p. 229 below).

The End and the Beginning

From the North African perspective, the four centuries from 400 to 800 were a period of massive change as the old pagan Roman world became Christian, only to disintegrate to be replaced by Arab rule and the Muslim faith. For those living in the Sahel the perspective was very different. In the western and central regions the communities continued their trajectory of development unhindered, increasing in size and developing into small polities that could come together in confederations. In the east—the middle Nile valley—it was a similar picture of continuity, with individual states existing in harmony. The two sides of the desert, north and south, experienced dramatically different rates of social change.

The other characteristic of the period was the growth of connectivity across the desert. This was already under way early in the first millennium but intensified over time, facilitated by the movement of Berber pastoralists south into the desert, their mobility enhanced by the speed and reliability of the camel. Once the networks had begun to coalesce, the demand for commodities, both from the north and from the south, introduced a new dynamic, greatly increasing the volume of trade and, in doing so, intensifying mobility.

7

EMERGING STATES
AD 760–1150

T HE conquest of North Africa by the Muslim armies had been largely achieved
under the energetic leadership of the Umayyad dynasty based at Damascus,
but growing discontent, particularly among non-Arab Muslims, and sectarian
differences within, led, in 740, to outright rebellion. Out of the chaos Abu al-Abbas
al-Saffah emerged as victor, becoming the first caliph of the Abbasid dynasty centred
on a new capital built at Baghdad in Mesopotamia. Under the Abbasids the influence
of the Arab elite was considerably reduced, and the power of the caliph was curtailed
by the appointment of viziers and emirs, who became increasingly responsible for
regional government. The loosening of central authority had little effect on continuing
discontent. Indeed it exacerbated the collapse of Abbasid authority as regions broke
away to become independent states. In the west, al-Andalus (Spain) ceded to Umayyad
rule in 756, followed by the Ibadis in Algeria in 777, the Idrisids in Morocco in 788, the
Aghlabids in Ifriqiya in 800, and the Tulunids in Egypt in 807. Within sixty years of
the Abbasid revolution the whole of North Africa had been lost.

Behind all the superficial fluttering in the politics of leadership, what was really happening in North Africa was a subtle interaction between the forces of change and those
of continuity. The spread of the new religion, Islam, had introduced, alongside the various sects of Christianity, Judaism, and paganism, a powerful new belief system that
in its different interpretations could be used to support deep-rooted political or tribal
identities. It was also a facilitator of trade since it strengthened the trust networks and

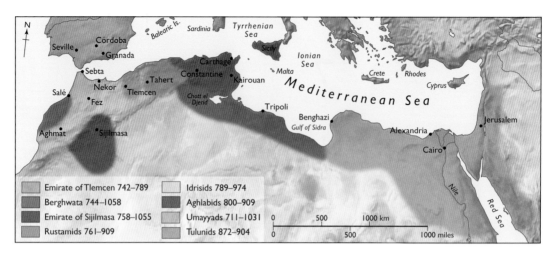

7.1 In the middle of the eighth century, the unity of the Muslim rule began to fragment into a number of smaller competing polities.

provided a set of standards that could transcend tribal and ethnic entities. Another feature of the period was an increased mobility and, in particular, the influx of people from the Near and Middle East. At the beginning a large number of Arabs arrived with the Muslim armies. Under the Abbasids, Persians were often appointed to senior administrative posts, while later the Fatimid army relied heavily on Turks and black African troops imported from the Sudan. Later, in the mid eleventh century, there was a substantial incursion of Banu Hilal Bedouins from the Hejaz and Najd, western and central regions of Arabia, who caused much upset in the Maghrib (p. 226 below). While all these incomers, together with lone traders, teachers, and missionaries, added to the ethnic mix, there remained beneath it all the ever-powerful indigenous Berber population, many of whom had now converted to Islam. They remained territorial and tribal throughout, as they had for the millennium or more before, coming together in confederations whenever it was to the mutual benefit, and splitting up to resume ancient rivalries when new opportunities were presented. It was this deeply rooted tribal dynamic driving the Berbers that lay behind the rise and fall of the Muslim polities of North Africa.

The Northern Polities in the Eighth and Ninth Centuries

The revolt of the Berbers, which began in 740 and was followed by a rebellion that heralded the assent of the Abbasids, caused the tenuous unity of North Africa to

fragment into tribal factions owing allegiance to different religious leaders. The Ibadi movement, which had reached North Africa by 719, grew in strength, its influence stretching from Zawila in the Fazzan westwards to western Algeria. After attempts to suppress it by the Abbasid caliphate, the centre of power shifted to Tahert in western Algeria, and in 777 Ibn Rustam, born in Ifriqiya but of Iranian origin, became imam. Although they were strict Kharijites, the Ibadis created a cosmopolitan state in which Christians and Muslims of other sects were welcome, together with refugees driven out of Tunisia and Tripolitania. Tahert became an intellectual centre, attracting many scholars. Another faction of the Kharijites, the Sufriyya, who ruled from Tlemcen, went on to found the oasis trading centre at Sijilmasa on the northern edge of the desert in 758, requiring all the nomadic Berbers of the area to settle within the city bounds. Sijilmasa became a vibrant trading centre. It was walled in the ninth century and a hundred years later the historian al-Masadi described it as so large that it took half a day to walk its length.

One of the refugees from the conflicts now playing out in Arabia was Idris ibn Abd Allah, who traced his ancestry back to Fatima, the daughter of the Prophet. Idris fled to the Maghrib in 788 and settled in Volubilis, a town founded in the Roman period and now the centre of the powerful Awraba Berbers. He was immediately accepted as imam, the tribe regarding someone of such distinguished descent as enhancing its standing. He was poisoned in 791 by an Abbasid assassin and succeeded by his son Idris II, who went on to build a powerful state. To consolidate his position Idris first killed the tribal chief and then established a new capital at Fez, welcoming Arab settlers, some of whom became high officials in his administration. By the time of his death in 828 the Idrisid state had grown, extending from western Algeria to the flanks of the Atlas Mountains, but it was a fragile construct and in the more remote regions the Berber population remained a law unto itself. A further weakness was that after the death of Idris II, when the kingdom passed to his son Muhammad, it was further divided into polities for each of Muhammad's seven brothers. Over the years the ruling family became increasingly Berberized. For a brief period from 917 to 925 the Idrisids accepted the overlordship of the Fatimids but continued to hold power until 974.

By the end of the eighth century, the old province of Ifriqiya, that is, eastern Algeria, Tunisia, and Tripolitania, though still under the direct authority of the Abbasid caliphate, had declined into anarchy. In 800, in an attempt to restore order, the caliph appointed an Arab, Ibrahim ibn al-Aghlab, as hereditary emir. He was de facto ruler, but his dynasty, the Aghlabids, acknowledged subservience to the caliph and paid an annual tribute. Ibrahim quickly brought the province under control, but it was an unwieldy territory to govern. The main cities, Kairouan, Tunis, and Tripoli, and the smaller cities in the agricultural lowlands presented little problem. The land was fertile and produced abundant grain and oil, which formed the basis of a profitable trade with the Byzantine world and with Italy. But the territory also included the mountainous uplands of Numidia occupied by Berber tribes who were loosely self-governing. They had converted to Islam but were forced to pay taxes in the guise of alms, which caused much resentment. Some of the discontent was mitigated by providing opportunities, for those who wanted adventure, to serve in the conquest of Sicily and the raids which followed on the towns of the Italian mainland, including Rome. Such enterprises could be profitable. Berber fighters also played a part in quelling rebellion among the Arab troops, which broke out in 824 and lasted for twelve years.

Egypt remained part of the Abbasid caliphate until 868, when a Turkic officer, Ahmad ibn Tulun, set himself up as governor. The Tulunids went on to secure Syria, parts of Jordan, the Hejaz, Cyprus, and Crete, but were considered by the Abbasids as vassals. Their strength rested upon a highly professional army composed of Turkic and black Sudanese slave soldiers strengthened by Greeks and Persians, and was underpinned by the prosperous Egyptian economy owing its resilience to agricultural productivity and a growing linen industry, creating commodities much in demand in the Byzantine world.

Standing back from the flurry of political confusion that characterized the late eighth and ninth centuries in North Africa, a few broad generalizations can be made. The population was impressively cosmopolitan, but that mixture, comprising descendants of the Carthaginians, Romans, Byzantines, Jews, and Arabs, tended to be mainly concentrated in the coastal cities, which continued to act as magnets for visitors from the Near and Middle East. Religious beliefs varied. There were enclaves of Christians and Jews, mainly urban-based, but large numbers of the Berber population had converted to Islam, favouring the puritanism of the Kharijite sect. Devout Muslim scholars were revered, especially those with a good pedigree, and could quickly rise to become religious leaders, but in many of the more remote areas the Muslim faith was lightly worn and local custom prevailed, especially in the case of law. There were also regions where paganism remained strong. The tribal system dominated everything. North Africa was a kaleidoscope of small tribal entities coalescing with each other, breaking apart, and coming together in new configurations. There were also traditional friendships and enmities forging boundaries evident over long periods of time. And behind it all there lay the varied structure of the land, the coastal strip, the arable plains, the mountain ranges and their valleys, and the desert edge, each region constraining or enabling connectivity between the communities living within them.

Against all these deep-rooted structures and systems a privileged few of the transient elite, the Idrisids, Rustamids, Aghlabids, and Tulunids, strutted and fretted their hour and created the headlines of history. It was, indeed, a busy time, of intrigue and murder, and of battles and pillage, but what began to emerge, as the Muslim faith became better understood and was more widely practised, was the acceptance of a scheme of values which allowed communities, whatever their tribal affiliations, to join together in systems of trade, soon to embrace the whole of North Africa, and to shrink momentous journeys across the breadth of the continent, from Senegal to Mecca, to the commonplace. These networks had already begun, but now, with the stimulus of growing demand coming from Muslim North Africa, the pace and volume of trade quickened dramatically. We will return to these issues after the political events of the tenth and eleventh centuries have been outlined.

The Rise of the Fatimids

When Muhammad died in 632, the question of succession became a contentious issue, one which has divided the Muslim world ever since. The problem was that the Prophet had no sons. Some of the community believed that legitimacy lay with the Prophet's closest followers. These became known as Sunni, from *sunnah*, meaning lawful, that is, following the teachings of the Prophet. Others argued that leadership should pass to Muhammad's cousin Ali, who had married the Prophet's daughter Fatima, since they believed that the spirit which had inspired Muhammad had passed to him and his descendants. These were the Party of Ali (the Shia-t-Ali), who became known as the Shia. Ali's great-great-grandson had two sons, Musa and Ismail, and a schism arose as to who had inherited the spirit. Those who followed Ismail, the Ismailis, were presented as heretics by the Abbasid caliphate. One of their beliefs which traditionalists found it hard to accept was that a messianic figure, the Mahdi, descended from the Prophet through his daughter Fatima, would one day return to the world and sweep away all the tyrannies, bringing peace and justice.

In 893 an Ismaili missionary, Abu Abd Allah, who had made his way to North Africa and was preaching to the Kutama, a Berber tribe living in the mountainous region of northern Algeria, found that they were receptive to his message that the Mahdi would soon come among them. The tribe made their *islam* (submission) to the Muslim community, recognizing Abu Adb Allah as prophet, judge, and commander. Under his leadership they became a highly effective force and began to drive out the Aghlabids, establishing a new order. After successes in western Algeria in 907–8 they launched their attack on Ifriqiya, eventually taking Kairouan in March 909, displacing the Aghlabid elite.

Meanwhile, an Ismaili imam, Abdullah al-Mahdi Billah (873–934), disguised as a merchant, was waiting in Sijilmasa. Abu Adb Allah declared him to be the Mahdi, announcing his coming. In triumph the army set off to the west to meet him, conquering, en route, the Rustamid imamate and driving the Ibadis from their capital, Tahert. The Mahdi entered Kairouan in December 909 or January 910, becoming the first imam and caliph of the Fatimid dynasty (so named after the Prophet's daughter). It was an astonishing achievement, an obscure Berber tribe inspired by a charismatic religious leader making themselves masters of much of North Africa. It demonstrated the ferocious power of the remote tribesmen, yet for all its revolutionary fervour it did little more than effect a regime change. There were many who opposed the new Shi'ite elite, not least the Sunnis who lived in the coastal region and the stern Kharijites of the Atlas Mountains. Religious divides and personal rivalries provided fertile ground for discontent to grow.

The early Fatimid caliphate in North Africa was bent on expansion. To the west lay a number of petulant polities that needed to be brought to heel, but it would be hard work for little return. To the east, however, lay greater prizes, not least the prospect of taking over the whole of the faltering Abbasid empire. With this in mind, in 913 a force was sent to conquer Egypt. Alexandria fell, but the Fatimids failed to take the capital, Fustat, and after two unproductive years they returned to Ifriqiya. Another attempt made in 920 was also a failure: the lesson had been learnt and Egypt was left in peace, at least for a while. Attention now turned to the west, and in 922 an army was dispatched against the Idrisids, taking the capital Fez. The drive to the west may, at least in part, have been occasioned by the attractions of Umayyad Spain. At any event the Umayyad leader, Abd al-Rahman III, was alarmed and sent raiding parties to capture the North African coastal towns of Melilla and Ceuta, from which he could stir up Berber resistance against the Fatimids.

The resistance came to a head in 943 when Abu Yazid, a Kharijite, proclaimed jihad against the Shi'ite Fatimids. Abu Yazid was an Ibadi whose father was a Zenata Berber trader and his mother a black slave bought in the Saharan oasis town of Tadmekka. Presenting himself as an ascetic, dressed in rags and riding a donkey, he was accepted as a messiah come to rid the Berbers of Shi'ite domination. The speed and determination of his Berber army took the Fatimids by surprise. Many towns were captured, and Kairouan fell in October 944. The next target was the palace city of al-Mahdiyya, on the coast, where the Fatimids had taken refuge, but after a long siege Yazid withdrew, fearful of the nomadic Sanhaja, who had intervened on the side of the Fatimids. The war dragged on for another three years, by which time the rebels had been driven back into the Atlas Mountains, taking refuge in the fortress of Kiyana. In August 947 the fortress fell and Abu Yazid was killed. His body, stuffed with straw, was displayed for all to see at al-Mahdiyya.

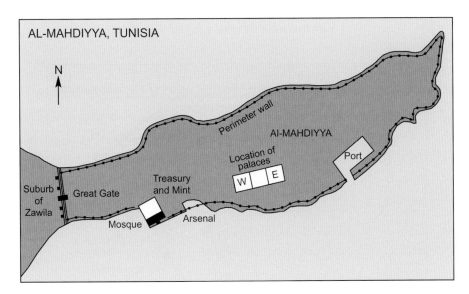

7.2 In the early tenth century, the Fatimids created the strongly fortified town of al-Mahdiyya, on the east coast of Tunisia, to serve as the capital of Ifriqiya. The area had already been occupied in Phoenician and Roman times but the Fatimids chose a narrow, easily defended promontory for their settlement. Fortifications were necessary. These were difficult times because the Shi'ite Fatimids were regarded with deep hostility by the local Sunnis. Al-Mahdiyya was replaced as the capital by Tunis, built by the Almohads in the early twelfth century.

7.3 The Great Mosque of al-Mahdiyya on the waterfront was incorporated in the fortifications of the city.

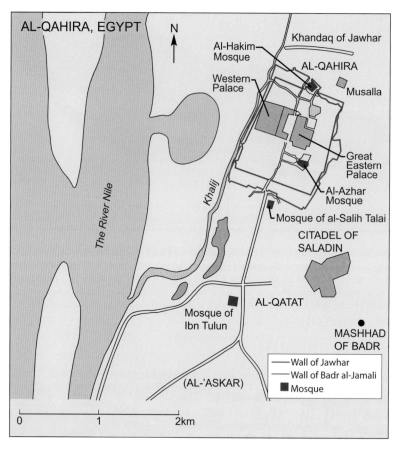

7.4 Following the conquest of Egypt by the Fatimids in 969, a fortified palace quarter was established outside Fustat. It was called Al-Qahira, 'the Victorious', and gives its name to Cairo.

Building on Abu Yazid's revolt, the Umayyads had stirred up the Berbers in Morocco, creating a separate focus of threat to the stability of the Fatimids, but it was not until 958 that they retaliated. Then, in a rapid thrust, they swept out of Kairouan, across North Africa, capturing Fez and Tangier and driving the Umayyads back across the Strait of Gibraltar to Andalusia. By 969 the Fatimids felt secure enough to make another attempt on Egypt: in August the army moved in and soon occupied the whole country unopposed. A new palace quarter was created outside Fustat. This became known as al-Qahira, 'the Victorious': modern Cairo.

The parallels between the Berber uprising inspired by Abu Adb Allah, which saw the installation of the Fatimids, and that led by Abu Yazid against them, are

interesting. Although both men were outsiders, their religious fervour stirred the Berbers into active rebellion. Yet there were always other Berbers who, for religious or tribal reasons, were ready to oppose. Fatimid rule did briefly unite large areas of North Africa, but tribalism was ever present, poised ready to shred the country into its many factions.

The Fatimids in Egypt

In 972 it was judged safe for the Fatimid court to move from Ifriqiya to Egypt. All those who wished to accompany their caliph, al-Mu'izz, congregated at Sardaniya, not far from Kairouan, and on 14 November a great column of people and animals set out for Egypt. The caliph was accompanied by his entire court, his treasure, and the coffins of his ancestors. The next year, on 10 June, al-Mu'izz crossed the Nile and entered Cairo. Here, seated on a golden throne, he received the Egyptian elite, who came to pay homage. Secure in their new capital, supported by their faithful army of Kutama Berbers, the Fatimids could now concentrate on consolidating their position in the east. North Africa was no longer of much interest and could be left to Berber nominees to govern.

By 990 the boundaries of the Fatimid caliphate had been extended to the east and north to include much of Syria, Jordan, and Palestine, as well as the Hejaz region of western Arabia. The Fatimids were now an independent imperial power in command of an empire that controlled the trade routes between Africa, the East, and the Mediterranean. The rest of the Muslim world, cut off from the Red Sea and the Mediterranean, turned their attention more to the Persian Gulf and the East. The Fatimids were now in a position to develop their trading enterprises with the Byzantine world, facilitating the interaction by establishing a customs system that treated Muslims and non-Muslims as equals.

But Egypt was not in a stable state. The period 935–1094 was a time of hot, dry weather with low Nile flood levels, leading to uncertain harvests with the consequent social unrest. The population in the tenth and eleventh centuries fell from 2.1 to 1.5 million, a sure sign of stress. Inability to deal with the fluctuating wheat prices had contributed to the collapse of the previous Abbasid regime, and two years after the Fatimid takeover famine and plague still gripped the country. But in 972 there was a marked improvement, and new laws, which kept wheat prices under strict control, soon began to bring stability. Each year the tax level was recalculated based on the extent of cultivable land assessed at the highest flood level at the start of the agricultural season. To keep the situation firmly in the hands of the government, the publication of data about the Nile floods below the level of 16 cubits was forbidden, the intention being to prevent panic, leading to hoarding and price inflation. Although the new system worked well, the actual output of grain fell because greater quantities of flax and sugar, both producing higher profits, were now being grown. Though financially beneficial, the policy brought long-term damage since in times of stress wheat had to be imported at inflated prices. The worst crisis came in the years 1063–1072, a period known as *al-shidda al-uzma*, when catastrophically low Nile levels continued year on year. It was a time of famine, plague, and price inflation.

The Fatimids recognized the importance of the Nile as a commercial highway bypassing the rest of the Muslim world. One of the first acts of the military commander, in 970, was to send a trade mission to Makuria in the middle Nile. It was led by Ibn Salim al-Aswani, who was later to write a history of Nubia based on his experience. The purpose of the mission was primarily to re-establish the terms of the previous agreement, the Baqt. The king of Makuria, Georgios III, was content to do this, but when he was invited to convert to Islam he replied by offering, instead, the opportunity for al-Aswani to become a Christian. The sparring over, a suitable accommodation was reached when al-Aswani was given permission to celebrate Eid outside Dongola, to the consternation of many of the local Christians.

7.5 The Coptic branch of the Christian Church remained strong in Egypt. This Lustre Ware bowl from Egypt, dating to the late eleventh century, depicts a Coptic priest.

The re-establishment of the trade corridor with the south considerably strengthened the Fatimid caliphate. Along it could pass commodities from the Indian Ocean and the East African coast as well as the black slaves gathered in Nubia for onward transportation. Black slave soldiers played an important part in the Fatimid army alongside Berbers and Turks, and the demand for annual replacement must have been considerable. There are hints, too, that the caliphate may have been proactive in searching out new opportunities for trade. Sometime during the *shidda*—the decade of famine and plague—a

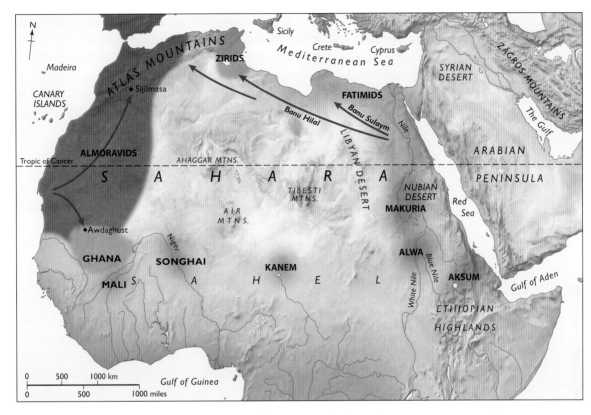

7.6 Northern Africa *c.*1055, showing the major polities and the movement of Bedouin tribes.

mission was sent to Abyssinia. Its purpose is obscure. It may have been simply to pro-cure grain supplies, but it would have provided the opportunity to seek out new routes to East Africa.

The Indian Ocean Coast

The maritime trading system which linked the coasts of Kenya and Tanzania to the Muslim world and to India and beyond was already well under way by the mid eighth century but grew in intensity after that, during which time a lingua franca, Swahili, developed to facilitate communication between local traders and incoming merchants. At many points along the coast, trading posts grew, places like Manda and Shanga on the Lamu archipelago, Tumbe on Pemba Island, Unguja Ukuu on Zanzibar, Dembeni on the Comoros Islands, and Chibuene on the coast of Mozambique between the

Zambezi and Limpopo rivers. They began as small agricultural settlements but by the tenth century had grown to sizeable communities covering 5–10 hectares.

At Shanga excavations have demonstrated that occupation began in the eighth century and continued to the fifteenth century, when the settlement was abandoned. Work on the site of the Friday mosque showed that the existing structure was built in the eleventh century, but the building preceding it, presumed to be the earlier mosque, dates back to the foundation of the trading settlement.

The long coastal zone, with its many offshore islands, produced a range of desirable commodities: elephant ivory, mangrove wood, ambergris, the shells of hawk's-bill turtles, rock crystal, some gold, and, of course, slaves. The traveller al-Masudi, writing in the early tenth century, mentions the hunting of wild elephants, the tusks of which were usually sent to Oman and from there transported to India and China. He was particularly impressed by leopard skins: 'The people wear them as clothes or export them to Muslim countries. They are the largest leopard skins and the most beautiful for making saddles.' These products were exchanged for manufactured goods such as pottery, textiles, metalwork, and glass. Much of the imported material came from the Persian Gulf, with some arriving from India and East Asia. What is noticeable is the dearth of goods from the Mediterranean and the Red Sea before the thirteenth century, apart from a little Mediterranean glass and coral and a few Fatimid coins. This suggests that it was the Abbasid network, with its capital at Baghdad, accessed through the gulf, that was at this time dominating East African trade. With the establishment of the Fatimid caliphate in Egypt and along the west coast of Arabia, there would have been an incentive for the Red Sea route to be reinvigorated. That rivalry existed cannot be doubted, and if the volume of traded goods found in archaeological contexts is a fair measure of the intensity of trade, then the Fatimids had to compete hard for their share of the market. Perhaps this was one of the reasons why they sent a mission to Abyssinia: to spy out the possibilities of an overland route between East Africa and the Nile corridor.

Meanwhile, in the Maghrib

When, in November 972, the Fatimid caliph al-Mu'izz and his entourage left Ifriqiya for Egypt, the intention was not to abandon the Fatimid domain in Ifriqiya and the Maghrib but to leave its administration in the hands of trusted Berbers, the Zirids, one of the Sanhaja tribes who lived in the highlands south of Algiers. They had supported the Fatimids in helping to stamp out the rebellion of Abu Yazid, and had brought regions in the west under the control of the caliphate. With the departure of the Fatimid rulers the whole of North Africa was, for the first time since the arrival of the Phoenicians in the ninth century BC, under the control of Berbers, albeit at first as clients of the Fatimids.

In the years to follow, tribalism and ambition were to play their part, much as they always had done. In 984, under their leader, al-Mansur, the Zirids established themselves in Kairouan and for thirteen years North Africa and Sicily were peaceful and prosperous. But on al-Mansur's death in 996 his brother Hammad refused to acknowledge the authority of al-Mansur's young son and broke away, establishing a separate polity in the central Maghrib. About the same time, another tribe, the Zenata, who had ousted the Idrisids further to the west, also proclaimed their independence. North Africa had now reverted to the twofold division determined by its geography, the settled, prosperous east, integrated with the central Mediterranean maritime networks

7.7 The fortified palatial city of Qal'a Bani Hammad, in the Hodna Mountains of northern Algeria, was built in 1007 to serve as the capital of the Hammadid dynasty. It was raided by the Bedouin Banu Hilal and abandoned in 1090.

under the control of the Zirids, and the more fragmented, backward west, divided between the Hammadids and the Zenata.

Contacts between the Zenata and the Umayyad caliphate of Córdoba had been close, the Umayyads giving support to the Zenata war-leaders, who took control of Tlemcen, Sijilmasa, and Fez. Large numbers of Berbers, mainly Zenata, but also discontented Zirids, had gone to serve in Iberia, where they formed alien communities hated by the local people. Revolution and civil war in the early eleventh century led to the emergence of city states, many of them controlled by Berber warlords. The flow of Berbers into Iberia had begun with Tariq in 711 (p. 199 above). The influx in the late tenth century had swelled the numbers. It was a prelude to the coming of the Almoravids in the eleventh century (pp. 230–4 below).

Relations between the Zirids and the Fatimid caliphate in Egypt were uneasy, not least because the Zirids favoured Sunni Islam, and in the uprising that broke out in Ifriqiya in 1016 large numbers of Shi'ites were killed. It was about this time that Tripolitania broke away from the Zirids, an action supported by the Fatimids. Matters finally came to a head in 1048 when the Zirids formally broke with the Fatimids, recognizing instead the legitimacy of the Sunni Abbasid caliphate.

The Fatimid response to the secession was to unleash Bedouin nomads, the Banu Hilal and the Banu Sulaym, on Zirid-held territories. The story of the migration of the Bedouins to North Africa is told in the *Taghriba* (March West), a poem composed by the twentieth-century Egyptian poet Abdel Rahman el-Abnudi based on oral traditions gathered in Upper Egypt. It is of its kind, highly romanticized, but the basic facts are not in doubt. The Banu Hilal and Banu Sulaym belonged to a confederation of Bedouin nomads whose homeland lay in the Hejaz and Najd regions of the Arabian peninsula. In the early eleventh century they had migrated to Egypt, driven perhaps by the onset of drier climatic conditions, and were contained by the Fatimids in the desert in the south of the country. Their numbers were considerable, though whether they reached the 150,000–300,000 quoted by some sources is debatable. In 1050 or 1051 they were sent west by the Fatimids, so the story goes, to wreak havoc on the Zirids following their secession from the caliphate. While this could have been part of a policy to regain North Africa from the rebels, it seems more likely that, by encouraging the Bedouins to travel west, the Fatimids were simply ridding themselves of a threat to Egypt, which at the time was suffering from famine and political instability.

The Banu Sulaym first settled in Cyrenaica and Tripolitania, while the Banu Hilal continued west into Ifriqiya, taking Kairouan in 1057. Later, in the mid twelfth century, the Banu Sulaym forced the Banu Hilal out of Ifriqiya, driving them to the west and south. The initial onslaught defeated the Zirids, who were able to hold only a few coastal cities, and greatly weakened the Hammadids and Zenata. While there can be no doubt that the influx of large numbers of Bedouin had a significant effect in Arabizing the North African population, reports of their devastating impact on the prosperity of the country were exaggerated. According to the fourteenth-century writer Ibn Khaldun, they settled on the land like 'a swarm of locusts', turning it into an arid desert. It is true that those who made their homes in the desert fringes continued with their pastoral nomadic lifestyle, but others embraced a more settled agricultural existence, intermarrying with the local population. The ethnic and cultural difference between Arab and Berber was, however, to remain a significant factor in later history.

The Western Arc

The many Berber tribes occupying the western and northern Sahara at first sight form a confusing palimpsest. Ibn Khaldun tried to introduce some order by suggesting that they divided into two distinct groups: the Butr and the Baranis. The best known of the confederacies, the Zenata, belonged to the Butr, while the Sanhaja and Masmuda were of the Baranis. That the divide was significant is shown by the fact that the Zenata and Sanhaja spoke different dialects of the Berber language. Tribes belonging to the Zenata confederacy occupied much of the northern belt of the Sahara and were largely transhumant pastoralists. The Masmuda were sedentary agriculturists living further north in Morocco, their focus being Aghmat and the High Atlas. The Sanhaja encompassed many different tribes spread over a large area. Included in their number were the Kutama, agriculturists who had settled in Kabylia in northern Algeria, and who provided the military strength of the Fatimid army. Nomadic Sanhaja occupied much of the western Sahara, from southern Morocco, through Mauritania, to northern Mali. They were divided into three main tribes: the Lamtuna in the north, living in the alluvial basin of the river Sous and the Adrar plateau in Mauritania; the Godala, who occupied the Atlantic coastal region from southern Morocco to the mouth of the Senegal; and the Masufa of northern Mali. All of these tribes were to feature large in the events of the eleventh century, which saw the rise of the Almoravids.

The Sanhaja tribes controlled the trade routes across the western Sahara between the kingdom of Ghana in the Sahel and the Zenata in the north. The main caravan route in the eighth century lay between two terminal markets, Sijilmasa in the north and Awdaghust in the south, a distance of 1,660 kilometres, recorded by a contemporary writer as 'fifty stages', each stage representing a day's travel averaging 33 kilometres.

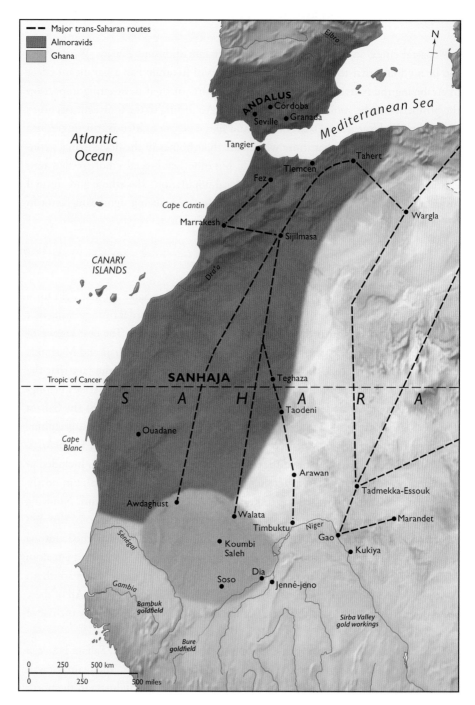

Major trans-Saharan routes
Almoravids
Ghana

ANDALUS
• Córdoba
Seville • • Granada
Tangier •
Tlemcen •
Fez • Tahert •
Cape Cantin
Marrakesh • Wargla •
Sijilmasa •

Atlantic Ocean

CANARY ISLANDS

Tropic of Cancer — — — — — — — — — — — — — SANHAJA • Teghaza
S A H A R A
• Taodeni
Cape Blanc • Ouadane
• Arawan
Tadmekka-Essouk •
• Awdaghust • Marandet
• Walata
Timbuktu *Niger* Gao •
Koumbi Saleh • • Kukiya
• Dia
Soso • • Jenné-jeno
Bambuk goldfield
Gambia *Sirba Valley gold workings*
Bure goldfield

Mediterranean Sea

Dra'a

Senegal

0   250   500 km
0   250   500 miles

7.8 The rise of the Almoravids in the middle of the eleventh century impacted on the empire of Ghana, but the two were interdependent, Ghana providing gold for the desert traders, who, in turn, supplied Ghana with salt.

228

Awdaghust, modern Tegdaoust, was one of the major centres of the Lamtuna. At the end of the ninth century it was described by the geographer al-Yaqubi as 'the residence of a king who has no religion or law. He raids the land of the Sudan who have many kingdoms.' By Sudan he is referring to the kingdom of Ghana, implying that at this time it was a federation of different polities. A century or so later the situation had developed, since we learn from the writer Ibn Hawqal that 'the king of Awdaghust maintains relations with the ruler of Ghana', who had considerable supplies of gold which he was pleased to exchange for salt coming from the Sahara. From Awdaghust to the capital of Ghana was a ten-day journey 'for a lightly loaded caravan'.

The geographer al-Bakri (1040–94) gives a lively description of Awdaghust, probably based on an account written in the previous century. It lay in a barren region but had a copious supply of fresh water. It was a large and well-populated town with a number of mosques, and all around were gardens of date palms. Wheat was grown, together with figs, vines, and 'excellent cucumbers'. There were also large plantations of henna, and sheep and cattle were numerous. To add to the good life, abundant honey was imported from the south. It was a comfortable, prosperous town peopled largely by traders from Ifriqiya who were served by armies of slaves 'so numerous that one person ... might possess a thousand servants or more'.

The wealth of the merchants depended largely on their ability to manipulate the trade in Saharan salt for gold acquired by the Soninke people of the kingdom of Ghana from the goldfields to the south. But many other goods would have been traded on the back of these staples. The merchants from the north could offer textiles and brass, while, as we have seen, the Soninke provided honey and unlimited numbers of the black slaves so much in demand in the Muslim north. The scale and sophistication of the trade, made possible by the trust networks binding the Muslim traders, is evident from a remark by Ibn Hawqal that an inhabitant of Sijilmasa was in debt to a merchant of Awdaghust for a sum of 40,000 gold dinars.

The relationship between the Sanhaja Lamtuna and the Soninke of Ghana was ambivalent. Both benefited considerably from trade, and it was in the interests of both that it should be managed in an atmosphere of mutual trust, but that did not stop individuals on both sides pursuing their personal ambitions. The chief of the Lamtuna, Tilutan, with his army of camel-mounted nomads attacked peripheral Soninke polities while the Soninke raided caravans before they reached Awdaghust. How the city itself fared is unclear, but by the middle of the eleventh century it seems to have been under the authority of the king of Ghana, at which moment, in 1054 or 1055, it was attacked and pillaged by the Almoravids (p. 232 below). Thereafter it seems not to have recovered. A hundred years later al-Idrisi describes it as 'a small town in the desert, with little water.... Its population is not numerous and there is no trade.' The archaeological evidence bears this out, showing that, by the end of the twelfth century, large parts of the town had been abandoned. It would seem that by now a more easterly route across the desert was favoured, starting from Sijilmasa and passing through Taghaza to Walata, which now served as the terminal market for the Sahel kingdoms.

Sijilmasa, at the northern end of the western trans-desert route, had been founded by the Kharijites at the time of the Berber revolt in the mid eighth century. Situated south of the Atlas Mountains on the fringe of the Sahara, it was ideally located to articulate the trade between the south and the Maghrib al-Aqsa (the Western Maghrib). Ibn Hawqal, who visited the region in the middle of the tenth century, ascribes its rapid growth to a reorientation of trade routes. It appears that the direct route from the kingdom of Ghana to Egypt had become difficult, possibly because of the onset of drier weather conditions making parts of the route hazardous. The preferred route was now along the North African coast to Sijilmasa and then south across the desert. The discovery, during the excavations, of pottery from the middle Niger and of glass from Egypt reflects the breadth of the trading links. The city was taken over by the Maghrawa, one of the Zenata Berber tribes from north-west Algeria, in 980. Within a generation they had captured Fez and had consolidated the routes through central and northern Morocco.

By the end of the millennium, the Sanhaja, who commanded the western Sahara and oversaw the trade between the Zenata of the Maghrib and the kingdom of Ghana, had become powerful and ambitious. Something of the scale of their power is shown by the fact that Tilutan, leader of the Lamtuna, is believed to have commanded a hundred thousand camel troops. The strength of the confederacy lay in their unity of purpose and their religious zeal as recent converts to Islam. But the situation was not to last. In the early decades of the eleventh century, the Maghrawa, who had taken over Sijilmasa, began to expand their sphere of control, ousting the Sanhaja tribes from the Sous and Dra'a valleys of southern Morocco, thus assuming control of the northern end of the trans-Saharan trading network. It was about this time that the Soninke of Ghana established themselves in Awdaghust. In the face of these threats the Sanhaja confederacy began to fragment.

The Almoravids

Attempts by the Lamtuna to unite the Sanhaja sometime about 1035 failed, but five years or so later the sudden appearance of a charismatic religious leader inspired the desert tribes with a new sense of purpose, which led to the rise of the Almoravid empire.

It was, in many ways, an echo of the process that had brought the Idrisids to power in the late eighth century and the Fatimids in the early tenth century, and reflected the eagerness with which Berber tribesmen were prepared to respond to the call of a messiah.

The story begins with the well-meaning initiative of Yahya ibn Ibrahim, a chieftain of the Gudala, one of the Sanhaja tribes living in the Atlantic coastal region of Mauretania. Yahya was a devout, but rather ill-educated, Muslim who went on the pilgrimage to Mecca. On his way back, he stopped at Kairouan, where he met a jurist of the Sunni Maliki school and, bewailing the lack of religious education among his tribesmen, asked for guidance. The jurist advised him to visit the *ribat* (fortified monastery) of the Maliki scholar Waggag ibn Zalwi in the Sous valley and ask him to provide a teacher to instruct his people. Ibn Ibrahim followed the advice, calling at the *ribat* on his way home, meeting Ibn Zalwi, who proposed sending Abdullah ibn Yasin, a recent convert with a puritan adherence to the dictates of the Koran, to guide the tribesmen.

The Gudala found Ibn Yasin's teaching harsh. He demanded absolute obedience even for quite minor misdemeanours. For missing Friday prayers the penalty was twenty lashes. Like many zealots he displayed a level of ignorance. According to the near-contemporary historian al-Bakri, his understanding of Muslim law was primitive and many among the Gudala questioned his opinions and demands. His response was to assert that those who disobeyed him were cutting themselves off from the Islamic community and could, therefore, lawfully be killed, a sentence which he was not reluctant to impose. While the tribal chief, Yahya ibn Ibrahim, lived, his authority gave Ibn Yasin protection, but on his death in the 1040s Ibn Yasin was expelled. With his few faithful followers he made for the seclusion of an island somewhere on the coast or in a river estuary and there set up a *ribat*. His fame spread and more people joined him, inspired to fight a Holy War against the ignorant and the wicked who opposed the word of God. The enemy included not only pagans and Christians but also any Muslim who did not follow Maliki Sunnism.

As Ibn Yasin's power grew, he was accepted by the Lamtuna tribe, whose chief, Yahya ibn Umar, saw in the religious leader the dynamic force needed to re-establish the Sanhaja confederation and restore the authority they had once enjoyed. This was in harmony with Ibn Yasin's teaching, which believed tribalism to be contrary to the interests of Islam. Ethnic differences and family loyalties were to be swept away since all Muslims were equal and subservient to the sacred Law. So it was that in the 1050s the Lamtuna set out, under the joint leadership of Ibn Yasin and Yahya ibn Umar, to re-establish the greatness of the Sanhaja. They now called themselves al-Murabitun ('the Bound Together'), which in Spanish becomes Almoravids.

The advance was rapid, and they had soon established their control over the whole of the trading network in the western Sahara. In 1055 Sijilmasa was taken from the Maghrawa and a strict Islamic regime imposed: all musical instruments were smashed and wine shops were closed down, an event reflected in the archaeological record by the sudden disappearance of grape pips. The next year it was the turn of Awdaghust. The town was, said al-Bakri, 'inhabited by Zenata together with Arabs who were always at loggerheads with each other', but because it was now under the authority of the Soninke rulers of Ghana, all constraints were lifted. 'The Almoravids violated its women and declared everything they took to be the booty of the community.'

With the capture of Sijilmasa, Ibn Yasin had reached the northern limit of the desert and was now faced with the considerable challenge of the Atlas Mountains. By crossing the range to confront the Berghwata, whose territory lay between the mountains and the Atlantic, he opened up a new world for the conquering Almoravids, but soon after, on 7 July 1059, he was killed in battle and was buried near Rabat.

Two years earlier, Yahya ibn Umar had died fighting and was succeeded by his brother Abu Bakr ibn Umar, who carried on with the campaign, in 1061 or 1062 establishing the garrison town of Marrakesh, a few kilometres from the old merchant city of Aghmat, thus consolidating his conquests in Morocco. But then he learnt that fighting had broken out among the tribes in the south. It was a serious problem requiring his personal attention. There was nothing for it but to leave the continuation of the northern campaign, following the death of Ibn Yasin, to his cousin Yusuf ibn Tashfin. Ibn Tashfin showed himself to be an able leader. From his base in Marrakesh, he completed the conquest of the Berghwata, and in 1063 went on to take Fez. He then moved north to capture Tangier and from there turned east to Tlemcen, continuing the advance along the coast to Algiers. By the early 1070s he had extended the Almoravid empire to the Mediterranean shore of Morocco and Algeria. With the exception of the Andalusian enclave at Ceuta, he was now firmly in charge of Maghrib al-Aqsa.

Abu Bakr, realizing that it was unwise to attempt to re-establish his command of the north, decided to remain in the south, where the tribal disputes were still causing problems. The Gudala were now in open rebellion, and trouble had broken out between the Lamtuna and their neighbours the Masufa. The situation was quickly restored, but to provide a new sense of purpose to deflect the tribal bickering, Abu Bakr decided to lead a campaign against the Soninke of the kingdom of Ghana sometime about 1076. How extensive and persistent the intervention was is unclear, but eventually, while fighting somewhere just north of the river Senegal in November 1087, Abu Bakr was felled by an arrow.

7.9 Marrakesh was founded in 1070 as the capital of the Almoravid empire. Little survives of the architecture of the period except for the Koubba, probably a pavilion belonging to the mosque built in the early twelfth century. While the outside of the building is austere, the inside of the cupola of the dome is alive with intricate decoration expressing the energy and exuberance of the age.

While Yusuf ibn Tashfin was consolidating his conquests in the north, he was invited by the princes of the *taifas*—the fractious polities into which Muslim Iberia was now divided—to help them hold back the Christians, who, under the inspired leadership of Alfonso VI of Castile, had captured Toledo and were advancing on the south. There had been much debate among the princes about the wisdom of the invitation, some fearing that Yusuf would refuse to leave once he had enjoyed the opulence of the country, but it was not so. Having successfully defeated the Christian army at Zallaqa (Sagrajas), near Badajoz, he sailed with his army back to Africa, leaving only a token force of three thousand men to assist the Andalusian leaders. Al-Bakri gives a vivid account of the Almoravids in battle, the infantry advancing with pikemen in front keeping the enemy at bay, while the troops behind hurled their javelins, supported by riders on horses and camels ready for the final charge. And all this time the steady drum beat controlling their inexorable advance, never letting them falter, never permitting uncontrolled pursuit.

From 1086 the situation in Iberia began to deteriorate. Internal dissent, with the people turning against their exploitative princes, and the Christians continuing to make advances, led to further fragmentation. Four years later, in 1090, Ibn Tashfin was back once more, this time unifying the country under Almoravid rule, an act which was given legitimacy by clerics who issued a *fatwa* (ruling) stating that he was morally just and had the right to dethrone leaders he considered to be of unsure faith. Within four years he had deposed most of the princes, sending them into exile in North Africa, and had contained the Christians at the battle of Consuegra. In 1097 he assumed the title Amir al-Muslimin (Commander of the Muslims), having made his peace with the caliph of Baghdad. He died in 1106 at the age of 100 and was buried in Marrakesh. His son Ali ruled for thirty-six years, enjoying the enervating luxury of Andalusia.

The Almoravid achievement was astonishing. In a mere fifty years these austere desert tribesmen, guided by their puritan faith, had become masters of a territory that stretched across two continents, from the river Senegal to the Ebro, a distance of 3,500 kilometres. More to the point, they had vindicated the belief of their Berber predecessors, the Kharijites, that the *umma* (community) should be governed by the most godly, irrespective of ethnicity or status.

The Empire of Gold

The empire of Ghana occupied a central position between the upper reaches of the Senegal and the Niger and the desert margin stretching from southern Mauritania to south-west Mali. Located between the desert and the forest, it was a place where goods changed hands as they passed from one mode of transport to another, from camels to donkeys and then to boats or to the shoulders of humans. At every transition there was the opportunity to make a profit, and it was from this trade that the kingdom drew its power. But this power was founded on the long-term productivity of the region, animal husbandry, fishing, and cereal growing, which allowed large agglomerations of population to congregate in favoured locations (pp. 172–3 above). These polities were ruled by kings, and over time came together under the leadership of a high king, the extent of the confederacy depending on the ability and ambition of the leader at the time.

Around the fringes of the empire were other polities, the agriculturists of Takrur and the nomadic Fulani on the desert margin to the west, the Susu to the south in the upper reaches of the Senegal, Kaw Kaw to the east with its centre at Gao on the Niger Bend, and the various desert tribes to the north unified as the Almoravids in the middle of the eleventh century.

The empire takes its name from its ruler, the Ghana. The people were the Waganda, of Niger–Congo descent, who spoke Soninke. The first mention of Ghana, at the end of the eighth century, describes it as 'the land of gold'. Between the ninth and eleventh centuries, when the empire was at the height of its powers, it occupied much of the west of the Sahel. The Andalusian writer al-Bakri gives a vivid impression of the city of Ghana in the middle of the eleventh century, gathered from merchants who knew it at first hand:

> The city of Ghana consists of two towns situated on a plain. One of these, which is inhabited by the Muslims, is large and possesses twelve mosques in which they assemble for Friday prayer. There are salaried imams and muezzins, as well as jurists and scholars. In the environment there are wells of sweet water ... The king's town is six miles distant ... Between the two towns are continuous habitations ... In the king's town, and not far from his court of justice, is a mosque where the Muslims who visit the court pray. Around the king's town are domed buildings and groves and thickets where the sorcerers of these people, men in charge of the religious cult, live. In them, too, are the idols and the tombs of their kings.
>
> (*Book of Routes and Realms* 3–6)

He goes on to explain that the majority of the king's officials, including his treasurer and interpreters, are Muslims. When the king sits in audience in his domed pavilion, he wears regalia including gold necklaces and bracelets and a high hat decorated with gold and wrapped in fine cotton. Standing around are ten horses covered with gold embroidery. Behind the king stand ten pages holding shields and swords decorated with gold,

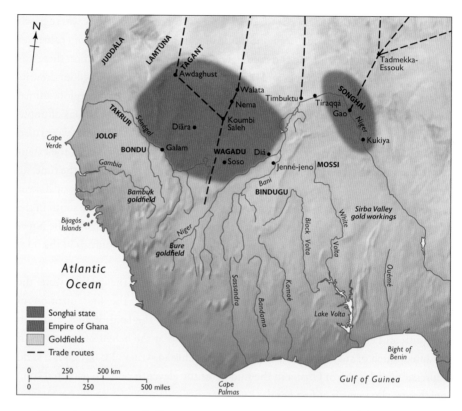

7.10 The empire of Ghana reached its maximum extent *c*.1050. Its power was founded upon the ability of its rulers to command the trade with the north. The empire of Songhai, based on Gao, also articulated trade between the north and south.

and on his right hand are the sons of the kings of his country wearing splendid garments, their hair plaited with gold. The governor of the city sits on the ground before the king and around him are ministers similarly seated. Even the guard dogs at the door have collars decorated with gold and silver. There is a lot more besides: the use of a hollow-log drum to call the meeting, the men shaving their beards, the women their heads, and the fact that the king's heir apparent is the son of his sister. There is much detail of this kind: al-Bakri was evidently fascinated by anthropology.

The description explains much about the working of the state, the way in which the confederacy was held together by the sons of the vassal kings remaining as hostages in the king's court, and the matrilineal form of succession. We can also see the good sense in separating the commercial operations, where the Muslim traders congregate, from the regal and ceremonial activities of the pagan Soninke. Such arrangements helped to provide the delicate balances and controls so necessary to keep the system working in harmony.

Where exactly this city described by al-Bakri lay is unclear. Some observers have argued it to be Koumbi Saleh in the southern Mauritanian desert, but what is known of the site does not fit well with al-Bakri's description. Another source, al-Idrisi, writing in the twelfth century, notes that the city was sited on the banks of the Nile, by which he means the Niger. The question must remain unresolved pending new archaeological evidence.

One of the reasons why Koumbi Saleh is in doubt as the capital of Ghana is that no royal burials have been identified there, and al-Bakri is quite specific about their presence and their form. He tells us that, when a king died, he was placed on a bed covered with carpets and cushions set within a large wooden chamber surrounded by his personal ornaments and weapons, together with quantities of food and drink and the bodies of those who served him. Then they piled more mats over the chamber and 'the people assemble, who heap earth upon it until it becomes as big as a hillock and they dig a ditch around it'. After that, sacrifices were made to the dead and offerings of intoxicating drink placed nearby. Clearly the burial mounds of the kings were substantial structures. Mounds of this kind are well known in Mali. An example excavated at El-Oualedji, dating to between 1030 and 1120, was some 12 metres high and contained a burial chamber with two burials, provided with copper alloy bracelets and rings, iron weapons, necklaces with beads of copper, agate, and jasper, as well as finely made pottery. Another group of tombs of about the same date was found at Koï Gourrey (Killi), upstream from Timbuktu. The largest, 15–18 metres high, contained three groups of skeletons. In the centre was a jumble of between twenty-five and thirty females and children, some wearing copper alloy arm-rings, bracelets, and necklaces, as well as head ornaments composed of beads of glass, agate, and carnelian, and above the bodies was placed a group of copper alloy and terracotta figurines. To the north were the bodies of two male warriors with weapons and iron arm-rings, surrounded by lamps, while to the south was a single burial wearing a necklace of wooden and stone beads and accompanied by a fine stone axe. The quality of the excavation, carried out at the beginning of the twentieth century, did not allow the relationship of the burial groups or the process of burial to be distinguished.

The kings of Ghana were evidently powerful men. One king was, according to al-Bakri, able to call upon an army of two hundred thousand, of whom more than forty thousand were archers. The wealth of the state derived from trade, most particularly the gold and slaves which Ghana was able to offer in exchange for salt, copper, and trinkets coming from the north across the desert. The best gold, says al-Bakri,

EMERGING STATES, AD 760–1150

7.11 (*Top*) The great tumulus (burial mound) of El-Oualedji, Mali, dominates the landscape. It marks the grave of a member of the elite interred sometime between 1030 and 1120.

7.12 (*Bottom*) The tumulus of El-Oualedji, some 12 metres high, posed problems for archaeologists, but a gaping trench was hacked into it in 1901, producing an impressive array of grave goods displayed in this contemporary photograph.

comes from the town of Ghijaru, which is eighteen days distant from the king's town …
The nuggets found in the mines of his country are reserved for the king, the gold dust being
left for the people. But for this, the people would accumulate gold until it lost its value.

The size of the largest gold nugget owned by the king was a subject of wonder. Al-Idrisi
says it weighed 30 pounds, so large that the king could tether his horse to it. If this was
not ostentatious enough, a fourteenth-century writer claimed that the nugget, eventually sold to Egyptian merchants, weighed a ton. Leaving aside the more colourful spec-
ulations, we can assume that gold was plentiful and probably came from the goldfields
to the south at Bambuk and Bure.

Some indication of the processes involved in the gold trade is given in a twelfth-
century account which describes how gold merchants from the north travelled to the

7.13 Little is known about the process of gold working in the medieval period except that the gold probably
came from alluvial deposits. The image, showing present-day gold panning at Kalsaka village, Yatenga
province, Burkina Faso, gives an idea of the simplicity of the process.

7.14 The rich grave excavated at Rao/Nguiguela, Senegal, dating to the twelfth to thirteenth century, produced an intricately decorated gold pectoral (disc worn on the chest) 184 millimetres in diameter.

capital of Ghana, where they met agents who took them south to the river Senegal, a journey of about twelve days. On the banks of the river they laid out their trade goods, announcing their presence with drums before retiring. The natives then arrived with their gold, placing it next to the goods, retiring in their turn. If the merchants were content, they took the gold and departed, if not they walked away and waited for more gold to be added. It was an example of silent trade exactly like that described by Herodotus seventeen hundred years before (p. 107 above). Whether this is the report of an actual contemporary observation or the repetition of a traditional myth must remain unknown.

No doubt the merchants would have had to pay their agents and provide a tithe for the king. Al-Bakri mentions customs duties. He is not specific about gold, but 'on every donkey-load of salt, when it is brought to the country the king levies one dinar and two dinars when it is sent out'. For every load of copper a tithe was taken equivalent to the weight of 5 dinars: for other goods the tithe was twice as much.

The quantity of copper alloy items buried in the great mound at Koï Gourrey gives an indication of how much was being consumed in the empire of Ghana. All had to be imported. Analysis of the alloy used to make the jewellery found in the burial has shown that most of it was brass containing up to 15 per cent zinc. Clearly, it was the quality of the alloy, especially its yellow colour, that gave it value. The point is precisely made by the mid tenth-century writer Ishaq ibn al-Husayn, who said of the people of Ghana, 'Their country has much gold, but the people prefer brass to gold. From the brass they make ornaments for their women.' Brass is likely to have been imported from the north. In 1964 an abandoned caravan shipment of over two thousand bars of brass was found at Ma'den Ijafen in the desert of Mauritania. The bars were in bundles wrapped in mats and bound with ropes. The bindings were radiocarbon-dated to between 1000 and 1280. Analysis of the metal suggested that it was probably of European origin.

The kingdom of Ghana depended for its Saharan trade on the city of Awdaghust, which lay to the north of the kingdom on the edge of the desert. Ibn Hawqal, writing in the mid tenth century, stresses the importance of salt coming from the desert, for which the Soninke were prepared to pay 200–300 dinars a load. The kings of the two cities maintained good relations for some time, but between 970 and 1054 Awdaghust was brought under Ghana's control. The rise of the Almoravids in the late eleventh century began to put pressure on the empire. Al-Idrisi can still describe the capital of Ghana as the greatest of all towns in the south with the most extensive trade, but by the late fourteenth century Ghana had lost its centrality and was eventually incorporated into the empire of Mali (pp. 274–83 below).

Neighbouring Polities in the Western Sahel

The empire of Ghana was surrounded by other, smaller states with which it maintained contact. To the west, in the valley of the lower Senegal river, was the kingdom of Takrur, which, like Ghana, grew rich through articulating the gold trade between the goldfields of Bambuk and the desert tribes on its northern border. It was to facilitate the trade that the king and his court converted to Islam in the 1030s. In addition to gold and slaves, they were able to trade sea salt from Aulil, at the mouth of the Senegal, and coarse cloth, which they manufactured themselves. In the region between the rivers Senegal and Gambia the tradition of erecting megalithic monuments and large burial mounds continued. Although dating is imprecise, the most intensive period of monument building is thought to be from the eighth to the eleventh century, but elite burial in large mounds continued into the thirteenth century. The magnificent gold pectoral and the gold beads from the burial at Rao in north-west Senegal bear witness to the growing power of the elite at the time before the impact of Islam had made itself widely felt. As the power of Ghana waned, Takrur grew, but it, too, was soon to be incorporated into the empire of Mali.

South of Ghana was another powerful tribe, the Susu, who lived in the mountainous region on the Mali–Guinea border, from which location they could control the movement of gold and iron and products coming from the rainforests to the south. They, too, briefly benefited from the decline of Ghana, occupying the capital in the early thirteenth century before they were eventually absorbed by the growth of Mali.

To the east of Ghana lay the Songhai-speaking kingdom of Kaw Kaw with its capital at Gao on the river Niger. It was first referred to as a major regional power in the ninth century (p. 209 above); by the tenth century, the king had embraced Islam. At

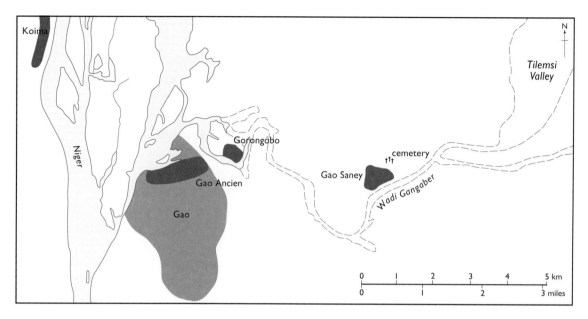

7.15 The trading centre of Gao, situated on the banks of the Niger, began to develop in the eighth century. There may have been another centre of activity across the river at Koima. Both Gao Ancien and Gao Saney have been subject to modern excavation.

this time the documentary sources record that there were two towns: one on the east bank of the river, where the markets were held and the merchants lived, and the other on the west bank, where the king and his entourage lived and where he had his treasure house filled with salt and his own private mosque. The archaeological evidence has identified two separate settlements: Gao Ancien and Gao Saney, but both are on the east bank of the Niger. Gao Saney was occupied from the eighth to the twelfth century and Gao Ancien from the sixth to the sixteenth. There is the possibility that the settlement where the king was said to reside on the west bank is to be identified with a large sand-dune, La Dune Rose, but no archaeological evidence of the crucial period has yet been found there. It is, of course, possible that Gao Ancien and Gao Saney are the two settlements referred to in the early sources and that the writer misunderstood the lie of the land, assuming the tributary river that divides them to be the main course of the Niger.

Both settlements were functioning in the tenth and eleventh centuries. Gao Ancien has produced evidence of high-status buildings, including one with a pillared hall, associated with gold and other elite goods. At another location, a pit dating to the ninth century was found containing fifty hippopotamus tusks, possibly a merchant's

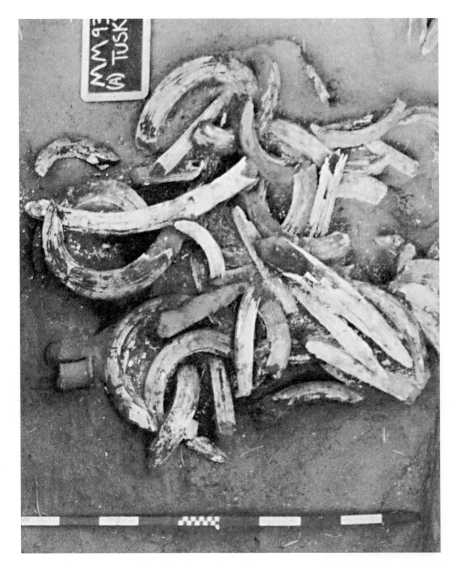

7.16 One of the more remarkable of the discoveries made at Gao Ancien was of a pit dating to the ninth century containing fifty hippopotamus tusks, perhaps the stock of a trader gathered for transhipment to the north.

stock awaiting transit across the desert. Other finds, including glass beads from Egypt and North Africa, reflect the reach of the trading networks now passing through Gao. While discoveries at Gao Ancien are consistent with a resident elite, those from Gao Saney, including metalworking and bead manufacture, imply commercial activity. The

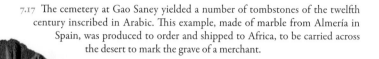

7.17 The cemetery at Gao Saney yielded a number of tombstones of the twelfth century inscribed in Arabic. This example, made of marble from Almería in Spain, was produced to order and shipped to Africa, to be carried across the desert to mark the grave of a merchant.

size of the mound at Gao Saney, 26 hectares in extent and 6–7 metres high, speaks of the vitality of its enterprise.

Nearby a Muslim cemetery developed, the graves identified by inscribed tombstones dating to between 1100 and 1300. Five of the early twelfth-century tombstones were made from marble imported from Almería in southern Spain: they had been carved before being dispatched. The cemetery evidence offers strong support for al-Bakri's reference to there being resident merchants from the north. The strong links between Gao and the Umayyad leadership in Spain are reflected in diplomatic gifts—a sword, a signet ring, and a copy of the Koran—that were said to have been sent to the Gaoan leader, addressed as 'the Commander of the Faithful'.

Gao was well integrated in the trading network at least as early as the eighth century, serving as a commercial centre on the Niger at the end of the cross-desert route, and a place with easy access to the Sirba goldfield to the south. Some 300 kilometres to the north-east of the city, in the Adrar des Iforas, was the town of Tadmekka (modern Essouk). It was an important Berber-controlled trading centre from which three trans-desert routes fanned out, leading to Kairouan via Wargla, to Tripoli via Ghadames, and to Egypt via Ghat. Al-Bakri tells us that

7.18 One of the main routes north from Gao passed through the town of Tadmekka (Essouk) in the Iforas Mountains, which became an important trading centre occupied by Berbers. The ruins of the town lie in the valley between two ranges of hills.

of all the towns in the world [this] is the one that resembles Mecca ... It is a large town amidst mountains and ravines and is better built than Ghana or Kaw Kaw [Gao]. The inhabitants of Tadmekka are Muslim Berbers who veil themselves as the Berbers of the desert do ... They wear clothes of cotton, *nuli*, and other robes dyed red. Their king wears a red turban, yellow shirt, and blue trousers ... Their women are of perfect beauty ... but adultery is allowed among them. They fall on any merchant ...

(*Book of Routes and Realms*)

Such a colourful and enticing place must have been attractive to its many visitors. It became a centre for lively trade. Among the many commodities passing through from

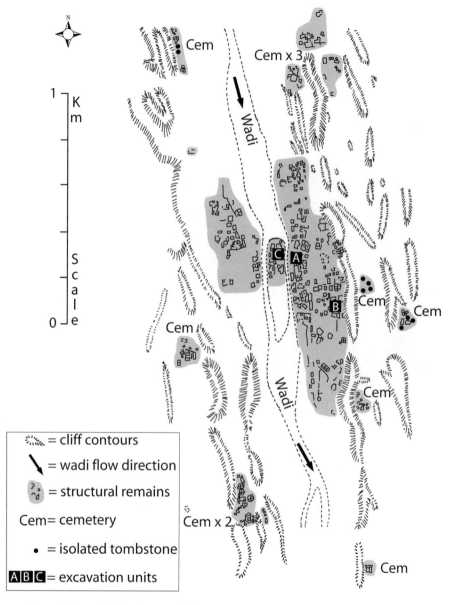

7.19 The settled area of Tadmekka extended for 2 kilometres along the valley, with the cemeteries located on the periphery.

the south were the customary gold, slaves, and ivory, together with 'sorghum and other grains ... From the land of the Sudan', a reminder of the great importance of the agricultural products of the Sahel to the desert communities.

The ruins of ancient Tadmekka now extend for a kilometre along both sides of a wadi, with its cemeteries in the flanking hills. Excavation has shown that settlement began at least as early as the ninth century and continued into the fourteenth century. Among the detritus recovered was a quantity of imported pottery from North Africa and Egypt. There were also more exotic finds like the sherd of a Chinese celadon bowl of the Northern Song dynasty dating to the eleventh or twelfth century, cowrie shells from the Indian Ocean, and fragments of silk, all reflecting the extent of the community's trading network.

Activities under way at Tadmekka included gold working. The evidence, dating to the tenth or eleventh century, comes from the discovery of crucibles in which the gold was purified using glass as a flux, and moulds for casting small, semi-spheroid gold pellets to serve as blanks for coin striking. These are referred to by al-Bakri when he writes that 'their dinars are called "bald" because they are of pure gold without any stamp'. By producing gold coin blanks to a standard weight, the gold traders of Tadmekka were providing their markets in the north with a convenient unit to strike with their own dies to add their authority to the issue. How early this process began at Tadmekka or elsewhere is not known, but the fact that gold coins, known as globular *solidi*, issued by the Byzantines from Carthage in the seventh century, were struck from subspheroidal blanks hints that the practice may have begun some centuries earlier than its first attestation at Tadmekka.

The Communities of the Central and Eastern Sahel

The peoples living around Lake Chad in the central Sahel continued to benefit from the traditional trade routes across the central Sahara, which linked them to the Fazzan and to the North African coast beyond. The earliest mention of the region, from an Arab geographer in the eighth century, refers to the people as Zaghawa. Later, in the ninth century, al-Yaqubi writes of 'the Zaghawa who live in a place called Kanem', who sell slaves to the north. 'Their dwellings are huts made of reeds and they have no towns.' He adds that they were nomads famous for their cavalry. Kanem is the region to the north-east of Lake Chad, between the lake and the Bahr el-Ghazal, which was already occupied by agriculturists and pastoralists. It seems that the Zaghawa were horse-riding nomads, originally living in the central Sahara, who had migrated to

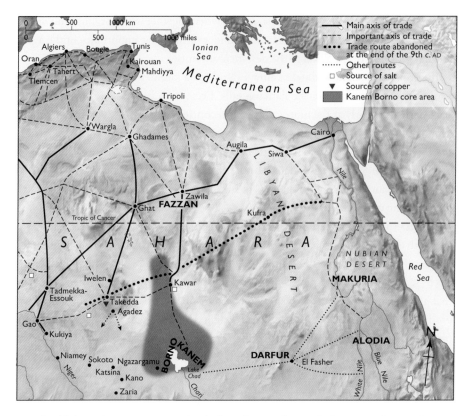

7.20 In addition to the many routes crossing the desert from north to south, there were others running east to west through the Sahel, linking the communities of the Niger Bend, the Kanem Borno state, Darfur, and the Nubian polities occupying the middle Nile.

Kanem in the early first millennium, where they settled among the indigenous agriculturists, driven perhaps by the onset of harsher climatic conditions. By the twelfth century there were, according to al-Idrisi, two towns in Kanem: Manan and Anjimi. Trade with the Ibadi Muslims was probably under way by the eighth century, but it was not until 1067–71 that the ruler of Kanem, Hawwa, who may have been female, was converted to Islam.

Al-Muhallabi, writing about 990, observes that 'the kingdom of Zaghawa is one of the most extensive. To the east it borders on the Nubian kingdom in Upper Egypt and between them is a ten-day march.' This raises the interesting possibility that the influence of Kanem might have extended eastwards along the Sahel as far as Darfur, from where trading contacts might have continued to the middle Nile kingdoms of Makuria and Alodia, giving the rulers of Kanem access to commodities coming via the Nile and the Red Sea. It could have been from the middle Nile states, as well as from North Africa, that the horses for which they were famous came. It was along such a route that chicken, coming from the Indian Ocean region, are likely to have been introduced into West Africa. East–west trade would not have competed too seriously with the caravans crossing the desert to the north, carrying ivory, ostrich feathers, and black slaves to the Mediterranean. By the thirteenth century, when the influence of Kanem had spread to the Fazzan, the king could delight the people of Tunis by sending the sultan the present of a giraffe.

Comparatively little is known of the communications between Kanem, in the central Sahel, and the Nile valley, but by the twelfth century the Darfur region was occupied by the Tora, probably a Berber people, who had introduced megalithic building techniques, farming, and irrigation to the region. Routes led north to Egypt, to Cyrenaica, and to Tripoli. There were also routes crossing the desert eastwards to Alodia and Makuria on the middle Nile, but they had the reputation of being more hazardous. It remains a possibility, however, that they were used to transport slaves and other goods acquired from the south to the Nubian kingdoms. The tradition that the Daja, the elite who replaced the Tora in the twelfth century, came from the middle Nile may be a memory of an influx of Nubians intent on exploiting the potential of Darfur.

The Forests of the South

Going south from the Sahel, the natural vegetation passes through a zone of savannah and moist woodland, giving way to equatorial forest, which forms a near-continuous band 300–400 kilometres wide running along the southern coast of West Africa from Sierra Leone to Cameroon. Through the forest, two major rivers, the Volta and the Niger, flow to the sea, the Niger creating a huge delta. It was a zone where yams, oil palm, and kola nuts could be grown, but tsetse fly infestation, causing sleeping sickness, made it unsuitable for domestic animals. Among the products of the region that might have been expected to feed into the trade network were slaves, ivory, and gold from the Akan goldfield, together with the kola nuts which produced a stimulant acceptable to Islam. There were also extensive supplies of copper in Nigeria, which were being worked in the tenth century, as well as sources of tin and silver that may have been exploited about this time. The commodities being traded in exchange were brass, textiles, beads, horses, and salt, though salt was also produced locally along the Atlantic coast.

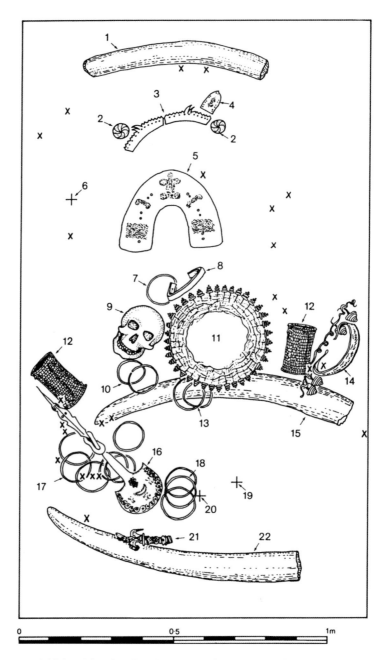

7.21 The remarkable burial found at Igbo Ukwu, Nigeria, dating to the ninth century, belongs to a member of the elite able to command a wide range of resources. The copper alloy objects associated with the burial show a very high degree of technical skill.

At various points within the forest zone, powerful polities developed, based on concentrations of wealth acquired through trade and warfare. One of these is represented by a burial complex found at Igbo Ukwu, near Onitsha in Nigeria, dating to the ninth century. The elite individual whose grave this was, was buried sitting on a stool, in a wood-lined burial chamber at the bottom of a deep pit, surrounded by his regalia, including three elephants' tusks. Above the chamber was another containing the remains of at least five attendants, and nearby were two separate deposits of offerings, one with the items carefully laid out, the other with them jumbled in a pit. The most remarkable of the grave goods were a number of highly ornate bronze castings with delicate surface decoration. They were made by the lost-wax process, which involved modelling the desired object in wax (or perhaps latex), covering it carefully in clay, and then firing it to harden the clay and melt the wax so that it could be poured out. The space which the wax had occupied could then be filled with molten copper alloy. That the items were locally made is suggested by the fact that the metal used to make a number of them had a high silver content comparable to ores from mines at Abakaliki about 100 kilometres away. Others, however, were made from copper sourced in Tunisia or Algeria.

Clearly, the individual buried at Igbo Ukwu was a person of high status whose lineage had access to an impressive array of material resources and was able to command the efforts of a wide range of specialists. This implies the development of a complex society like a small state, its power deriving from access to the trading networks of the north. The 160,000 beads of glass and carnelian found with the burial indicate the range of the contacts enjoyed by the elite. The carnelian may have come from the Fazzan or India, while the composition of the glass suggests an Egyptian origin. By what routes these items arrived is unknown, but most likely they came through the kingdom of Kanem, in the Chad basin, either via Cairo and the Fazzan or by way of the easterly route from the middle Nile through Darfur. In return the forest chiefs may have offered slaves, ivory, or possibly silver and tin.

That bronze castings of such astonishing skill and originality suddenly appear in the forest zone with no obvious antecedents is, at first sight, surprising, but little is known of the archaeology of the area, making it difficult to place Igbo Ukwu in the context of regional cultural development. However, close stylistic comparison with local pottery decoration is sufficient to show that the bronze castings belong to a local tradition rather than being inspired by alien imports.

Igbo Ukwu is only one of several polities that began to develop in the lower Niger region in the ninth to eleventh centuries. To the west, in the territory of the Yoruba, Old Oyo, Ife, and Benin all became important centres, with craftsmen working to very

7.22 Cast copper alloy head from Igbo Ukwu.

high standards in bronze, stone, and ter-racotta. At Igbo Olokun, within the walls of Ife, craftsmen were making glass beads for regional distribution perhaps as early as the eleventh century. They were easily distinguishable from imported beads by their distinctive high lime, high alumin-ium composition. There can be no doubt that by this time the communities of the equatorial zone had begun to share in the trading networks linking them with the whole of northern Africa.

The Beginning of a World System?

Sufficient will have been said in the earlier chapters to show that there were, by the middle of the first millennium AD, net-works of connectivity linking the Medi-terranean zone of North Africa with the sub-Saharan zone, and that, already, com-munities in the western Sahel had devel-oped in size and complexity and were engaging in long-distance exchange, albeit of the simple down-the-line type. The Roman presence in North Africa had given a significant boost to the trading activity, especially along the central Saha-ran routes by way of the Garamantes. The systems collapse which engulfed the Med-iterranean world from the fourth to the seventh centuries AD seems to have had little effect on the polities of the Sahel. Later, with the Arab advance through North Africa and the dissemination of Islam, a new dynamic was introduced. Succes-sive Berber tribes in the north, inspired by religious leaders teaching puritan versions

7.23 Leaded bronze vessel from Igbo Ukwu. The container was cast by the lost-wax method. Other parts were cast separately and attached by 'burning in', a process requiring much skill.

of the faith, came to control increasingly large territories, spreading their influence deep into the desert. This process culminated with the rise of the Almoravids in the late eleventh century, whose empire stretched across the desert from the Sahel to the Maghrib, and beyond to Iberia.

It was during this time that certain polities in the western and central Sahel began to develop into powerful states benefiting from intensification of trade in the commodities so much in demand in the Mediterranean and the Near East: gold, ivory, and slaves. The Sahel also began to serve as a corridor of connectivity, with the different polities living along it interacting with each other. There are signs that the network now extended across the eastern Sahel, connecting with the Nubian kingdoms on the middle Nile. As more leaders of the Sahel states accepted Islam and took the hajj, so the Sahel corridor developed as a convenient route to the Red Sea, and to Mecca. By the middle of the twelfth century, all the components of the Saharan network were functioning, and even the more remote regions in the forest zone were now fully engaged.

tota aquesta muntaya
de lonch / es apellade carena per
serrayns / e crestians / es apelade muntz
clars / e sapiats q en aquesta dita muntaya ha
moltes bones villes / e castels les quals con
baten los huns ab lus altres / e sapiats q la dita mun
taya es abundant de payscuy / e doli / e de totes bones
fruytes

sigilmessa   tebelbet   mpsa

                                              tacazt

                    tadia

da tenen gens q son
leu hon sino los vils
/ e san cavalcades al   aquest
es qui jamay nom temps   musser
n les bones marques   tagaza   de sir
                                                   rich / e
                                                   esta r
                                                   qual s
                GOGVIA

        fudam

            tenoath

ciutat de melli

8

WIDENING HORIZONS
1150–1400

FROM the beginning of the twelfth century, North Africa, from the equatorial forest to the Mediterranean and from the Atlantic to the Red Sea, was bound in a network of connectivity more extensive and more intensive than anything the continent had experienced before. Much of the vast region, as far south as the edge of the Sahel, had accepted Islam, to a greater or lesser degree, and Islam was now a way of life, extending along the African shore of the Gulf of Aden and far down the Indian Ocean coast, isolating the Christian communities of the middle Nile and Abyssinia.

Yet Christians and Muslims engaged in ways beneficial to both. Religious belief could be harnessed to maintain identity, but the dynamic that drove everything, irrespective of creed, was trade. Consumer durables, raw materials, and human power flowed on an ever-increasing scale. The middle years of the thirteenth century saw changes in the political structure of North Africa that were to initiate two hundred and fifty years of potential political stability. In the Maghrib, the Almohad empire developed and then fragmented into three polities, the Marinids, the Zayyanids, and the Hafsids, their territories roughly equating to Morocco, Algeria, and Tunisia, while in Egypt the Ayyubids were replaced by the Mamluks. These new tribal and dynastic confederations were to last until the arrival of the Ottoman Turks in the early sixteenth century. Meanwhile, to the south of the Sahara, the empires and city states of the Sahel were continuing their own trajectory of development, kept safe in their remote world by the protective waste of the desert.

Interfering Europeans

The period covered by this chapter saw comparatively little interference in African affairs by the European states except on the Iberian peninsula, where the Christian powers of the north were pushing relentlessly south against the Muslim polities. At the battle of Las Navas de Tolosa (1212), Alfonso VIII of Castile broke Almohad morale and soon the Christian armies had conquered the crucial valley of the Guadalquivir, taking Córdoba (1236), Jaén (1246), and Seville (1248). By 1275 Muslim-held territory had been reduced to the kingdom of Granada. In the Mediterranean, Sicily, which had been occupied by the Moors since 831, had become a prosperous, cosmopolitan place, managing the trade between North Africa and Italy, but in 1071 Norman mercenaries, led by Roger I, landed to establish the county of Sicily, though it took twenty years before the whole island was in Norman hands. The Norman regime in Sicily and southern Italy was in a strong position, and it was only a matter of time before they turned their attention to neighbouring Ifriqiya. Tripoli was attacked in 1142 or 1143 and eventually captured in 1146. Other coastal towns, Gabès, Tunis, Sfax, and Annaba, were soon to follow, leading to the creation of the Norman kingdom of Africa. It was a short-lived enterprise, swept away by the Almohads in 1160.

Africa remained largely unaffected by the Crusades, mounted by the European states against the Muslim rulers of Palestine, which had begun in 1096. But in the early thirteenth century, attention began to turn to the strategic position of Egypt and the part it might play in the fortunes of the contestants. The first direct intervention came during the Fifth Crusade (1217–21) when the Europeans captured the Egyptian town of Damietta at the mouth of the Nile. In the event, the flooding of the river prevented the advance on Cairo and the campaign was aborted. Nor did the French king Louis IX fare any better when he led the Seventh Crusade (1248–54), setting out from Cyprus in 1249 to capture Damietta. It was his intention to advance on Cairo, but his campaign ended in failure and humiliation (p. 266 below). A decade later, undaunted by his sobering experience, he decided to mount a new crusade, the eighth, this time with the aim of taking Tunis, a potentially profitable goal. The army landed in July 1270 and marched on the city to lay siege, but it was the height of summer and dysentery spread quickly through the army, killing the unfortunate Louis. In the negotiations that followed it was agreed that Christian merchants in Tunis should be granted free trade rights and Christian priests and monks be allowed to reside in the city. The sensible bargain, driven entirely by commercial imperatives, was beneficial to both sides, but had little to do with the ideals that had inspired the first Crusaders 170 years earlier.

8.1 The battle of Tunis was fought outside the town in July 1270, when Crusaders, led by the French king, Louis IX, tried to capture the city. The king, shown lying in his tent, caught dysentery and died. The illustration dates to the fifteenth century.

New Observers, New Sources

Our understanding of the Saharan and sub-Saharan populations is greatly enlivened by the work of a small group of Arab geographer-historians who wrote between 900 and 1400 offering vivid accounts of the African sites and the peoples they met on their travels or learnt about from others. We have already had cause to refer to the work of two of the tenth-century scholars, al-Masudi and Ibn Hawqal, contemporaries from Baghdad, and the eleventh-century Andalusian geographer al-Bakri, whose observations add detail to the story. Outstanding among the twelfth-century writers is Muhammad al-Idrisi (*c.*1100–1165), a member of the Andalusian elite whose family had been exiled to Ceuta, where he was born and died. He travelled widely in Europe, spending eighteen years in the court of Roger II, the Norman king of Sicily, where in 1154 he created the famous *Tabula Rogeriana*, a map of Eurasia and North Africa with a commentary and illustrations. It was a work of great accuracy based on the information gleaned from merchants and other travellers as well as his own more limited observations. He was followed by Yaqut al-Hamawi (1179–1229), born in Constantinople of Greek parents, who became apprentice to a Baghdadi trader and wrote extensively on history and geography.

The fourteenth century was blessed with three great writers. Shihab al-Din al-Umari (1301–49) lived in Damascus, where he wrote a history of the Mamluks in Egypt and Syria, and happened to visit Cairo not long after the famous visit of Mansa Musa, which he described in fascinating detail (p. 288 below). He was a near-contemporary of Ibn Battuta (1304–69), born in Tangier of Berber parents, who became one of the greatest travellers and travel writers of his time. Ibn Battuta began his journeying by making the hajj, from Mecca going on to visit Mesopotamia, Persia, Arabia, and the East African coast before setting off to the Pontic steppe, Central Asia, India, and China. His last itinerary, which encompassed Iberia, the western Sahara, and West Africa, and lasted from 1349 to 1354, will be considered in more detail below (pp. 279–83). The third of the fourteenth-century geographer-historians is Ibn Khaldun (1332–1406). Born in Tunis, he worked his way round the cities of North Africa, ending in Cairo. His great work *Kitab al-'Ibar* (Book of Lessons), begun as a history of the Berbers, was expanded into a world history. Its introduction, *Al-Muqaddimah* (The Prolegomena), reflecting on the socio-economic and geographical aspects of history, is one of the most thoughtful and advanced analyses to be written in the Middle Ages.

We are fortunate, indeed, that the works of this small, but distinguished, group of geographer-historians has survived. They capture the observer's sense of wonder at the world of others, but sometimes their ill-disguised disapproval of the people encountered is all too evident. Referring to the natives of the Sudan, the tenth-century writer Ibn Hawqal explained that he had not bothered to describe the peoples of 'the torrid zone' because, as a civilized person, 'loving wisdom, ingenuity, religious justice and regular government, how could I notice such people as these, or magnify them by inserting an account of their countries?' Fortunately his successors showed themselves to be more balanced and more anthropologically minded.

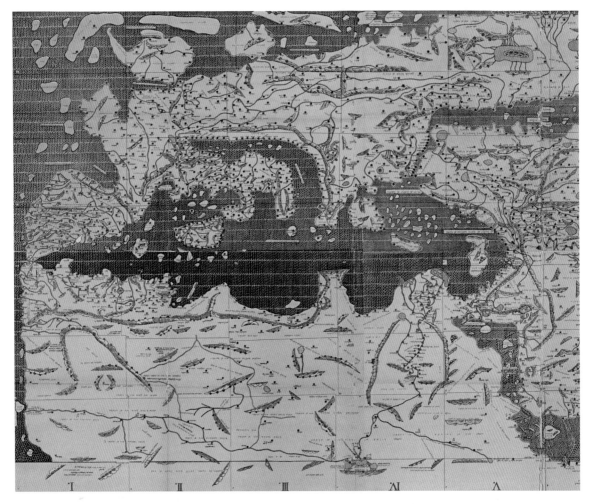

8.2 A map of the known world, called the *Tabula Rogeriana*, was drawn in 1154 for Roger II of Sicily by the geographer Abu Abdullah Muhammad al-Idrisi. Only the western half of the map is shown here. The cartographer's knowledge of Africa was limited, but he clearly believed that the Niger and the Nile were the same river, an idea proposed by Herodotus in the fifth century BC.

The Almohads and Thereafter

With the Almoravids firmly entrenched in southern Iberia at the beginning of the twelfth century, the energy that had sustained the movement and had led to spectacular territorial gains was all but spent. Their new leader, Ali ibn Yusuf (r. 1106–42), a young man of 23 when he came to power, devout, but inexperienced in the harsh reality of desert warfare, settled down in Iberia to the life of a zealot, while his courtiers enjoyed all the luxuries that Andalusia had to offer. As one astute observer wrote, the emir was content with 'the proceeds of taxation as he withdrew into his religion, praying at night and fasting by day. So the welfare of his subjects was utterly ignored.' Left unchecked, his elite followers seized power for themselves and, 'even worse, their wives took charge, involving themselves in every vice, not least the drinking of wine and prostitution'. For some it must have seemed like the end of the world order.

One such was Ibn Tumart, a Masmuda Berber, son of a village leader in the High Atlas. He had spent some years studying theology in Baghdad and, on his return home, was shocked by what he saw: young women, their faces exposed, while it was the men, in true Almoravid fashion, who wore veils. About 1122 he began to teach a new form of puritanism, setting himself up as the Mahdi: the saviour who had come to overthrow the corrupt Almoravids and establish peace. To this end he transformed the stateless Berbers of the High Atlas into a zealous army ready to take the field in the name of God. It was the now-familiar story. When Ibn Tumart died in 1129, his cause was taken up by his follower Abd al-Mumin, the sect being called al-Muwahhidun ('those who recognize the unity of God'), the Almohads.

Bursting out of their mountain stronghold, the Almohads captured Marrakesh in 1147 and went on to take the rest of Morocco and eastern Algeria. At this time the Normans living in Sicily were consolidating their hold on Ifriqiya, and by 1148 they had established control of the entire coast from Tunis to Tripoli, much to the dismay of the local Muslim authorities, who turned to the Almohads for help. In 1159 Abd al-Mumin led his army from Marrakesh and drove the Normans out, thus establishing his authority across the whole of North Africa from Morocco to Tripolitania. The success of the campaign was in no small part due to the efficiency with which the Almohads had used their fleet to gain mastery of the western Mediterranean. With North Africa now free of Christian garrisons, it was not long before Abd al-Mumin decided to lead his army into Andalusia in support of the faltering Muslim cause. There were some initial successes against the Christian forces, but the disastrous defeat, in July 1212, at Las Navas de Tolosa marked the beginning of the long retreat.

Not only had the hundred and forty years or so of the Almohad empire been a considerable political and military achievement, bringing together the disparate people of North Africa under one authority, but it had encouraged a resurgence of all aspects of culture. Ibn Tumart was, himself, an accomplished scholar, while his successors were civilized men who rebuilt their faith, freeing it from the rigid constraints of Maliki doctrines. Science, the arts, and architecture saw great advances. It was through the efforts of Muslim scholars working in the Andalusian court that the scientific knowledge of the classical world was transmitted to medieval Europe and great scholars flourished: men like Ibn Rushd (known as Averroes), a polymath who combined

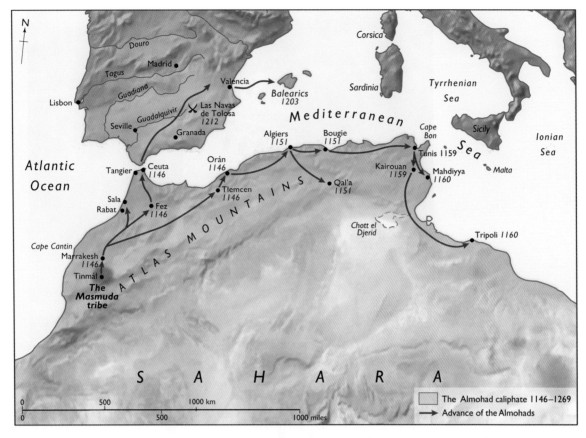

8.3 From their home in the Atlas Mountains the Almohads established their authority over much of North Africa and southern Iberia in the twelfth and thirteenth centuries.

the posts of chief judge and court physician to the Almohad caliph as well as being a prolific author contributing to medicine, philosophy, mathematics, and linguistics. Architecture, too, benefited from Almohad patronage, which inspired masterpieces such as the minarets of the Kutubiyya Mosque in Marrakesh, the Hassan Mosque in Rabat, and the Giralda in Seville, all that is left of the great mosque after demolition to make way for the Christian cathedral. It was a time of stunning achievement made possible by a succession of educated and enlightened caliphs.

But it was not to last. The defeat at Las Navas de Tolosa in 1212 had been devastating, marking the demise of Almohad power in Iberia. In Africa, too, their authority came under increasing threat, and over the next half-century the fragile unity fell apart. The first region to break away was Ifriqiya when, in 1229, the Hafsid governor, Abu Zakariyya, proclaimed independence. Then followed, in 1235, the Zayyanids, a Zenata

8.4 The Almohads sponsored great architects who built many fine buildings, including the minaret of the Kutubiyya Mosque in Marrakesh, shown here, which has strong similarities to those in Rabat and Seville.

Berber tribe who ruled from Tlemcen in north-west Algeria. While these secessions were going on, the Marinids, another Zenata Berber tribe living in north-east Morocco, were making trouble. Eventually, about 1215, they were expelled from their home territory and forced to the Rif Mountains, but in 1244–8 they surged forth to take control

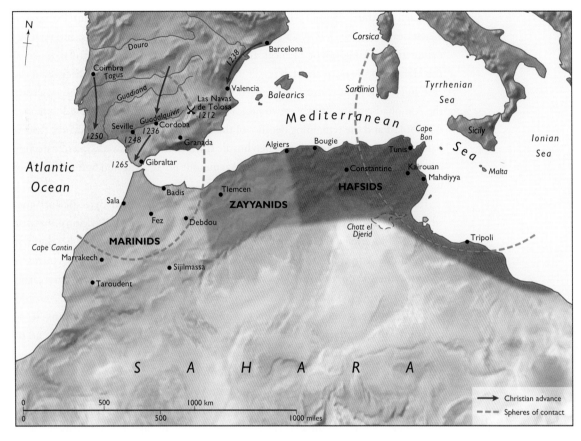

8.5 The collapse of the Almohads led to the Maghrib splitting into three polities. The Hafsids, in Tunisia and eastern Algeria, developed trading networks in the central Mediterranean, while the Marinids of Morocco traded largely with Iberia. The Zayyanids occupied an intermediary position subservient to their neighbours.

of a number of cities including Rabat, Salé, Meknes, and Fez, using the last as a base to attack the Almohads. The final act came in 1269, when they captured Marrakesh. The break-up of the political unity of the Maghrib was now complete.

What is remarkable is that the three new polities, in spite of almost continual territorial conflicts, were able to maintain their identities into the sixteenth century. The Hafsids and Marinids were the stronger states with well-defined territories, while the Zayyanids, situated uncomfortably between them, tended to be the victims of their aggression. The Hafsids were the first to engage in expansionist activities, conquering the Zayyanid kingdom of Tlemcen in 1242 and imposing overlordship. In the fourteenth century it was the Marinids who dominated the Maghrib, especially during the reign of Abu al-Hassan Ali (1331–48), when the army could boast forty thousand Zenata cavalry as well as Arab nomad cavalry and Andalusian archers. In 1337 they conquered the kingdom of Tlemcen and ten years later briefly took control of much of the Hafsid empire until an Arab revolt in southern Tunisia drove them back from the east. In 1358 they lost control of Tlemcen, bringing to an end their attempt to re-create the Almohad empire. They were to take Tlemcen again in 1370, but their dominance did not last and the remaining decades of the century saw their power decline, exacerbated by separatist movements. When hostile tribes in the Atlas swept down to occupy Marrakesh, the Atlantic trading town of Azemmour broke away and Sufi militants set up their own polity south of Marrakesh.

Transcending the unedifying details of tribal struggles and dynastic intrigue, what stands out is the way in which the three broad geographical regions imposed a degree of internal cohesion over the two and a half centuries from the break-up of the Almohad empire in the mid thirteenth century to the major changes brought about by the Ottoman incursions in the early sixteenth century. The prime reason was that each region benefited from a coherent commercial network. The Marinid region of Morocco enjoyed a growing maritime trade, connecting with its trans-Saharan routes and interfacing with Iberia through ports like Tangier. At the other end of the Maghrib, the Hafsids controlled the major port of Tunis with easy access to the networks of the central Mediterranean, offering opportunities for trade and piracy, while Kairouan served as the focal point on the overland route to Egypt. Between the two powerful dynasties, each with its own separate trading systems, lay the kingdom of Tlemcen, which dominated the east–west routes through the Maghrib and also the north–south routes across the central Sahara from the gold- and slave-producing regions of the south. Yet again, it was the simple realities of geography that shaped history.

Egypt: The Ayyubids and the Mamluks

The hold of the Fatimid caliphate on Egypt began to falter in the eleventh century when dissent broke out among the different ethnic groups that constituted the army. The Berbers made up the largest component, but increasing numbers of Turks were now causing trouble and in 1020 the black Sudanese troops rebelled against them. Tensions simmered until, in 1060, open war broke out. The outcome was that the Berbers, siding with the Sudanese troops, took over much of the countryside, while the Turks held Cairo. The serious unrest among the military, combined with a period of droughts and famine, dramatically undermined the stability of the state. The secession of North African territories, troubles with desert Bedouins, followed by the loss of the Levant and Syria, finally led to the complete collapse of the system.

With Egypt now in a state of anarchy, and Christian Crusaders threatening to set up a base in the delta, firm action was needed, and in 1164 the decision was taken to send in a Kurdish commander, Asad al-Din Shirkuh, a member of the Ayyub family, to re-establish order. Shirkuh was accompanied by his nephew Salah al-Din, better known in the West as Saladin, and the force quickly assumed control of Egypt, providing support for the vizier. When, in 1169, the vizier died, Shirkuh took over the post but died later in the year to be succeeded by Saladin. The appointment was authorized by the Fatimid caliph, having satisfied himself that Saladin was too young and too weak to pose a threat to his authority. He was mistaken. In the event, Saladin embarked upon a highly successful series of campaigns, helped by his older brother Turan Shah, who was responsible for smashing the revolt of the black Sudanese soldiers then stationed at Cairo. Two years later, in 1171, Saladin seized power, thus establishing the Ayyubid dynasty, at the same time switching allegiance from the Fatimids to the Abbasid caliphate based in Baghdad.

Having strengthened his position by appointing members of his family to many of the senior positions, Saladin set out to expand his empire. In 1171 his nephew led a small expedition along the North African coast to deal with the Bedouin tribes in the region of Barqa in Cyrenaica. The next year, in response to a raid on Aswan from Makuria, Turan Shah took a contingent of Kurdish troops into Nubia, leaving them to raid at will. It was at this time that the cathedral at Faras was destroyed. But when reports were received from Dongola suggesting that the country was in an impoverished state hardly worth the effort of conquest, it was decided to accept a guarantee from Makuria to protect Aswan and Upper Egypt, and to withdraw the Ayyubid force now established in Qasr Ibrim. North Africa required a little more attention. A campaign in 1174 expelled the Normans from Tripoli, and in 1188 Kairouan was taken. In parallel with the consolidation of Africa, Saladin extended his power to the Levant, Syria, and Mesopotamia, while in the Red Sea he appropriated the Hejaz and Yemen, thus taking full control of the lucrative Red Sea trade and the routes to East Africa and the Indian Ocean.

It was not a centralized empire that Saladin wished to found, but rather a series of states ruled by his kinsmen. The weaknesses inherent in such a system are self-evident. When he died, in 1193, discord erupted, focused mainly in the Levant and Syria, where the active presence of Crusaders and Mongols introduced additional tensions and opportunities to form protective alliances. Another factor in the complex mix was the growing power of the Mamluks in the Ayyubid army. The Mamluks were an elite force composed of troops brought as boys from their homeland on the steppe and given special military training. The name means 'owned', reflecting the fact that they belonged to the Muslim leader they served. Many of them were Kipchak Turks, horsemen from the steppe; others were Circassians from the Caucasus. They lived and trained together and became a closely knit corps, always aloof from the people of the countries in which they served.

For Ayyubid Egypt the beginning of the end came in 1248 when Louis IX of France set out for Cyprus on the Seventh Crusade hoping to gain the support of the Mongols, now in the Near East, for his plan to conquer Egypt. His idea was to use it as a base from which to free the Holy Land from the Muslims. When it became evident that no alliance was possible, Louis sailed, in 1249, with a fleet of vessels for the Egyptian port of Damietta on the Nile delta, capturing it with his twenty-thousand-strong force. The Ayyubids, supported by their Mamluk army, chose to base themselves at al-Mansurah, commanding the line of advance from Damietta to Cairo. At the crucial moment when the two armies were preparing for confrontation, the Egyptian sultan, al-Salih Ayyub, died. It could have spelt disaster for the Egyptians had it not been for his indomitable wife, Shajar al-Durr, said to be beautiful, pious, and intelligent, taking control and, with the aid of the Mamluk generals, defeating the Christian forces in a battle at al-Mansurah, in the aftermath of which Louis was captured. Only after paying a massive ransom were he and twelve thousand of his imprisoned troops allowed to sail to Acre in May 1250.

With Ayyubid power fragmented and the Mamluks in Egypt becoming increasingly dominant, the situation was very unstable. The Ayyubid heir, al-Mu'azzam Turan Shah, assumed power but was assassinated in April 1250, bringing the Ayyubid dynasty to an end. In his place the Mamluks appointed Shajar al-Durr, known as queen of the Muslims, as sultana. But within three months she had been forced to marry the Mamluk general Izz al-Din Aybak and then to abdicate, leaving Aybak as the first Mamluk sultan. Factionalism among the Mamluks grew worse, and disagreements between the strong-willed Shajar and her husband intensified, only to be resolved when, in 1257, she had him murdered in his bath. In the uproar that followed she was arrested, stripped, and beaten to death with clogs by the servants of her stepson and his mother, and her body thrown into the citadel ditch. It was an ignominious end for a woman whose energy and leadership had saved Egypt from the rampages of the Crusaders.

The long rule of the Mamluks can be divided into two periods. The first, 1250–1381, was dominated by the Bahri dynasty, who were Kipchak Turks from the Pontic steppe. The second, lasting from 1381 to the coming of the Ottoman Turks, was under the control of the Burji, who were Circassians. Much of the political and military activity was concentrated in the first period and was concerned with extending Mamluk control into the Levant, Syria, and the Hejaz.

8.6 In 1249 King Louis IX of France set out from Cyprus with 1,800 ships bound for the Egyptian coastal port of Damietta, intending to establish the Crusades in Egypt as a preliminary to attacking the Holy Land from the south. He took the port, but he and his force were later captured, to be released only after the payment of a massive ransom. In the illustration, from John the Good's *Grandes Chroniques de France*, the French are shown arriving at Damietta.

In the south, in Nubia, Makuria was in steep decline, largely because of changes in trade routes, which tended now to bypass the middle Nile, but also because of the onset of periods of drier, hotter weather, which tended to encourage raiding by the desert Bedouin. In the second half of the thirteenth century, the Mamluks began to take an interest in the area, raiding Dongola in 1265. Ten years later the Makurians attacked Aswan and in reprisal the Mamluks invaded the south, winning many battles in the Dongola region, killing the king, and installing a nominee of their own, thus making Makuria a vassal state of Egypt. A rebellion in 1286 gave Makuria a few years of independence, but the kingdom was reoccupied in 1312 when a Muslim was put on the throne, and five years later, in a highly symbolic act, the throne hall of Old Dongola was converted into a mosque. Christianity survived, and some of the later kings were Christian, but civil war, anarchy, and plague devastated the region, hastening its decline.

Meanwhile, under the Mamluks, Egypt flourished. The population probably reached 3.3 million, but they were mostly dispersed in the thousands of small villages scattered along the river. Only some 230,000 lived in towns, the largest now being

8.7 The throne hall of Old Dongola, on the middle Nile, was built by the Makurian kings in the ninth century. Makuria was occupied by the Mamluks early in the fourteenth century, and in 1317 the throne hall was converted into a mosque.

Cairo with a population of sixty thousand, followed by Alexandria at about half that size. Agriculture was the prime source of revenue, which, under Mamluk rule, was efficiently centralized, but trade between the Mediterranean world and the East via the Red Sea added to the wealth of the empire. The Mongol presence in the Near East and the Pontic steppe, and the disruption consequent upon that, meant that the overland routes to the East were no longer reliable. By occupying both sides of the Red Sea, the Mamluks now controlled the flow of products entering the Mediterranean world coming from Persia, India, and South-East Asia. These included textiles, spices such as pepper, cloves, and cinnamon, indigo, and a range of medicinal drugs, in return for which gold, silver, woollen fabrics, linen, furs, wax, honey, and cheeses were exchanged. The Mamluks now had treaties with the major maritime trading states of Europe—Genoa, Venice, and Barcelona—and with far-flung places like Ceylon. Cairo and Alexandria grew rich on the commerce. Although internal conflicts were many, and few of the Mamluk sultans died a natural death, the embedded nature of the commercial system and the vested interests in maintaining it kept the Mamluk elite in power for 250 years.

Exploring the Land of Barbur, Zanj, and Sofala

By the middle of the twelfth century, the communities living along the east coast of Africa were well integrated into the trading system controlled by Muslim entrepreneurs. Arab geographers recognized three regions. From the Horn of Africa south to Mogadishu was Barbur, or Berbera, equivalent now to the Somali coast. Further south lay the land of Zanj, a name used to describe both the region—the coast of Kenya, Tanzania, and northern Mozambique—and its inhabitants. The southern extremity of Zanj was also referred to as Sofala, after the town, and beyond that lay the little-known land of Wak Wak, merging into the realm of the fabulous. The original population was Bantu, but in the trading towns that developed along the coast, often on offshore islands, Arabs and Persians had settled and the population had largely accepted Islam. Al-Idrisi, writing in the first half of the twelfth century, was familiar with the region (pp. 223–4 above), but he was relying on information gathered by others. A later writer, Abu al-Fida (1273–1331), assembled basic geographical information on the towns of Malindi, Mombasa, and Sofala, while Zhao Rukuo, a Chinese official in charge of external trade in Fujian province, offered some anecdotes about the island of Zanzibar (Ts'ong-po) and the Berbera coast (Pi-P'a-Lo) in his book *Description of the Barbarians* (*Zhufan zhi*), published in 1226. He describes the trade goods sent from China to Zanzibar, 'white cotton cloth, porcelain, copper, and red cotton', which were exchanged for ivory, gold, ambergris, and sandalwood. Nor could he resist describing the exotic animals found along the Berbera coast: ostriches 'six to seven feet tall', the zebra, 'a kind of mule'. And the giraffe (*tsu-la*), which 'resembles a camel in shape' and has skin an inch thick. 'The inhabitants of this country, who are great hunters, hunt this animal with poisoned arrows.'

These writers, composing in comfort at a distance, made good use of details they could glean from others. But for a vivid first-hand account we must turn to the famous traveller Ibn Battuta, who visited the East African coast in 1331 and wrote about it in his *Travels* (*The Rihla*). Beginning his journey in the Gulf of Aden he gives a brief sketch of Zeila on the Somali coast, a major market, but 'one of the dirtiest towns in existence, vile and evil smelling. The cause of the stench is the great quantity of fish which is brought there, as well as the blood of camels, which are slaughtered in the streets.' The conditions were so noxious that the party preferred to sleep overnight on the boat. From Zeila it was a fifteen-day journey to Mogadishu, a large town of wealthy merchants, where they were hospitably received and entertained by the sultan. On

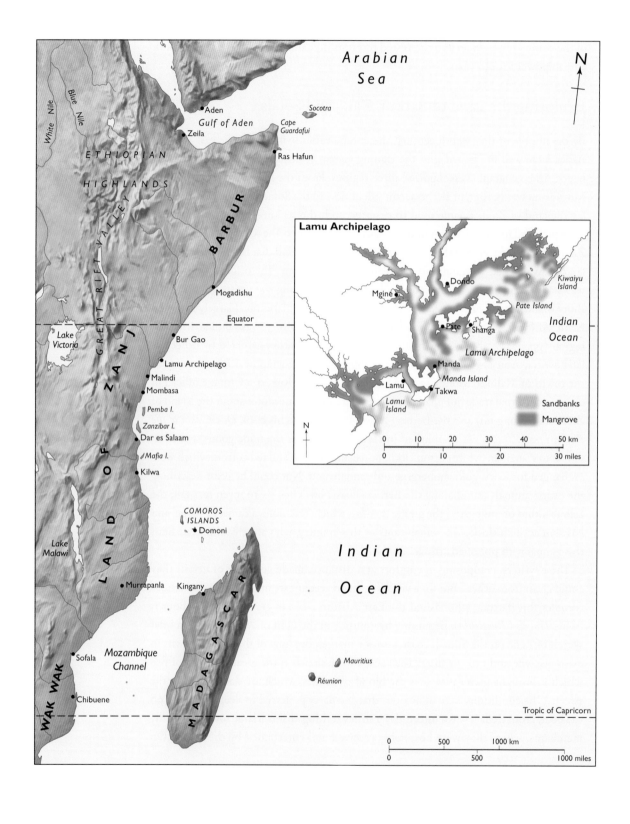

Arabic
Sea

N

White Nile
Blue Nile
• Aden
Gulf of Aden
Socotra
• Zeila
Cape Guardafui
E T H I O P I A N
H I G H L A N D S
• Ras Hafun

B A R B U R

Mogadishu •
Equator
Lake Victoria
• Bur Gao
• Lamu Archipelago
• Malindi
• Mombasa
◁ Pemba I.
◁ Zanzibar I.
• Dar es Salaam
◁ Mafia I.
• Kilwa

L A N D   O F   Z A N J

G R E A T   R I F T   V A L L E Y

Lake Malawi

COMOROS ISLANDS
◁ • Domoni

• Murrapanla   Kingany •

I n d i a n

O c e a n

M A D A G A S C A R

W A K   W A K
• Sofala
Mozambique Channel
• Chibuene

Mauritius
Réunion

Tropic of Capricorn

| 0 | 500 | 1000 km |
| 0 | 500 | 1000 miles |

Lamu Archipelago

Dondo •
Kiwaiyu Island
Mginé •
Pate Island
Pate • • Shanga
Indian Ocean
Lamu Archipelago
Manda •
Manda Island
Lamu • • Takwa
Lamu Island

N

Sandbanks
Mangrove

| 0 | 10 | 20 | 30 | 40 | 50 km |
| 0 | 10 | 20 | 30 miles |

8.8 (*Opposite*) By the twelfth century, the east coast of Africa was regularly visited by Muslim traders sailing from the Red Sea and the Persian Gulf. Trading enclaves were established at intervals, often on offshore islands, which offered a degree of protection.

the Friday they were brought suitable clothes so that they could worship in the chief mosque. The next day they attended an open meeting in the sultan's audience hall, which began with a communal meal. After the sultan had retired, 'the qadi and viziers, the private secretary and four of the chief amirs sit to hear causes and complaints. The questions of religious law are directed to the qadi: other cases are judged by the council, that is, the viziers and amirs'. Ibn Battuta was evidently well satisfied with the prosperous and well-ordered Muslim community whose hospitality he had enjoyed.

Next it was Mombasa, 'a large island two days' journey from the land of the Swahili', where the mosques were strongly constructed of wood. After a night's sleep, they were on their way again, making for Kilwa, 'the principal town on the coast, the greater part of whose inhabitants are Zanj of very black complexion and many displayed [ritual] facial scarring'. Kilwa, he thought, was one of the most beautiful and well-constructed towns in the world. 'The people are engaged in a holy war, for their country lies beside that of the pagan Zanj. Their chief quality is piety.' The sultan, revered for his generosity, 'frequently makes raids into the Zanj country, attacks them, and carries off booty, of which he reserves a fifth, using it in a manner prescribed in the Koran'. But in spite of his enthusiasm for the elite sport of raiding, the sultan was very humble: 'He sits and eats with beggars, and venerates holy men and descendants of the Prophet.' Kilwa was the last of the East African ports he visited; from there he sailed back to Arabia.

The picture which Ibn Battuta paints is of well-ordered cosmopolitan towns, visited by foreign merchants and by holy men from the Hejaz and Iraq, run by an urban elite of dedicated Muslims. Beyond, in the hinterland, things were very different. Here lived unbelievers, who, while they might be trading partners, were also fair game for raiding parties in search of loot and slaves.

The archaeological evidence is consistent with the descriptions given by travellers. At Shanga excavations have shown how, from the eighth to the fifteenth century, the settlement grew, beginning with timber buildings, later to be replaced by structures of mud and coral, which, in turn, gave way to buildings constructed only of coral. By the early thirteenth century, coral structures were widespread. At its maximum extent the town covered some 15 hectares and is thought to have comprised some 220 houses and at least three mosques. Settlement came to an end in the early decades of the fifteenth century. There is ample evidence of commerce which was managed through a locally issued silver coinage. At Kilwa the Great Mosque, originally built in the eleventh century, was quadrupled in size in the early fourteenth century, at which time a palace

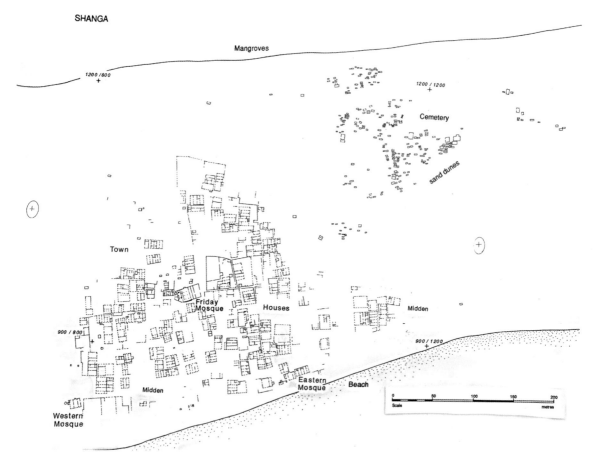

8.9 The trading port of Shanga, on the shore of the Indian Ocean, had grown, by the thirteenth century, to become a town of 15 hectares.

8.10 (*Opposite top*) Some of the trading ports grew to become sophisticated cities. Kilwa, in Tanzania, was one of the finest. The Great Mosque was founded in the eleventh century but was improved on several occasions until the early fourteenth century.

8.11 (*Opposite bottom*) Just outside Kilwa was the Husuni Kubwa, a palace built in the fourteenth century for Sultan al-Hasan ibn Sulaiman.

complex was built at Husuni Kubwa on an elevated, airy position, its style and sophistication suggesting that it was the work of a Middle Eastern architect. Seeing familiar buildings like these, it is little surprise that Ibn Battuta was enthusiastic in his praise of the city.

The merchants who passed through these coastal towns have left detritus allowing archaeologists to track their movements. The quantity of glazed pottery from

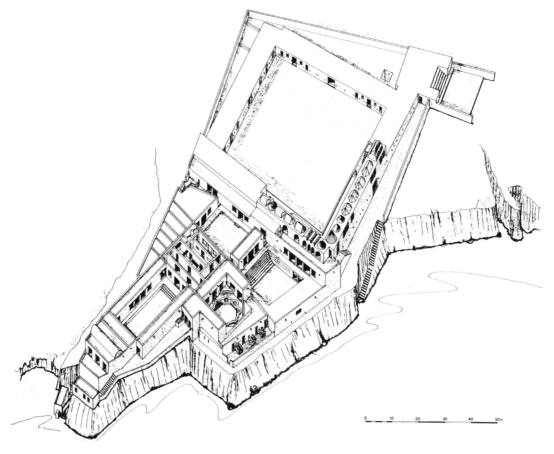

Arabia, the Persian Gulf, and China, and the very many glass beads from India and Egypt, speak of far-flung trade rising to a peak in the fourteenth century. Most of these imports were absorbed by the urban populations and used to define and display their status. It was here that a range of consumer products and foodstuffs was generated to trade with the communities of the interior for the products for which Africa was famous: ivory, animal skins, and slaves. By the fourteenth century, gold, probably coming from the Zambezi region and passing through the southern port of Chibuene, was beginning to enter the network, making the trading opportunities of East Africa even more attractive.

The power and longevity of the Mamluk regime in Egypt and the Red Sea meant that, from the middle of the thirteenth century, the trading systems of the Indian Ocean and the Mediterranean could develop apace, secure in the systems of trust, respect, and hospitality that governed commercial interactions in the Islamic world.

The Empire of Mali

The kingdom of Ghana (or Wagadu), which had dominated the western Sudan for several hundred years, began to decline in the twelfth century, eventually, by the early decades of the thirteenth century, to be replaced by the even larger empire of Mali, which grew from a Malinke chiefdom to become a decentralized multi-ethnic state. Mali remained at the peak of its power throughout the fourteenth century, by the end of which the Songhai had begun to challenge, eventually eclipsing their rivals altogether. The rise and fall of states in western Sudan between the ninth and fifteenth centuries is little more than the passing of the baton of power from one dominant polity to another as the continuous power struggle between elites takes its course. The dynamic comes, in part, from the personalities of individual leaders, but behind it all lie the demands imposed by changing patterns of trade.

The story of this period to the end of the fourteenth century is told in some detail by the Arab historian Ibn Khaldun, who based his narrative on the oral traditions of the Mali people. With admirable brevity he summed up the complex picture:

> Later the authority of Ghana waned and its power declined whilst that of the veiled people, their neighbours on the north next to the lands of the Berbers, increased. The latter overcame the Sudanese, plundered their territories, imposed upon them tribute, and converted many of them to Islam. As a result, the authority of the rulers of Ghana dwindled away, and they were overcome by the Susu, their Sudanese neighbours, who subdued and crushed them completely.

Later the people of Mali outnumbered the Sudanese peoples in their neighbourhood and expanded over the whole region. They conquered the Susu and took over all their possessions, both their original territory and that of Ghana, as far as the Ocean to the west.

(*Kitab al-'Ibar*)

The Susu, who were themselves Soninke, occupied the region south of Wagadu, in the upper reaches of the rivers Senegal and Niger, their territory extending across a range of environments including good farmland and pastures and woodland savannah. Their land was productive of iron, but, of more significance, they were able to control the flow of gold from the Bure goldfields, and malagueta pepper and kola nuts from the rainforest zone to the south. Herein lay their power. In the twelfth century they began to extend their authority over their neighbours to the north, the empire of Ghana,

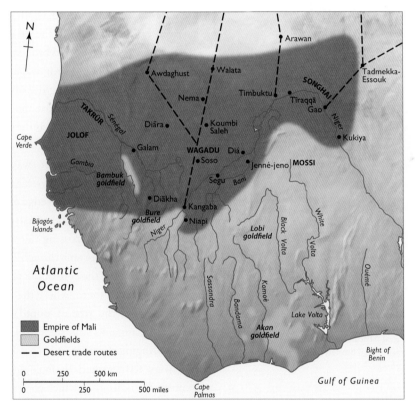

8.12 The empire of Mali had grown to its greatest extent by 1300, absorbing the lands ruled by Ghana as well as many of the surrounding tribes, and extending northwards to the edge of the desert. The Songhai, occupying the Niger Bend, were brought under its jurisdiction.

and to the south, where lived the Malinke. The old empire of Ghana, already weakened by attacks from the desert nomads, succumbed, but the Malinke fought back fiercely against Susu aggression, inspired by an effective war-leader, Sundjata. About 1240 he defeated the Susu and drove them out, and over the next forty years, created the empire of Mali, incorporating the territory of Ghana as well as much of the land once controlled by the Susu. Subsequent leaders extended the authority of the empire by subjugating states in the lower Gambia and Senegal river regions as far west as the Atlantic. To the east, further conquests brought the Niger Bend, down-river to Kukiya, under the control of Mali, drawing the important trading cities of Timbuktu and Gao into the Malian sphere, as well as the oasis town of Tadmekka.

Mali now governed a great swath of the western Sudan stretching for 2,000 kilometres along the southern edge of the desert, commanding the terminal markets of all the routes crossing the western Sahara. But important though these trading nodes were, the core of the power of Mali lay to the south, where the land could support the size of population needed to maintain a large standing army.

The bringing together of such a large and diverse territory under a single authority created conditions in which commerce could develop new systems of complexity. This, in turn, gave rise to increased productivity within the boundaries of the empire, as well as leading to an intensification of trade with the south, particularly with the all-important goldfields of Bure and Akan. Peace

8.13 The peoples of the West and Central African Sahel were dependent on horse riding and are shown, in models in terracotta and bronze, to be accomplished riders. This example comes from Bura-Asinda-Sikka, Niger.

brought with it opportunity, and allowed the development of specialist merchant elites bound by family ties. In the east of the empire were the Juula, in the west the Jakhanke, while along the desert boundary Soninke merchants were at work. These specialist groups expanded the trading reach of the empire into territories beyond, the Juula opening contacts with the Akan goldfield through the town of Begho, the Jakhanke developing markets in Gambia and Senegal, while the Soninke extended their activities eastwards along the Sahel to the city states of Hausaland.

By the late thirteenth century, under the leadership of Uli (r. 1260–77), the empire had gained power and stability. In the words of Ibn Khaldun,

> During his powerful government their domains expanded and they overcame neighbouring peoples ... Their authority became mighty and all the nations of the Sudan stood in awe of them. Merchants from the Maghrib and Ifriqiya travelled to their country.

The diversity of commercial enterprise brought wealth to the state, enhancing the power of successive kings, men like the famous Mansa Musa, who, in the 1320s, entranced the world with his lavish displays of wealth (pp. 287–8 below). But the empire was a fragile construct built of smaller polities with competing loyalties, held together only by strong leadership. With the death of Mansa Sulayman in 1360,

> dissension broke out among the people of Mali. Authority over them became divided and their rulers contested the kingship. They killed each other and were preoccupied with civil war until finally Mansa Djata came out [victorious] and consolidated power in his hands.

Although a degree of order had been restored, the situation was very unstable. In the 1360s a large region made up of a number of small polities between the lower Senegal and Gambia rivers broke away to become a separate Jolof empire, and it may have been about this time that the kingdom of Susu ceased to accept the authority of Mali. There were also troubles in the east, which required a military force to be sent, ultimately unsuccessfully, to secure Tadmekka about 1380. The loss of the caravan city was a serious blow to Mali's links with Ifriqiya, Tripolitania, and Egypt. By the end of the fourteenth century, Mali had become a shadow of its former self, weakened by internal dissent and by attacks from the desert Tuareg and the Mossi living in the Upper Volta region. The Songhai, with their capital at Gao, had achieved independence, and over the next century were to overrun much of the old empire of Mali to become the successor power in the western Sudan. The much-reduced core that remained maintained its identity until the late seventeenth century.

Crossing the Desert

By the end of the thirteenth century, the desert-edge town of Walata had replaced Awd-aghust as the southern destination favoured by desert caravans. It was better connected with the main centres of the empire of Mali and the cross-desert route leading to it had the advantage of passing through Taghaza, a major supplier of salt. Over time the alternative route through Taghaza to Timbuktu began to gain in popularity. Timbuktu, sited on the edge of the desert only 20 kilometres from the river Niger, was linked directly to the riverine transport system, facilitating the wide distribution of goods. The town had begun as a small settlement set up by Tuareg, but with the expansion of the empire in the mid thirteenth century, it grew and took on greater significance, eventually, in the fifteenth and sixteenth centuries, becoming widely renowned as a centre of learning and commerce. By this stage the city had grown, with a densely packed nucleus, but in its topography and the siting of its mosques it is possible to discern two distinct

8.14 The Great Mosque of Djenné, Mali. The present building, dating to 1907, replaces earlier mosques dating back to the thirteenth century. Although built in traditional style by the local guild of masons, some reject its authenticity, seeing it as an interference in local culture by the French colonial administration.

agglomerations, which suggests that it may originally have been two communities, one of native peoples, the other for the commercial community. Its beneficial siting, linking desert and river networks, led to it becoming the preferred terminal, leaving Walata to decline. The disadvantage of the site lay in its vulnerability to attack. In the late fourteenth century it was pillaged and burned by the Mossi, pagans who lived south of the Niger Bend, but was quickly restored to Mali. Early in the fifteenth century it was again raided, this time from the north, by Tuareg, who in 1433 or 1434 moved in and settled. Even so, the town continued to be administered by governors appointed by Mali until the 1470s, when it was incorporated into the Songhai empire.

The city of Gao, further down-river, was vital to the prosperity of the empire of Mali since it commanded a different route network. From Gao it was possible to travel eastwards across the desert, through Tadmekka, thereafter selecting one of several routes to the Maghrib, to Ifriqiya, to Tripolitania, or to Egypt. A more easterly route led through Takedda in south-west Aïr, where supplies of copper were to be had, and then on to the central and eastern Sahel. To the south, Gao had access to the valleys of the Volta and to the goldfields of Akan. It is easy to understand why the rulers of Mali sought to control it and the networks it commanded. Its loss, at the end of the fourteenth century, was a devastating blow from which the kingdom of Mali never recovered.

The great traveller Ibn Battuta explored some of the desert routes in the western Sahara in the middle of the fourteenth century and has left vivid first-hand accounts

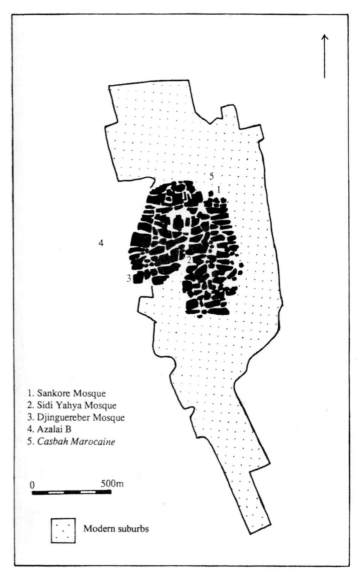

1. Sankore Mosque
2. Sidi Yahya Mosque
3. Djinguereber Mosque
4. Azalai B
5. *Casbah Marocaine*

0   500m

[∴] Modern suburbs

8.15 The plan of the core of the ancient centre of Timbuktu suggests that the town may have developed as two separate communities, the merchants keeping themselves separate from the local people.

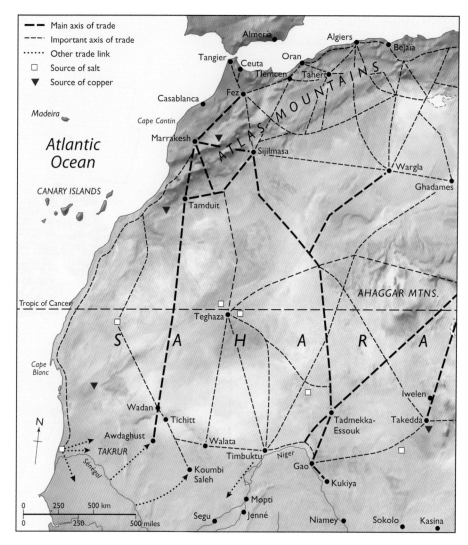

8.16 Crossing the desert from the Maghrib to the Sahel was a dangerous undertaking and success depended on the skill of the Berber leaders who could guide the caravan safely across the featureless desert using the stars to navigate. The impetus to trade, driven by the Muslim states in the north, saw the cross-desert routes become more numerous and much more intensively used.

of life on the road. His route from Fez to the empire of Mali passed through Sijilmasa, where he stopped to prepare for his trans-Saharan journey, buying camels and amassing fodder sufficient to feed them for four months. In February 1352 he set out for Walata in the company of a merchant caravan, on a journey that was to take two months. They passed through Taghaza and then, at Tasarahla, the caravan rested to prepare for

the final leg of the journey, taking the opportunity to repair and refill the waterskins. Before they set off, they hired a local messenger (*takhshif*) and sent him on ahead to their agents in Walata to announce their imminent arrival and ask for water to be sent out to meet them in the desert four days from the city. The service of the *takhshif* was rewarded with a hundred gold *mitkal*, the price of a good riding horse, but then, as Ibn Battuta explains, his task was vital.

> Sometimes the *takhshif* perishes in the desert and the people of Walata know nothing of the caravan, and its people or most of them perish too ... There is no road to be seen in the desert, and no track, only sand blowing about in the wind.
>
> (*The Travels*)

But on this occasion the system worked well. When they were still seven days out from Tasarahla they were relieved to see, in the distance, the fires of those who had been sent to meet them.

Ibn Battuta knew a merchant living in Walata and had written to him asking him to rent a house for his stay. Fifty days later he was on the road again, travelling south to the capital of Mali. The journey was rather different. He was passing through inhabited territory, no longer desert. It was much safer for the traveller, and accordingly the group need not be large: in this case he was accompanied by only three companions and a guide. There was no need to carry supplies of food since the locals would provide it in return for 'pieces of salt, glass trinkets, and some articles of perfume'. This was a barter economy and there was no use for 'dinars and dirhams'. They crossed the Niger and arrived in the capital twenty-four days later. Here he stayed for eight months, probably longer than intended, but he had to recover from a bout of severe food poisoning which had killed one of his companions—one of the recurring dangers of eating unfamiliar street food.

It was now February 1353 and time to begin his homeward journey. Since he could not afford a horse, he set out on a camel for Timbuktu, a city with which he was not impressed, and then took to the river, travelling by canoe to Gao, stopping en route to barter trade goods with local villagers for meat and butter. He also acquired a slave boy, who remained in his service for years. Gao was much more to his liking and he stayed there for a month before joining a caravan of merchants who had come from Ghadames and were travelling back home. He had got as far as Takedda when he received a summons from his patron, the sultan Abu Inan, calling him back to Fez. For the long journey back across the desert region of Touat to Sijilmasa he purchased two camels and supplies for seventy days and joined a large caravan leaving in mid September. Among his travelling companions were six hundred female slaves. They arrived in Sijilmasa in early December and, after two weeks resting, set out, at the end of the month, on the final leg of the journey across the Atlas Mountains. 'It was a time of intense cold, and a great deal of snow had settled on the road. I had seen difficult roads and much snow in Bukhara, Samarqand, Khurasan and in the country of the Turks, but never saw one more difficult than this.' It was a memorable homecoming.

Ibn Battuta's account of his journeys through western Africa gives an incomparable impression of life on the caravan routes and the effectiveness of its organization. Large numbers of people and goods in quantity moved, irrespective of time of year, and in the size of the travelling community lay the assurance of a safe passage. At the time he was making his journey across the western Sahara the progress of Arabization was well under way. Already nomadic Arabs, the Banu Maqil, had penetrated southern Morocco and had taken over the valleys of the Sus region and the Dra'a, and the Bani Hasan had begun their advance to the south, gradually replacing the Sanhaja Berbers. But Berber communities continued to occupy the lands bordering the northern limit of the empire of Mali and, according to Ibn Khaldun, they were subject to the king and paid him a tribute, some serving in his army. It was, clearly, in his interests to maintain a hold over the desert nomads through whose territory the caravan routes passed. Once the caravans had reached Walata, they were under the direct jurisdiction of Mali. The central route, as far as Tadmekka, was also controlled by Mali, but beyond that the traveller was in the hands of the Tuareg. The route through their domain was, however, safe, as witnessed by the fact that caravans of twelve thousand camels made the journey from the Malian capital to Cairo on a regular cycle.

Once he had reached the well-ordered empire of Mali, Ibn Battuta found travelling much easier and had time to observe the people. He did so, not entirely without prejudice, but was prepared to agree that 'the negroes possess some admirable qualities. They are seldom unjust and have a greater abhorrence of intolerance than any other people.' But he found some of their behaviour not entirely to his liking. 'The women servants, slave-girls, and young girls go about in front of everyone naked, without a stitch of clothing on them. Women go into the sultan's presence naked, and without any covering, and his daughters go about naked.' For a devout Muslim this was unnerving. So too was the custom of people putting ashes on their heads as a mark of respect. These alien behaviours he regarded as 'reprehensible practice[s]'.

In a rather less censorious passage he records the visit of tribesmen from Wangara:

> The sultan received them with honour, and gave them as his hospitality-gift a servant, a negress. They killed her and ate her, and having smeared their faces and hands with her blood came to the sultan to thank him. I was informed that this was their regular custom whenever they visit his court.

After two years travelling across the desert and through Mali, he must have been relieved to arrive back in the civilized and predictable comfort of Fez.

The Kingdoms of the Central and Eastern Sudan

The empire of Kanem, which occupied a large area to the east of Lake Chad, was under the control of the Sayfawa dynasty from the eleventh century. In the early thirteenth century, driven by the energy of the *mai* (king) Dunama Dabbalemi (1210–59), who was said to have commanded 41,000 cavalry, the territory of the empire was extended in all directions. An advance northwards along the caravan route to the Fazzan enabled him to take over the oasis of Traghan in the Murzuq desert in south-west Libya, appointing a governor to oversee the empire's trading interests. Elsewhere, in frontier territories, military commanders were installed and given land. It was probably at this time that the empire extended its authority over the town of Takedda in the Aïr Mountains, commanding an important route node to the north and north-west as well as valuable copper resources. In the fourteenth century, in exchange for copper, Kanem was exporting slaves and saffron-dyed cloth. In addition to territorial expansion, the king was also initiating diplomatic exchanges with the sultan of Tunisia, sending gifts like the giraffe mentioned above (p. 249), and establishing a madrasa in Cairo for the benefit of pilgrims on the hajj.

The late thirteenth century was a very unsettled time, possibly exacerbated by climatic degeneration in the north, with continuous conflicts with neighbouring tribes, first with the So and later the Bulala, during which eight *mai* were killed. The result of these conflicts saw the Kanembu people and their ruling Sayfawa dynasts forced to abandon their capital of Nijimi and to move to the Borno region west of Lake Chad. Eventually, in 1472, after a century of instability, a new capital was founded at Birni Gazargamo in the fertile valley of the river Komadugu Gana. The city, protected by a rampart 6.7 kilometres in circumference, with its palaces, mosques, and trading quarters, flourished until the early nineteenth century, when it was destroyed during the invasion of the Fulani.

The strength of Gazargamo lay in its domination of the intersection of two major routes, the one leading north across the Sahara, through the Fazzan to the North African coast, the other running east–west through the Sahel. With the development of the empire of Mali, the Sahel route came to be more widely used, eventually giving access to the kingdoms of the middle Nile. Between Mali and Kanem Borno, in the savannah and open woodlands north of the Niger and Benue (now northern Nigeria), land occupied by Hausa agriculturists, a series of small city states developed.

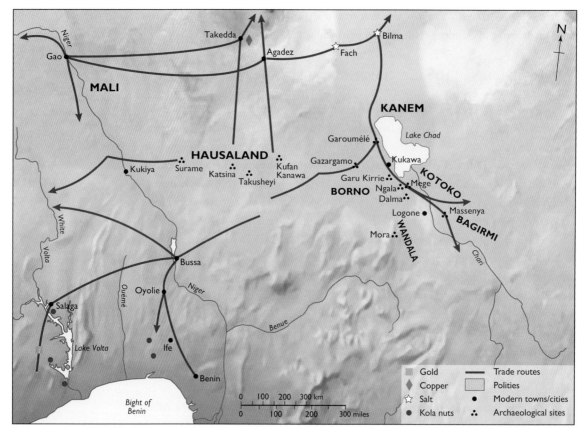

8.17 The Hausa city states developed in the region between the empires of Mali and Kanem Borno. They were well placed to trade with the forest zone to the south and were linked by trans-desert routes to the Maghrib.

The states, of which there were traditionally seven, were each focused on a walled city built in a prominent position, often on a granite outcrop with good reserves of water. Some eventually grew to considerable proportions. Kano, for example, had walls in excess of 9 metres high and 30 kilometres in circumference. The walls reflected not only the autonomy and identity of the state, but also the need for defence in times of intense competition and conflict.

The states were self-contained but were known for their specializations: Rano and Kano were called the chiefs of indigo; Zaria, the chief of slaves; Gobir, the chief of war; and Katsina and Daura, the chiefs of markets. Katsina, sited midway between the Niger and the Chad basin, was the most powerful mercantile centre. Its craftsmen produced leatherwork, textiles, and iron, which were exported by resident traders,

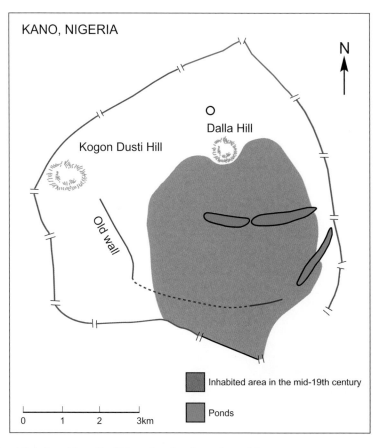

KANO, NIGERIA

N

Dalla Hill

Kogon Dusti Hill

Old wall

Inhabited area in the mid-19th century

Ponds

0   1   2   3km

8.18 Simplified plan of the walls of Kano, the urban focus of one of the Hausa city states.

together with gold, kola nuts, and slaves coming from the south. Hausa tradition records the appearance of Wangara (that is, Soninke) merchants arriving from the west in the thirteenth century bringing Islam, but Islam may already been introduced earlier, in the tenth or eleventh century, through links with Kanem. That merchants were arriving from both east and west accounts for the rise in prosperity of Hausaland.

The extent of these trade links is vividly demonstrated by the cemetery of Durbi Takusheyi, which dates to the thirteenth to fourteenth century. Here three burial mounds in a group of eight have been scientifically excavated. Each contained a female burial, arranged in a sitting position, accompanied by jewellery and other grave goods. Among the items buried with the dead were a cowrie-shell head-covering and belt, the shells coming from the Indian Ocean, a necklace of carnelian beads with a silver

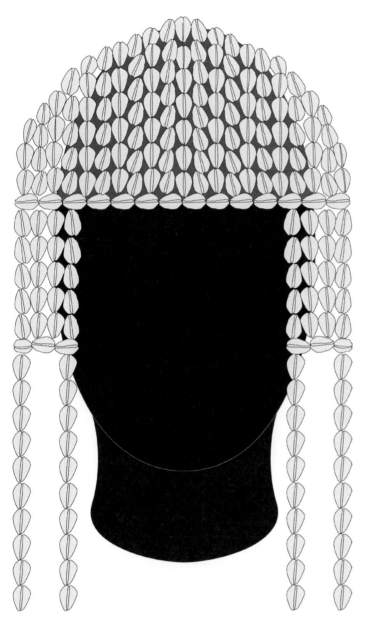

8.19 The female buried in grave 4 in the cemetery of Durbi Takusheyi, northern Nigeria, in the thirteenth–fourteenth century was wearing a head-covering made from cowrie shells brought from the Indian Ocean. It is shown here in reconstruction.

plaque, gold earrings, finger rings, and pendants from the western Sahel, ivory bracelets, a copper alloy Mamluk bowl from Egypt, two buckets, one from the Near East, a belt of beads, some of which were Chinese, and large ingots of brass like those found in the abandoned caravan at Ma'den Ijafen. The remarkable variety of the goods with which these Hausa women were provided is witness to the widely flung trading relationships enjoyed by the Hausa.

The close-packed, largely independent city states result from a very different socio-economic system from that underlying the empires of Mali and Kanem Borno. The explanation probably lies in the fact that, in Hausaland, no one city had exclusive control of all the valuable goods coming from the south. These products found different routes through Hausa territory, benefiting the towns through which they passed. The towns were also generating exploitable commodities in their own right. Without the centralization of commercial power, a single large state could not emerge. Although there were episodes of centralized control, the city states maintained their identity until the beginning of the nineteenth century.

To the east of Kanem Borno, in the Darfur region, a polity continued to work the land and control trade routes to the north and east. They were ruled by the Daju, who were traditionally believed to have come from the middle Nile valley in the twelfth century. Among the valuable resources to hand were the pagan tribes in the Dar Fertit region to the south, who, through raid or trade, provided slaves for the markets in Nubia, Egypt, the Fazzan, and the North African coast.

Exploring the World

The spread of Islam throughout much of northern Africa by the fourteenth century encouraged the imperative to travel. Before the arrival of Islam, the Berber tribes who inhabited the Sahara, by the very nature of their nomadic existence, were travellers. But these journeys were prescribed by economic factors and were usually practised within a limited range of familiar environments. Acceptance of Islam required the faithful, at least once in a lifetime, to make the hajj—the pilgrimage to Mecca—if they had the health and means to do so. Such a journey took people into new worlds in the company of others of different ethnicities, who carried with them unfamiliar knowledge.

One of the most famous of the pilgrimages, which became a sensation in its time, was that of Mansa Musa, who ruled Mali from 1312 to 1337. In 1324 he set out on the hajj, starting at Walata and travelling through Touat. The exact route he took through North Africa is not known but he may have gone by way of Wargla, Ghadames, and Siwa to reach Cairo, where he stayed for some time before travelling on to Medina and Mecca. He rode on horseback in great splendour, with five hundred slaves holding golden staffs preceding him. Among his great entourage and baggage train were between eighty and a hundred camels, each carrying up to 130 kilograms of gold dust, which he dispersed as charitable gifts and used for purchases in Egypt with such abandon that the value of gold was depressed for ten years. Having been so lavish on his outward journey, on his way back he was forced to borrow gold from moneylenders, one of whom, an Alexandrian merchant, accompanied him home to be sure of repayment. The route back from Cairo is not recorded, but the procession passed through Gao, which had just been captured by the Malian army. Here an Andalusian poet and architect, al-Sahil, who had joined the king's entourage at Mecca, was given the task of building a grand new mosque. He used fired brick, a material previously unknown in the region. From Gao the route home led through Timbuktu.

The journey, with its flamboyant display of wealth and power, became a legend. That gold came from the western Sudan was widely known, but the exotic splendour of Mansa Musa's court and its sheer extravagance must have come as a shock. It was a story widely reported. In 1339, not long after Musa's return, the Majorcan cartographer Angelino Dulcert produced a *mappa mundi* in which Mansa Musa was depicted sitting on a throne in the centre of Africa, resplendent in a gold crown and holding a sceptre. The famous Catalan Atlas, drawn in 1375, shows a similar figure holding out what appears to be a gold nugget to an approaching rider. The caption reads, 'This negro lord is called Mansa Mali, lord of the negroes of Guinea. So abundant is the gold which is found in his country that he is the richest and most noble king in all the land.' Musa would have been well pleased if he had known what worldwide fame his pilgrimage would bring, but then, perhaps that was his intention.

When in Egypt, Mansa Musa told many stories which were recorded by the scholar al-Umari. One concerned his immediate predecessor, Muhammad ibn Qu (not Abubakri Keita II as is often stated), who developed a deep curiosity about the Atlantic Ocean and refused to believe that the far side could not be reached:

> So he equipped two hundred boats full of men, and the same number filled with gold, water, and food, sufficient for several years. He ordered the leader not to return until they had reached the extremity of the Ocean or until they had exhausted the provisions and the water.
>
> (Ibn Fadlallah al-Umari, *Masalik al-absar fi mamalik al-amsar*)

After a long time had passed, only one boat returned, reporting that the others had perished in a whirlpool. Not to be deterred, Muhammad called for an even bigger expedition to be prepared, which he intended to lead himself: 'two thousand ships for him and his men and one thousand more for water and provisions'. When all was ready, he appointed Mansa Musa as his regent and then set off, 'never to return nor to give a sign of life'. It is a fascinating story, even if the size of the fleets has, surely, been exaggerated.

One can understand the intense curiosity that the Ocean must have generated, especially for inland people who had never seen the sea before. The Arabs were fearful of the Sea of Perpetual Gloom, as they called it, but, at a time when knowledge of the wider world was growing, it need occasion no surprise that one of the elite of Mali, in command of unlimited resources, should rise to the challenge, driven on by his curiosity.

By far the most remarkable of the medieval African explorers was Ibn Battuta (1304–69), who, for thirty years of his life, travelled the world, reaching as far as China. He eventually returned home to Morocco in 1354, where he dictated his adventures to Ibn Juzayy, choosing the somewhat immodest title *A Masterpiece to Those Who Contemplate the Wonders of Cities and Marvels of Travelling*, a work more usually known as *The Travels* (*The Rihla*). Ibn Battuta was born in Tangier and at the age of 21 decided to set off on the hajj:

8.20 The king of Mali, Mansa Musa, famed for his flamboyant journey across the desert to Cairo and on to Mecca, was featured on maps of the period. In this extract from the Catalan Atlas, drawn by the Majorcan cartographer Abraham Cresques (1325–87), the king, wearing a crown and with a sceptre in one hand, is shown seated on a throne, holding up a nugget of gold. He dominates Africa.

> I departed alone, without the companionship of fellow travellers, or in the assembly of a caravan, but swayed by an overmastering impulse within me ... to visit those illustrious sanctuaries. So I resolved to leave my loved ones behind, female and male, and abandon my home, as birds their nests.

The young lone explorer is a compelling image, but he was soon to join caravans, find congenial travelling companions, and acquire wives, the first only a few months after leaving home.

He journeyed along the coast of North Africa to Alexandria and then to Cairo. After exploring the region he set off down the Nile, intending to cross the Eastern Desert to

 289

the port of Aydhab and from there to take a ship across the Red Sea to Arabia, but the coastal region was in a state of rebellion so he was forced to return to Cairo and travel on to Damascus to find a caravan going south to the city of Medina, from where he made his way to Mecca.

His wanderlust had now taken hold and he was soon on the road again, in November 1326 travelling throughout Iraq and into Persia before returning the following September, ill with diarrhoea, to Mecca, where he stayed for two years until local riots made it advisable to move on. His journey took him south along the Red Sea to Somalia, and then down the coast of East Africa to Kilwa (pp. 269–71 above), returning to Arabia and Mecca in time for the hajj of 1332. For the next fifteen years he was involved in a remarkable progress, through Anatolia to the Black Sea, across the sea to the Pontic steppe, and then through Central Asia to India, making for Delhi, where he spent six years. After various adventures in southern India, including spending time in the Maldives and Sri Lanka, he made for Chittagong in Bangladesh. In 1345 he sailed south, through the Strait of Malacca and then north through the South China Sea to the Chinese port of Quanzhou in Fujian province, at the time under the control of the Mongols. After travelling in China as far as Beijing he returned to Quanzhou in 1346 and began his long journey home. He voyaged mostly by sea as far as the Persian Gulf, arriving in Damascus in 1348 to find the Black Death raging through the Near East and the Mediterranean, devastating populations. Even so, he made the hajj to Mecca again before returning to Tangier, via Sardinia, arriving home in 1349. But after a few days he was off again, this time to southern Spain to help avert a Christian attack on Gibraltar. His final journey, through West Africa (pp. 279–83 above), began in autumn 1351. Four years later he was finally back in Fez, there to organize his memories, proclaiming the world he had experienced.

Ibn Battuta's thirty years of travel is exhausting, even to read about in brief summary. He had faced debilitating illness, attacks by robbers, and the threat of the Black Death, yet by his own account he was able to live a comfortable life with servants, buying the occasional slave girl when the mood took him. He was able to sustain his lifestyle because he was a man of learning. He had studied the Maliki school of Sunni Muslim law, and his skills as a judge were welcomed wherever there were Maliki communities. Even more to the point, as he progressed, he acquired a wealth of esoteric knowledge. Scholars of this kind were highly respected by the leaders of the countries through whose territories they passed. A sultan or a khan would gain status by having such a learned man in his entourage, as if by retaining a man of knowledge he owned the knowledge. So valuable were they that it was often difficult for an honoured guest to escape and move on, as Ibn Battuta himself found on several occasions.

The three examples of the travellers chosen here, displaying extremes of wealth, curiosity, and persistence, reflect the increasingly mobile population among whom those who could afford it could make the pilgrimage to Mecca, or could follow up that nagging desire to explore what lay beyond the familiar. The innate compulsion to acquire knowledge drove many souls.

Stability and Intensification

Taking the long view of the period 1150–1400, it is clear that in the middle of the thirteenth century new political structures, robust enough to create a stability lasting centuries, came into being in three regions of northern Africa. In Egypt the Mamluk dynasty stamped their authority, remaining in power into the early sixteenth century; in western Sudan the empire of Mali rose to power to be replaced by an even stronger Songhai empire lasting to the late sixteenth century; and in the Maghrib, three small polities, locked together in an unstable equilibrium, kept control of the territory well into the sixteenth century.

The relative stability of these three state systems ensured that the trading networks which bound them flourished. In the east the Mamluks commanded the flow of goods between the Indian Ocean and the Near East and Mediterranean, while in the west the dual nodes of the empire of Mali and the Maghrib states, linked by the trans-Saharan caravans, controlled the movement of commodities and trade goods between West Africa and the Mediterranean. These two systems accounted for the bulk of the trade flow across Africa by 1400. Between them Kanem Borno and the Hausa city states may have functioned on a lesser scale, but the leaders of Kanem Borno attempted, through diplomacy, to establish themselves as international players. It was the stability of the commercial networks and the wide acceptance of the values of Islam that made travel comparatively safe and opened up the world to merchants and those with the curiosity to explore.

franca

itali

a

bordeq

as Illhas terceiras

seciria

tunis

as canareas

te,us claros

Mõ

seuta

Duraon

Africa

Ilhas do cabo vo de

Serra lioa

mina

Reino d
be nins

9

AFRICA AND THE WORLD
AD 1400–1600

ITHIN the space of three years, in the early fifteenth century, two quite separate events occurred signifying the sudden interest of the outside world in the affairs of Africa. The first, in 1415, was a Portuguese expedition to Morocco, led by King John I, and the establishment of a permanent Portuguese enclave at Ceuta on the North African coast. The second was the visit of a Chinese fleet under the command of Admiral Zheng He to several of the trading ports along the East African coast in 1417. King John's venture was the beginning of the Portuguese takeover of the West African gold trade and, within a century, was to see Portugal establishing trading bases around the coast of Africa and then moving on to dominate the Indian Ocean trade. The Ceuta raid was the first small step in what was eventually to become the European colonization of Africa. Zheng He's mission was to open diplomatic relations between the East African port cities and the Ming dynasty in China with the intention, perhaps, of close commercial engagement and even the prospect of territorial acquisition. In the event, the mood in China changed and the Ming emperors gave up all interest in the West, reverting to a policy of isolationism. It was left to the Portuguese to absorb the East African ports into their growing empire ninety years later.

Throughout this period much of North Africa remained largely unchanged. The Mamluks continued to command Egypt and the Red Sea and the trade which flowed between the Indian Ocean and the Mediterranean. And in the Maghrib the three dynasties, fractious as always, remained in power, except that, in Morocco in 1459, the

Marinids were replaced by the Wattasids, Zenata Berbers from a related family. The trans-Saharan trade networks continued to function much as before but with greater intensity, and in the western Sudan, as the empire of Mali failed, the Songhai became the dominant force. Their command of Gao and Timbuktu gave them control of the all-important river network, and from this central position on the east–west and north–south routes the elite were able to grow rich, manipulating the throughput of the gold and slaves so much in demand in the north. The Songhai empire, following Mali and Ghana before it, was the last of the empires of the western Sudan. With the development of Portuguese trading ports along the coast of West Africa, a completely new dynamic was created. Commodities from the forest zone could now be loaded onto ships rather than the backs of humans, donkeys, and camels.

The Chinese Arrive

In 1405 a remarkable fleet set out from China under the command of Admiral Zheng He (*c*.1371–1433) on the first of seven expeditions designed to spread Chinese influence throughout the Indian Ocean region. Zheng He was a Muslim from Yunnan province who, at the age of 10, entered the entourage of Yongle, who was to become the Ming emperor in 1403. By this time Zheng He had proved his worth. He was well educated, a successful military commander, and a trusted supporter of the emperor. So when Yongle decided to open up the 'western oceans' to Chinese diplomacy and trade, Zheng He, with his Muslim upbringing, was the obvious choice to be appointed admiral of the fleet.

The first expedition, which set sail in 1405, was large by any standards. It comprised 317 ships, including sixty large treasure junks. Each of the treasure junks was up to 120 metres long and fitted with nine masts supporting one or two bamboo sails per mast. The total complement numbered about 28,000 people. Besides being stocked with everything necessary to support and maintain the armada, the vessels carried gifts of silk, tea, painted scrolls, gold, silver, textiles, and porcelain. The size and magnificence of the fleet was designed to proclaim the might of China, the immediate aim being to build alliances with the powerful polities around the Indian Ocean and to attract ambassadors to return with them, bearing gifts, to make their supplication to the Ming emperor.

The first three expeditions, setting out in 1405, 1408, and 1409, followed the established trade routes around South-East Asia and reached as far as Sri Lanka. The fourth expedition, 1413–15, visited some of the same places but expanded further west to Calicut, in south-west India, before making for Hormuz on the Persian Gulf. From there they sailed down the coast of Arabia and into the Red Sea, landing at Jeddah,

9.1 When the Ming admiral Zheng He set out with his great fleet in 1405, he must have caused a sensation at every port he visited. One of his sixty large treasure junks, reputed to be up to 120 metres long with nine masts, is imagined on this Chinese postage stamp issued to commemorate the six-hundredth anniversary of the first voyage.

from where a party travelled on to Mecca. The fifth expedition, 1417–19, was even more adventurous. It began by returning ambassadors to their homes in various parts of South-East Asia and then made for Aden before sailing south to explore the East African coast, visiting various ports including Mogadishu, Brava, and Malindi. The sixth venture, 1421–3, returned ambassadors to the Persian Gulf, the Red Sea, and the east coast of Africa. Some vessels were then sent off to explore still further south, perhaps as far as Sofala. The fruits of these African journeys included lions, leopards, camels, ostriches, rhinos, zebras, and giraffes, together with gems, spices, medicines, and cotton. The final journey, made in 1431–3, visited places in South-East Asia and India, continuing on to Hormuz, Aden, and the Red Sea. It was on the way home, at Calicut in 1433, that Zheng He died.

The sudden appearance of the massive and opulently stocked Chinese fleet in the Red Sea and along the East African coast must have been an unwelcome shock to the Arab traders who habitually worked these shores, and the intruders were greeted with some hostility, but the Arabs need not have worried. Yongle had greatly overextended the resources of the Ming empire, and famine and floods were also taking a toll. Eventually, the anti-expansionist faction in the Ming court prevailed and extravagant maritime ventures became a thing of the past. Ming China turned in upon itself, adopting a determined isolationist stance that was to last for many centuries. For the

Mamluks in Egypt the threat had passed and the traditional trading systems could continue undisturbed, at least until the end of the century, when the Portuguese burst in with cannons blazing.

The Portuguese Imperative

The independent kingdom of Portugal was proclaimed in 1139 following the battle of Ourique, but it was not until 1249, when the Moors were finally driven from the Algarve, that the kingdom expanded to its present borders. Hostilities with neighbouring Castile continued, but finally came to an end in 1385 when the Portuguese emerged triumphant from the battle of Aljubarrota and John I, of the house of Aviz, became king. Portugal was a poor, underpopulated country on the fringe of Europe. Culturally rather backward, its elite still clung to the ideals of the past chivalric age. But a sense of adventure, combined with a deep-seated crusading spirit, created an energy driving them on to explore, to convert, and to colonize. With their last enemy on the Iberian peninsula beaten, this energy had to be channelled. The location of the country, clinging to the Atlantic fringe, meant, inevitably, that it was the sea that offered the opportunity.

The driving force in the early years was the infante Dom Henrique (1394–1460), the third surviving son of John I. Dom Henrique, or Henry the Navigator as he became known, is credited with encouraging the maritime exploration of West Africa. Stories that he set up a school of navigation on the Sagres peninsula may well have been far-fetched or exaggerated, and the sobriquet 'the Navigator' was not assigned to him until the nineteenth century, but, that said, there can be little doubt that, from the Algarve, the province of which he was governor, he encouraged the enthusiasm for exploration of the Atlantic coast and provided the patronage needed to make it a reality. The motives for such expeditions were mixed. Commercial imperatives were never far from the surface, and locating the source of the gold brought in quantity from the south by the caravans crossing the Sahara to the Maghrib was a prime concern. But religion also played an important part. The aspiration of converting non-believers to the Christian faith provided a driving force for some, and a convenient justification for others. Henry had been appointed Grand Master of the Military Order of Christ, a successor organization to the Knights Templar, at the age of 26 and took his duties, to save the heathen, seriously. That the Order of Christ was wealthy and well able to sponsor expeditions gave welcome reassurance to the ships' captains who were required to face the challenge of the oceans. But the prime reason for Henry's enthusiasm for exploration, so his biographer assures us, was his desire to fulfil the predictions of his horoscope. Henry, then, was a driven man. What made him effective was that the Portuguese elite, at last freed from internal warfare, now had the energies to invest in overseas adventures.

Portugal's expansion began in 1415 with the capture of the Moroccan port of Ceuta, which, until then, had served as the terminal for the gold caravans from the south. The expedition was led by King John I, supported by his four sons, for whom it was an opportunity to win honours. A large force of 45,000 men, transported in two hundred ships, caught the defenders by surprise and the town was quickly taken. The 21-year-old Dom Henrique, who fought well in the brief event, was rewarded with the governorship of the Algarve, while his older brother Duarte was put in charge of the new colony. The Moors, who had previously used Ceuta, responded by switching their trading activities to Tangier, leaving Ceuta to become a backwater of little or no commercial value. The situation remained for a while, while the exploration of the Atlantic islands and the African coast got under way, but eventually Dom Henrique and his brother Ferdinand persuaded Duarte, now king, that they should capture Tangier. A force, dispatched in 1437 under Dom Henrique's command, laid siege to the town but was quickly encircled by the Marinid army sent to relieve the siege. The debacle ended only when the Portuguese agreed to terms. The army would be allowed to leave on condition that Ceuta was handed back to the Marinids. Ferdinand was to stay behind as a hostage to ensure that the terms were honoured. In the event, once the Portuguese force was safely on its way home, it became clear that they had no intention of quitting Ceuta. As a consequence, Ferdinand remained a captive and died six years later. It was hardly a creditable outcome, and further attempts to take Tangier in 1458 and 1463 met with an equal lack of success. The town was finally captured in 1471.

In the twenty years following the capture of Ceuta, Dom Henrique had concentrated his interests on the Atlantic islands and the Atlantic coast of Africa down to Cape Bojador. The Canary Islands were particularly desirable, but the Catalans had already begun their conquest in 1402 and considered the islands to be within their sphere of interest. Various Portuguese interventions were made, but ownership was not finally settled until 1479 when the treaty of Alcáçovas assigned the whole island group to Castile. Meanwhile, the Portuguese were becoming more adventurous, exploring the Atlantic and discovering unoccupied island groups. Madeira and Porto Santo were first sighted in 1419 but were not considered to be of much interest. The Azores were known as early as 1375, since islands in this approximate position appeared on the Catalan Atlas of that date, but it was not until 1427 that one of Dom Henrique's captains rediscovered them. Settlement of both island groups began in earnest in 1439 when Dom Henrique began to send out organized bands of colonists financed by investors from Italy and the Low Countries. Soon the islands were making a significant contribution to the European economy, with Madeira exporting sugar and the Azores, grain. Later

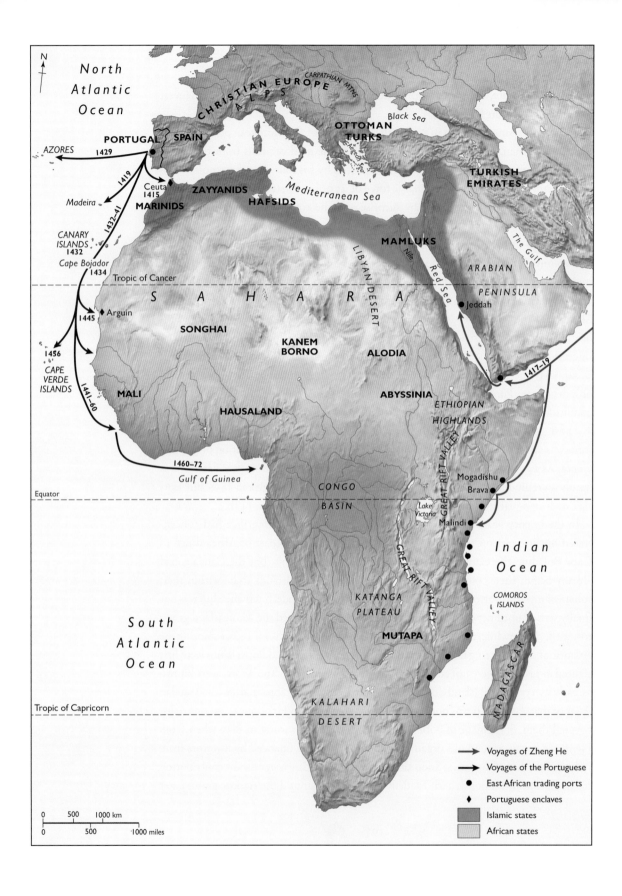

N

*North
Atlantic
Ocean*

CHRISTIAN EUROPE

CARPATHIAN MTNS

A L P S

Black Sea

**OTTOMAN
TURKS**

Aegean Sea

PORTUGAL **SPAIN**

AZORES   1429

1419

Mediterranean Sea

**TURKISH
EMIRATES**

Ceuta
1415
MARINIDS

ZAYYANIDS

HAFSIDS

Madeira

1432-41

The Gulf

MAMLUKS

Nile

ARABIAN

*CANARY
ISLANDS*
1432

Cape Bojador
1434

Tropic of Cancer

S   A   H   A   R   A

*LIBYAN
DESERT*

Red Sea

PENINSULA

Jeddah

1445   ◆ *Arguin*

SONGHAI

**KANEM
BORNO**

ALODIA

1456

*CAPE
VERDE
ISLANDS*

1441-60

MALI

HAUSALAND

ABYSSINIA

ETHIOPIAN

HIGHLANDS

1417-19

1460-72

Gulf of Guinea

GREAT RIFT VALLEY

Mogadishu
Brava

Equator

CONGO

BASIN

*Lake
Victoria*

Malindi

*Indian
Ocean*

GREAT RIFT VALLEY

*KATANGA
PLATEAU*

*COMOROS
ISLANDS*

*South
Atlantic
Ocean*

MUTAPA

MADAGASCAR

KALAHARI

Tropic of Capricorn

DESERT

0   500   1000 km

0   500   1000 miles

→ Voyages of Zheng He

→ Voyages of the Portuguese

● East African trading ports

◆ Portuguese enclaves

■ Islamic states

▨ African states

9.2 (*Opposite*) Maritime visitors to Africa from Portugal and China, 1415–72. While the Chinese soon lost interest, the Portuguese persisted.

the Azores became a vital port of call for vessels returning from America and the Indian Ocean, using the westerlies to bring them safely to European shores.

The discovery of the islands came about as part of a systematic exploration of the West African coast begun about 1421. The sheer excitement of discovery, and the comfortable reassurance that one was doing God's will, played an important part, but the driving force was to find ports where gold carried by the desert caravans across the Sahara could be intercepted before reaching the Maghrib. This was one of the reasons why control of the Canary Islands first featured large, but as coastal exploration thrust further south, closer to the supposed goldfields, the islands became less significant. Not far south of the latitude of the Canaries was the infamous promontory known as Cape Non, beyond which, it was believed, the heat would burn a white man to death. South by another 400 kilometres was Cape Bojador, a treacherous place where the shallows stretched far out to sea and the currents ran fast. It took all of Dom Henrique's powers of persuasion to encourage his ships' captains not to turn back. Eventually, in 1434, one brave soul, Gil Eannes, rounded Bojador to find calmer seas beyond.

Into the Unknown

After their failure to take Tangier in 1437, the Portuguese began to thrust south again, spurred on by the enthusiasm of Dom Henrique's second brother, Dom Pedro, who had recently become regent. Rapid progress was made. In 1442 Nuno Tristão sighted the great landmass of Cap Blanc, protecting an extensive bay. Within the bay, shielded from the full force of the Atlantic by recurving headlands, lay the island of Arguin. Realizing the potential of the island, Tristão returned in 1445 to establish a trading post there. By this time, he had reached as far south as the river Senegal. In the same year another captain, Dinís Dias, sailed past Cape Verde and landed on Palma Island (Gorée), off the Senegal coast. By 1446 Nuno Tristão, now on his fourth voyage, had pushed still further south, probably to the mouth of the Gambia, where, according to one story, his launch was ambushed by natives in canoes and he and most of his men were killed. After another expedition, sent out the following year, also sustained considerable casualties, Dom Henrique decided to halt operations.

Something of the ethos of these pioneer expeditions can be appreciated by the way in which the indigenous population were treated: they were regarded simply as commodities. On his first voyage, Tristão, learning of the location of a Sanhaja fishing village, immediately attacked it, taking ten prisoners to sell as slaves. On his next

9.3 The island of Arguin, on the coast of Mauritania, was well protected from the force of the Atlantic by Cap Blanc and Cap d'Arguin. The first Portuguese landing took place in 1442.

voyage, a raid on another Sanhaja village secured him fourteen slaves. The third voyage yielded twenty-one. News of his lucrative activities soon spread, and between 1446 and 1456 dozens of ships, armed with licences to trade in slaves issued by Dom Henrique, descended on the Bay of Arguin to decimate the local population. Arguin Island became the first European slave-trading colony in Africa.

Ten years later Dom Henrique began sponsoring new expeditions of discovery. In 1455 he selected a young Venetian merchant venturer, Alvise Cadamosto, to spearhead the advance, providing him with a caravel and the necessary crew and provisions, on the understanding that he, Dom Henrique, would receive half the spoils. Travelling south via Madeira, the Canaries, and Arguin Island, Cadamosto made for the river Senegal and then south again to Mboro, where a base had already been established by the Portuguese to trade with the native Wolof peoples. He carried with him, as trade goods, woollen cloth and Spanish horses, which were much in demand. For a single

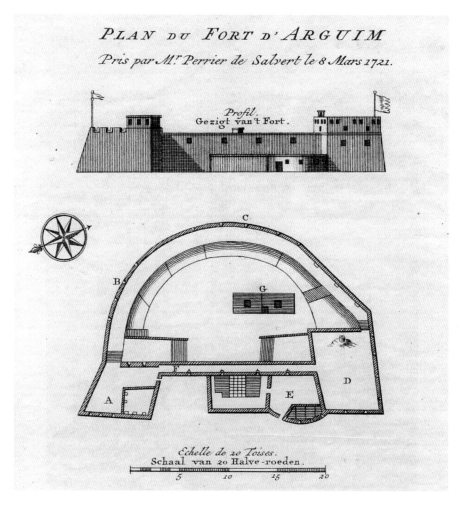

9.4 Arguin Island was established as a trading post by the Portuguese in 1445 and was held by Portugal as a fortified colony until it was taken by the Dutch in 1633. The illustration shows the fort as it was in 1721.

horse he expected to receive between nine and fourteen black slaves. His negotiations with the natives were friendly and he spent a month as a guest of a local king before sailing on, around Cape Verde, to the mouth of the Gambia. Here he was confronted by hostile Mandinka, who mounted massed canoe attacks. It was now late in the season so he decided to return to Portugal to share the profits with his sponsor, Dom Henrique.

Cadamosto has left a detailed account of the coast and the people he encountered. Visiting Arguin Island, he found the trading colony well organized and under strict regulations laid down by Dom Henrique.

9.5 The Portuguese success in navigating the Atlantic and Indian oceans was due in part to the development of the caravel with its stern-mounted rudder and lateen-rigged sails, which enabled the vessels to sail close to the wind. The painting is by Rafael Monleón, 1885.

No person must enter the Gulf or trade with the Arabs, except those who are licensed according to the ordinance, and have habitation and factors on the island, and have been accustomed to transact business with the Arabs on that coast. The items of merchandise chiefly provided for trade are woollen cloth and linen, silver trinkets, *aldtizeli* or frocks, and cloaks, and other things, above all wheat: and the Arabs give in return negro slaves and gold. A castle has been built on the isle of Arguin, by order of the prince, to protect this trade, on account of which caravels or ships arrive there every year from Portugal.

(*Original Journals of the Voyages of Cada Mosto and Pedro de Cintra to the Coast of Africa*, chapter 4)

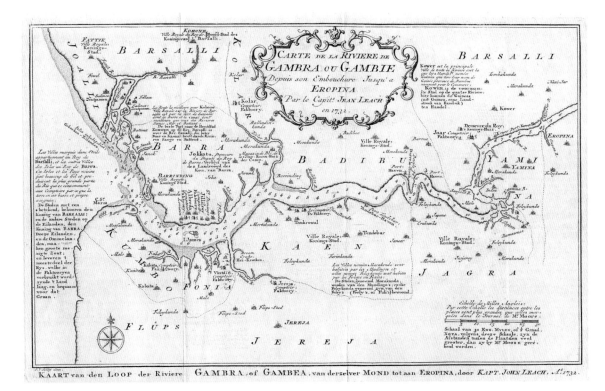

9.6 The two West African rivers the Senegal and the Gambia provided the Portuguese with routes to the African interior. It was probably while exploring the Gambia that Nuno Tristão and his crew were ambushed by the local tribesmen. This map of the Gambia was drawn by Jacques Nicolas Bellin in 1732, on information supplied by Captain John Leach.

It was only ten years earlier that the first Portuguese ships had terrorized the local Sanhaja Berbers and carried them off as slaves.

Cadamosto made a second voyage south, in 1456, this time with three ships. The intention was to make for the river Gambia, but rounding Cape Verde in a storm they were driven out into the Atlantic, fortuitously discovering the uninhabited Cape Verde islands. Having explored them and concluded they were of little interest, they made for the Gambia. This time they met no aggression and were able to sail 90 kilometres up-river to the court of the Mandinka king, Battimansa, where they found there to be little gold available. Moving on again they explored the coasts and rivers of Guinea-Bissau and the Bijagós Islands before turning back to Portugal. Further expeditions by Pedro da Cintra sometime about 1462 probed the coast of Sierra Leone and reached as far as Nigeria, but, with the death of Dom Henrique in 1460, enthusiasm for exploration abated. The trading colony on Arguin Island and the friendly relations enjoyed with the native elites controlling the rivers Senegal and Gambia were sufficient to satisfy the commercial aspirations of the Portuguese merchants. Attention now turned to the need to establish firmer control of the Strait of Gibraltar. The Moroccan town of Ksar es-Seghir had been taken in 1458, and Tangier and Arzila were added in 1471, giving Portugal a much stronger hold on the coast of the western Maghrib.

Exploring the Gulf of Guinea

Opening up trade routes along the African coast was an expensive business and it was a matter of concern that other nationalities, not least the Castilians, were showing an interest in the commercial possibilities. In 1454 and 1456 Dom Henrique managed the diplomatic coup of persuading the pope to issue bulls recognizing Portugal's monopoly of the entire coastline 'extending from Cape Bojador and Cape Non through all Guinea and passing beyond the southern parts'. Anyone breaking the monopoly would be excommunicated. It must have given Dom Henrique and his supporters a degree of assurance and seems to have been honoured, at least for a while.

Reluctance to invest in the exploration of West Africa's southern coast after Dom Henrique's death was due partly to the uncongenial nature of the coastline with its difficult winds and currents, vast marshy deltas, and mangrove swamps, and partly to the unwillingness of sailors to enter these southern latitudes where the North Star was no longer visible. But the potential for discovering new markets remained, and in 1469 the new king, Alfonso V, granted Fernão Gomes, a Portuguese merchant, the monopoly to trade in the Gulf of Guinea for a five-year period in return for an annual rent and on the understanding that his ships explored 100 leagues of new coast every year. Gomes chose his captains well. By the end of the contract he had become a wealthy man and nearly 3,200 kilometres of coast had been explored, including the coasts of present-day Ghana, Nigeria, and Cameroon as far as Cape Santa Catarina in Gabon. Among his discoveries was the port which became known as Elmina, where gold from the Akan goldfields was available in plenty. Other parts of the coast were rich in ivory, slaves, and malagueta pepper.

Gomes did not renew his lease in 1475. One reason was that the War of the Castilian Succession which had broken out between Portugal and the Castilians had begun to interfere with Portugal's maritime trade after Isabella of Castile had authorized her subjects to trade with Africa in defiance of the original papal bulls. Castilian privateers

9.7 (*Opposite*) By 1563, when the Portuguese cartographer Lázaro Luis published this nautical chart, the coast of West Africa was becoming well known. The building shown on the African mainland is the fort of São Jorge at Elmina.

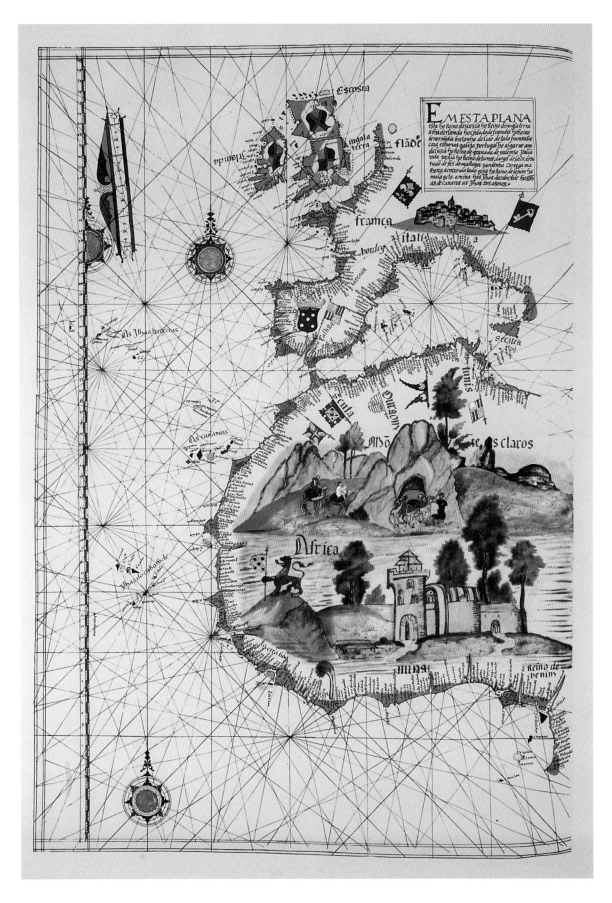

9.8 The fort of São Jorge, modified by the Dutch after they took it over in 1637, still watches over the port of Elmina.

rushed to the Guinea coast and brutal confrontations ensued. The situation remained tense until 1479, when the treaty of Alcáçovas confirmed Portugal's monopoly of the Guinea trade together with ownership of Madeira, the Azores, and the Cape Verde islands.

Central to the success of the Guinea trade was the port of Elmina, opened up by Gomes in 1471. It became a prize to be fought over during the War of Succession, and in 1478 a Castilian force of thirty-five caravels confronted the Portuguese fleet nearby. The Portuguese won, but the incident had exposed the vulnerability of Elmina and the need to consolidate the foothold. In 1482, after negotiation with the local chiefs, the fort of São Jorge da Mina was built using stone shipped out from Portugal. It was to be manned by sixty soldiers and soon became the centre of a thriving community. Gold was the most important export, together with malagueta pepper, with lesser quantities of other local products—ivory, gum, wax, and palm oil—passing through the port. But from the beginning the Portuguese refused to deal in locally procured slaves for fear that slave wars would disrupt the flow of gold. This did not prevent them from acquiring slaves captured in Benin and exported from the Portuguese factory of Gato on the river Benin, though numbers were never great, reaching about five hundred a year by the end of the century. The principal imports were cloth, much of it obtained in Morocco, together with copper, iron, and hardware of various kinds from Europe. The presence of local trading factories was also a stimulus for local trade between the different West African communities with access to the coast. Benin, in addition to supplying slaves, was also a source of cloth and glass beads, which the merchants tran-shipped along the coast to the Gold Coast, where such commodities were much in demand.

The Kingdoms of the Forest Zone

The forest zone extends in a belt some 400 kilometres wide between the forest savan-nah in the north and the coast of the Bay of Guinea, lined with mangrove swamps. Although domesticated animals do not thrive because of diseases, especially sleeping sickness spread by the tsetse fly, the forest is a rich environment, producing an abun-dance of crops including millet, yams, and palm oil, allowing settled communities to develop. As other products of the region, such as gold, ivory, and slaves, began to be demanded by traders from the Sahel, so a series of small states emerged. Some had ori-gins as early as the eleventh century, but by the fourteenth century there were many with thriving cities. One of the largest was Begho, near the Black Volta river, sited just north of the forest margin. Excavations show that the town was divided into separate quarters for local artisans and foreign merchants. Its great attraction to the traders was the gold coming from the Akan goldfield to the south, but local craftsmen were work-ing iron, casting brass, and making and dyeing cloth, all commodities that could be dis-tributed through the trade networks.

Further east, in what is now Nigeria, was the city of Ife, which grew to considera-ble proportions in the fourteenth and fifteenth centuries from much earlier origins. It, too, is located on the interface between the forest and the savannah, controlling trade with the forest zone west of the Niger delta. Ife is known, in Yoruba mythology, as the place where the god Oduduwa separated the earth from the water and created all liv-ing things. It is famous now for the superb quality of the highly realistic figures made by its craftspeople in terracotta and brass. The city spread over several square kilometres and was enclosed by a series of walls reflecting its growth from the eleventh to the late fifteenth century, when it was abandoned. The reason for its demise is unknown but it may have been related to changes consequent on the arrival of the Portuguese on the coast, which encouraged the rise of Benin some 200 kilometres to the south-east. Benin was enclosed by a massive bank and ditch with a total circumference of 11.6 kilometres

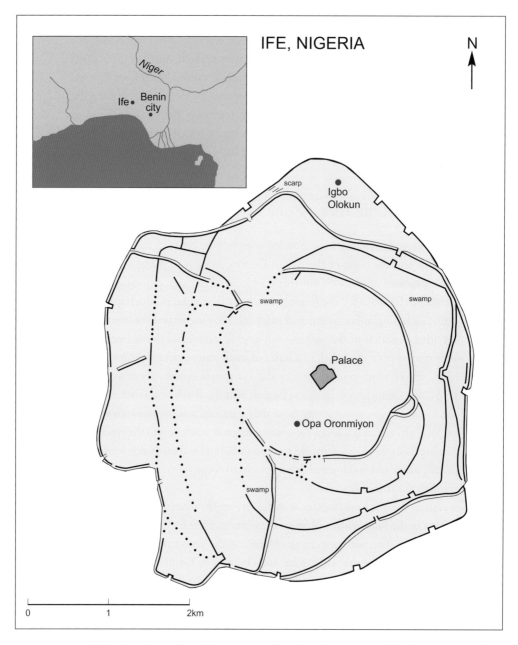

9.9 In Yoruba tradition, Ife, in Nigeria, is the place where the supreme god, Olodumare, ordered the creation of the world. The site was occupied from *c.*AD 800 and developed into a walled city between the twelfth and fifteenth centuries. The multiple defensive enclosures are largely undated, and the later phases may be comparatively recent. The Opa Oronmiyon is a stone pillar of early date. At Igbo Olokun excavations exposed an early glass-bead-making site.

and is surrounded by a vast network of enclosures. Precise dating is not available but there are suggestions that the system was already well developed by the twelfth century. Benin city was certainly occupied by the thirteenth century and reached its peak in the fifteenth century when fine bronze castings, owing much to the style of those found in earlier contexts at Ife, were being manufactured. From the early sixteenth century, Benin was in direct contact with the Portuguese merchants.

The city states of the forest zone had long been integrated with the trans-Saharan trading networks, well before the arrival of Europeans, but with the opening up of the maritime routes by the Portuguese around 1470, and the foundation of the factory at Elmina in 1471, a completely new dynamic was introduced. It was now possible for the forest polities to trade their goods directly with the agents of the consumers rather than through the series of middlemen needed to transport them north across the desert. Contact with the Portuguese traders also meant that they could have a direct influence on the range of goods offered to them in exchange. Another advantage, as has been mentioned, is that there now developed a cabotage trade carrying local products between ports along the coast. The benefits of all this to the forest communities were considerable.

9.10 This nearly life-size head from Ife was cast by the lost-wax method in heavily leaded zinc brass in the fourteenth or fifteenth century. The head, originally wearing an elaborate headdress, was found with sixteen others. Its striking naturalistic style is characteristic of the Ife workshops producing these masterpieces.

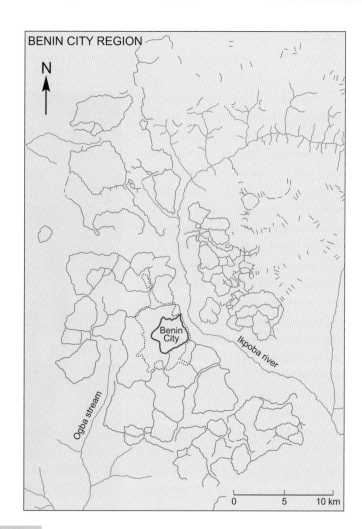

BENIN CITY REGION

N

Benin
City

Ogba stream

Ikpoba river

0   5   10 km

9.11 (*Above*) The city of Benin, in southern Nigeria, was in occupation by the thirteenth century and was enclosed by a massive bank and ditch, with a circumference of 11.6 kilometres, probably by the mid fifteenth century, before the appearance of Europeans. The city was surrounded by an extensive network of interlocking enclosures.

9.12 (*Left*) Benin is famous for its heads, plaques, and animals cast in copper alloy. They were manufactured in the court of the *oba* (king) from the sixteenth century. The illustrated example is the head of an *oba* dated to 1525–75.

9.13 (*Opposite*) The Portuguese continued their progress along the African coast, eventually rounding the Cape of Good Hope in 1488. After a pause, during which the complexities of Atlantic sailing were explored, Vasco da Gama made his epic voyage into the Indian Ocean in 1498, visiting some of the trading ports along the East African coast.

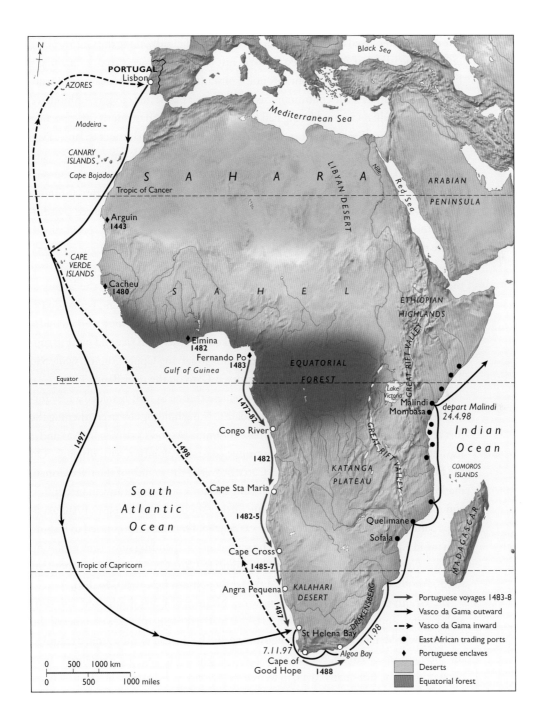

N

PORTUGAL
Lisbon

AZORES

Madeira

CANARY
ISLANDS

Cape Bojador

Black Sea

Mediterranean Sea

S A H A R A

LIBYAN DESERT

Nile

Red Sea

ARABIAN
PENINSULA

Tropic of Cancer

Arguin
1443

CAPE
VERDE
ISLANDS

Cacheu
1480

S A H E L

ETHIOPIAN
HIGHLANDS

Elmina
1482
Fernando Po
1483

Gulf of Guinea

EQUATORIAL

FOREST

Lake
Victoria

GREAT RIFT VALLEY

Equator

1497

1498

1472-82

Congo River

1482

Cape Sta Maria

1482-5

South
Atlantic
Ocean

KATANGA
PLATEAU

GREAT RIFT VALLEY

Malindi
Mombasa

depart Malindi
24.4.98

Indian
Ocean

COMOROS
ISLANDS

Quelimane

Sofala

MADAGASCAR

Cape Cross

1485-7

Tropic of Capricorn

Angra Pequena

KALAHARI
DESERT

1487

DRAKENSBERG

1.1.98

St Helena Bay

7.11.97
Cape of
Good Hope

Algoa Bay

1488

Portuguese voyages 1483-8
Vasco da Gama outward
Vasco da Gama inward
● East African trading ports
♦ Portuguese enclaves
   Deserts
   Equatorial forest

0   500   1000 km
0   500   1000 miles

 311

Consolidation and Forward Again

The captains employed by Fernão Gomes had advanced rapidly along the Guinea coast, reaching the island of Fernando Po (Bioko), just off the north west coast of mainland Equatorial Guinea, in 1472. From this point onwards the coast of Africa turned stubbornly south rather than continuing eastwards, as was expected, to give unhindered access to the Indian Ocean. Having had his ships follow the coast south for some 600 kilometres to Cape Santa Catarina, Gomes decided to allow his contract to lapse. Even if it was possible to get to the Indian Ocean, there were no quick returns to be made. Anyway, the Guinea coast still offered huge opportunities. So it was that the onward push was halted while the gains were consolidated. The building of the fort at Elmina in 1482 was a clear statement of intent, and it was soon to be supplemented by additional forts at Axim, Shama, and Accra along the Ghana coast designed specifically to ensure that the local communities sold their gold only to accredited Portuguese traders.

A major step in the consolidation of the Portuguese commercial infrastructure was the establishment of colonies on offshore islands, the first at Santiago, the largest of the Cape Verde islands, in 1462, and later on the islands of São Tomé and Fernando Po, at the eastern end of the Gulf of Guinea, in 1493 and 1494. The colonies, worked under slave labour, produced sugar for the export market, together with rice and meat to supply the residents of the coastal factory forts, Santiago serving Upper Guinea, while São Tomé served the gulf, providing for the factory at Gato on the river Benin.

The accession of King John II to the Portuguese throne in 1481 heralded a new forward push. His first concern was to consolidate existing holdings by strengthening the fort at Arguin and building the fortified base at Elmina. As soon as this work was under way, he commissioned Diogo Cão to continue coastal exploration with dispatch. On the first voyage, which set out in 1482, Cão discovered the mouth of the river Congo, marking it with a stone pillar (*padrão*) bearing the arms of Portugal and an inscription commemorating the event, before pushing further south along the coast of Angola to Cape Santa Maria, where another *padrão* was erected. From here he returned to Lisbon, arriving in April 1484. Later in the year he set out again, spending some time exploring the river Congo before making another leap south to Cape Cross in Namibia, about 21° south. Another *padrão* commemorated the landing. It was here that Cão died.

The race to the Indian Ocean was now on. Hearing of Cão's death, John immediately commissioned a new expedition to be led by Bartholomeu Dias, a member of the royal household. Dias departed in August 1487 and by the end of the year had rounded the southern tip of Africa, too far out to sea to sight land, reaching Kwaaihoek, near the mouth of the Boesmans River, in March 1488. Finding his crew reluctant to go on, he turned back, this time sighting the southernmost cape, which he called the Cape of

Storms (Cabo das Tormentas). It was aptly named. Twelve years later, returning after a voyage to the Indian Ocean, the convoy of four ships with which he was travelling was lost at sea in a great storm on 29 May 1500. That King John had by then renamed the promontory the Cape of Good Hope (Cabo da Boa Esperança) is not without a certain irony.

The way to the Indian Ocean was now open, but the long, arduous journey along the west coast of Africa was expensive and daunting. Enthusiasm seems to have faltered, and nothing is heard of further expeditions in the decade between 1488 and 1497. This does not, however, mean that ships were inactive, but simply that such voyages as there were, exploring the winds and currents in the Atlantic, were kept secret. This was a tense time, with Spain and Portugal vying with each other for maritime supremacy. Matters came to a head in 1493 when Christopher Columbus, returning from the Caribbean, where he had made land the previous year, sailed into Lisbon harbour announcing that he had found a way to the East by sailing west across the Atlantic. That Columbus had been sponsored by the king of Spain increased the rivalry between the two states. The immediate result was frantic diplomatic activity, which culminated in the signing of the treaty of Tordesillas in June 1494, by which it was agreed that a meridian 370 leagues west of the Cape Verde islands marked the line of divide between the interests of the two countries. To the west of the line Spain could claim ownership of all the new territories discovered, while to the east all was the preserve of Portugal. There was now a renewed impetus for Portugal to advance into the Indian Ocean and beyond. Thus, in July 1497 Vasco da Gama, a Portuguese nobleman tasked with leading a new expedition, set sail from Lisbon.

The remarkable thing about da Gama's expedition was that, instead of following the African coast, he made straight for the Cape Verde islands and then sailed in a great loop, on a south-west course, out into the Atlantic before swinging round to the southeast, steering towards Africa with the intention of passing south of the Cape of Good Hope. A slight miscalculation meant that he hit land at St Helena Bay, too far north, and had to sail south along the coast to round the cape. The voyage from the Cape Verde islands had taken three months—an astonishing time to be at sea—but this was twice as fast as it would have been had he followed the coast. One can only suppose that, in the decade of apparent inactivity, ships' captains had been actively researching the winds and currents of the Atlantic to chart the ideal passage.

The rest of the story can be briefly told. Once past the Cape, da Gama sailed up the east coast of Africa, exploring the ports frequented by Muslim traders. The first he put into was Quelimane, having missed Sofala, further south. The intrusion of this foreigner, with his heavily armed ships, was received with some hostility by the local communities, particularly at Mombasa, but the inhabitants of nearby Malindi were more

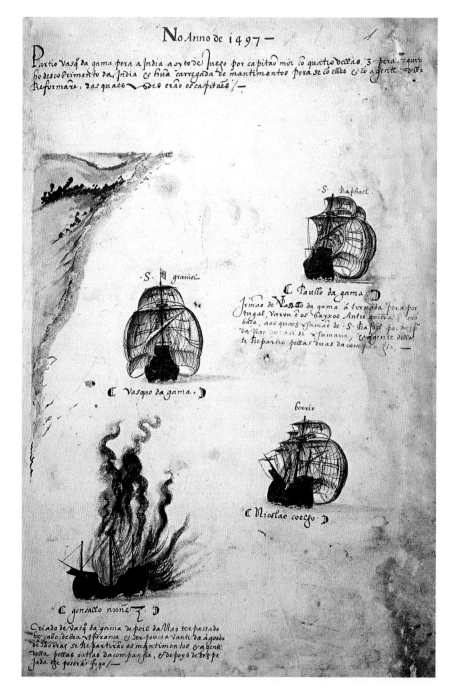

9.14 The *Memória das Armadas* of 1568 illustrates the four vessels which accompanied Vasco da Gama into the Indian Ocean.

friendly and here he was able to hire an experienced Gujarati navigator to guide them safely across the Indian Ocean to Calicut on the west coast of India, where he landed in May 1498. Having established relations with the local elite, and acquired a small cargo of cinnamon and pepper, he set sail for home, arriving in September 1499: only half his original ship's company were still alive. The magnitude of his achievement and its anticipated impact on Portugal's economy was celebrated by the construction of the monumental church and monastery of Jerónimos at Belém, which graces the river approach to Lisbon. It was partly funded by gold reluctantly donated by the sultan of Kilwa, who in 1502 found himself confronted by da Gama's fleet of fourteen warships.

The Portuguese went on to establish a maritime empire in the Indian Ocean by maintaining mastery of the sea and by taking hold of strategic places commanding

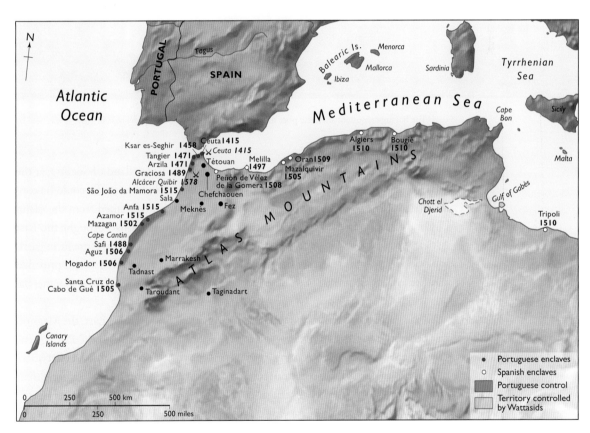

9.15 The Portuguese capture of Ceuta in 1415 inspired Portugal, and later Spain, to establish commercial enclaves along the Atlantic and Mediterranean coasts of the Maghrib. By agreement Portugal focused on the Atlantic while Spain was left with the Mediterranean, extending as far east as Tripoli.

9.16 The Portuguese established the port town of Mazagan on the Moroccan coast in 1502. It was held by Portugal until 1769.

the major routes. When attempts to capture Aden failed, the island of Socotra, at the eastern end of the Gulf of Aden, was taken, from where Red Sea traffic could be controlled. Likewise, oversight of the Persian Gulf trade was maintained from the island of Ormuz, captured in 1515. By this time gunboat diplomacy had brought the East African ports under Portuguese domination with a minimum of investment in garrison troops. The capture of the island of Goa on the west coast of India in 1510 provided another vital link in the chain by which Portugal gathered to itself the commercial opportunities of the Indian Ocean.

While Portuguese admirals were consolidating their power in the East, the Maghrib was becoming a source of renewed interest for both the Spanish and the Portuguese. One by one, coastal towns serving as terminals for the trans-Saharan trade networks were appropriated. The two countries had signed an agreement in 1496 defining their separate spheres of interest. Portugal concentrated on the Atlantic coast, capturing Mazagan in 1502, Agadir in 1505, and Mogador in 1506, adding them to Tangier and Ceuta, which they already held. Meanwhile, in the Mediterranean, Spain took Melilla in 1497, Mazalquivir in 1505, Peñón de Vélez de la Gomera in 1508, Oran in 1509, and Algiers, Bougie (Bejaïa), and Tripoli in 1510. The ease of the land grab was a reflection of the increasing weakness of the Berber states.

The opening up of the whole of the African coast to the predatory Europeans in the fifteenth and early sixteenth centuries was facilitated by a rapid advance in shipbuilding technology and navigation. It marked the beginning of a new political reality.

The Empire of Songhai

The western Sudan in the fifteenth century saw the demise of the empire of Mali and the rise of the Songhai, who were to rule over an even greater territory, creating one of Africa's largest states. The Songhai, a Nilo-Saharan-speaking people, had established their capital at Gao on the river Niger at least by the eleventh century, probably earlier. The commercial importance of Gao was recognized by the leaders of Mali who had conquered the city at the end of the thirteenth century and held it for a hundred years until a rebellion in 1395 returned it to independence. Thereafter the Songhai began to increase in power, building their strength around their cavalry and the fleet of river-craft manned by Sorko fisherman. The earliest territorial advances they made were in Méma in the 1460s, but it was the famous king Sonni Ali (r. 1464–92) who was credited with the foundation of the Songhai empire. The seventeenth-century Timbuktu chronicle *Tarikh al-Sudan*, completed by the scholar Abd al-Sa'di, sums up his career. He reigned 'for twenty-eight years, waged thirty-two wars, of which he won every one, always the conqueror, never the conquered'.

Soon after coming to power, Sonni Ali began a campaign of determined territorial expansion characterized by the deployment of overbearing force and speed. Since he relied heavily on his river-based navy, most of his successes were won along the Niger waterways. In 1469 he drove the Tuareg from Timbuktu. By this time the town had a population of a hundred thousand and not only was a great emporium but was well on the way to becoming a major centre of learning. In 1471 Sonni Ali was attacking the territory of the Mossi tribes south of the Niger Bend, and two years later he began what became a protracted siege of Djenné, which was to last for several years. All this time the Mossi were a persistent threat, raiding the middle Niger, invading Macina, and pushing north to Walata, the caravan city on the edge of the desert. But in 1483 they were decisively beaten by Sonni Ali and driven back. Much of his effort was spent in taking over territories which had been appropriated by Mali and adding them to the new empire. He made two attempts at the core of the Mali kingdom but found the frontiers along the rivers Niger and Bani too heavily fortified to allow much headway to be made.

The second stage of the expansion of the Songhai empire was masterminded by Askiya Muhammad I (r. 1493–1528), an army commander who had usurped power from Sonni Ali's son. Building a much stronger, professional army, with well-ordered

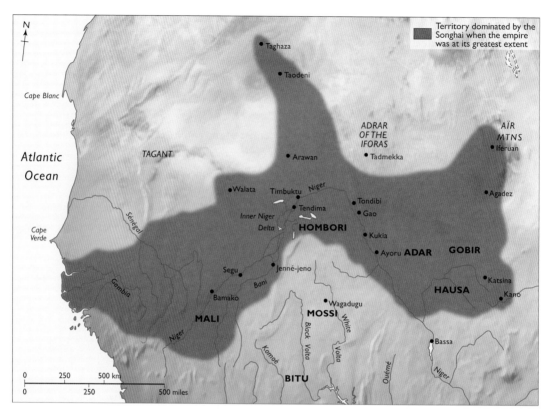

9.17 The rebellion of the Songhai against the empire of Mali in 1395 freed the city of Gao and marked the beginning of the rise of the Songhai as a powerful state. At its greatest extent the empire of Songhai incorporated a huge swath of territory from the Atlantic to the boundaries of the empire of Kanem Borno in the central Sahel.

units of infantry and cavalry, he was able to extend his reach well beyond the Niger valley, west into Senegal, north into the desert as far as the commercially important town of Taghaza, and west along the Sahel to Hausaland, where he attacked the city states of Gobir, Katsina, and Zaria, while forcing the main city, Kano, to pay a massive tribute. In addition to his military prowess, Askiya Muhammad was an inspired administrator who created a centralized government with ministers to oversee all aspects of the empire's economy, while the country was divided into provinces under regional governors. The senior positions were held by members of his family and by other noble families, but below them was an extensive civil service of highly educated individuals, many of whom were slaves.

Unlike Sonni Ali, who was content to play to the pagan beliefs of his subjects while acknowledging Islam when dealing with the merchants settled in the towns, Askiya

Muhammad was a faithful Muslim and established Islam as the official religion of the nobility. His faith became more fervent after his pilgrimage to Mecca in 1496–7, from which he returned believing himself to be caliph with the authority of God to rule. For some, his regime was too strict. Discontent in the court grew, until 1528, when he was deposed by his son and banished to a mosquito-ridden island in the river while his sons fought each other for control of the state. Eventually, in 1537, old, blind, and embittered, he was recalled to Gao, but died the following year. The dynastic squabbles continued for a while, but during the long reign of Askiya Dawud (r. 1549–82) the Songhai state experienced a period of peace and prosperity. It was the calm before the final storm (pp. 329–32 below).

While the empire of Songhai flourished and extended its boundaries, the Malinke core of the old empire of Mali, between the upper Niger and the coast of Gambia, continued to maintain a degree of independent cohesion. When Cadamosto visited the West African coast in 1455–6, he learnt much of the kingdom of Mali, and of the trade in salt coming from the desert to be exchanged for gold from the Bambuk and Bure goldfields. Later, in 1512, when the geographer and diplomat Leo Africanus visited the western Sudan, his description of the kingdom implies that it was still of considerable size, but he notes, 'the last of the rulers of Melli [Mali] became a tributary to the *ischia* [*askiya*]. The latter's attacks are so heavy that the king cannot give food to his family.' Yet thirty years later, when the Songhai invaded the capital of Mali, they were unable to bring the kingdom under control and it remained a recognizable entity for another two centuries.

Until the appearance of the Portuguese in West Africa, beginning about 1440, the gold trade, which so benefited the successive empires of Ghana, Mali, and Songhai, was in the hands of entrepreneurs who congregated in the towns at the southern terminals of the trans-Saharan routes, but, with the establishment of Portuguese entrepôts around the coast from Arguin to Elmina, the dynamic of the gold trade changed, allowing those controlling the goldfields of Bambuk and Bure in the west and Akan to the south-east to negotiate directly with the European merchants. The obvious advantage for the Europeans was that they could, at least in theory, get the gold at a lower price, without the mark-up charged by the Sudanese states, the desert caravan traders, and the dynasts controlling the Maghrib. That said, the west coast trading enclaves seem to have had only limited access to gold. In the mid fifteenth century, Cadamosto was disappointed to find little gold available to him on the river Gambia, and in the late fifteenth and early sixteenth centuries the annual throughput at Arguin was only 20–25 kilograms. In contrast, at the same time Elmina was exporting 400 kilograms. Several factors caused these discrepancies. One was that the yields of the various western goldfields were declining by this time, while the Akan field was prolific, but there were also

9.18 The final stages of Songhai expansion came under Askiya Muhammad I (r. 1493–1528), whose tomb, in slightly modified form, still stands in Gao.

other reasons. While the traders at Elmina were in direct contact with the Akan producers, those working the west coast of Africa were dependent on drawing off gold from the existing caravan routes. It may also be that the agents at Arguin, who were responsible for managing the royal monopoly, had less incentive to be energetic than did the traders at Elmina, who were looking after their own interests.

The quantity of gold, slaves, ivory, and malagueta pepper now passing through the coastal ports rather than through the hands of the Songhai cannot have failed to have an impact on the Songhai economy. Indeed, it may have been these new pressures that drove Askiya Muhammad to take more direct control of the caravan routes across the desert by capturing the salt mines at Taghaza, thus acquiring the essential salt without having to pay for it with gold. At the same time, he founded a colony at Agadez, on the southern edge of the Aïr Mountains, the better to control another of the desert routes. Nor is it impossible that their push eastwards, into Hausaland, was an attempt to develop new markets to compensate for the decline of goods coming from the forest zone in the south. It is difficult to distinguish direct causes and effects, but one can be sure that the Portuguese presence on the south coast after 1470 must have dislocated the systems underpinning the Songhai economy and thus the stability of the state. More dislocation was soon to come from a different direction.

The Ottomans in the North

During the thirteenth century, Anatolia was divided into a series of independent prin-cipalities known as beyliks. One of these, located in Bithynia, on the frontier of the Byzantine empire, was populated by Ottoman Turks, people of Turkic origin who had come under Persian influence. Under successive leaders they grew in strength and spread westwards into Europe, capturing the Byzantine capital of Constantinople in 1453 and transforming it into the capital of the Ottoman empire.

In the early years of the sixteenth century, the Turks were fighting in the East against the Safavid Persians, who were being supported by the Mamluks of Egypt. To halt this dangerous collusion the Ottoman sultan Selim I (r. 1512–20) decided, in 1516, to attack the Mamluk army in Syria, and when the Mamluks refused to come to terms, he marched on Egypt, defeating the defending army just outside Cairo in 1517. To control the newly conquered country he appointed his trusted supporter Hayır Bey, who gov-erned as a vassal of the sultan until his death, after which Egypt was ruled by a viceroy (pasha) sent from Constantinople. Selim I was a clear-sighted leader able to deal with the political intrigues of the time. He gained his sobriquet, the Grim, from the simple decisive action he took to ensure the peaceful succession of his son Suleiman. He had all his other sons killed, together with his own brothers and nephews. It was an effective solution. Suleiman the Magnificent was to rule for forty-six years, during which time the empire flourished, and to die a natural death, an unusual achievement for the age.

While Egypt and Cyrenaica were now formally part of the Ottoman empire, much of the Mamluk state system remained unchanged and the Mamluk elite retained posi-tions of power in both the army and the civil administration. Under the Ottomans, lethargy set in: there was no innovative architecture, nor did Egypt produce histo-rians or other scholars of note. It was, however, a stable polity, with a high level of agricultural productivity providing revenue for Constantinople. It also continued to command the Red Sea, but here some consolidation was required. To this end an expe-dition was sent to annex Nubia as far south as the Third Cataract, and in the Red Sea the establishment of a garrison at Zeila on the African coast in 1520 and the occu-pation of Yemen and Aden between 1535 and 1546 brought the Gulf of Aden firmly under control as a counter to growing Portuguese interference (pp. 326–7 below).

The Maghrib and the Western Mediterranean

With the growing power of the Ottomans in the Balkans, the annexation of Egypt in 1517, and the expulsion of the Knights of Rhodes in 1522, the Ottomans gained control over the eastern Mediterranean. In the expansive mood that prevailed under

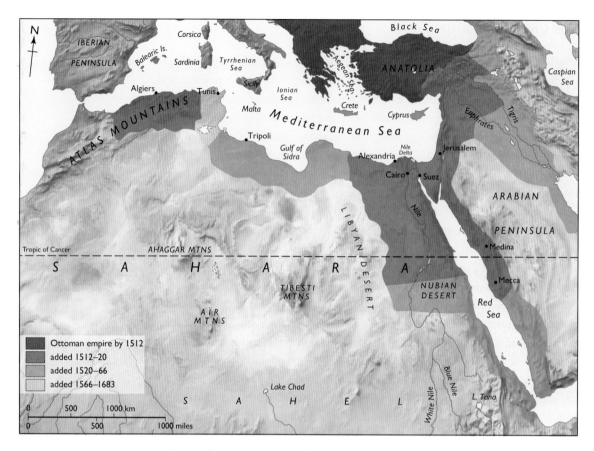

9.19 By 1566 the Ottoman empire had expanded in Africa to include the entire coast from the centre of Morocco to the Gulf of Aden.

Suleiman the Magnificent (r. 1520–66), attempts were made by land forces to advance through Europe, but the way was blocked by Vienna. After an unsuccessful siege in 1529 and a failed direct attack four years later, no further advances by land were attempted. But the sea offered easier and more varied opportunities, particularly for privateers, who could make a good living intercepting ships and raiding ports under licence from the sultan. Two entrepreneurs who were famously successful were the brothers Aruj and Hayreddin Barbarossa, born on the island of Lesbos, then part of the Ottoman empire. In the first decade of the sixteenth century, under the patronage of members of the sultan's household, they were active in the western Mediterranean, disrupting the Spanish and Portuguese ships engaged in servicing the garrisons set up along the North African coast following the fall of Granada to the Christians in 1492 (pp. 316–17 above).

9.20 The great harbour of Alexandria remained one of the most active ports in the Mediterranean, serving as an outlet not only for the produce of Egypt but also for the commodities carried by the Red Sea traders. The fortress on the spit of land (top) was built by the Mamluk sultan Qaitbay in 1477 to command the harbour, and stood to protect the city thereafter. The city continues to thrive.

Their activities ranged wide, but after the loss of their patron in one of the many palace upheavals, the brothers thought it wise to stay in the west, making a good living by offering assistance to the North African leaders in warding off Spanish interference. In 1516 they took Algiers from the Spanish and made it the base for their operations. Two years later, Aruj was killed during an attack on Tlemcen, but by then the success of the Barbarossa brothers had become well known in Constantinople and when Hayreddin offered submission to the new sultan in return for military assistance, he once more became an agent of the state. Under Suleiman he was given the title of grand admiral, and in 1532 coastal Algeria became part of the Ottoman empire. Over the next twenty years or so, control was gradually extended into the hinterland, and on one expedition Barbarossa reached as far south as the oasis of Touggourt, well into the Sahara.

9.21 Hayreddin Barbarossa (c.1478–1546). For a man whose reputation was as a swashbuckling corsair, the picture, painted by Nakkep Reis Haydar in 1540, projects a rather more muted image.

The situation in Tunisia was a little more complex. While the Hafsids continued to hold much of the territory, the Spanish had seized several of the coastal cities. In 1534 Barbarossa took Tunis and made it a base for raids at sea, but it was retaken by Spain the following year. There matters rested until 1569 when the city was seized by the *bey* (governor) of Algiers, who held it until the Spanish once more took it back in 1573. The loss of this vital port was a serious setback and so, the next year, Selim II sent out a fleet of 250–300 ships carrying 75,000 troops determined to win it back and to hold onto it. It was at Goleta, on the approach to Tunis, that the Ottomans won a decisive battle, finally ending Hafsid and Spanish rule, after which they incorporated the whole of Tunisia into the Ottoman empire. By this time much of Libya was also in Ottoman hands. The Spanish had invaded Tripoli in 1510, handing it over to the Knights of St John, but in 1551 Admiral Sinan Pasha captured it on behalf of the Ottomans, and by the 1580s the tribes of the Fazzan had been brought into the alliance.

From the Barbarossas' speculative enterprise in capturing Algiers in 1516 to the incorporation of the Fazzan in the 1580s, the Ottomans had acquired the whole of Tripolitania and much of the Maghrib as far as Tlemcen in Morocco. It was only in the western Maghrib that the successors of the Berber dynasties held out against the land-hungry aggression of the Portuguese, the Spanish, and the Ottomans.

For a while it looked as though the Ottomans were going to be successful in taking control of the maritime networks in the central and western Mediterranean. In 1565 they had attacked the Knights Hospitaller on Malta, striking fear into the hearts of the Christian West. But when the great maritime confrontation finally came at Lepanto, off the east coast of southern Greece, in 1571, the Spanish and Venetian fleet demonstrated that the Ottomans were far from invincible. The Turks lost two hundred ships and thirty thousand men. In the aftermath, a peace treaty was signed with Venice in 1573, under the terms of which the Turks were allowed to expand and consolidate their North African interests. This is why their capture of Tunis the following year went unopposed by the European allies.

9.22 Ottoman troops led by Uluç Ali, pasha of Algiers, are pictured here marching on Tunis in 1569. From *Şehname-i Selim Han* by Seyyid Lokman (1581).

The Struggle for Abyssinia

The Christian community surviving in the remoteness of Ethiopia maintained close links with the Coptic Church in Egypt, but it was also in touch with the wider Christian world, sending embassies to the pope and to various Christian churches. Although not directly involved in the Crusades, a steady stream of Ethiopian pilgrims made visits to Jerusalem. The presence of the Christian enclave provided a focus of hostility for the Somali Muslims who lived on the western coast of the Red Sea. Already, by the tenth century, they had come together as the sultanate of Adal with their capital at Zeila. By the fourteenth century, they were sporadically raiding the Christian Abyssinians, and in the early fifteenth century, when the capital was moved further inland to Dakkar, attacks on the Christians became easier to stage and more frequent.

Matters came to a head in 1529 when the Somali sultan Ahmad ibn Ibrahim al-Ghazi (r. 1506–43) decided on an all-out invasion of the Ethiopian empire. No doubt, religious fervour played a part, not least the desire to protect Muslim minorities living among the Christians, but another attraction was the focal position of the Ethiopian Highlands in the complex route networks linking the inner highlands to the Red Sea port of Mitsiwa (Massawa, in Eritrea). The economic rewards of conquest would not have been overlooked.

The first campaign, in 1529, saw Ahmad's Somali army defeat an Ethiopian expeditionary force at the battle of Shimbra Kure, near Mojo. Two years later Ahmad won another decisive victory using cannon to panic the Ethiopians, and later the same year dispersed another Ethiopian force, capturing the royal regalia, before entering and occupying the Ethiopian Highlands, sacking and burning churches as he went. He was now master of three-quarters of the Christian territory. The conflict continued using the accoutrements of modern warfare: cannon, matchlock muskets, and arquebuses. It was a war of attrition watched with interest by the Ottomans and the Portuguese, who were now, themselves, in conflict over the command of sea routes in the Indian Ocean.

Open hostilities between the Ottomans and Portuguese broke out in 1538 when the Ottomans sent help to the sultan of Gujarat, who was besieging the Portuguese base at Diu. In retaliation the Portuguese decided to send a force to destroy the Ottoman fleet at Suez. The expedition was led by Estêvão da Gama, the second son of Vasco da Gama. By February 1541 the force had reached Mitsiwa, and here they were met by urgent requests for help from the Ethiopians. The best da Gama could do was to send a detachment of four hundred musketeers under his younger brother, Cristóvão, and continue with his mission. Although the cohort of Portuguese troops was small, with their help the Ethiopians were able to reclaim most of the Ethiopian Highlands in a hard-fought struggle.

Once the Portuguese had become involved, it was inevitable that the Ottomans would be drawn in. Ahmad sought assistance, and was rewarded when the Ottoman governor of Yemen sent two thousand Arab musketeers, nine hundred Turkish pikemen, and a thousand Turkish foot musketeers, together with Turkish horsemen. The opposing armies met at Wofla, near Lake Ashenge in Eritrea, in August 1542. The Portuguese expeditionary force was crushed, and its commander, Cristóvão da Gama, was killed, but the Ethiopians rallied and six months later, in February 1543, at Wayna Daga, near Lake Tana, the Ethiopians, with Portuguese help, defeated the Adal–Ottoman army, killing the commander, Ahmad. With Ahmad's death the Somali force disintegrated.

The clash between the Muslim Somalis and the Christian Ethiopians was very much a local conflict fuelled by ethnic and religious differences, but behind it all lay the age-old desire to control the trade networks upon which the elites depended to maintain their supremacy. There was little to interest the external powers, the Portuguese and the Ottomans, whose prime concern was to keep the sea routes in the Indian Ocean open for the benefit of their entrepreneurs. Da Gama's dispatch of a small contingent of musketeers to aid the Ethiopians looks more like the token gesture of a man whose mind was on greater goals. But the Portuguese action forced the Ottomans to respond by supporting the Somalis. When the war was over, rather than become further embroiled, the Ottomans took the simple way out by occupying the Red Sea port of Mitsiwa in 1557, which effectively cut off the Ethiopians from further Portuguese support.

Thereafter, for the next half-century, the history of Ethiopia was dominated by the migration of inland peoples, notably the Oromo from the south-east of the country. In an amusing twist to events, in the early seventeenth century the Ethiopian king appealed to the Ottomans in Mitsiwa, asking them to prevent Catholic Portuguese missionaries from entering the country since they would disrupt the deep-rooted Christian faith of his subjects.

Meanwhile, in Morocco

With the fall of the kingdom of Granada in 1492, the Spanish and Portuguese began, as we have seen, to establish fortifications and trading bases along the coast of the Maghrib, taking over a number of Berber cities, stretching from Agadir to the Libyan city of Tripoli. These bases were in place by 1510. The Wattasids, who at this time still ruled Morocco, accepted their Portuguese incumbents. Indeed, there were economic advantages in the arrangement since the presence of the foreign enclaves facilitated trade between Morocco and Europe. But not all were happy with the situation, especially the Sa'di family, who claimed descent from the Prophet and whose power base lay in the south-west of the country. Opposed to the Wattasid–Portuguese alliance, in 1525 they marched on Marrakesh. By 1541 they had ousted the Portuguese from Agadir and several other enclaves, and by 1550 had established themselves in the Wattasid capital of Fez. The country was still politically divided, but success against the Portuguese had created a new national pride and, by playing on fear of Ottoman expansion from Algeria, the Sa'dis were able to build a new identity and sense of purpose among the Moroccan people.

The test came in 1578, in a period of dynastic turmoil, when the deposed sultan, aided by a Portuguese army led by the 24-year-old king Sebastian I, confronted the Sa'dis at the battle of Alcácer Quibir on the banks of the river Loukkos. Sebastian saw the fractious situation in Morocco as an opportunity for the Portuguese to gain land and for missionary activity, bringing personal acclaim. In preparation he had assembled a multinational force from Spain, Flanders, Germany, and Italy numbering as many as twenty thousand men and had transported them to North Africa in a fleet of five hundred vessels. Among his close supporters were the flower of the Portuguese nobility eager to serve their king in what could be presented as a crusade against the infidel. The opposing Sa'di forces were led by Abd al-Malik, an elderly man suffering a terminal illness and barely able to ride a horse, yet the result of the confrontation was a devastating defeat for Sebastian, who died in battle together with most of the Portuguese elite. The ailing al-Malik also died, though of his illness, but not before appointing his brother Ahmad as sultan. Ahmad was quick to embrace the glory of the battle and thereafter adopted the name al-Mansur ('the Victorious').

The battle of Alcácer Quibir was far more than a local event. It had absorbed a great deal of Portugal's financial reserve. The death of so many of the country's nobility, the loss of prestige, and the crippling cost of getting the hostages returned greatly undermined the state. When Sebastian's successor died two years later, in 1580, the Spanish king, Philip II, exploited Portugal's weakness by invading the country, incorporating it into the new Iberian Union. Portugal was to lose its identity as a nation state for the next sixty years. In Morocco the Sa'di dynasty was greatly strengthened by its stunning victory and, under Ahmad al-Mansur's astute and intelligent leadership, went from strength to strength. In early life al-Mansur had spent seventeen years among the Ottomans, returning to his country well versed in the arts of diplomacy, which he now put to good use. Ambassadors arrived from many countries bringing expensive gifts. The Portuguese and William of Orange sent embassies to negotiate the return of hostages, the pasha of Algiers was eager to establish friendly relations, the French did their best to ingratiate themselves, while the Spanish arrived with gifts of vulgar opulence. The English were less flamboyant in their approach, not least because they wanted to ensure that their illicit trade, selling arms to the Moroccans in return for saltpetre, an essential component of gunpowder, continued unnoticed by the other European powers. Al-Mansur's regime benefited from the gifts and the ransoms they were able to gather in, but the Europeans and Ottomans proved to be fickle friends who all had designs on Moroccan territory. However, with the Ottomans now involved in costly conflict with the Persians, Portugal no longer a functioning entity, and Spain and England beginning to face up to each other in a serious confrontation, al-Mansur was free, as never before, to follow his own ambitions, unassailed by worries of interference from without.

9.23 The battle of Alcácer Quibir, fought between the Portuguese and the Moroccans on 4 August 1578, lasted only four hours, but it was time enough for the slaughter of almost all of Portugal's elite. The devastating Portuguese defeat opened the way for the rise of the Moroccan leader Ahmad al-Mansur.

Invasion across the Desert

Al-Mansur's grand scheme was, quite simply, to send an army across the Sahara to conquer the empire of Songhai and thus to bring the whole of the hugely lucrative gold trade under the control of the Moors. Once his aspiration became known, his counsellors unanimously opposed it, giving sound reasons for doing so. To these al-Mansur offered a forceful response, the simple thrust of which was that the desert was not a barrier since merchants had been making the crossing for many hundreds of years and that the tribesmen of the western Sudan, whose only weapons were swords and spears, were no match for battle-hardened troops using gunpowder. His arguments won the

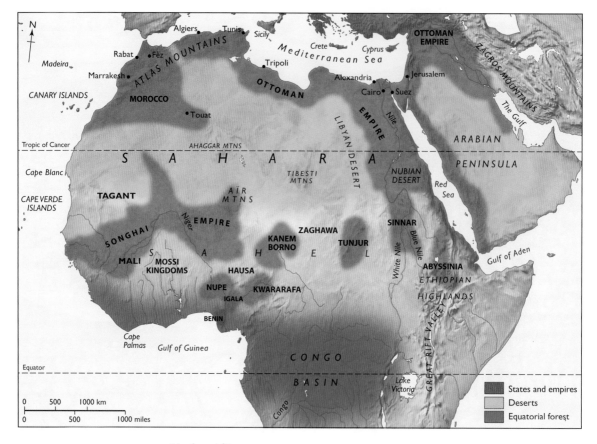

9.24 Northern Africa, c.1550.

day. Al-Mansur was a man of action whose success, in the febrile times in which he lived, depended on military achievement. Morocco was hemmed in. To the north the way was blocked by the strong Christian states of Iberia. To the east lay the kingdom of Algiers, ruled by the Ottomans: to try to drive them out would call for much effort, winning little gain. The only opportunity for military success, given the constraints imposed by Europe, Algiers, and the Atlantic, was to look south across the desert, where unlimited landscapes for conquest lay open, offering the prospect of massive reward.

Relations between the Moors and the Songhai had sometimes been a little strained. Troubles focused around ownership of the salt mines at Taghaza on the main north–south caravan route. The mines were worked by black slaves under the control of Masufa nomads and, as we have seen (p. 318 above), they had been taken over by the Songhai in one of their periods of expansion. In 1546 al-Mansur's father had asked the *askiya* of Songhai to cede the mines to him, but the request was flatly refused and, in a show of strength, the *askiya* dispatched two thousand Tuareg to raid the Dra'a region of Morocco with the instruction to extend their activities to Marrakesh if the opportunity allowed. The *askiya* had made his point forcefully, and it was ten years before the Moors thought it worth responding by sending a raiding party to Taghaza, killing the Songhai governor. The scores levelled, matters rested until, after the success of Alcácer Quibir, al-Mansur reopened the issue by offering to lease the mines from the *askiya*. The deal was agreed and presents were exchanged in Gao. By this time the Songhai had developed the highly productive salt mines at Taodeni, in the Sahara desert north of Timbuktu, and had little need for the almost worked-out deposits at Taghaza. It is difficult to see why the Moors should have bothered with the deal unless it was to provide them with the opportunity to visit Gao to assess the strength of the Songhai.

Al-Mansur was now making preparations for the invasion. Exploratory expeditions had been sent to the oases of Touat and Gorain, probably to test the logistics of crossing stretches of desert. There was also the story of a large force being sent through Wadan to upper Senegal with the intention of attacking Timbuktu. Another rumour of an army being lost in the desert adds to the belief that one or more abortive attempts were being made to explore routes to the south. But al-Mansur was now well advanced in planning his great invasion, and in autumn 1590 the force was dispatched.

The army was placed under the command of Judar, a eunuch who had been born in Spain, captured in a raid, and brought to Morocco, where he was raised in the palace at Marrakesh. He was a skilled and trusted member of al-Mansur's court with a proven ability as an organizer, a skill vital for a man tasked with leading an army across 1,400 kilometres of desert. The core of his fighting force was small: a mere four thousand men. Of these, 2,500 were light infantry armed with arquebuses, about a thousand being Moors from Andalusia, the rest renegade mercenaries of varying origins, including deserters who had fought with the Ottomans in Algeria. Then came fifteen hundred light cavalry, mostly Moors armed with lances. Though small, the carefully chosen forces were highly professional, with extensive experience. Additional armaments consisted of six large cannons and a number of smaller pieces carried two to a camel. These were managed by a specialist team of gunners, including seventy musketeers, all from Christian countries. Ammunition consisted of 31,000 pounds of gunpowder and an equivalent amount of shot. In addition to the arms, the baggage train included bullock hide waterskins, quantities of wheat, oats, and pressed dates, and 180 tents. To carry all this, eight thousand camels, looked after by a thousand camel-drivers, and a thousand packhorses were needed. Maintenance and labouring were carried out by six hundred sappers. The ratio of fighting men to animal and human support is a stark reminder of the difficulties involved in transporting a military force across a desert. That the army made the crossing without significant incident shows that the lessons of earlier expeditions had been well learnt.

The main force set out from Marrakesh on 16 October 1590 and crossed the Atlas Mountains to Lektawa, where other elements of the expedition joined them, and from there followed the well-used route through Taghaza, Taodeni, and Walata to Arawan, where the desert begins to give way to pasture as the Niger is approached. What state Judar's force was in when it arrived is not recorded, but the depletion of both men and beasts must have been considerable. That Judar fielded only a thousand of his men in his first engagement with the Songhai may reflect the scale of the losses he suffered during the twenty weeks it had taken to make the journey from Marrakesh.

Al-Mansur had painted an optimistic picture about confrontation with the Songhai in his speech to his counsellors. 'Today the Sudanese have only spears and swords, weapons which will be useless against modern arms. It will be easy for us to wage a successful war against these people and to prevail over them.' When the time came, the leader of the Songhai, Askiya Ishak, was able to assemble eighteen thousand cavalry armed with spears and 9,700 infantry, mostly bowmen. For Judar the odds did not look good, but he had the firepower and the discipline. The Songhai began the engagement by driving a vast herd of cattle towards the opposing force, hoping to cause confusion, but the tactic failed when the animals were panicked by the noise of the cannon, and it was not long before the flanks of the well-trained Moorish army were able to close in on the disorganized Songhai mass. Even though the desert crossing had taken its toll of the Moors, al-Mansur's confident assessment of the outcome had proved correct, but in the rout that followed, many of the Songhai were able to escape across the Niger on boats, leaving the Moors unable to follow. The battle of Tondibi, as it became known, had been a military success for the Moors, but there were disappointments to follow when they entered Gao. The city did not match up to their high expectations and, more to the point, the occupants had already carried off everything of value.

Disillusion

While the desert crossing and the battle of Tondibi were significant achievements, the toll on the Moorish force had been great, and the disappointment with Gao even greater. As men and pack animals began to succumb to disease at an alarming rate, Judar became anxious to negotiate an agreement with Askiya Ishak and depart for home. The *askiya*, for his part, wanted the invaders gone, so terms were quickly agreed. Ishak was prepared to offer allegiance to the ruler of Morocco, together with trade concessions, sweetened by the gift of 350 kilograms of gold and a thousand slaves. The deeply disillusioned Judar was ready to accept, but had to refer the offer to al-Mansur. While waiting for a reply, however, he agreed to move his troops out of Gao, in return for a gift of horses, to Timbuktu, a town he found to be more congenial. Though its architecture was built of mud, it was the intellectual capital and a far more sophisticated place than Gao. Here he settled with the remnant of his force to await al-Mansur's reply.

When news of the successful desert crossing and the battle of Tondibi reached Morocco, there was jubilation, but al-Mansur was deeply unimpressed by Judar's bleak report stressing the poverty of the Songhai state, and by the terms negotiated. Given that he had argued so eloquently for the expedition, al-Mansur had to present it in a far more favourable light, even if this meant grossly distorting the reality. Some were prepared to be convinced by his optimism, but others, especially the merchants who had their own sources of information, expressed considerable doubts about the wisdom and value of the enterprise. It was essential for his credibility that the operation be re-energized. To do this he decided to replace Judar with a new commander, Mahmud ibn Zarqun.

Mahmud and his escort of forty reached Timbuktu in seven weeks, and on arrival set about building boats to transport troops. When ready, they set off down the river to confront Ishak. At Bamba the Songhai army was met and defeated, and Ishak, now cut off from his base, was captured and murdered by local tribesmen. The new *askiya* appointed to replace him had little option but to send their submission to the Moors, but when he and his counsellors arrived to agree a peace treaty, they were all slaughtered.

Mahmud had briefly gained the advantage, but famine was now beginning to take its toll, and, to make matters worse, the Songhai had appointed a skilful and energetic new leader, Askiya Nur, whose strategy was to draw the Moors further south into the malarial swamps and the fringes of the forest zone, where the advantage of their firearms was negated, and where he could harass them using guerrilla tactics. After two years Mahmud admitted failure and sent a dispatch to al-Mansur explaining the seriousness of the situation. This time al-Mansur accepted reality and responded with reinforcements. They did little good, and in 1593 Mahmud, realizing that further campaigning in the south was pointless, withdrew to the right bank of the Niger, holding a small strip between Jenné and Gao with his main base at Timbuktu, leaving a garrison to watch over Gao. The energy and enthusiasm of the Moors was now spent.

In the rest of the Songhai empire, anarchy prevailed. The situation was summed up by Abd al-Rahman al-Sa'di, an Andalusian who worked in Timbuktu, in his chronicle *Tarikh al-Sudan*:

> Security gave place to danger, wealth to poverty, distress and calamities and violence succeeded tranquillity. Everywhere men destroyed each other; in every place and in every direction there was plundering, and war spared neither life nor property nor persons. Disorder was general and spread everywhere, rising to the highest degree of intensity.

Perhaps a little overdramatic, but it characterizes the uncertain times which gripped the old empire as the tribes around the periphery flung themselves on the weakened Songhai carcass. These internal conflicts were managed for a while by Askiya Nur, who also had to counter the activities of the Moors, but on his death all semblance of organized resistance collapsed and the old empire fragmented into a multitude of tribal polities.

The Moors held onto their riverbank for a while, fighting off attacks from Tuareg and the Sanhaja nomads, but with the death of al-Mansur came the turmoil of succession in Morocco and little attention was paid to the fate of distant western Sudan. Formal abandonment came in 1618, leaving the remaining expatriate Moors to manage the best they could.

Standing back from the detritus of thirty years of conflict, what had al-Mansur's desert adventures achieved? He had hoped to gain control of the gold sources south of the Sahel but had failed to understand the geographical complexity of the region and the fact that the Songhai were really only middlemen. The huge expenditure of material and manpower on the trans-desert campaign had certainly increased the flow of gold, but not to the extent he had expected. Nonetheless, he made good use of the extra wealth, investing in improving the defences of Morocco, erecting mosques and madrasas for public use, and developing a sugar industry in Sus. The enterprise had also captured the public imagination, even of his detractors; it was grand theatre and gave him an enviable status among his Ottoman and European neighbours, providing a bargaining power that, for a while, elevated Morocco to being one of the big players on the world scene.

Across Two Hundred Years

Two themes dominate the two hundred years from 1400 to 1600: the absorption of Egypt and much of the rest of North Africa into the fast-growing Ottoman empire, and the rapid spread of Portuguese interests around the Atlantic and Indian Ocean coasts of Africa. The two were very different phenomena. The Ottomans took over existing state systems, generally stifling development and innovation, being content to take the profits of local productivity and trade while their energies focused on trying to dominate the Mediterranean and to make land conquests in Europe. The Portuguese worked under different imperatives. Their interests, at this stage at least, lay in establishing a viable maritime route to the markets of India and the Far East and to setting up enclaves, at select points on the African coast, through which to exploit local commercial opportunities. There was no intention, in these early years, of making significant territorial gains on the continent. The Portuguese had neither the manpower nor the will to do so. Occasionally, as in the case of Abyssinia, they found themselves to be under pressure from allies to provide military help, but this was reluctantly done.

The presence of the Ottomans in North Africa and Egypt did little to change the now long-established patterns of connectivity which bound these regions to their African hinterland: the same trade routes saw the flow of much the same range of goods, though it is likely that the demand for slaves increased. The impact of the Portuguese was more varied. In East Africa they simply took over the trading centres that had, for centuries, been worked by Muslims arriving via the Red Sea or the Persian Gulf, but around the coasts of West Africa they were setting up their enclaves in virgin territory. Such a sudden innovation cannot have failed to have an impact on native exchange systems. The demand for slaves, ivory, gold, and malagueta pepper suddenly increased, drawing on supplies that had once gone north across the Sahara to the markets of the Maghrib. It is difficult to trace the effect of this in the archaeological or historical record, but it may have been the disruption to the system that drove the Songhai to extend their control northwards to the salt-producing Taghaza Oasis and eastwards to the city states of Hausaland. It is not at all unlikely that concern about the potential of the Portuguese trading enclaves to draw gold and other commodities out of the trans-Saharan system was one of the reasons why al-Mansur decided upon the invasion of the Songhai.

The Moroccan campaign to western Sudan was a high-risk enterprise of the kind that is unlikely to have been contemplated before accessibility of gunpowder gave an advantage to the north. A few decades earlier, firearms and cannon had been used for the first time in Abyssinia, but these had been available to both sides. In the case of the Moors versus the Songhai, asymmetric availability favoured the Moors irrespective of the size of the force. It was now a changed world in which gunpowder would play an increasing part.

Globalization and firepower were to dominate Africa henceforth, but what made the world seem suddenly smaller was the achievement of that tiny army making its four-month trek across the Sahara.

10

RETROSPECT
AND PROSPECT

THE story of the Sahara and of the people who lived around its fringes is the story of two contests: the one between humans and their environment, the other between polities for the control of resources. Thus it has always been, and always will be. In the distant past we have only the detritus of human existence—archaeological evidence—to base the story on, but for more recent times, when oral and written histories become available, it is possible to consider the deeds of powerful individuals, of battles and the growth of empires. These stories are compelling but can easily become too dominant. The personalities, and the narratives they help to generate, are superficial, rather like the glittering choppiness on the surface of the deep Ocean. What really determines the course of events is the interplay of human agency, driven by imperatives controlled by genetics, with landscape, constantly reshaped by environmental change.

North Africa is a large slab of old, hard rocks floating on the magma of the earth's core, breaking from and colliding with other slabs through deep time. These forces and readjustments have given the landmass special characteristics, and these have affected human activity. Perhaps the most important is the complex of rift valleys created when the eastern part of the landmass began pulling away from the rest. These East African rifts provided habitats and corridors of migration for early humans. Further north they were flooded by the sea, becoming the Gulf of Aden and the Red Sea, which, in later history, allowed maritime trade routes to develop, linking the Mediterranean to the Indian Ocean. Plate tectonics also led to the formation of the Mediterranean Sea, as the Eurasian and African plates swung together. The near-enclosed stretch of water was a congenial place for human groups to live and to interact, and it fast became a hothouse for cultural innovation and a zone of rapid population growth, developments which were to have a major impact on Africa. Plate tectonics also provided northern Africa with a long ocean coastline which, when maritime technology became sufficiently developed, allowed new connectivities to evolve.

Superimposed upon this bedrock base was a network of rivers, themselves the creation of the interaction of climate and geology. Of these, the most important in terms of their effects on human development were the Nile, flowing from the East African Highlands, and the Niger, with its source in the Guinea Highlands. Both provided fertile soils suitable for the development of agriculture and corridors of communication where communities could flourish, grow, and interact.

The second formative factor is climate. By virtue of its position on the globe, northern Africa spans a number of east–west climatic zones. Although these have shifted over time as the earth's axis has altered, the basic pattern has remained: a wide central desert flanked by narrower zones grading from steppe, through bushy grassland savannah, to woodland or forest. Over the last five thousand years the desert has been the dominant feature, separating the Mediterranean coastal zone from the Sahel in the south. For much of that time the defining narrative has been the way in which the peoples of these two favoured areas have interacted.

The Human Contribution

The impact of climate on solid geology creates a series of microenvironments—biomes—offering conditions conducive to the development of plant and animal life. One component of the biome is the human species. The archaeological and historical evidence allows a narrative to be constructed describing the growing impact of humans on the environment and of the increasing complexity of their society. Human behaviour is conditioned largely by genetic makeup. As an animal, the human's prime concern is to feed and to reproduce. Humans also form social groups with hierarchical structures, which help care for old and young. But, unlike other animals, they have two additional, genetically determined traits: the ability to imagine, and the desire to acquire. These imperatives have driven the human species, creating the complexity of events we choose to call history.

The successful search for food, reproduction, and social being enabled humans to build viable communities that could maintain themselves in a variety of different eco-zones, utilizing whatever resources were available. At first, for an extended period of time, they were hunter-gatherers, but the introduction of domesticated cattle, sheep and goats, and pigs, and of cultivated wheat and barley from the Near East into the North African coastal zone and the Nile valley, allowed a more sedentary way of life to develop, encouraging a growth in population. In the western Sudan, the equatorial zone, and the Ethiopian Highlands a range of staple crops developed from the indigenous flora, ensuring that, in these regions too, a more sedentary way of life could develop. In the areas between, less suitable for crop growing, pastoralism became the dominant subsistence strategy, augmented by hunting and fishing. Changes in climate, particularly the desertification of the Sahara, which was under way by 3000 BC, drove populations to move away, leaving some areas, which had previously supported large communities, depopulated, while others, in receipt of migrants, became more densely occupied.

Natural population rise consequent upon a more sedentary lifestyle, and dislocations of population caused by climate change, created tensions, especially when the population in any given region reached the holding capacity of the land. Since human societies are naturally aggressive, the tensions could quickly build to outright conflict, usually directed at neighbours, beginning with raids to acquire food and goods and culminating in the takeover of new territory. The raid was also the way in which aspiring young males could gain status. Once the process had begun, the endemic nature of aggression ensured that, for many societies, warfare became a regular and self-sustaining part of the social system, a reality all too evident in the narratives examined in the previous chapters.

Aggression also played a role in satisfying the desire to acquire. Acquisition can take many forms, the most obvious being the accumulation of wealth in the form of goods like gold and other rare materials, but it could also be manifested in owning herds of cattle, bevies of servants or slaves, and, for men, displays of wives. A more subtle form of acquisition is that of knowledge. A person with exotic knowledge, gained from study, travel, or revelation, was someone of value. A lord who could coerce such a person to remain in his court had possession of that knowledge and would be seen to be the greater for it. The human need to acquire, on whatever level, energized society. At the most basic it encouraged trade in exotic materials, be it a few coloured beads or many camel loads of gold dust. Some of the commodities, like slaves, slabs of salt, or malagueta pepper, were essentially currency with which rarer, more desirable products could be bought. So it was that networks of connectivity grew up, across the deserts and by river and sea, and the flow of commodities created systems that became integral to the social structure. Trade networks will exist wherever there are humans. What gave such dynamism to those in northern Africa was the vigorous consumer world of the Mediterranean and the Near East, spread along its northern flank, with its boundless demand for quantity and quality.

10.1 Salt, so long a vital commodity in trans-Saharan commerce, continues to feature large in trade across the desert. The image is timeless.

That humans have the power of imagination and abstract thought also sets them aside from other animals. They are able to create complex belief systems and to frame them in a way that can be communicated and shared through stories, rituals, structures, and artefacts. A belief system accepted by the elite became a powerful tool for social coercion. The religion of ancient Egypt provides a vivid example of this, with its huge investment in religious architecture. Shared religions also provide brotherhoods across ethnic divides. The spread of Islam through northern Africa greatly facilitated the trans-Saharan trade networks. It provided an ethical system, giving assurance that trade deals would be honoured by distant participants, and was therefore rapidly adopted by elites and entrepreneurs. The story told of Mansa Musa, king of Mali in the fourteenth century, is revealing. Having dissipated his stock of gold on the outgoing stage of his pilgrimage to Mecca, he had to borrow gold from Egyptian merchants, one of whom decided to return with the *mansa* to Mali to make sure he was paid back. Though the merchant died on the way, Mansa Musa took trouble to find out who his heirs were so that they could be reimbursed in full.

Religious beliefs could also provide a convenient structure to legitimize aggression. The Islamic leaders who declared jihad against unbelievers were matched by Christian Crusaders who could even persuade themselves that the sack and looting of Christian Constantinople in 1204 was justified in the pursuit of God's will. The conversion of heathens provided Dom Henrique and the Portuguese nobles with the justification for their military interventions in North and West Africa, which later opened up the continent to Portuguese trading interests.

The three principal drivers embedded in our human genetic structure, aggression, acquisition, and the propensity to construct binding belief systems, are a potent combination. By understanding them we can better appreciate the narrative of history.

Zones of Innovation

Within an area the size of northern Africa, the interplay of solid geology and climate has created many different ecozones, some of which are hostile to human communities while others are congenial and have encouraged rapid development and innovation. These differences hold true over long periods of the past and help to explain the course of history. Such issues have been stressed throughout this book, but it is well to stand back here to see, in perspective, just how crucial were the zones of innovation to the history of Africa. The northern part of Africa may be perceived to be an insular mass, bounded largely by the sea and the equatorial forest, with two principal interfaces with the rest of the world: the Mediterranean and the coast of East Africa. The Mediterranean, by virtue of its ecology, ease of maritime connectivity, and the plethora of niches around its highly convoluted coastline, where humans can live well in comparative comfort, saw the rapid development of society and the early emergence of complex polities. The long North African interface was an integral part of this zone of innovation, which dominated the *longue durée* from the time when hunter-gatherers spread along the coast from the Levant to the contest between the Ottoman Turks and the Christian states of Spain and Portugal for control of the seaways. Throughout this span of time, the Mediterranean and its adjuncts, the Near East and Europe, were to have a constant effect on North Africa, not least because its fast-growing population made it a huge consumer market drawing in African products. The East African coast was rather different since it was open to the vagaries of Indian Ocean contacts, which, from an early stage, saw exchanges of cultivated plants and domesticated animals. Later it was drawn into a more regular trade network, organized initially by the Romans and later taken over by Muslim merchants, until the Portuguese began their domination of Indian Ocean trade.

Besides these two crucial maritime interfaces there were four other zones of innovation within the northern African landmass. The best known is the Nile valley, a long, high, fertile strip of land isolated by the protective desert. A hothouse for the early development of settled farming, by 3000 BC it had begun to evolve into a highly distinctive complex society benefiting not only from its own productivity but from the throughput of commodities as trade intensified. The other great river, the Niger, in its middle course, also provided a varied and productive environment for the development of complex societies reliant on locally cultivated crops, pastoralism, and fishing. Dispersed urban agglomerations characterized the early stages, but out of these beginnings grew larger political configurations, the empires of Ghana, Mali, and Songhai. These developments concentrated in the western Sudan, but elsewhere along the great Sahel corridor other manifestations of social complexity emerged: the Hausa city states, Kanem Bornu, and eventually Wadai, a state to the east of Lake Chad, and Darfur. These were essentially sedentary communities whose strength lay in their ability to control the south–north trade routes. It is an interesting speculation that, had it not been for the Mediterranean demand for commodities from the south, the Sahel corridor might have developed a more mobile pastoral society comparable to that of the nomads of the Eurasian steppe. The final zone of innovation is the Ethiopian Highlands, which occupy a unique position between the southern and northern parts of Africa. Rapid variation in altitude, combined with the local climatic pattern, means that many different ecozones exist in close proximity, offering an exceptional range of plant cultivars. From the beginning, Ethiopia has developed a distinctive culture, which it has maintained to the present day, latterly as a Christian enclave in a sea of Islam.

The persistence of these four zones of innovation over long periods of time is one of the more remarkable features of African prehistory and history. Geography is clearly an important factor, but behind it also lies the stability of the population. Although there were, of course, large-scale movements of people from time to time, and changes in elite governance, these were insignificant beside the rootedness of the basic populations in their traditional territories. Compared to the mass movements that at certain times flooded through Eurasia, the population of the northern part of Africa exhibited a remarkable stability.

Corridors of Communication

The movement of people and commodities across North Africa in the past favoured various routes: the Nile corridor, the Red Sea, along the Atlantic coast, and the numerous caravan routes criss-crossing the desert. Sufficient will have been said to show that these connectivities, already in use by the first millennium, persisted over time, carrying

10.2 The sinuous band of the Nile, and its neighbour the Red Sea, provided the essential routes by which goods moved between the Indian Ocean and East Africa, and the Mediterranean world. The fertile expanse of the Nile delta, fronting the desert, has provided an interface linking Africa, the Near East, and the Mediterranean.

increasingly large flows of commodities. Each route will have been in the hands of specialists. The Nile needed experienced boatmen used to running with the flow and returning with sail when the winds were right. The Red Sea and the Indian Ocean also required sailors and navigators whose knowledge accumulated over time, and which was eventually committed to writing, generating sets of sailing instructions like the remarkable *Periplus of the Erythraean Sea*. As knowledge expanded, so vessels could venture further south along the East African coast. But when, eventually, the Portuguese admiral Vasco da Gama forced his way into these waters from the west, he found it necessary to take on board a specialist navigator to guide him across the Indian Ocean. Knowledge was there for the hiring.

The Atlantic coast of Africa was a little more problematical. Reefs made inshore sailing hazardous, while far out, ships were at the mercy of the prevailing winds and currents, benign for those sailing south but contrary for those trying to beat a north-erly course. That said, it is evident that, in the mid first millennium BC, Mediterranean explorers were pushing south and returning to tell the tale. One, the Carthaginian Hanno, may even have reached the Bight of Bonny. Recent commentators who doubt that such journeys were possible underestimate the ability of Phoenician sailors to man-age the Atlantic using a combination of sails, rowing, and careful use of inshore pas-sages. Even so, it was not easy, and it was not until the development of the caravels in the fourteenth century, with their lateen rig and stern-mounted rudders, that coastal journeys could be made on a more regular basis. By the end of the fifteenth century, sailors had learnt how to make a wide sweep out into the open Atlantic before swinging round to sail past the Cape of Good Hope to reach the Indian Ocean.

The many trans-Saharan routes were also managed by specialists, the descendants of the Berber pastoralists who had once wandered the region when it was clothed with vegetation before desiccation set in five thousand years ago. These were the ancestors of the Sanhaja and the Tuareg, who were to rule the desert routes, providing guid-ance and protection for those who wished to make the journey across the waste. Their mobility made them a formidable force, as on the occasion when, inspired by a char-ismatic religious leader, many banded together to become the Almoravid movement. Later the Tuareg put constant pressure on the Songhai empire, attacking and holding the important centre of Timbuktu. The desert nomads have continued to be a signifi-cant presence. A UNESCO report of 1962 refers to them as 'a people perfectly adapted to the natural environment, not only physically, through the sharpness of their senses, the sureness of their instincts, the speed of their reflexes, but also by their social organi-zation and their sense of honour'. They are 'a lordly people who command our respect by the dignity of their attitudes and the wisdom of their rare utterances'. The author of the report bewails their fate in the fast-changing world, many being forced to adapt to jobs as labourers in the oilfields.

The mobility of the desert nomads facilitated the movement of entrepreneurs, usu-ally people of Berber origin, who congregated in the trading centres both to the north and to the south of the desert in considerable numbers and helped in the transport of their goods across the desert. Something of the complexity of the organization can be glimpsed through the activities of the al-Makkan family in the fourteenth century. There were five brothers who were partners in the firm. Two lived in Walata on the southern fringe of the desert. It was their job to accumulate stocks of gold and ivory from markets further south. Two other brothers lived in Tlemcen in the Maghrib, where they acquired European trade goods. The fifth brother, who had overall control of the flow of goods, was based in the great trading centre of Sijilmasa on the north-ern edge of the desert, where he could keep abreast of market values and instruct his

10.3 To cross the desert needed skills based on experience passed down through the generations. The Berbers from North Africa moved gradually into the desert in the first millennium AD, adapting to the harsh conditions. Their descendants are still there. One of these groups, embracing the whole of the central Sahara, is the Tuareg.

brothers when best to dispatch goods and what prices to charge. The desert-edge trading centres were full of merchants of this kind.

The other form of mobility evident on the desert caravan routes was pilgrimage. The vast entourage that accompanied Mansa Musa from Mali to Mecca may well have been an exceptional display of affluence, but pilgrimage played an important part in the life of the devout who could afford the time and cost of the long journey to Mecca. Pilgrim caravans, usually travelling through Cairo, would have been an annual feature of life on the trans-desert routes. The round journey from the western Sudan took about a year. How many people were travelling at any one time it is impossible to say, but the journeys of the devout must have noticeably swelled the number of people on the move. Far from being a hostile barrier, the great desert was alive with travellers.

10.4 Pilgrimage to Mecca had become big business by the thirteenth century and involved much organization. Something of the clamour and colour of it all is captured by this painting, of *c.*1236, by Yahya ibn Mahmud al-Wasiti for the *Maqamat* written by al-Hariri of Basra.

The Last Four Hundred Years

Until the middle of the nineteenth century, developments in Africa were essentially continuations of trajectories already well established in the region, largely conditioned by geographical constraints. The states of the Sudan continued to evolve as isolated polities strung out along the Sahel, while Abyssinia maintained its identity in the face of pressure from its neighbours. Egypt, after Napoleon's brief and ineffectual adventure (1789–1801), was restored under the Turkish general Muhammad Ali, who was able to revitalize the military and succeeded in conquering Nubia. In North Africa the

Moroccan state continued under Berber rule much as before, while Algeria, Tunisia, and Tripoli broke away from Ottoman domination, though coastal areas of Tripoli were regained by the Ottomans in 1835 and the Fazzan recolonized seven years later.

The European states, for their part, were holding onto their trading concessions, though there was some change. In 1653 the Omanis from Arabia ousted the Portuguese from much of the East African coast, leaving them with Mozambique and, for a while, Mombasa. Meanwhile, the Dutch had entered the competition for trading rights, taking over some of the stations on the Gold Coast and establishing Cape Colony in 1652, later to be appropriated by the British. The French, apart from establishing their presence in Senegal, had shown comparatively little interest in Africa, but political intervention in Algeria in 1830 opened their eyes to the opportunities to be had in North Africa. Within ten years they had taken over much of coastal Algeria, and, with the collapse of local resistance in 1847, France acquired the whole of Algeria, opening the territory to a flood of some 170,000 settlers, who poured in from Spain, Italy, and Malta, as well as some from France. This sudden grab of territory by the Europeans set in motion the 'Scramble for Africa', which was to characterize the latter part of the nineteenth century.

The slave trade, which, since at least the middle of the first millennium BC, had dominated patterns of trade in North Africa, began to trouble the conscience of the more enlightened Europeans by the end of the eighteenth century, and in 1807 the British government outlawed the slave trade (though not slavery) within its dominions and began to bring pressure to bear on other states to do likewise, even establishing a naval detachment to patrol the coast of West Africa to apprehend ships of any nation thought to be carrying slaves. It was a small beginning to a process that was to struggle to have a significant effect. The repatriation of slaves to West Africa was already under way in 1792, when Freetown was established in Sierra Leone to provide a home for slaves who had served on the British side in the American War of Independence. Comparatively few returned, but after 1808 it became the base where slaves, freed by the Royal Navy's anti-slavery patrols, were landed for resettlement. In all, some hundred thousand were repatriated here in the first half of the nineteenth century.

A number of Americans, though for mixed motives, considered slavery to be a social problem in need of a solution, and in 1816 the American Colonization Society was founded to repatriate Africans. Prominent among the members were Quakers who believed that, since all Africans had a better chance of surviving in their own country, it was a moral imperative to return them. Others, the slave owners, were opposed to sending back slaves but agreed to repatriate free Africans, whom they regarded as socially disruptive. The returnees were transported to Monrovia in Liberia, which, in 1847, proclaimed itself to be an independent republic. The numbers were not large, probably no more than sixteen thousand by 1867. The experiment was not an unqualified success,

10.5 Freetown, in Sierra Leone, was first settled in 1787 by four hundred black Africans freed from America, the West Indies, and elsewhere, travelling via London. After initial difficulties the colony was refounded in 1792 by eleven hundred former American slaves who sailed from Nova Scotia in fifteen ships. In the face of attacks by the French, and by indigenous Africans, the British took over the territory, declaring Sierra Leone a Crown colony in 1808.

largely because those who returned, brought up in American culture, considered themselves to be superior to the local population, who were forced to serve as an underclass.

It was not until the 1860s that the Royal Navy's West Africa Squadron finally brought the West African slave trade to an end. It was a victory for those Europeans and Americans who abhorred slavery, but for the West African states whose economies were dependent on the sale of slaves it was a disaster, the more so because slavery provided a profitable way to rid society of dissidents. For many African rulers it was a time of economic decline, leading to poverty, sufficiently disruptive for the British government to feel it necessary to offer them compensation.

The 'Scramble for Africa' got under way in the early 1880s with the French taking over Tunisia, Senegal, and Gabon, the British finding themselves in possession of Egypt, the Spanish colonizing coastal Mauritania, the Portuguese taking a firmer hold on Angola and Mozambique, and other European states beginning to establish a first foothold on the continent, the Germans in Cameroon and South-West Africa, the Italians in Eritrea, and King Leopold of Belgium investing in a personal empire in the Congo. From this early beginning the land-hungry rampage continued until, by 1925, only Liberia and Abyssinia remained free of European domination. But the colonial episode was brief. In the aftermath of the Second World War a new nationalist feeling was beginning to emerge. Britain was first to respond by quitting Egypt, except for the Suez Canal Zone, in 1947. By 1960 most of the northern part of Africa was free of Europeans except for the French in Algeria, the British in Gambia, Sierra Leone, and Cameroon, the Spanish in western Mauritania (the Spanish Sahara), and the Portuguese in Guinea and the Cape Verde islands. On 3 February 1960, after making an extended tour of Africa, the British prime minister, Harold Macmillan, gave a historic speech to both houses of parliament of the Union of South Africa. Referring to the post-war independence movements in Asia, he continued:

> Today the same thing is happening in Africa, and the most striking of all impressions I have formed since I left London a month ago is the strength of African national consciousness. In different places it takes different forms, but it is happening everywhere. The wind of change is blowing through this continent, and, whether we like it or not, this growth of national consciousness is a political fact. We must all accept it as a fact, and our national policies must take account of it.

The success of the African National Congress in South Africa and the election of Nelson Mandela as president in 1994 marked the symbolic end of the colonial era. But not quite. The ports of Ceuta and Melilla on the coast of Morocco, acquired by the Spanish in the sixteenth century, remain the only colonial enclaves to survive on the African continent.

Climate and Population Again

Finally, we must return to the two crucial drivers, climate change and population growth, to understand what is happening now and how the future may pan out. At the present time, much of the Sahel is gripped with serious social unrest, which has been steadily increasing over the last forty years. The situation is exemplified by a news report of a minor incident which took place in the far west of the modern state of Sudan in August 2019 at the moment when Sudan's military council and civilian opposition leaders were signing a peace agreement after a long period of conflict:

> About 25 armed herders, riding camels and motorcycles, opened fire on people working on farms next to an internally displaced persons camp in Shangil Tobaya locality.
> According to people in the camp it was a 'revenge attack'. A few days earlier, the farmers had impounded the herders' camels and other livestock as they trespassed on farms and handed over the animals to the police.
>
> (Snigdha Das, *Down to Earth*, 2019)

 349

The story reflects the age-old tension between pastoralists and farmers, in this case driven to extremes by the rapid change in climate. Through time, human existence in the Sahel had depended upon the symbiotic relationship between pastoralists and farmers, the herders driving their cattle, sheep, and goats south to graze on the farmland after it had been cropped, their presence adding much-needed fertilizer to the land. It was a delicate system, its harmony managed by customary agreement and the mediation skills of trusted local leaders. But, from the middle of the twentieth century, the equilibrium has been increasingly upset. Climate change, leading to droughts and famine and to desertification, has made the search for pasture more desperate and has driven pastoralists to push further and further south, while population increase among the farmers is forcing them to extend further north into the traditional pasturelands. Given these pressures, conflicts have become inevitable, and with increasing desertification much of the Sahel has descended into violence.

The figures are stark. In the Sahel, temperatures are currently rising at a rate one and a half times faster than the global average, and the United Nations estimates that about 80 per cent of the farmland has now been degraded. Droughts are nothing new in the region, but the number has been increasing since the nineteenth century, and from the 1960s they have become particularly frequent. In the drought of 1968, 50–70 per cent of the cattle died. During the drought years 1972–5, a hundred thousand people were starving, while the drought of 1982–5, even more severe, drove many societies into armed clashes, leading in some places to full-scale warfare. Since the 1930s, the boundary between the desert and the Sahel has shifted southwards by up to 200 kilometres. At the same time the population is rising. In 2016, 60–70 per cent were under 24 years old, and if the growth continues, it is estimated that the population of the region will have nearly tripled by 2050. Already pressures are building, leading to a greatly increased rate of migration, some moving south into the savannah and forest zones, but many more joining the growing numbers of refugees making their way across the desert in the hope of reaching Europe. One estimate suggests that every year 12 million people leave their homes in West and Central Africa looking for work.

The droughts continue, the most serious in recent years being in 2010 and in 2012, which, according to the United Nations, left fifteen million people in the region undernourished. The personal misery, and the desperate mobility it has engendered, have led to an upsurge in violent conflict. Marginalized pastoralists, already suffering from social exclusion, have become easy prey to the radical Islamist groups who have made the Sahel their home, and to the criminal organizations dealing in arms, drugs, and people smuggling who have moved in to profit from the volatile situation. Nomads like the Tuareg, Dossak, and Fulani have provided willing recruits.

10.6 Since the middle of the twentieth century, the Sahel has suffered from droughts of growing frequency and intensity, resulting in greatly increased mobility among the population and an ensuing social instability. During this time, the boundary between the desert and the Sahel has moved south by between 50 and 200 kilometres, bringing hardship to many.

10.7 Insurgent groups flourish in the lawlessness created by the desertification of the Sahel. In 2012 Timbuktu was taken by Islamic fundamentalists, who destroyed shrines and burned books and manuscripts. The situation has been restored and the ancient buildings repaired. Although many books were lost, local inhabitants did much to save the old libraries and salvage manuscripts from the destruction.

The alliance of separatist and other groups led to a security crisis in 2012: Gao was attacked and Timbuktu was taken by fundamentalists, who demolished historic shrines and burned rare books and manuscripts. As the insurgency intensified and the Malian capital, Bamako, began to look vulnerable, French troops were sent in at the request of the government and with the support of the United Nations. A peace deal between the Tuareg and the government of Mali was signed in June 2013 and the situation largely restored. But unrest simmered, and by 2018 organized violence in the Sahel had reached new levels, with Mali and Burkino Faso registering the highest number of civilian deaths in the region.

It is widely accepted that desertification is the major underlying cause of social upheaval and regional insecurity. In an attempt to combat the worst excesses of this, a conference held in Chad in 2002 proposed that a band of trees 15 kilometres wide should be planted, running the whole length of the Sahel from the Atlantic to the Red Sea, a distance of 8,000 kilometres. The Great Green Wall for the Sahara and the Sahel Initiative, as it became known, was formally endorsed by the African Union in 2007. Since then the original idea has expanded, taking on a broader brief to encourage the development of a mosaic of land use practices beneficial to the environment, to halt the spread of the Sahara, to create rural jobs reducing migration and improving food

10.8 The Great Green Wall for the Sahara and the Sahel Initiative, formally endorsed in 2007, proposed to create a belt of woodland 15 kilometres wide from the Atlantic to the Red Sea to keep the desert at bay, to encourage other agricultural enterprises, and, in doing so, to provide work opportunities and stability for the population. It is a work in progress.

security, and to absorb 250 million tons of carbon dioxide from the atmosphere. The project was embraced with enthusiasm by the states of the Sahel and is already bringing relief to many people. By 2022, 20 million hectares of land had been restored and 350,000 jobs created. The target is to restore 100 million hectares by 2030.

But, in spite of human ingenuity and efforts to mitigate the devastation and misery caused by desertification, climate change is largely a force of nature. Detailed studies of the Sahara have shown that the desert has increased in area by 10 per cent over the last hundred years and that the prime factor was the Atlantic Multidecadal Oscillation, a natural climatic cycle that affects the sea temperature in the North Atlantic which, in turn, moderates the West African Monsoon system bringing rain to northern Africa. The Oscillation runs on a fifty- to seventy-year cycle, varying from cold and dry to warm and moist. Since the 1970s, northern Africa has been experiencing a cold, dry phase, leading to greater desertification. Distinguishing between the effects of the natural cycle and anthropogenic factors, like global warming resulting from greenhouse gases, deforestation, and soil degeneration initiated by overgrazing, is not easy, but recent research has suggested that the desertification of the Sahel is about two-thirds due to the natural Oscillation. Whatever the causes, human efforts like the Great Green Wall will make a real difference.

The Oscillation is now moving into a warm, moist phase, but it will not affect the Sahel evenly. The projection suggests that precipitation will increase in the central and eastern Sahel but will decrease in the west. Since 1990, rainfall in the Sahel has begun to increase, but the Atlantic Multidecadal Oscillation may not be the only natural factor. Others, such as changes in the surface temperature of the Sahara and the effects of high-altitude winds, may also have played a part. These are complex issues still to be worked out in detail. The reality is, however, that since the last decade of the twentieth century, in spite of occasional devastating droughts, the Sahara has been getting steadily wetter and greener. Whether this is the result of a short-term oscillation or of a much longer trend it is impossible yet to say. Maybe, in the millennia to come, the Sahara will become green, the lakes will fill, and wild animals will again roam its bush and woodland.

A GUIDE TO FURTHER READING

Acontinent as large and complex as Africa will generate an extensive literature. In offering a selection for further reading I have had to be highly selective, focusing on works that cover specifically the subject matter of this book: connectivity in the northern part of the continent, north of the equatorial forest, in the period up to the early seventeenth century. Even so, the range of works is considerable. Here I have concentrated on general studies providing the broad context but have included references to more detailed pieces of research to allow the reader, if so inclined, to delve into the evidence and to explore some of the principal debates. We begin with useful general works before looking in more detail at the literature relevant to each chapter.

Some General Works

Two classic series, which together form an invaluable resource, are *The Cambridge History of Africa*, published in eight volumes between 1975 and 1986, and the UNESCO *General History of Africa*, to be completed in eleven volumes, the first of which was published in 1981. Of the *Cambridge History*, the first three volumes are relevant to this book: i: *From the Earliest Times to c.500 BC*, ed. J. D. Clark (1982); ii: *From c.500 BC–AD 1050*, ed. J. D. Fage (1979); and iii: *From c.1050–c.1600*, ed. R. Oliver (1977). Of the UNESCO *General History of Africa*, the first four volumes cover the timespan dealt with here: i: *Methodology and African Prehistory*, ed. J. Ki-Zerbo (1981); ii: *Ancient Civilizations of Africa*, ed. G. Mokhtar (1981); iii: *Africa from the Seventh to the Eleventh Century*, ed. M. Elfasi (1988); iv: *Africa from the Twelfth to the Sixteenth Century*, ed. D. T. Niane (1984). The UNESCO volumes are available online, open access, in several languages, at <https://unesdoc.unesco.org/search/8aea7bc6-6e4e-4299-80fe-3378eb992176> (accessed 28 July 2022). It should be noted that the texts of most of these works were completed more than thirty years ago. For a more up-to-date and attractively produced single-volume work it is difficult to do better than C. Ehret, *The Civilizations of Africa: A History to 1800* (2nd edn, Charlottesville, 2016). An invaluable accompaniment to any reading are the brilliant maps, with short texts, offered in C. McEvedy, *The Penguin Atlas of African History* (revised edn, London, 1995).

On African archaeology, four major books, which together give an unrivalled overview of the richness of the continent, may be recommended: G. Connah, *African Civilizations: An Archaeological Perspective* (3rd edn, Cambridge, 2015); P. Mitchell, *African Connections: Archaeological Perspectives on Africa and the Wider World* (Walnut Creek, 2005); L. Barham and P. Mitchell, *The First Africans: African Archaeology from the Earliest Toolmakers to the Most Recent Foragers* (Cambridge, 2008); and D. W. Phillipson, *African Archaeology* (3rd edn, Cambridge, 2005). To these should be added the invaluable *Oxford Handbook of African Archaeology*, edited by P. Mitchell and P. Lane (Oxford, 2013), a compendium of seventy chapters written by specialists presenting the most recent thought in their particular area of study, each chapter with a thorough bibliography.

For readers who want to follow current discoveries and debates there are three principal journals dealing with the archaeology of the continent: *Journal of African Archaeology* (since 2003); *Azania: Archaeological Research in Africa* (since 1966); and *African Archaeological Review* (since 1983). For African history, much of the current research is published in *Journal of African History* (since 1960); *International Journal of African Studies* (since 1971); *African Historical Review* (since 2007, formally *Kleio*, 1969–2006); and *African Economic History* (1976–2016). These journals, it should be stressed, are for those who want to delve deep into current research.

For those who wish to be led gently into the main theme of this book, which is the Sahara and the peoples who helped to connect all the regions of northern Africa, there are several excellent introductions. A good place to start is with E. Gearon, *The Sahara: A Cultural History* (Oxford, 2011). An absolute must is E. W. Bovill's classic, first published in 1958, *The Golden Trade of the Moors* (2nd edn, Princeton, 2009). R. A. Austen, *Trans-Saharan Africa in World History* (Oxford, 2010) has much to add. Strongly to be recommended are two superb exhibition catalogues, both brilliantly illustrated and supported by informative essays, written by scholars involved in the new research featured in the volumes: A. LaGamma (ed.), *Sahel: Art and Empires on the Shores of the Sahara* (New York, 2020) and K. B. Berzock (ed.), *Caravans of Gold, Fragments in Time: Art, Culture, and Exchange across Medieval Saharan Africa* (Princeton, 2019). Another enjoyable source, offering entertaining vignettes of African medieval history, is F.-X. Fauvelle, *The Golden Rhinoceros: Histories of the African Middle Ages* (Princeton, 2018). Finally, for something rather different, though relevant to our theme, C. English, *The Book Smugglers of Timbuktu* (London, 2017) is a fascinating read. It gives an incomparable insight into the travellers who, in the eighteenth and nineteenth centuries, explored the desert routes, intercut with the story of the race to save the ancient libraries of Timbuktu from destruction during the Islamic insurgency of 2012. It is a vivid reminder that history is a continuum.

Chapter 1 The Desert, the Rivers, and the Oceans

The chapter explores aspects of the physical geography of Africa, an essential beginning for an understanding of how humans have responded to the constraints and opportunities of the landscape. By far the best introduction to the subject is W. M. Adams, A. S. Goudie, and A. R. Orme (eds.), *The Physical Geography of Africa* (Oxford, 1996), which contains essays on many of the topics discussed in this chapter: plate tectonics, the rift valley systems, climate and climate change, the river systems, and the different climatic zones, all clearly described with useful bibliographies. This is the place to begin. A more detailed consideration of the rift valley systems is given in J. Chorowicz, 'The East African Rift System', *Journal of African Earth Sciences*, 43 (2005), 379–410. The effect of climate change on the vegetational history of the Sahara has generated a considerable literature. The complexities of the Milanković cycles are reviewed in A. Berger, 'Milankovitch Theory and Climate', *Reviews of Geophysics*, 26/4 (1988), 624–57, and, more recently, R. K. Kaufmann and K. Juselius, 'Testing Competing Forms of the Milankovitch Hypothesis: A Multivariate Approach', *Palaeooceanography*, 31 (2016), 286–97. The Intertropical Convergence Zone and its effects on Africa are considered in S. Nicholson, 'The ITCZ and the Seasonal Cycle over Equatorial Africa', *Bulletin of the American Meteorological Society*, 99/2 (2018), 337–48. The use of multiple strands of evidence to build up a picture of climate change in the Sahara is clearly reviewed in P. B. de Menocal and J. E. Tierney, 'Green Sahara: African Humid Periods Paced by Earth's Orbital Changes', *Nature Education*, 3/10 (2012), 12–18, with full bibliography. The specific study of the effects of climate change on settlement in the eastern Sahara, referred to in this chapter, is presented in R. Kuper and S. Kröpelin, 'Climate-Controlled Holocene Occupation in the Sahara: Motor of Africa's Evolution', *Science*, 313/5788 (2006), 803–7. Other classic studies have been brought together in F. A. Hassan (ed.), *Droughts, Food and Culture: Ecological Change and Food Security in Africa's Later Prehistory* (New York, 2002). Further references to climate change in the desert and the Sahel are given below (p. 384).

The environmental zones of northern Africa—desert, Sahel, savannah, and forest—are well presented in the relevant chapters in Adams *et al.* (eds.), *Physical Geography of Africa*. The remarkable Ethiopian Highlands, which distort the neat regularity of the climatic zones, are introduced in D. W. Phillipson, *Ancient Ethiopia: Aksum, its Antecedents and Successors* (London, 1998), chapter 1, and G. Connah, *African Civilizations: An Archaeological Perspective* (3rd edn, Cambridge, 2015), chapter 3.

Of the two great African rivers, the Nile is introduced in P. Mitchell, *African Connections: Archaeological Perspectives on Africa in the Wider World* (Walnut Creek, 2005), 65–78, while Connah, *African Civilizations*, chapter 2, provides a careful analysis of the middle Nile region with its great bends and cataracts. The Nile is thoroughly described in H. J. Dumont, 'The Nile River System', in B. R. Davies and K. F. Walker (eds.), *The Ecology of River Systems* (Dordrecht, 1986), 61–88. The same volume contains a detailed study of the Niger by R. L. Welcomme, 'The Niger River System', 9–59. The variety of the riverine environments of the Niger and their effects on human settlements is carefully considered in R. J. McIntosh, *The Peoples of the Middle Niger* (Oxford, 1998).

The Mediterranean and the people who lived around it feature large in this book. A review of the characteristics of the Mediterranean from the point of view of sailors is given in B. Cunliffe, *On the Ocean: The Mediterranean and the Atlantic from Prehistory to AD 1500* (Oxford, 2017), 41–8, and aspects of Mediterranean culture are considered throughout. There are three excellent books dealing with the peoples living around the Mediterranean: P. Horden and N. Purcell, *The Corrupting Sea: A Study of Mediterranean History* (Oxford, 2000); C. Broodbank, *The Making of the Middle Sea: A History of the Mediterranean from the Beginning to the Emergence of the Classical World* (London, 2013); and D. Abulafia, *The Great Sea: A Human History of the Mediterranean* (London, 2011). The Phoenicians, who were responsible for opening up the Mediterranean and its Atlantic approaches, are treated in detail in M. E. Aubet, *The Phoenicians and the West: Politics, Colonies, and Trade*, trans. M. Turton (2nd edn, Cambridge, 2001). The Red Sea and Indian Ocean trading system in the Ptolemaic and Roman period is introduced in *The Periplus Maris Erythraei: Text with Introduction, Translation, and Commentary*, ed. L. Casson (Princeton, 1989). A more recent assessment is given in R. Tomber, *Indo-Roman Trade: From Pots to Pepper* (London, 2008). The Indian Ocean system in relation to Africa is presented in a broader context in Mitchell, *African Connections*, chapter 4. Translations of the major documentary sources relating to East African coastal trade are presented in *The East African Coast: Select Documents from the First to the Earlier Nineteenth Century*, ed. G. S. P. Freeman-Grenville (Oxford, 1962). The sailing conditions along the Atlantic coast are discussed in Cunliffe, *On the Ocean*, 49–67. We will return to the question of the Carthaginian exploration of the West African coast later.

While this book does not deal in any detail with the fascinating story of the evolution of modern humans in Africa and their spread to Eurasia, the subject is summarized in brief outline. It is fast-changing as new finds and revised dates become available. Four chapters in P. Mitchell and P. Lane (eds.), *The Oxford Handbook of African Archaeology* (Oxford, 2013) set the scene: R. A. Foley, 'Human Evolution as the Context for African Prehistory', 269–87; M. Domínguez-Rodrigo, 'The Oldowan: Early Hominins and the Beginning of Human Culture', 289–306; M. Sahnouni, S. Semaw, and M. Rogers, 'The African Acheulean: An Archaeological Summary', 307–23; and M. M. Lahr, 'Genetic and Fossil Evidence for Modern Human Origins', 325–40. For a more recent assessment of the fossil evidence, C. Stringer, 'The Origin and Evolution of *Homo Sapiens*', *Philosophical Transactions of the Royal Society*, ser. B, 371 (2016) gives an insight into the intricacies of the debate. The question of language can be approached through B. Heine and D. Nurse (eds.), *African Languages: An Introduction* (Cambridge, 2000). The use of ancient DNA analysis to identify population movements is beginning to show just how complex is the subject. Two recent scientific papers demonstrate the point: G. B. J. Busby *et al.*, 'Admixture into and within Sub-Saharan Africa', *eLife*, 21 June 2016 (doi: 10.7554/eLife.15266); and A. Choudhury *et al.*, 'African Genetic Diversity Provides Novel Insights into Evolutionary History and Local Adaptations', *Human Molecular Genetics*, 27/R2 (2018), R209–R218.

Chapter 2 The Long Beginning

For a well-balanced overview of the formative period, see D. W. Phillipson, *African Archaeology* (3rd edn, Cambridge, 2005), chapters 3 and 4. Clark's model for characterizing stone tools is explained in G. Clark, *World Prehistory in New Perspective* (3rd edn, Cambridge, 1977), 23–38. L. Wadley's brief chapter, 'Theoretical Frameworks for Understanding African Hunter-Gatherers', in P. Mitchell and P. Lane (eds.), *The Oxford Handbook of African Archaeology* (Oxford, 2013), 355–66, introduces some of the important considerations. A good introduction to the methods used to study past climates, including the Marine Isotope Stages, is given in T. M. Cronin, *Paleoclimates: Understanding Climate Change Past and Present* (New York, 2010). The spread of humans out of Africa is a fast-developing study. For a very readable account giving the broad context, see C. Stringer, *Lone Survivors: How We Came to Be the Only Humans on Earth* (London, 2013). Among the more recent papers the following add interesting detail: T. Rito *et al.*, 'A Dispersal of *Homo Sapiens* from Southern to Eastern Africa Immediately Preceding the Out-of-Africa Migration', *Science Reports*, 9/4728 (2019) (doi: 10.1038/s41598-019-41176-3) and C. J. Bae, K. Douka, and M. D. Petraglia, 'On the Origin of Modern Humans: Asian Perspectives', *Science*, 358/6368 (2017) (doi: 10.1126/science.aai9067). An overview of early hunter-gatherer groups in northern Africa is given in E. Garcea, 'Hunter-Gatherers of the Nile Valley and the Sahara before 12,000 Years Ago', in Mitchell and Lane (eds.), *Oxford Handbook of African Archaeology*, 419–30. See also E. A. A. Garcea, 'The Spread of Aterian Peoples in North Africa', in E. A. A. Garcia (ed.), *South-Eastern Mediterranean Peoples between 130,000 and 10,000 Years Ago* (Oxford, 2010), 37–53. An important contribution to dating is published in R. N. E. Barton *et al.*, 'OSL Dating of the Aterian Levels at Dar es-Soltan I (Rabat, Morocco) and Implications for the Dispersal of Modern *Homo Sapiens*', *Quaternary Science Reviews*, 28 (2009), 1914–31. Excavations relevant to this period include Uan Tabu and Haua Fteah in Libya, described in E. A. A. Garcea (ed.), *Uan Tabu in the Settlement History of the Libyan Sahara* (Florence, 2001); C. B. M. McBurney, *The Haua Fteah (Cyrenaica) and the Stone Age in the South-East Mediterranean* (Cambridge, 1967); and K. Douka *et al.*, 'The Chronostratigraphy of the Haua Fteah Cave (Cyrenaica, Northeast Libya)', *Journal of Human Evolution*, 66 (2014), 39–63. For an interesting regional study, see A. L. Hawkins, 'The Aterian of the Oases of the Western Desert of Egypt: Adaptation to Changing Climatic Conditions?', in J.-J. Hublin and S. P. McPherron, *Modern Origins: A North African Perspective* (New York, 2012), 157–75. The intricacies of Middle Stone Age technology are thoroughly reviewed in E. M. L. Scerri and E. E. Spinapolice, 'Lithics of the North African Middle Stone Age: Assumptions, Evidence and Future Directions', *Journal of Anthropological Sciences*, 97 (2019), 9–43.

The later hunter-gatherer period in North Africa is conveniently summarized in R. N. E. Barton and A. Bouzouggar, 'Hunter-Gatherers in the Maghreb, 25,000–6000 Years Ago', in Mitchell and Lane (eds.), *Oxford Handbook of African Archaeology*, 431–43, and in R. N. E. Barton *et al.*, 'The Late Upper Palaeolithic Occupation of the Moroccan Northwest Maghreb during the Late Glacial Maximum', *African Archaeological Review*, 22/2 (2005), 77–100. More specifically, for the Capsian culture, M. Jackes and D. Lubell, 'Early and Middle Holocene Environments and Capsian Cultural Change: Evidence from the Télidjène Basin, Eastern Algeria', *African Archaeological Review*, 25/1 (2008), 41–55. For the Iberomaurusian culture, see R. N. E. Barton *et al.*, 'Origins of the Iberomaurusian in NW Africa: New AMS Radiocarbon Dating of the Middle and Later Stone Age Deposits at Taforalt Cave, Morocco', *Journal of Human Evolution*, 65/3 (2013), 266–81. The practice of dental evulsion is reviewed in L. T. Humphrey and E. Bocaege, 'Tooth Evulsion in the Maghreb: Chronological and Geographical Patterns', *African Archaeological Review*, 25/1 (2008), 109–23. An insight into burial practice is given in L. Humphrey *et al.*, 'Infant Funerary Behavior and Kinship in Pleistocene Hunter-Gatherers from Morocco', *Journal of Human Evolution*, 135/102637 (2019) (doi: 10.1016/j.jhevol.2019.07.001).

The Iwo Eleru burial was first published in D. Brothwell and T. Shaw, 'A Late Upper Palaeolithic Proto-West African Negro from Nigeria', *Man*, 6/2 (1971), 221–7, with a later, more detailed study in K. Harvati *et al.*, 'The Later Stone Age Calvaria from Iwo Eleru, Nigeria: Morphology and Chronology', *PLoS One*, 6/9 (2011) (doi: 10.1371/journal.pone.0024024). Its biological context is further examined in C. M. Stojanowski, 'Iwo Eleru's Place among Late Pleistocene and Early Holocene Populations of North and East Africa', *Journal of Human Evolution*, 75 (2014), 80–9.

References for the climatic factors affecting the greening of the Sahara have been given in the Further Reading for Chapter 1. For an excellent overview with copious references, see F. S. R. Pausata *et al.*, 'The Greening of the Sahara: Past Changes and Future Implications', *One Earth*, 2/3 (2020), 235–50. Other relevant papers include P. B. de Menocal *et al.*, 'Abrupt Onset and Termination of the African Humid Period', *Quaternary Science Reviews*, 19/1 (2000), 347–61, and M. R. Talbot *et al.*, 'An Abrupt Change in the African Monsoon at the End of the Younger Dryas', *Geochemistry, Geophysics, and Geosystems*, 8/3 (2007) (doi: 10.1029/2006GC001465). The effects of climate change on human populations in the Sahara are discussed in K. Manning and A. Timpson, 'The Demographic Response to Holocene Climate Change in the Sahara', *Quaternary Science Reviews*, 101 (2014), 28–35, and J. C. Larrasoaña, A. P. Roberts, and E. J. Rohling, 'Dynamics of Green Sahara Periods and their Role in Hominin Evolution', *PLoS One*, 8/10 (2013) (doi: org/10.1371/journal.pone.0076514).

The importance of lakes and rivers to the economy of the hunter-gatherers in northern Africa is discussed in J. E. G. Sutton, 'The Aquatic Civilization of Middle Africa', *Journal of African History*, 15/4 (1974), 527–46. The hut shelters excavated at Ti-n-Torha in Acacus, providing evidence of the community's subsistence strategy, are reported in B. E. Barich, 'La Serie stratigrafica dell'Uadi Ti-n-Torha (Acacus, Libia): per una interpretazione delle facies a ceramica saharo-sudanesi', *Origini*, 8 (1974), 7–157. Evidence for the early origin of pottery production in northern Africa is presented in E. Huysecom *et al.*, 'The Emergence of Pottery in Africa during the Tenth Millennium cal. BC: New Evidence from Ounjougou (Mali)', *Antiquity*, 83/322 (2009), 905–17, and in F. Jesse, 'Early Pottery in Northern Africa: An Overview', *Journal of African Archaeology*, 8/2 (2010), 219–38. The dugout canoe from Dufuna, Nigeria, is described in A. Garba, 'The Architecture and Chemistry of a Dug-Out: The Dufuna Canoe in Ethno-Archaeological Perspective', *Berichte des Sonderforschungsbereichs*, 268/8 (1996), 193–200.

Chapter 3   Domesticating the Land, 6500–1000 BC

The most convenient place to begin with this complex but intensely interesting topic is with two overviews in P. Mitchell and P. Lane (eds.), *The Oxford Handbook of African Archaeology* (Oxford, 2013): D. Gifford-Gonzalez and O. Hanotte, 'Domesticating

Animals in Africa', 491–505, and S. di Lernia, 'The Emergence and Spread of Herding in Northern Africa: A Critical Reappraisal', 527–40. For earlier debates about cattle found in the Egyptian Sahara, see F. Wendorf and R. Schild, 'Are the Early Holocene Cattle in the Eastern Sahara Domestic or Wild?', *Evolutionary Anthropology*, 3/4 (1994), 118–28, and A. Gautier, 'Archaeozoology of the Bir Kiseiba Region, Eastern Sahara', in F. Wendorf, R. Schild, and A. E. Close (eds.), *Cattle-Keepers of the Eastern Sahara: The Neolithic of Bir Kiseiba* (Dallas, 1984), 49–72. More recently there have been several studies of the genetics of cattle, of which the most useful are M. Brass, 'Early North African Cattle Domestication and its Ecological Setting: A Reassessment', *Journal of World Prehistory*, 31 (2018), 81–115, and D. Pitt *et al.*, 'Domestication of Cattle: Two or Three Events?', *Evolutionary Applications*, 12/1 (2019), 123–36. The key site of Nabta Playa is described in F. Wendorf and R. Schild *et al.*, *Holocene Settlement of the Egyptian Sahara*, i: *The Archaeology of Nabta Playa* (New York, 2001); the megalithic alignments are discussed on pp. 489–502, and more recently in J. M. Malville, 'Astronomy at Nabta Playa, Southern Egypt', in C. L. N. Ruggles (ed.), *Handbook of Archaeoastronomy and Ethnoastronomy*, ii (New York, 2015), 1079–91.

The climatic event of 6200 BC is discussed in T. Kobashi *et al.*, 'Precise Timing and Characterization of Abrupt Climate Change 8,200 Years Ago from Air Trapped in Polar Ice', *Quaternary Science Reviews*, 26/9 (2007), 1212–22.

The subject of rock art in the Sahara, which has generated a considerable literature, can best be approached through A. Muzzolini, *Les Images rupestres du Sahara* (Toulouse, 1995); J.-L. Le Quellec, *Art rupestre et préhistoire du Sahara* (Paris, 1998); and F. Mori, *The Great Civilisations of the Ancient Sahara: Neolithisation and the Earliest Evidence of Anthropomorphic Religions* (Rome, 1998). See also B. E. Barich, *People, Water and Grain: The Beginnings of Domestication in the Sahara and the Nile Valley* (Rome, 1998).

The development of domestic crops in Africa is summarized in three chapters in P. Mitchell and P. Lane (eds.), *The Oxford Handbook of African Archaeology* (Oxford, 2013): D. Fuller and E. Hildebrand, 'Domesticating Plants in Africa', 507–25; R. Haaland and G. Haaland, 'Early Farming Societies along the Nile', 541–53; and P. Breunig, 'Pathways to Food-Production in the Sahel', 555–70. The Mediterranean and Near Eastern contribution to the spread of farming to northern Africa is a subject being actively debated. As background to the spread of the Neolithic system through the Mediterranean, see J. Zilhão, 'Early Food Production in Southwestern Europe', in C. Renfrew and P. G. Bahn (eds.), *The Cambridge World Prehistory*, iii: *West and Central Asia and Europe* (Cambridge, 2014), 1818–34. Four detailed studies can be recommended that are specific to North Africa: J. Linstädter, 'The Epipalaeolithic–Neolithic-Transition in the Mediterranean Region of Northwest Africa', *Quartär*,

55 (2008), 41–62; J. Morales *et al.*, 'The Introduction of South-Western Asian Domesticated Plants in North-Western Africa: An Archaeobotanical Contribution from Neolithic Morocco', *Quaternary International*, 412B (2016), 96–109; C. Broodbank and G. Lucarini, 'The Dynamics of Mediterranean Africa, *ca.* 9600–1000 BC: An Interpretative Synthesis of Knowns and Unknowns', *Journal of Mediterranean Archaeology*, 32/2 (2019), 195–268; and G. Lucarini, Y. Bokbot, and C. Broodbank, 'New Light on the Silent Millennia: Mediterranean Africa, *ca.* 4000–900 BC', *African Archaeological Review*, 38/1 (2021), 147–64. The possibility that there was an influx of population from the Levant is discussed in R. Fregel *et al.*, 'Ancient Genomes from North Africa Evidence Prehistoric Migrations to the Maghreb from both the Levant and Europe', *Proceedings of the National Academy of Sciences*, 115/26 (2018), 6774–9. That they brought their dogs with them is argued in A. Bergström *et al.*, 'Origins and Genetic Legacy of Prehistoric Dogs', *Science*, 370/6516 (2020), 557–64.

The independent domestication of native African crops is succinctly presented in Fuller and Hildebrand, 'Domesticating Plants in Africa'. In more detail, for the early cultivation of pearl millet, see K. Manning *et al.*, '4500-Year-Old Domesticated Pearl Millet (*Pennisetum glaucum*) from the Tilemsi Valley, Mali: New Insights into an Alternative Cereal Domestication Pathway', *Journal of Archaeological Science*, 38/2 (2011), 312–22. For early rice cultivation, S. S. Murray, 'Identifying African Rice Domestication in the Middle Niger Delta (Mali)', in R. Cappers (ed.), *Fields of Change: Progress in African Archaeobotany* (Groningen, 2007), 52–62. Ethiopian domesticates are discussed in D. W. Phillipson, 'The Antiquity of Cultivation and Herding in Ethiopia', in T. Shaw *et al.* (eds.), *The Archaeology of Africa: Food, Metals and Towns* (London, 1993), 344–57, updated by A. Negash, 'Enset (*Ensete ventricosum*) and the Archaeology of Southwestern Ethiopia', *African Archaeological Review*, 37/4 (2020), 627–37.

The changing climate is summarized in S. Kröpelin *et al.*, 'Climate-Driven Ecosystem Succession in the Sahara: The Past 6,000 Years', *Science*, 320/5877 (2008), 765–8. Early farming in the western Sahel is discussed in K. Neumann, 'Early Plant Food Production in the West African Sahel: New Evidence', in M. van der Veen (ed.), *The Exploitation of Plant Resources in Ancient Africa* (New York, 1999), 73–80; K. Neumann, 'The Late Emergence of Agriculture in Sub-Saharan Africa: Archaeobotanical Evidence and Ecological Considerations', in K. Neumann, A. Butler, and S. Kahlheber (eds.), *Food, Fuel and Fields: Progress in African Archaeobotany* (Cologne, 2003), 71–92; and S. Kahlheber and K. Neumann, 'The Development of Plant Cultivation in Semi-Arid West Africa', in T. P. Denham, J. Iriarte, and L. Vrydaghs (eds.), *Rethinking Agriculture: Archaeological and Ethnoarchaeological Perspectives* (Walnut Creek, 2007), 320–46. The complexities of the middle Niger region are explored in R. J. McIntosh, *The Peoples of the Middle Niger* (Oxford, 1998). A useful summary of the development of farming in Ethiopia is given in M. Curtis, 'Archaeological Evidence for the Emergence of Food-Production in the Horn of Africa', in Mitchell and Lane (eds.), *Oxford Handbook of African Archaeology*, 571–84.

The movement of crops into and out of Africa across the East African–Indian Ocean interface is discussed in D. Q. Fuller, 'African Crops in Prehistoric South Asia: A Critical Review', in Neumann *et al.* (eds.), *Food, Fuel and Fields*, 239–71; D. Q. Fuller and N. Boivin, 'Crops, Cattle and Commensals across the Indian Ocean: Current and Potential Archaeobiological Evidence', *Études Océan Indien*, 42/43 (2009), 13–46; D. Q. Fuller *et al.*, 'Across the Indian Ocean: The Prehistoric Movement of Plants and Animals', *Antiquity*, 85 (2011), 544–58; and R. C. Power *et al.*, 'Asian Crop Dispersal in Africa and Late Holocene Human Adaptation to Tropical Environments', *Journal of World Prehistory*, 32/4 (2019), 353–92.

Contacts between Iberia and North-West Africa in the third and second millennium have not been extensively studied but the distribution of Beaker pottery and associated artefacts are discussed in R. J. Harrison and A. Gilman, 'Trade in the Second and Third Millennia BC between the Maghreb and Iberia', in V. Markotic (ed.), *Ancient Europe and the Mediterranean* (Warminster, 1977), 91–104, and M. del C. Poyato Holgado and A. Hernando Grande, 'Relaciones entre la Península Ibérica y el Norte de Africa "marfil y campaniforme"', in E. Ripoll Perelló (ed.), *Actas del Congreso Internacional 'El Estrecho de Gibraltar', Ceuta, 1987* (Madrid, 1988), i, 317–29. The sources of ivory found in contexts in Iberia are discussed in T. X. Schuhmacher, J. L. Cardoso, and A. Banerjee, 'Sourcing African Ivory in Chalcolithic Portugal', *Antiquity*, 83/322 (2009), 983–97.

The special characteristics of the Nile valley are nicely brought out in F. A. Hassan, 'The Dynamics of a Riverine Civilization: A Geoarchaeological Perspective on the Nile Valley, Egypt', *World Archaeology*, 29/1 (1997), 51–74, and a careful consideration of the early farming system is provided by Haaland and Haaland, 'Early Farming Societies along the Nile'. A very thoughtful discussion of the archaeological evidence for early developments in Egypt, presented in the broader regional setting, is offered in D. Wengrow, *The Archaeology of Early Egypt: Social Transformations in North-East Africa, c.10,000–2650 BC* (Cambridge, 2006). A useful source for the Pharaonic period in Egypt is the collection of essays brought together in I. Shaw (ed.), *The Oxford History of Ancient Egypt* (Oxford, 2000). The middle Nile valley, Nubia, is thoroughly introduced in G. Connah, *African Civilizations: An Archaeological Perspective* (3rd edn, Cambridge, 2015), chapter 2. For a broad overview of the development of the region, see also D. A. Welsby, *The Kingdom of Kush: The Napatan and Meroitic Empires* (London, 1996) and the same author's 'Kerma and Kush and their Neighbours', in

Mitchell and Lane (eds.), *The Oxford Handbook of African Archaeology*, 751–64. The position of Kush in the regional trading network is explored in H. Hafsaas-Tsakos, 'The Kingdom of Kush: An African Centre on the Periphery of the Bronze Age World', *Norwegian Archaeological Review*, 42/1 (2009), 50–70. The Land of Punt is discussed in R. Fattovich, 'Punt: The Archaeological Perspective', *Beiträge zur Sudanforschung*, 6 (1996), 15–29, and K. Kitchen, 'The Land of Punt', in T. Shaw *et al.* (eds.), *The Archaeology of Africa: Foods, Metals and Towns* (London, 1993), 587–608.

Chapter 4   Creating Connectivities, 1000–140 BC

The *Histories* of Herodotus features large in the discussion of the early travellers' tales. There are many good translations. The classic is by G. Rawlinson, *The History of Herodotus* (1858–60), available, edited by E. H. Blakeney, as *The Histories of Herodotus* (London, 1964). A more recent version is translated by T. Holland as *Herodotus: The Histories* (London, 2013). The text ascribed to Hanno, describing his Atlantic venture, is available in a translation by A. N. Oikonomides, *Periplus; or, Circumnavigation (of Africa)* (Chicago, 1977). There have been many attempts to reconstruct the geography of the voyage. Among the best are M. Cary and E. H. Warmington, *The Ancient Explorers* (London, 1929); R. Carpenter, *Beyond the Pillars of Hercules: The Classical World Seen through the Eyes of its Discoverers* (New York, 1966); and D. W. Roller, *Through the Pillars of Herakles: Greco-Roman Exploration of the Atlantic* (New York, 2006). This last volume, as its subtitle implies, includes details of other attempts to explore the Atlantic coast of Africa. A thorough discussion of scholarship surrounding Hanno's journey is provided in A. Mederos Martín and G. Escribano Cobo, 'El periplo norteafricano de Hannón y la rivalidad gaditano-cartaginesa de los siglos IV–III a.C.', *Gerión*, 18 (2000), 77–107. For arguments that it would not have been possible to sail north along the coast in classical times, see R. Mauny, 'La Navigation sur les côtes du Sahara pendant l'antiquité', *Revue des Études Anciennes*, 57/1–2 (1955), 92–101.

The Phoenicians made a significant impact on the North African coast and the Atlantic coast of Morocco. The most convenient background study is M. E. Aubet, *The Phoenicians and the West: Politics, Colonies, and Trade*, trans. M. Turton (2nd edn, Cambridge, 2001). Evidence for the Phoenician trading enclave at Huelva is discussed in F. González de Canales Cerisola, L. S. Pichardo, and J. L. Gómez, *El emporio feniso precolonial da Huelva, c.900–770 BC* (Madrid, 2004) and F. González de Canales, L. Serrano, and J. Llompart, 'The Precolonial Phoenician Emporium of Huelva, *ca.*900–770 BC', *Bulletin Anticke Beschaving*, 81 (2006), 13–29. The trading enclaves along the Portuguese coast are described in A. M. Arruda, *Los fenicios en Portugal: fenicios y mundo indigena en el centro y sur de Portugal, siglos VIII–VI a.C.* (Barcelona, 2000).

The archaeological evidence for Phoenician, Carthaginian, and early Roman settlement along the Atlantic coast of Africa has been gathered together in a major work, A. Mederos Martín and G. Escribano Cobo, 'Oceanus Gaditanus': ora, púrpura y pesca en el litoral atlántico norteafricano y las Islas Canarias en época fenicia, cartaginesa y romana republicana (Santa Cruz de Tenerife, 2015).

For Carthage, the earliest archaeological evidence for settlement is discussed in R. F. Docter et al., 'New Radiocarbon Dates from Carthage: Bridging the Gap between History and Archaeology?', in C. Sagona (ed.), Beyond the Homeland: Markers in Phoenician Chronology, supplement to Ancient Near Eastern Studies, 28 (2008), 379–422, and R. F. Docter et al., 'Punic Carthage: Two Decades of Archaeological Investigation', in J. L. López Castro (ed.), Las ciudades fenicio-púnicas en el Mediterráneo occidental (Almería, 2008), 85–104.

The classic treatments of the Berbers of North Africa are G. Camps, Les Berbères: mémoire et identité (2nd edn, Paris, 2007) and M. Brett and E. Fentress, The Berbers (Oxford, 1996). The rise of Carthage and its interaction with the Numidian kingdom and the Roman world is treated in S. Lancel, Carthage: A History (Oxford, 1995). The Numidians are considered in G. Camps, 'Les Numides et la civilisation punique', Antiquités Africaines, 14 (1979), 43–53. For the Numidian king Masinissa, see P. G. Walsh, 'Masinissa', Journal of Roman Studies, 55 (1965), 149–60. Numidian monuments like the Medracen tomb are discussed in J. C. Quinn, 'Monumental Power: "Numidian Royal Architecture" in Context', in J. R. W. Prag and J. C. Quinn (eds.), The Hellenistic West: Rethinking the Ancient Mediterranean (Cambridge, 2013), 179–215.

The development of complex societies in the Sahel is introduced in two chapters in P. Mitchell and P. Lane (eds.), The Oxford Handbook of African Archaeology (Oxford, 2013): K. MacDonald, 'Complex Societies, Urbanism, and Trade in the Western Sahel', 829–44, and D. Gronenborn, 'States and Trade in the Central Sahel', 845–58. The complex developments in the middle Niger region are set out in extenso in R. J. McIntosh, The Peoples of the Middle Niger (Oxford, 1998) and the same author's Ancient Middle Niger: Urbanism and the Self-Organizing Landscape (Cambridge, 2005). Of the important sites in the region, Dhar Tichitt is discussed in S. Amblard-Pison, Communautés villageoises néolithiques des Dhars Tichitt et Oulata (Mauritanie) (Oxford, 2006), and Jenné-Jeno in S. K. McIntosh (ed.), Excavations at Jenné-Jeno, Hambarketolo and Kaniana (Inland Niger Delta, Mali): The 1981 Season (Berkeley, 1995). The growing social complexity in the region is carefully analysed in S. K. McIntosh and R. J. McIntosh, 'Cities without Citadels: Understanding Urban Origins along the Middle Niger', in T. Shaw et al. (eds.), The Archaeology of Africa: Food, Metals and Towns (London, 1993), 622–41; K. C. MacDonald, 'Before the Empire of Ghana: Pastoralism and the Origins of Cultural Complexity in the Sahel', in G. Connah (ed.),

Transformations in Africa: Essays on Africa's Later Past (London, 1998), 71–103; and R. J. McIntosh, 'The Pulse Model: Genesis and Accommodation of Specialization in the Middle Niger', *Journal of African History*, 34/2 (1993), 181–220.

The complex questions surrounding the development of bronze and iron metallurgy in Africa are ably summarized in B. Mapunda, 'The Appearance and Development of Metallurgy South of the Sahara', in Mitchell and Lane (eds.), *Oxford Handbook of African Archaeology*, 615–26. This updates the classic studies of D. Killick *et al.*, 'Reassessment of the Evidence for Early Metallurgy in Niger, West Africa', *Journal of Archaeological Science*, 15/4 (1988), 367–94, and A. F. C. Holl, 'Metals and Precolonial African Society', in M. S. Bisson *et al.*, *Ancient African Metallurgy: The Socio-Cultural Context*, ed. J. O. Vogel (Walnut Creek, 2000), 1–82. The debate is taken further in É. Zangato and A. F. C. Holl, 'On the Iron Front: New Evidence from North-Central Africa', *Journal of African Archaeology*, 8/1 (2010), 7–23, and the critique, P. Craddock, 'New Paradigms for Old Iron: Thoughts on É. Zangato and A. F. C. Holl's "On the Iron Front"', in the same journal, 29–36. A broad overview of copper working is provided in E. W. Herbert, *Red Gold of Africa: Copper in Precolonial History and Culture* (Madison, 1984). For details of copper production in Mauritania, N. Lambert, 'Les Industries sur cuivre dans l'Ouest Saharien', *West African Journal of Archaeology*, 1 (1971), 9–21. The Nok culture is fully covered in a series of excellent papers brought together in P. Breunig (ed.), *Nok: African Sculpture in Archaeological Context* (Frankfurt, 2014).

Evidence for desert crossings in this period is plentiful. A useful starting point is M. Liverani, 'The Libyan Caravan Route in Herodotus IV. 181–185', *Journal of the Economic and Social History of the Orient*, 43/4 (2000), 496–520. A range of archaeological evidence is presented in K. C. MacDonald, 'A View from the South: Sub-Saharan Evidence for Contacts between North Africa, Mauritania and the Niger, 1000 BC–AD 700', in A. Dowler and E. R. Galvin (eds.), *Money, Trade and Trade Routes in Pre-Islamic North Africa* (London, 2011), 72–82; S. Nixon, 'Excavating Essouk-Tadmakka (Mali): New Archaeological Investigations of Early Islamic Trans-Saharan Trade', *Azania*, 44/2 (2009), 217–55; and S. Magnavita, 'The Oldest Textiles from Sub-Saharan West Africa: Woolen Facts from Kissi, Burkina Faso', *Journal of African Archaeology*, 6/2 (2008), 243–57. Other relevant papers will be found in S. Magnavita *et al.* (eds.), *Crossroads: Cultural and Technological Developments in First Millennium BC/AD West Africa* (Frankfurt, 2009) and D. J. Mattingly *et al.* (eds.), *Trade in the Ancient Sahara and Beyond* (Cambridge, 2017).

Engravings of horse-drawn chariots on rock faces in the Sahara have long been a subject of interest. The two classic studies are H. Lhote, *Les Chars rupestres sahariens: des Syrtes au Niger, par le pays des Garamantes et des Atlantes* (Toulouse, 1982) and G. Camps, 'Beginnings of Pastoralism and Cultivation in North-West Africa and the

Sahara: Origins of the Berbers', in *The Cambridge History of Africa*, i: *From the Earliest Times to c.500 BC*, ed. J. D. Clark (Cambridge, 1982), 548–623. It is now thought that the horse and chariot reflected status rather than representing the transport of goods. The use of the camel is discussed in B. D. Shaw, 'The Camel in Roman North Africa and the Sahara: History, Biology, and Human Economy', *Bulletin de l'Institut Fondamental d'Afrique Noire*, ser. B, 41/4 (1979), 663–721. For the early occurrence of camels, P. Rowley-Conwy, 'The Camel in the Nile Valley: New Radiocarbon Accelerator (AMS) Dates from Qaṣr Ibrîm', *Journal of Egyptian Archaeology*, 74/1 (1988), 245–8, and for camels in Senegal, K. C. MacDonald and R. H. MacDonald, 'The Origins and Development of Domesticated Animals in Arid West Africa', in R. M. Blench and K. C. MacDonald (eds.), *The Origins and Development of African Livestock: Archaeology, Genetics, Linguistics and Ethnography* (London, 2000), 127–62.

The Garamantes of the Fazzan have been the subject of intensive study. Among the pioneer early works are two general discussions by C. M. Daniels: *The Garamantes of Southern Libya* (London, 1970) and 'The Garamantes of the Fezzan', in F. F. Gadallah (ed.), *Libya in History* (Benghazi, 1971), 261–85. Early excavation reports by Charles Daniels include 'Garamantian Excavations: Zinchecra, 1965–67', *Libya Antiqua*, 5 (1968), 113–94, and 'Excavation and Fieldwork amongst the Garamantes', *Libyan Studies*, 20 (1989), 45–61. To these should be added M. S. Ayoub, *Excavations in Germa between 1962 and 1966* (Tripoli, 1967). The more recent programme by David Mattingly is thoroughly presented in his *The Archaeology of Fazzan*, i: *Synthesis* (London, 2003). More detailed studies generated by the work appear in volumes ii (2007), iii (2010), and iv (2013). The role of the Garamantes in trans-Saharan trade is explored in an important chapter, D. J. Mattingly, 'The Garamantes and the Origins of Saharan Trade: State of the Field and Future Agendas', in D. J. Mattingly *et al.* (eds.), *Trade in the Ancient Sahara and Beyond* (Cambridge, 2017), 1–52.

For a brief but perceptive overview of Egypt from the third to the first millennium, see I. Shaw, 'Pharaonic Egypt', in Mitchell and Lane (eds.), *Oxford Handbook of African Archaeology*, 737–50. More detailed essays are brought together in I. Shaw (ed.), *The Oxford History of Ancient Egypt* (Oxford, 2000), each with suggestions for further reading. The international trading centre at Naukratis in the delta is fully treated in A. Möller, *Naukratis: Trade in Archaic Greece* (Oxford, 2000). A reader wishing to explore the conflict between the Greeks and Persians cannot do better than to invest time in R. Lane Fox, *Alexander the Great* (London, 1973).

The background for Nubia and the kingdom of Kush in the first millennium BC is given in D. A. Welsby, *The Kingdom of Kush: The Napatan and Meroitic Empires* (London, 1996) and L. Török, *The Kingdom of Kush: Handbook of the Napatan-Meroitic Civilization* (Leiden, 1997). A number of specialist papers relevant to the region will be found in R. Friedman (ed.), *Egypt and Nubia: Gifts of the Desert* (London, 2002). For Ethiopia in the first millennium BC useful background is given in D. W. Phillipson, *Ancient Ethiopia: Aksum, its Antecedents and Successors* (London, 1998) and the same author's 'Complex Societies of the Eritrean/Ethiopian Highlands and their Neighbours', in Mitchell and Lane (eds.), *Oxford Handbook of African Archaeology*, 799–815. More specialist papers include R. Fattovich, 'The Development of Ancient States in the Horn of Africa, *c.*3000 BC–AD 1000: An Archaeological Outline', *Journal of World Prehistory*, 23 (2010), 145–75, and D. W. Phillipson and P. R. Schmidt (eds.), *Re-evaluating the Archaeology of the First Millennium BC in the Northern Horn*, special issue of *African Archaeological Review*, 26/4 (2009). The Red Sea trading system is considered in its Indian Ocean context in R. Tomber, *Indo-Roman Trade: From Pots to Pepper* (London, 2008). The archaeology of the Red Sea trading ports is described in a number of individual reports, including D. Peacock and L. Blue (eds.), *The Ancient Red Sea Port of Adulis, Eritrea: Results of the Eritro-British Expedition, 2004–5* (Oxford, 2007); by the same editors, *Myos Hormos—Quseir al-Qadim: Roman and Islamic Ports on the Red Sea. Survey and Excavation, 1999–2003* (Oxford, 2006); S. E. Sidebotham, *Berenike and the Ancient Maritime Spice Route* (Berkeley, 2011); and M. Woźniak, 'Shaping a City and its Defenses: Fortifications of Hellenistic Berenike Troglodytika', *Polish Archaeology in the Mediterranean*, 26/2 (2017), 43–60.

Chapter 5 The Impact of Empire, 140 BC–AD 400

There are several general works dealing with the Roman period in North Africa. A straightforward introduction is provided in S. Raven, *Rome in Africa* (London, 1993). M. Brett and E. Fentress, *The Berbers* (Oxford, 1996) and C. Briand-Ponsart and C. Hugoniot, *L'Afrique romaine de l'Atlantique à la Tripolitaine, 146 av. J.-C.–533 ap. J.-C.* (Paris, 2006) offer more up-to-date surveys. For Tripolitania, see D. J. Mattingly, *Tripolitania* (London, 1995), and for Egypt, A. K. Bowman, *Egypt after the Pharaohs, 332 BC–AD 642* (London, 1986). See also D. J. Mattingly and R. B. Hitchner, 'Roman Africa: An Archaeological Review', *Journal of Roman Studies*, 85 (1995), 165–213. The contribution of Juba II is thoroughly discussed in D. W. Roller, *The World of Juba II and Kleopatra Selene: Royal Scholarship on Rome's African Frontier* (London, 2003).

   On the early desert expeditions of Cornelius Balbus and Julius Maternus, see J. Desanges, *Recherches sur l'activité des Méditerranéens aux confins de l'Afrique, VIᵉ siècle avant J.-C. – IVᵉ siècle après J.-C.* (Rome, 1978). The revolt of Tacfarinas is analysed in some detail in W. Vanacker, 'Adhuc Tacfarinus: Causes of the Tiberian War in North Africa (AD *ca.*15–24) and the Impact of the Conflict on Roman Imperial Policy',

Historia, 64/3 (2015), 336–56. Nero's interest in exploring the Nile is briefly considered in E. Buckley and M. Dinter, *A Companion to the Neronian Age* (Chichester, 2013), 364–5.

The effects of the Roman administration on the native population is the subject of E. Fentress, 'Romanizing the Berbers', *Past and Present*, no. 190 (Feb. 2006), 3–33. Investment in agriculture is treated in D. L. Stone, 'Culture and Investment in the Rural Landscape: The North African *Bonus Agricola*', *Antiquités Africaines*, 34 (1998), 103–13. For the development of Dougga, see M. Khanoussi, 'L'Évolution urbaine de Thugga (Dougga) en Afrique proconsulaire: de l'agglomération numide à ville africo-romaine', *Comptes-Rendus des Séances de l'Académie des Inscriptions et Belles-Lettres* (2003), 131–55, and the same author's *Dougga* (Tunis, 2008). The anomalous position of Egypt in the Roman empire is well brought out in A. K. Bowman, *Egypt after the Pharaohs, 332 BC–AD 642* (London, 1986).

The kingdom of Meroe can most conveniently be accessed through D. A. Welsby, *The Kingdom of Kush: The Napatan and Meroitic Empires* (London, 1996); L. Török, *The Kingdom of Kush: Handbook of the Napatan-Meroitic Civilization* (Leiden, 1997); D. N. Edwards, 'Meroe and the Sudanic Kingdoms', *Journal of African History*, 39/2 (1998), 175–93; and the same author's *The Archaeology of the Meroitic State: New Perspectives on Social and Political Organization* (Oxford, 1996). See also I. Vincentelli, 'Trade and Caravan Routes in Meroitic Times', in M. Liverani and F. Merighi (eds.), *Arid Lands in Roman Times* (Florence, 2003), 79–86. The Aksumite kingdom is presented in S. Munro-Hay, *Aksum: An African Civilisation of Late Antiquity* (Edinburgh, 1991); D. W. Phillipson, *Ancient Ethiopia: Aksum, its Antecedents and Successors* (London, 1998); and the same author's *Foundations of an African Civilisation: Aksum and the Northern Horn, 1000 BC–AD 1300* (Woodbridge, 2012). Trade along the East African coast is introduced in *The Periplus Maris Erythraei: Text with Introduction, Translation, and Commentary*, ed. L. Casson (Princeton, 1989). The question of Diogenes and the 'Mountains of the Moon' is exhaustively explored in G. Sidiropoulos and D. Kalpakis, 'The "Mountains of the Moon": A Puzzle of the Ptolemaic Geography', *Byzantina Symmeikta*, 24 (2014), 29–66.

We return in this chapter to the Garamantes, now during the Roman period. The references given in the Further Reading for Chapter 4 are relevant here as well. Additional works include D. J. Mattingly and A. I. Wilson, 'Farming the Sahara: The Garamantian Contribution in Southern Libya', in Liverani and Merighi (eds.), *Arid Lands in Roman Times*, 37–50; A. I. Wilson, 'The Spread of Foggara-Based Irrigation in the Ancient Sahara', in D. J. Mattingly *et al.* (eds.), *The Libyan Desert: Natural Resources and Cultural Heritage* (London, 2006), 205–16; D. J. Mattingly, 'Impacts beyond Empire: Rome and the Garamantes of the Sahara', in L. de Blois and J. Rich (eds.), *The Transformation of Economic Life under the Roman Empire* (Amsterdam, 2002), 184–203; and R. Pelling, 'Garamantian Agriculture and its Significance in the Wider North African Context: The Evidence of the Plant Remains from the Fazzan Project', *Journal of North African Studies*, 10/3–4 (2005), 397–412. The screen of forts built by the Romans in the early third century are discussed in G. Barker *et al.* (eds.), *Farming in the Desert: The UNESCO Libyan Valleys Archaeological Survey*, i: *Synthesis* (Paris, 1996), while the Garamantian traders encountered, mentioned on ostraca, are noted in R. Marichal, *Les Ostraca de Bu Njem* (Tripoli, 1989), 110–14. References to developments in the lands south of the desert listed in Chapter 4 are also relevant for this chapter. A number of additional papers are to be found in S. Magnavita *et al.* (eds.), *Crossroads Carrefour/Sahel: Cultural and Technological Developments in First Millennium BC/AD West Africa* (Frankfurt, 2009).

Commodities traded across the Sahara in the Roman period were many and varied and the literature is correspondingly large. Three books contain many of the major papers: M. I. J. Davies and K. MacDonald (eds.), *Connections, Contributions and Complexity: Africa's Later Holocene Archaeology in Global Perspective* (Cambridge, 2018); D. J. Mattingly *et al.* (eds.), *Trade in the Ancient Sahara and Beyond* (Cambridge, 2017); and A. Dowler and E. R. Galvin (eds.), *Money, Trade and Trade Routes in Pre-Islamic North Africa* (London, 2011). For a major review article bringing the evidence for Roman trade together, see A. Wilson, 'Saharan Trade in the Roman Period: Short-, Medium- and Long-Distance Trade Networks', *Azania: Archaeological Research in Africa*, 47/4 (2012), 409–49. Trade in gold is discussed in T. F. Garrard, 'Myth and Metrology: The Early Trans-Saharan Gold Trade', *Journal of African History*, 23 (1982), 433–61, and the trade in slaves in E. Fentress, 'Slavers and Chariots', in Dowler and Galvin (eds.), *Money, Trade and Trade Routes in Pre-Islamic North Africa*, 65–71. Routes across the desert are attractively presented in K. Braun and J. Passon (eds.), *Across the Sahara: Tracks, Trade and Cross-Cultural Exchange in Libya* (Freiburg, 2020).

On desert nomads and camels, a good place to begin is with J. Scheele, 'The Need for Nomads: Camel Herding, Raiding, and Sahara Trade and Settlement', in Mattingly *et al.* (eds.), *Trade in the Ancient Sahara and Beyond*, 55–79. Some papers on the early appearance of camels have been listed above (p. 368). A very helpful introduction to Sahara nomads is given in Brett and Fentress, *The Berbers*, chapter 6. For a detailed study of the Tuareg through time, see J. Nicolaisen and I. Nicolaisen, *The Pastoral Tuareg: Ecology, Culture and Society*, 2 vols. (London, 1997). The famous tomb of Tin Hinan is discussed in M. Reygasse, 'Fouilles de monuments funéraires de type "chouchet" accolés au tombeau de Tin Hinan à Abalessa', *Bulletin de la Société de Géographie et d'Archéologie d'Oran* (1940), 148–66, and M. Gast, 'Témoignages nouveaux sur Tine

Hinane, ancêtre légendaire des Touareg Ahaggar', *Revue d'Occident Musulman et de la Mediterranée*, 13–14 (1973), 395–400. The unrest along the Tripolitanian frontier in the third century is considered in D. J. Mattingly, *Tripolitania* (London, 1995) and the same author's 'The Laguatan: A Libyan Tribal Confederation in the Late Roman Empire', *Libyan Studies*, 14 (1983), 96–108.

Chapter 6 An End and a Beginning, AD 400–760

This chapter covers a particularly turbulent time in the history of Europe and the Near East, and inevitably North Africa got caught up in these events. For those wishing to explore the background history of the period, the following are recommended: A. Cameron, *The Mediterranean World in Late Antiquity, AD 395–700* (London, 2011); B. Ward-Perkins, *The Fall of Rome and the End of Civilization* (Oxford, 2005); P. Heather, *The Fall of the Roman Empire: A New History of Rome and the Barbarians* (Oxford, 2006); B. Dignas and E. Winter, *Persia and Rome in Late Antiquity: Neighbours and Rivals* (Cambridge, 2007); J. A. C. Brown, *Muhammad: A Very Short Introduction* (Oxford, 2011); K. Armstrong, *Muhammad: A Biography of the Prophet* (London, 1992); and A. Hourani, *A History of the Arab People* (London, 1991). Suitably prepared, we can now approach some of the specific issues raised in this chapter.

A concise history of the Vandals is provided in A. Merrills and R. Miles, *The Vandals* (Chichester, 2010). More specific to the Vandals in North Africa is A. Merrills (ed.), *Vandals, Romans and Berbers: New Perspectives on Late Antique North Africa* (Aldershot, 2004). Other relevant papers include P. Heather, 'Christianity and the Vandals in the Reign of Geiseric', *Bulletin of the Institute of Classical Studies*, 50/S91 (2007), 137–46, and J. Linn, 'The Roman Grain Supply, 442–455', *Journal of Late Antiquity*, 5/2 (2012), 298–321.

Two excellent introductions to the Byzantine world are A. Cameron, *The Byzantines* (Chichester, 2006) and C. Mango (ed.), *The Oxford History of Byzantium* (Oxford, 2002). More detailed works on North Africa include S. T. Stevens and J. P. Conant (eds.), *North Africa under Byzantium and Early Islam* (Cambridge, MA, 2010); W. E. Kaegi, *Muslim Expansion and Byzantine Collapse in North Africa* (Cambridge, 2010); and D. Pringle, *The Defence of Byzantine Africa from Justinian to the Arab Conquest: An Account of the Military History and Archaeology of the African Provinces in the Sixth and Seventh Centuries* (Oxford, 1981). For the towns and countryside in this period, see A. Leone, *Changing Townscapes in North Africa from Late Antiquity to the Arab Conquest* (Bari, 2007) and A. Leone and D. J. Mattingly, 'Vandal, Byzantine and Arab Rural Landscapes in North Africa', in N. Christie (ed.), *Landscapes of Change: Rural Evolutions in Late Antiquity and the Early Middle Ages* (Aldershot, 2004), 135–62;

also a wide-ranging review, E. Fentress and A. I. Wilson, 'The Saharan Berber Diaspora and the Southern Frontiers of Byzantine North Africa', in Stevens and Conant (eds.), *North Africa under Byzantium and Early Islam*, 41–63. For the complexity of tribal organization in Libya in the Late Roman period, two detailed studies by D. J. Mattingly are to be recommended: 'Libyans and the "Limes": Culture and Society in Roman Tripolitania', *Antiquités Africaines*, 23/1 (1987), 71–94, and 'The Laguatan: A Libyan Tribal Confederation in the Late Roman Empire', *Libyan Studies*, 14 (1983), 96–108.

The Arab conquest of North Africa is discussed in Kaegi, *Muslim Expansion and Byzantine Collapse in North Africa*; V. Christides, *Byzantine Libya and the March of the Arabs towards the West of North Africa* (Oxford, 2000); and the same author's chapter 'The Islamic Conquest and the Defense of Byzantine Africa: Reconsideration on Campaigns, Conquests, and Contexts', in Stevens and Conant (eds.), *North Africa under Byzantium and Early Islam*, 65–87. To put the North African advance in its broader context, see R. G. Hoyland, *In God's Path: The Arab Conquests and the Creation of an Islamic Empire* (Oxford, 2014) and J. M. Abun-Nasr, *A History of the Maghrib in the Islamic Period* (Cambridge, 1987). The legend and legacy of the Berber warrior queen Kahina is exhaustively treated in A. Hannoum, *Colonial Histories, Post-Colonial Memories: The Legend of the Kahina, a North African Heroine* (Portsmouth, NH, 2001). The unification of North Africa under Islam is the subject of a concise chapter (chapter 3) in M. Brett and E. Fentress, *The Berbers* (Oxford, 1996). For a more detailed study of the situation in Libya, see J. Thiry, *Le Sahara libyen dans l'Afrique du Nord médievale* (Leuven, 1995).

The history and archaeology of the polities along the middle Nile are fully discussed in W. Y. Adams, *Nubia: Corridor to Africa* (Princeton, 1977); D. A. Welsby, *The Medieval Kingdoms of Nubia: Pagans, Christians and Muslims along the Middle Nile* (London, 2002); and D. N. Edwards, *The Nubian Past: An Archaeology of Sudan* (London, 2004). Another useful source is V. Christides, 'Nubia and Egypt from the Arab Invasion of Egypt until the End of the Umayyads', in C. Bonnet (ed.), *Études nubiennes*, i: *Communications principales* (Geneva, 1992), 341–56. For the treaty of Baqt, see J. Spaulding, 'Medieval Christian Nubia and the Islamic World: A Reconsideration of the Baqt Treaty', *International Journal of African Historical Studies*, 28/3 (1995), 577–94. On slavery, D. N. Edwards, 'Slavery and Slaving in the Medieval and Post-Medieval Kingdoms of the Middle Nile', in P. Lane and K. C. MacDonald (eds.), *Slavery in Africa: Archaeology and Memory* (London, 2011), 79–108.

A thorough coverage of the situation in the western Sahel is given in R. J. McIntosh, *The Peoples of the Middle Niger* (Oxford, 1998) and the same author's *Ancient Middle Niger: Urbanism and the Self-Organizing Landscape* (Cambridge, 2005). Other important papers include K. C. MacDonald, 'Before the Empire of Ghana: Pastoralism and the Origins of Cultural Complexity in the Sahel', in G. Connah (ed.), *Transformations in Africa: Essays on Africa's Later Past* (London, 1998), 71–103, and K. C. MacDonald *et al.*, 'Exploratory Archaeology at Jenné and Jenné-Jeno, Mali', *Sahara*, 8 (1997), 19–28. For the settlements in the Méma region, T. Togola, *Archaeological Investigations of Iron Age Sites in the Mema Region, Mali (West Africa)* (Oxford, 2008). Excavations at Gao are described in three sources by T. Insoll: 'Iron Age Gao: An Archaeological Contribution', *Journal of African History*, 38/1 (1997), 1–30; 'Islamic Glass from Gao, Mali', *Journal of Glass Studies*, 40 (1998), 77–88; and *Urbanism, Archaeology and Trade: Further Observations on the Gao Region (Mali). The 1996 Fieldseason Results* (Oxford, 2000). Dates for the megalithic monuments at Tondidarou are given in J. F. Saliège *et al.*, 'Premières Datations de tumulus pré-islamique au Mali: site mégalithique de Tondidarou', *Comptes-Rendus des Séances de l'Académie des Sciences*, 291D (1980), 981–4. Evidence from Kissi is summarized in S. Magnavita, 'Sahelian Crossroads: Some Aspects on the Iron Age Sites of Kissi, Burkina Faso', in S. Magnavita *et al.* (eds.), *Crossroads Carrefour/Sahel: Cultural and Technological Developments in First Millennium BC/AD West Africa* (Frankfurt, 2009), 79–104.

The *Tarikh* of al-Yaqubi, translated by M. Th. Houtsma, is available in an edition by M. S. Gordon *et al.*, *The History (Ta'rikh) by Ibn Wāḍiḥ al-Yaʿqūbī*, 2 vols. (Leiden, 2017–18). References to the Tuareg have been given in the Further Reading for Chapter 5. Insights into the Sanhaja will be found in H. T. Norris, *Saharan Myth and Saga* (Oxford, 1972).

Chapter 7 Emerging States, AD 760–1150

Developments in the Islamic world of the Near and Middle East impacted heavily on North Africa. Discussion of the main events will be found in K. Armstrong, *Islam: A Short History* (London, 2000) and M. S. Gordon, *The Rise of Islam* (Westport, CT, 2005). A number of papers dealing with the Ibadis are brought together in A. Ziaka (ed.), *On Ibadism* (Hildesheim, 2014). A succinct account of the impact of Islam on North Africa is given in M. Brett and E. Fentress, *The Berbers* (Oxford, 1996), chapter 3. For a more detailed account, see J. M. Abun-Nasr, *A History of the Maghrib in the Islamic Period* (Cambridge, 1987). The rise of the Fatimids and the conquest of Egypt are fully treated in M. Brett, *The Fatimid Empire* (Edinburgh, 2017) and H. Halm, *The Empire of the Mahdi: The Rise of the Fatimids*, trans. M. Bonner (Leiden, 1996). The development of the polities of the middle Nile is described in D. A. Welsby, *The Medieval Kingdoms of Nubia: Pagans, Christians and Muslims along the Middle Nile* (London, 2002) and D. N. Edwards, *The Nubian Past: An Archaeology of Sudan* (London, 2004). A detailed account of the archaeological evidence for Islam outside

North Africa, but including the middle Nile, is presented in T. Insoll, *The Archaeology of Islam in Sub-Saharan Africa* (Cambridge, 2003).

Trading systems along the east coast of Africa are summarized in P. Mitchell, *African Connections: Archaeological Perspectives on Africa and the Wider World* (Walnut Creek, 2005), chapter 4, and in Insoll, *Archaeology of Islam in Sub-Saharan Africa*, chapter 4. Translations of texts of encounters with East African trading enclaves are brought together in *The East African Coast: Select Documents from the First to the Earlier Nineteenth Century*, ed. G. S. P. Freeman-Grenville (Oxford, 1962).

The Bedouin incursions into North Africa are treated briefly in Brett and Fentress, *The Berbers*, chapter 4, and discussed in more detail in M. Brett, 'Ibn Khaldun and the Arabisation of North Africa', *Maghreb Review*, 4 (1979), 9–16, and the same author's 'The Flood of the Dam and the Sons of the New Moon', in M. Brett, *Ibn Khaldun and the Medieval Maghreb* (Aldershot, 1999), 55–67. The incursion and its effects are also considered in A. S. Baadj, *Saladin, the Almohads and the Banū Ghāniya: The Contest for North Africa, 12th and 13th Centuries* (Boston, 2015), chapter 1.

For the people and events in the western Sahara the classic text has been N. Levtzion, *Ancient Ghana and Mali* (London, 1973) supported by *Corpus of Early Arabic Sources for West African History*, ed. N. Levtzion and J. F. P. Hopkins (Cambridge, 1981). A comprehensive new review, M. A. Gomez, *African Dominion: A New History of Empire in Early and Medieval West Africa* (Princeton, 2018), presents a much-expanded and more nuanced account. The great trading city of Sijilmasa is thoroughly treated in R. A. Messier and J. A. Miller, *The Last Civilized Place: Sijilmasa and its Saharan Destiny* (Austin, 2015). Other useful accounts include D. R. Lightfoot and J. A. Miller, 'Sijilmassa: The Rise and Fall of a Walled Oasis in Medieval Morocco', *Annals of the Association of American Geographers*, 86/1 (1996), 78–101, and J.-M. Lessard, 'Sijilmassa: la ville et ses relations commerciales au XIᵉ siècle d'après El Bekri', *Hespéris-Tamuda*, 10 (1969), 5–36. For the desert-edge town of Awdaghust (Aoudaghost), see E. A. McDougall, 'The View from Awdaghust: War, Trade and Social Change in the Southwestern Sahara, from the Eighth to the Fifteenth Century', *Journal of African History*, 26/1 (1985), 1–31, and N. Levtzion, 'Ibn Ḥawqal, the Cheque, and Awdaghost', *Journal of African History*, 9/2 (1968), 223–33. The archaeological site, now called Tegdaoust, was subject to excavation in the 1960s and the work is summarized in D. S. Roberts, 'Les Fouilles de Tegdaoust', *Journal of African History*, 11 (1970), 471–93. The Soninke people are introduced in Levtzion, *Ancient Ghana and Mali*, chapter 2.

The rise and expansion of the Almoravids is fully treated in A. K. Bennison, *The Almoravid and Almohad Empires* (Edinburgh, 2016) and R. A. Messier, *Almoravids and the Meanings of Jihad* (Santa Barbara, 2010). For more summary accounts, see Levtzion, *Ancient Ghana and Mali*, chapter 3, and Brett and Fentress, *The Berbers*,

105–13. There are also interesting discussions in D. Lange, 'The Almoravid Expansion and the Downfall of Ghana', *Der Islam*, 73/2 (1998), 313–51; H. T. Norris, 'New Evidence on the Life of Abdullah B. Yasin and the Origin of the Almoravid Movement', *Journal of African History*, 12/2 (1971), 255–68; and N. Levtzion, 'Abd Allah ibn Yassin and the Almoravids', in J. R. Willis (ed.), *Studies in West African Islamic History: The Cultivators of Islam* (London, 1979), 78–112. For the architecture of the period, X. Salmon, *Maroc almoravide et almohade: architecture et décors au temps des conquérants, 1055–1269* (Paris, 2018).

The empire of Ghana may be approached through Levtzion, *Ancient Ghana and Mali*; *Medieval West Africa: Views from Arab Scholars and Merchants*, ed. N. Levtzion and J. Spaulding (Princeton, 2003); D. Lange, *Ancient Kingdoms of West Africa: Africa-Centred and Canaanite–Israelite Perspectives* (Dettelbach, 2004); and Gomez, *African Dominion*. See also P. J. Munson, 'Archaeology and the Prehistoric Origins of the Ghana Empire', *Journal of African History*, 21/4 (1980), 457–66. The excavations at Koumbi Saleh are reported in S. Berthier, *Recherches archéologiques sur la capitale de l'empire de Ghana: étude d'un secteur d'habitat à Koumbi Saleh, Mauritainie. Campagnes II–III–IV–V (1975–1976)–(1980–1981)* (Oxford, 1997). On the trade in gold, T. Gerrard, 'Myth and Metrology: The Early Trans-Saharan Gold Trade', *Journal of African History*, 23/4 (1982), 443–61, and S. Nixon, 'Trans-Saharan Gold Trade in Pre-Modern Times: Available Evidence and Research Agendas', in D. J. Mattingly *et al.* (eds.), *Trade in the Ancient Sahara and Beyond* (Cambridge, 2017), 156–88.

The neighbouring polities to Ghana are considered in Levtzion, *Ancient Ghana and Mali*, chapter 4. For Takrur, see R. J. McIntosh, S. K. McIntosh, and H. Bocoum, *The Search for Takrur: Archaeological Excavations and Reconnaissance along the Middle Senegal Valley* (New Haven, 2016). For Gao, there is a useful summary of the evidence in Insoll, *Archaeology of Islam in Sub-Saharan Africa*, 232–50, with full references to earlier work, to which can be added M. Cissé *et al.*, 'Excavations at Gao Saney: New Evidence for Settlement Growth, Trade, and Interaction on the Niger Bend in the First Millennium CE', *Journal of African Archaeology*, 11/1 (2013), 9–37. The Islamic funerary inscriptions are published in P. F. de M. Farias, *Arabic Medieval Inscriptions from the Republic of Mali* (Oxford, 2005). The evidence for the important caravan town of Tadmekka (now Essouk) is fully discussed in S. Nixon (ed.), *Essouk-Tadmekka: An Early Islamic Trans-Saharan Town* (Leiden, 2017). A useful summary of the excavations is provided in S. Nixon, 'Essouk-Tadmekka: A Southern Saharan Center of the Early Islamic Camel Caravan Trade', in K. B. Berzock (ed.), *Caravans of Gold, Fragments in Time: Art, Culture, and Exchange across Medieval Saharan Africa* (Princeton, 2019), 123–37. Details of the gold-processing finds and their implications are explored in G. Pastorelli, M. Walton, and S. Nixon, 'Gold Processing at the Early

Islamic Market Town of Tadmekka, Mali: Preliminary Results from Experimental Replication', in the same edited volume, 213–21. The Byzantine globular *solidi* are discussed at length in D. W. Phillipson, 'Trans-Saharan Gold Trade and Byzantine Coinage', *Antiquaries Journal*, 97 (2017), 145–69. The Islamic inscriptions from the town are considered in P. F. de M. Farias, 'The Oldest Extant Writing of West Africa: Medieval Epigraphs from Essuk, Saney and Egef-n-Tawaqqast (Mali)', *Journal des Africanistes*, 60/2 (1990), 65–113.

For the Zaghawa and the origins of Kanem, see Insoll, *Archaeology of Islam in Sub-Saharan Africa*, 269–78; D. Lange, 'The Chad Region as a Crossroads', in M. El Fasi (ed.), UNESCO *General History of Africa*, iii: *Africa from the Seventh to the Eleventh Century* (London, 1992), 216–25; and D. Lange, 'Ethnogenesis from within the Chadic State: Some Thoughts on the History of Kanem-Borno', *Paideuma*, 39 (1993), 261–77. See also M. Last, 'The Early Kingdoms of the Nigerian Savannah', in J. F. A. Ajayi and M. Crowder (eds.), *History of West Africa*, i (New York, 1985), 167–224. The archaeological background will be found in G. Connah, *Three Thousand Years in Africa: Man and his Environment in the Lake Chad Region of Nigeria* (Cambridge, 1981). The sparse evidence for occupation in Darfur is summed up in A. McGregor, 'Palaces in the Mountains: An Introduction to the Archaeological Heritage of the Sultanate of Darfur', *Sudan and Nubia*, 15 (2011), 129–41.

Evidence for the development of towns in the equatorial forest zone to the south is conveniently presented in A. Ogundiran, 'Towns and States of the West African Forest Belt', in P. Mitchell and P. Lane (eds.), *The Oxford Handbook of African Archaeology* (Oxford, 2013), 859–73. For the burial from Igbo Ukwu, T. Shaw, *Igbo-Ukwu: An Account of Archaeological Discoveries in Eastern Nigeria* (London, 1970) and the same author's 'Further Light on Igbo-Ukwu, including New Radiocarbon Dates', in B. W. Andah, P. de Maret, and R. Soper (eds.), *Proceedings of the 9th Congress of the Pan-African Association of Prehistory and Related Studies, Jos, 1983* (Ibadan, 1995), 79–83. The implication of the burial for the movement of ideas and materials is considered in T. Insoll and T. Shaw, 'Gao and Igbo-Ukwu: Beads, Interregional Trade, and Beyond', *African Archaeological Review*, 9 (1997), 145–60; P. T. Craddock *et al.*, 'Metal Sources and the Bronzes from Igbo-Ukwu, Nigeria', *Journal of Field Archaeology*, 24/4 (1997), 405–29; and J. E. G. Sutton, 'Igbo-Ukwu and the Nile', *African Archaeological Review*, 18/1 (2001), 49–62. The manufacturing of glass beads at Ife is treated in A. B. Babalola, 'Emerging Perspectives on the Archaeology of Ile-Ife, Southwest Nigeria: Glass and Glass Beads Production', in A. S. Ajala (ed.), *Orality, Myth and Archaeological Practice* (Cologne, 2013), 56–77, and A. B. Babalola *et al.*, 'Ile-Ife and Igbo Olokun in the History of Glass in West Africa', *Antiquity*, 91/357 (2017), 732–50.

Chapter 8 Widening Horizons, AD 1150–1400

Events in the Mediterranean played an increasingly important part in developments in North Africa in the later medieval period. By far the best overview is provided by the relevant chapters in D. Abulafia, *The Great Sea: A Human History of the Mediterranean* (London, 2011). Another valuable source is offered by S. O'Shea, *Sea of Faith: Islam and Christianity in the Medieval Mediterranean World* (London, 2007). The Crusades had an, albeit limited, impact on North Africa. For background, two sources can be recommended: P. Lock, *The Routledge Companion to the Crusades* (London, 2006) and J. Richard, *The Crusades, c.1071–1291*, trans. J. Birrell (Cambridge, 1999). For Iberia in this period, W. M. Watt and P. Cachia, *A History of Islamic Spain* (Edinburgh, 1992) provides a sound background, while various chapters in R. Collins and P. Goodman (eds.), *Medieval Spain: Culture, Conflict and Coexistence* (Basingstoke, 2002) are of relevance to events impacting on North Africa. For the Arab geographer-historians the most thorough source is *Corpus of Early Arabic Sources for West African History*, ed. N. Levtzion and J. F. P. Hopkins (Cambridge, 1981), but E. W. Bovill, *The Golden Trade of the Moors* (2nd edn, Princeton, 1995), 61–6, provides a succinct summary of the principal writers.

The Almohads are fully treated in A. K. Bennison, *The Almoravid and Almohad Empires* (Edinburgh, 2016) and R. Le Tourneau, *The Almohad Movement in North Africa in the 12th and 13th Centuries* (Princeton, 2015). More specifically, for Ibn Tumart, see S. García, 'The Masmuda Berbers and Ibn Tumart: An Ethnographic Interpretation of the Rise of the Almohad Movement', *Ufahamu: A Journal of African Studies*, 18/1 (1990), 3–24. The great polymath Ibn Rushd (Averroes) is treated in some detail in P. Adamson and M. Di Giovanni (eds.), *Interpreting Averroes: Critical Essays* (Cambridge, 2019). For a shorter, more popular account, see L. Sonneborn, *Averroes (Ibn Rushd): Muslim Scholar, Philosopher, and Physician of the Twelfth Century* (New York, 2006). Events in the Maghrib following the Almohads are covered in J. M. Abun-Nasr, *A History of the Maghrib in the Islamic Period* (Cambridge, 1987), chapter 3. The contribution of Ibn Khaldun is described in A. J. Fromherz, *Ibn Khaldun: Life and Times* (Edinburgh, 2011). The Ayyubids in Egypt are the subject of M. C. Lyons and D. E. P. Jackson, *Saladin: The Politics of the Holy War* (Cambridge, 1984) and Y. Lev, *Saladin in Egypt* (Leiden, 1999). On the Mamluks, T. Philipp and U. Haarmann (eds.), *The Mamluks in Egyptian Politics and Society* (Cambridge, 1998) offers eighteen detailed and scholarly chapters on the subject. For the Seventh Crusade and its impact on Egypt, see W. B. Bartlett, *The Last Crusade: The Seventh Crusade and the Final Battle for the Holy Land* (Stroud, 2007). The impact of the Ayyubids and Mamluks on Nubia is considered in D. A. Welsby, *The Medieval Kingdoms of Nubia: Pagans,*

Christians and Muslims along the Middle Nile (London, 2002). The destruction of the Christian monuments at Qasr Ibrim is discussed in J. M. Plumley, 'Qasr Ibrim and Islam', *Études et Travaux*, 12 (1983), 157–70.

The exploration of the East African coast is referred to in a number of contemporary accounts. The most informative—al-Idrisi, Abu al-Fida, Ibn Battuta, and the Chinese writer Zhao Rukuo—are brought together in translation in *The East African Coast: Select Documents from the First to the Earlier Nineteenth Century*, ed. G. S. P. Freeman-Grenville (Oxford, 1962), 19–32. The anonymous history of Kilwa, compiled about 1520, is also transcribed: pp. 34–49. The archaeology and history of Kilwa are exhaustively treated in H. N. Chittick, *Kilwa: An Islamic Trading City on the East African Coast*, 2 vols. (Nairobi, 1974). Also of relevance are E. J. Pollard, 'The Maritime Landscape of Kilwa Kisiwani and its Region, Tanzania, 11th to 15th Century AD', *Journal of Anthropological Archaeology*, 27/3 (2008), 265–80, and S. Wynne-Jones, 'Creating Urban Communities at Kilwa Kisiwani, Tanzania, AD 800–1300', *Antiquity*, 81 (2007), 368–80. The excavations at Shanga are reported in M. Horton, *Shanga: The Archaeology of a Muslim Trading Community on the Coast of East Africa* (London, 1996). See also M. Horton, *Zanzibar and Pemba: The Archaeology of an Indian Ocean Archipelago* (London, 2017). For an interesting comparative study, see M. Horton, A. Crowther, and N. Boivin, 'Ships of the Desert, Camels of the Ocean: An Indian Ocean Perspective on Trans-Saharan Trading Systems', in D. J. Mattingly *et al.* (eds.), *Trade in the Ancient Sahara and Beyond* (Cambridge, 2017), 131–55. An overview of East African coastal trade is given in M. Horton, 'Early Maritime Trade and Settlement along the Coasts of Eastern Africa', in J. Reade (ed.), *The Indian Ocean in Antiquity* (London, 1996), 439–60. The crucial part played by Aden is explored in R. E. Margariti, *Aden and the Indian Ocean Trade: 150 Years in the Life of a Medieval Arabian Port* (Chapel Hill, 2007).

The empire of Mali may be approached through the classic work N. Levtzion, *Ancient Ghana and Mali* (London, 1973), but a more recent study, M. A. Gomez, *African Dominion: A New History of Empire in Early and Medieval West Africa* (Princeton, 2018), puts the empire into a broader context. Medieval trade across the desert is the leitmotiv of E. W. Bovill's classic book *The Golden Trade of the Moors* and is a theme that recurs in T. Insoll, *The Archaeology of Islam in Sub-Saharan Africa* (Cambridge, 2003). The desert trade is succinctly summed up in T. Insoll, 'Timbuktu and Europe: Trade, Cities, and Islam in "Medieval" West Africa', in P. Linehan, J. L. Nelson, and M. Costambeys (eds.), *The Medieval World* (2nd edn, London, 2018), 549–67. The evidence for Gao is presented in Insoll, *Archaeology of Islam in Sub-Saharan Africa*, 232–50. The mobile population of Walata is discussed in detail in T. Cleaveland, *Becoming Walata: A History of Social Formation and Transformation* (Portsmouth, NH, 2002).

Archaeological work in Timbuktu is presented in T. Insoll, 'Timbuktu the Less Mysterious?', in P. Mitchell, A. Haour, and J. Hobart (eds.), *Researching Africa's Past: New Contributions from British Archaeologists* (Oxford, 2004), 81–8. The route taken by Ibn Battuta across the desert and through Mali is considered in C. Meillassoux, 'L'Itinéraire d'Ibn Battuta de Walata à Malli', *Journal of African History*, 13/3 (1972), 389–95.

The developments in the central Sudan are summarized in D. Gronenborn, 'Kanem-Borno: A Brief Summary of the History and Archaeology of an Empire in the Central "Bilad el-Sudan"', in C. De Corse (ed.), *West Africa during the Atlantic Slave Trade: Archaeological Perspectives* (London, 2001), 101–30. See also B. Bakindo, 'The Early States of the Central Sudan: Kanem, Borno and Some of their Neighbours, to *c.*1500 AD', in J. F. A. Ajayi and M. Crowder (eds.), *History of West Africa*, i (New York, 1985), 225–54. There are also several relevant papers in D. Gronenborn (ed.), *Gold, Slaves and Ivory: Medieval Empires in Northern Nigeria* (Mainz, 2011). The Hausa city states are introduced in J. E. G. Sutton, 'Towards a Less Orthodox History of Hausaland', *Journal of African History*, 20 (1979), 179–201, and A. Haour, 'Power and Permanence in Precolonial Africa: A Case Study from the Central Sahel', *World Archaeology*, 37/4 (2005), 552–65. For a more recent and comprehensive review, see A. Haour and B. Rossi (eds.), *Being and Becoming Hausa: Interdisciplinary Perspectives* (Leiden, 2010). The archaeology of Kufan Kanawa, the possible precursor of Kano, is discussed in A. Haour, *Ethnochronology in the Zinder Region, Republic of Niger: The Site of Kufan Kanawa* (Oxford, 2003).

Mansa Musa and the empire of Mali are contextualized in Levtzion, *Ancient Ghana and Mali* and Gomez, *African Dominion*, chapter 6. See also N. M. Bell, 'The Age of Mansa Musa of Mali: Problems in Succession and Chronology', *International Journal of African Historical Studies*, 5/2 (1972), 221–34. Most of what is known about the unsuccessful Atlantic expeditions of Muhammad ibn Qu comes from the account recorded by Shihab al-Din al-Umari, an Arab scholar born in Damascus, translated in *Corpus of Early Arabic Sources for West African History*, ed. N. Levtzion and J. F. P. Hopkins (Cambridge, 1981), 268–9. The episode is discussed in F.-X. Fauvelle, *The Golden Rhinoceros: Histories of the African Middle Ages* (Princeton, 2018), 160–8, where the sultan in question is identified as Muhammad and not Mansa Musa's father, Abubakri, as is usually assumed. The travels of Ibn Battuta are described and discussed in R. E. Dunn, *The Adventures of Ibn Battuta, a Muslim Traveler of the 14th Century* (3rd edn, Berkeley, 2012) and D. Waines, *The Odyssey of Ibn Battuta: Uncommon Tales of a Medieval Adventurer* (London, 2010). The text written by Ibn Battuta is published in translation by the Hakluyt Society in H. A. R. Gibb, *The Travels of Ibn Battuta*, 3 vols. (London, 1956). A good general background to the hajj is given in M. Amin,

Journey of a Lifetime: Pilgrimage to Makkah (Northampton, MA, 2000), while the pilgrimage routes across northern Africa are considered in J. S. Birks, *Across the Savannas to Mecca: The Overland Pilgrimage Route from West Africa* (London, 1978). For a fascinating and broadly based study of pilgrimage and its role in developing socio-economic transactions, see J. McCorriston, *Pilgrimage and Household in the Ancient Near East* (Cambridge, 2011).

Chapter 9 Africa and the World, AD 1400–1600

The chapter begins with the remarkable voyages of Zheng He and his contacts with Africa. The context in which the journeys should be considered is given in *The Cambridge History of China*, vii: *The Ming Dynasty, 1368–1644*, ed. F. W. Mote and D. Twitchett (Cambridge, 1988). The voyages are presented in detail in L. Levathes, *When China Ruled the Seas: The Treasure Fleet of the Dragon Throne, 1405–1433* (New York, 1996) and E. L. Dreyer, *Zheng He: China and the Oceans in the Early Ming Dynasty, 1405–1433* (New York, 2007). A number of specific conference papers are brought together in C. L. Sien and S. K. Church (eds.), *Zheng He and the Afro-Asian World* (Malacca, 2012), presenting a range of scholarly work.

Much of the first part of the chapter deals with the Portuguese exploration of the African coast. The literature is very considerable. Two books which present the events in the broader context of world history are the classic J. H. Parry, *The Age of Reconnaissance: Discovery, Exploration and Settlement, 1450–1650* (London, 1963) and G. V. Scammell, *The First Imperial Age: Europe and Overseas Expansion, c.1400–1715* (London, 1989). For a specific study of the Portuguese endeavour, see M. Newitt, *A History of Portuguese Overseas Expansion, 1400–1668* (London, 2005). An essential text for the reader interested in the opening up of the Atlantic is F. Fernández-Armesto, *Before Columbus: Exploration and Colonisation from the Mediterranean to the Atlantic, 1229–1492* (Philadelphia, 1987). One of the principal characters in the early stages of the Portuguese exploration of the West African coast was Dom Henrique, or Prince Henry the Navigator as he later became known. Cutting through the myth about the man and offering a scholarly, but lively, narrative is the study by P. Russell, *Prince Henry 'the Navigator': A Life* (New Haven, 2001). It provides details of successive voyages and discoveries up to the time of Dom Henrique's death in 1460. A contemporary account of one phase of the discovery is published by the Hakluyt Society as Gomes Eanes de Zurara, *The Chronicle of the Discovery and Conquest of Guinea*, trans. C. R. Beazley and E. Prestage, 2 vols. (London, 1896–9). The exploits of Gil Eannes in rounding Cape Bojador are considered in P. Seed, 'Navigating the Mid-Atlantic; or, What Gil Eanes Achieved', in J. Cañizares-Esguerra and E. R. Seeman (eds.), *The Atlantic in Global*

History, 1500–2000 (Upper Saddle River, NJ, 2007), 77–89. Aspects of the voyage of Cadamosto are discussed in F. Verrier (ed.), *Voyages en Afrique noire d'Alvise Ca' da Mosto (1455 et 1456)* (Paris, 1994). For an English translation, see *'The Voyages of Cadamosto' and Other Documents on Western Africa in the Second Half of the Fifteenth Century*, ed. and trans. G. R. Crone (London, 1937). A detailed assessment of Cadamosto's achievements is given in Russell, *Prince Henry 'the Navigator'*, chapter 12. The exploits of Bartolomeu Dias are treated in E. G. Ravenstein, W. B. Greenlee, and P. Vaz de Caminha, *Bartolomeu Dias* (England, 2010). For Vasco da Gama two sources can be recommended: G. J. Ames, *Vasco da Gama: Renaissance Crusader* (New York, 2005) and S. Subrahmanyam, *The Career and Legend of Vasco da Gama* (Cambridge, 1998).

The physical remains of the Portuguese factory on Arguin Island were recorded over a century ago in A. Gruvel and R. Chudeau, *À travers la Mauritainie occidentale (de Saint-Louis à Port-Étienne)*, 2 vols. (Paris, 1901–11). The archaeological evidence for the factory and contemporary native settlement at Elmina is presented in C. R. DeCorse, *An Archaeology of Elmina: Africans and Europeans on the Gold Coast, 1400–1900* (Washington, 2001). Work on the later Dutch fort of St Jago is discussed in J. Anquandah, 'Archaeological Investigations at Fort St Jago, Elmina, Ghana', *Archaeology in Ghana*, 3 (1992), 38–45.

The kingdoms of the forest zone are introduced in A. Ogundiran, 'Towns and States in the West African Forest Belt', in P. Mitchell and P. Lane (eds.), *The Oxford Handbook of African Archaeology* (Oxford, 2013), 859–73, and in J. Anquandah, 'Urbanization and State Formation in Ghana during the Iron Age', in T. Shaw *et al.* (eds.), *The Archaeology of Africa: Food, Metals and Towns* (London, 1993), 642–51. There are a number of relevant papers in C. Monroe and A. Ogundiran (eds.), *Landscapes of Power: Regional Perspectives on West African Polities in the Atlantic Era* (Cambridge, 2012). For Benin, see G. Connah, *The Archaeology of Benin: Excavations and Other Researches in and around Benin City, Nigeria* (Oxford, 1975) and P. J. Darling, 'A Legacy in Earth: Ancient Benin and Ishan, Southern Nigeria', in K. W. Wesler (ed.), *Historical Archaeology in Nigeria* (Trenton, NJ, 1998), 143–97. For Ife, the context is described in S. A. Akintoye, *A History of the Yoruba People* (Dakar, 2010) and A. Ogundiran, 'Chronology, Material Culture, and Pathways to the Cultural History of Yoruba-Edo Region, Nigeria, 500 BC–AD 1800', in T. Falola and C. Jennings (eds.), *Sources and Methods in African History: Spoken, Written, Unearthed* (Rochester, NY, 2003), 33–79. The site of Ife is described in P. Ozanne, 'A New Archaeological Survey of Ife', *Odu*, new ser., 1 (1969), 28–45. Evidence for glass production in the city is presented in A. B. Babalola, 'Emerging Perspectives on the Archaeology of Ile-Ife, Southwest Nigeria: Glass and Glass Beads Production', in A. S. Ajala (ed.), *Orality, Myth and Archaeological Practice* (Cologne, 2013), 56–77. The economic context is discussed in

R. Horton, 'The Economy of Ife from *c.* AD 900–*c.* AD 1700', in I. A. Akinjogbin (ed.), *The Cradle of a Race: Ife from the Beginning to 1980* (Port Harcourt, 1992), 122–47.

The classic introduction to the empire of the Songhai is provided in N. Levtzion, *Ancient Ghana and Mali* (London, 1973) and now by M. A. Gomez, *African Dominion: A New History of Empire in Early and Medieval West Africa* (Princeton, 2018), which is essential reading. Another interesting paper is D. Lange, 'From Ghana and Mali to Songhay: The Mande Factor in Gao History', in D. Lange, *Ancient Kingdoms of West Africa: Africa-Centred and Canaanite–Israelite Perspectives* (Dettelbach, 2004), 495–544. One of the contemporary observers was Leo Africanus, whose life is briefly described in P. Masonen, 'Leo Africanus: The Man with Many Names', *Al-Andalus Magreb*, 8–9 (2021), 115–43. Some of the events he observed are discussed in H. J. Fisher, 'Leo Africanus and the Songhay Conquest of Hausaland', *International Journal of African Historical Studies*, 11/1 (1978), 86–112.

For a reader wishing to explore the nature and extent of the Ottoman empire, two works may be recommended: S. Faroqhi, *The Ottoman Empire: A Short History*, trans. Shelley Frisch (Princeton, 2009) and D. E. Pitcher, *An Historical Geography of the Ottoman Empire: From Earliest Times to the End of the Sixteenth Century* (Leiden, 1972). The Ottoman involvement in Africa begins with the conquest of Egypt, a subject discussed in A. C. Hess, 'The Ottoman Conquest of Egypt (1517) and the Beginning of the Sixteenth-Century World War', *International Journal of Middle East Studies*, 4/1 (1973), 55–76. The subsequent incorporation of the Maghrib is described in H. Touati, 'Ottoman Maghrib', in *The New Cambridge History of Islam*, ii, ed. M. Fierro, pt IV: *North and West Africa, Sixteenth to Eighteenth Centuries* (Cambridge, 2010), 503–46. For a spirited introduction to the Barbary pirates, see A. Konstam, *The Barbary Pirates, 15th–17th Centuries* (Oxford, 2016). A popular account of Barbarossa is given in E. Bradford, *The Sultan's Admiral: The Life of Barbarossa* (London, 1968).

The Portuguese involvement in Ethiopia is treated in considerable detail in *The Portuguese Expedition to Abyssinia in 1541–1543, as Narrated by Castanhoso*, ed. R. S. Whiteway (Abingdon, 2016; reprint of the Hakluyt Society edition, 2nd ser., 10, London, 1902). The famous battle of Alcácer Quibir (Alcazar) is given a full and lively treatment in E. W. Bovill, *The Battle of Alcazar: An Account of the Defeat of Don Sebastian of Portugal at El-Ksar el-Kebir* (London, 1952). The battle also features in the opening section of a book on al-Mansur, M. Garcia-Arenal, *Ahmad al-Mansur: The Beginnings of Modern Morocco* (Oxford, 2009), which provides a fine introduction to this formative period. The Moroccan invasion of the Songhai, the battle of Tondibi, and its aftermath are given full consideration in L. Kaba, 'Archers, Musketeers, and Mosquitoes: The Moroccan Invasion of the Sudan and the Songhay Resistance (1591–1612)', *Journal of African History*, 22/4 (1981), 457–75.

Chapter 10 Retrospect and Prospect

As the title of this chapter implies, it begins by looking back over the prehistory and history of northern Africa before 1600 in an attempt to try to discern the main drivers that have influenced human development. Selected background reading for this vast time span has been given in the preceding sections. We then fast-forward four centuries, a period of massive change which saw first the colonization of the continent by Europeans and then the rapid emergence of free nation states. One has only to flick through the excellent maps covering the period 1878 to 1994 in C. McEvedy, *The Penguin Atlas of African History* (revised edn, London, 1995) to appreciate the stunning pace of change. There are so many books dealing with the history of Africa in this period, good, bad, and indifferent, that it is almost invidious to be selective. That said, a good place to start is with J. Parker and R. Rathbone, *African History: A Very Short Introduction* (Oxford, 2007) to provide a perspective, and to follow on with K. Shillington, *History of Africa* (4th edn, London, 2019) and R. Oliver and J. D. Fage, *A Short History of Africa* (revised edn, London, 1990). Both books are classics, frequently updated, which have stood the test of time. To these should be added the very useful contributions brought together in J. Parker and R. Reid (eds.), *The Oxford Handbook of Modern African History* (Oxford, 2013). Readers seeking more detail could begin with the multiple volumes of the *Cambridge History of Africa* and the UNESCO *General History of Africa* (p. 355 above for publication details).

We end by returning to the vital drivers of climate change and population growth, which are having such a dramatic effect on the communities living within and around the Sahara. The subject is fast-changing, but the following selection of papers will give the flavour of the debate: N. Zeng, 'Atmospheric Science: Drought in the Sahel', *Science*, 302/5647 (2003), 999–1000; N. Thomas and S. Nigam, 'Twentieth-Century Climate Change over Africa: Seasonal Hydroclimate Trends and Sahara Desert Expansion', *Journal of Climate*, 31/9 (2018), 3349–70; C. Brierley, K. Manning, and M. Maslin, 'Pastoralism May Have Delayed the End of the Green Sahara', *Nature Communications*, 9 (2018), article 4018; and F. S. R. Pausata *et al.*, 'The Greening of the Sahara: Past Changes and Future Implications', *One Earth*, 2/3 (2020), 235–50. Trying to understand the complexities of the science and assessing the implications is a thought-provoking exercise. The social effects of climate change leading to the dislocation of communities and to mass migration are discussed in G. Ben-Arieh, 'Saharan Crossing: The Realities of Migration Today', in K. B. Berzock (ed.), *Caravans of Gold, Fragments in Time: Art, Culture, and Exchange across Medieval Saharan Africa* (Princeton, 2019), 283–93. It is a sobering reminder of the fragility of the world.

ILLUSTRATION SOURCES

Chapter 1 opener and 1.9: Peter Adams/Getty Images; **1.1** Photo12/Getty Images; **1.2** Multiple sources building on M. A. Summerfield, 'Tectonics, geology, and long-term landscape development' in W. M. Adams, A. S. Goudie and A. R. Orme (eds.) *The Physical Geography of Africa* (Oxford, 1996); **1.3**; Based on C. K. Nyamweru, 'The African rift system' in the above, figs, 2.2, 2.3, 2.4; **1.4** Sue Robinson/Alamy Stock Photo; **1.5** After D. J. Mattingly (ed.) *The Archaeology of Fazzan. Volume 1, Synthesis* (London, 2003), fig. 9.4; **1.6** After C. Scarre (ed.), *The Human Past. World Prehistory and the Development of Human Society* (London, 2005), fig. 10.10; **1.7** From R. Kuper and S. Kröpelin, 'Climate Controlled Holocene Occupation in the Sahara: motor of Africa's evolution' *Science* 313, August 2006, fig. 3; **1.8** Author, multiple sources; **1.10** Beata Tabak/Alamy Stock Photo; **1.11** Blickwinkel/Alamy Stock Photo; **1.12** Avatar_023/Getty Images; **1.13** Based on C. Scarre (ed.), *The Human Past* (London, 2005), fig. 10.1; **1.15** Author, multiple sources; **1.16** Jeff Schmaltz, MODIS Rapid Response Team, NASA/GSFC; **1.17** Author, multiple sources; **1.18** Michele Cattani/AFP/Getty Images; **1.19, 1.20, 1.21** Author, multiple sources; **1.22** © The Trustees of the British Museum; **1.23 (left)** After C. Ehret, *The Civilizations of Africa. A History to 1800* (Charlottesville, second edition 2016), map 4, and **(right)** P. Mitchell, *African Connections* (Walnut Creek, 2005), fig. 1.4.

Chapter 2 opener and 2.12a: The Metropolitan Museum of Art, New York, Creative Commons CC0, Gift of Albert Rothbart, 1933; **2.1** After L. B. Railsback et al., 'An optimized scheme of lettered marine isotope substages for the last 1.0 million years, and the climatostratigraphic nature of isotope stages and substages' *Quaternary Science Reviews* 111 (2015), 94–106, (fig.1); **2.2** D. W. Phillipson *African Archaeology* (Cambridge, 1985), figure 4.16, after Camps, 1974; **2.3** ASOR Photo Collection, licensed under CC BY-ND

4.0: Will Raynolds , May 2012, https://www.asor.org/wp-content/uploads/2020/08/
pid000190_Libya_HauaFteah_2012_05_Excavation-1024x683.jpg; **2.4** After N.
Barton and A. Bouzouggar, 'Hunter-gatherers of the Maghreb 25,000–6,000 years
ago' in P. Mitchell and P. Lane (eds.), *The Oxford Handbook of African Archaeology*
(Oxford, 2013), fig. 30.1; **2.5** Ibid., fig. 30.3: Joshua Hogue, copyright Nick Barton;
2.6, 2.7 Ian R Cartwright, Institute of Archaeology, University of Oxford; **2.8** Jacopo
Niccolò Cerasoni; **2.9** After S. Mithen, *After the Ice. A Global History 20,000–5000
BC* (London, 2003), p.12, with additions; **2.10** Multiple sources; **2.11** After C. Scarre
(ed.), *The Human Past* (London, 2003), fig. 5.5 with additions; **2.12b** Museo Egizio,
Turin; **2.13** akg-images / De Agostini Picture Lib. / G. Dagli Orti; **2.14** Antony Huan/
Wikimedia Commons (CC BY-SA-2.0) https://commons.wikimedia.org/wiki/
File:Pottery_bowl_fragments,_Early_Neolithic_Egypt,_Nabta,_7050-6100_BCE,_
British_Museum_EA76916_EA769046_EA76941_EA76943_EA76944.jpg; **2.15**
Institut für Archäologische Wissenschaften, Goethe-Universität Frankfurt.

Chapter 3 opener and 3.6: DPK-Photo/Alamy Stock Photo; **3.1** Anan Kaewkhammul
/Alamy Stock Photo; **3.2** Author, multiple sources; **3.3** Mike P Shepherd/Alamy
Stock Photo; **3.4** After D. J. Mattingly (ed.), *The Archaeology of Fazzan. Volume 1,
Synthesis* (London, 2003), fig. 8.1; **3.5** DEA / C. Sappa /Getty Images; **3.7** Author,
multiple sources including D. Fuller and E. Hilderbrand, 'Domesticating plants in
Africa' in P. Mitchell and P. Lane (eds.), *The Oxford Handbook of African Archaeology*
(Oxford, 2013), fig.35.2; **3.8** ©UCL, Institute of Archaeology; **3.9** © The Trustees of
the British Museum; **3.10** Arterra Picture Library / Alamy Stock Photo; **3.11** After C.
K. MacDonald, 'Before the Empire of Ghana: pastoralism and the origins of cultural
complexity in the Sahel' in G. Connah (ed.), *Transformations in Africa: Essays on Africa's
Later Past* (Leicester, 1998), fig. 4.5; **3.12** AFC Holl; **3.13** Author, multiple sources;
3.14 Author, multiple sources including G. Souville, 'Témoignages sur l'âge du Bronze
au Maghreb occidental' *Académie des Inscriptions et Belles-Lettres* (Paris, 1986), figs. 1
and 3, and G. Camps, 'Beginnings of pastoralism and cultivation in north-west Africa
and the Sahara: origins of the Berbers' in J. D. Clark (ed.), *The Cambridge History of
Africa*, Volume 1 (Cambridge, 1982), figs. 8.7, 8.8 and 8.17; **3.15** Author, multiple sources
including B. Midant-Reynes, 'The Naqada Period (*c*.4000–3200 BC)' in I. Shaw (ed.),
The Oxford History of Ancient Egypt (Oxford, 2000), p.45; **3.16** © The Trustees of the
British Museum; **3.17** Museo Egizio, Turin; **3.18** ©DAI Cairo, photo by Günter Dreyer;
3.19 The Picture Art Collection / Alamy Stock Photo; **3.20** Courtesy of the Oriental
Institute of the University of Chicago; **3.21** After B. M. Bryan, 'The Eighteenth Dynasty
before the Amarna Period (*c*.1550–1352 BC)' in I. Shaw (ed.), *The Oxford History of
Ancient Egypt* (Oxford, 2000), p. 227; **3.22** Walter Callens/Wikimedia Commons (CC

Archaeology of Fazzan. Volume 1, Synthesis (London, 2003), fig.6.14; **5.19** Details from D. J. Mattingly and G. D. B. Jones, 'A new clausura in Western Tripolitania: Wadi Skiffa South', *Libyan Studies* 17 (1986), fig. 1, and G. W. Barker (ed.), *Farming in the Desert. The UNESCO Libyan Valleys Archaeological Survey. Volume 1, Synthesis* (Paris, 1996); **5.20** After S. K. McIntosh, *Excavations at Jenné-jeno, Hambarketolo, and Kaniana (Inner Niger Delta, Mali), the 1981 season* (Berkeley, 1995), fig. 10.3; **5.21** Author, multiple sources including R. Mauny, *Tableau géographique de l'Ouest Africain au Moyen-Age d'après les sources ecrites, la tradition et l'archéologie* (Dakar, 1961), fig. 55; **5.22** After A. Wilson, 'Saharan trade in the Roman period: short–medium distance trade networks', *Anzania Archaeological Research in Africa* 47.4 (2012), fig. 1; **5.23** © The Trustees of the British Museum.

Chapter 6 opener and 6.12: Frans Lemmens/Alamy Stock Photo; **6.1** Author; **6.2** © The Trustees of the British Museum; **6.3** akg-images/Gilles Mermet; **6.4** Wikimedia Commons (CC BY-SA 4.0) https://commons.wikimedia.org/wiki/File:Djeddar_Monuments_fun%C3%A9raires_%C3%A0_Frenda_wilaya_de_Tiaret_14.jpg; **6.5** Author, multiple sources; **6.6** Issam Barhoumi/Wikimedia Commons (CC BY-SA 4.0) https://commons.wikimedia.org/wiki/File:Ksar_Lemsa_01.jpg; **6.7** Author, multiple sources including J. Haywood, *The Cassell Atlas of World History* (London, 1997), map 3.13; **6.8** Roger Wood/Getty Images; **6.9** Florentina Georgescu Photography/Getty Images; **6.10** Courtesy of the Polish Centre of Mediterranean Archaeology of the University of Warsaw, photo by Miron Bogacki; **6.11** After R. J. McIntosh, *The Peoples of the Middle Niger* (Oxford, 1988), maps 6.4 and 8.3; **6.13** Photo © Musée du quai Branly-Jacques Chirac, Dist. RMN-Grand Palais, Paris; **6.14** Musée du quai Branly-Jacques Chirac, Paris. Photo by Michel Urtado/Thierry Ollivier. © 2021. RMN-Grand Palais / Dist. Photo SCALA, Florence.

Chapter 7 opener and 7.14: akg-images/André Held; **7.1** Author, multiple sources; **7.2** After M. Brett, *The Fatimid Empire* (Edinburgh, 2017), map 2.1; **7.3** Ullstein bild /Getty Images; **7.4** After M. Brett, *The Fatimid Empire* (Edinburgh, 2017), maps 3.1 and 4.2; **7.5** ©Victoria and Albert Museum, London; **7.6** Author, multiple sources; **7.7** Zedam Nabil Photography/Getty Images; **7.8** Author, multiple sources including N. Levtzion, *Ancient Ghana and Mali* (London, 1973), maps 1 and 2; **7.9 (top)** Dipak Pankhania / Alamy Stock Photo; **7.9 (bottom)** imageBROKER / Alamy Stock Photo; **7.10** Author using N. Levtzion, *Ancient Ghana and Mali* (London, 1973), map 1 and other sources; **7.11** Wikimedia Commons CC0 licensed, https://commons.wikimedia.org/wiki/File:Tumulus_d%27El-Oualedji_(AOF).jpg; **7.12** BNF; **7.13** Universal Images

Group/Getty Images; **7.15** After T. Insoll, *The Archaeology of Islam in Sub-Saharan Africa* (Cambridge, 2003), fig.5.7, and M. Cissé, 'Gao, a Middle Niger city in medieval trade', in K. B. Berzock (ed.), *Caravans of Gold, Fragments in Time* (Princeton, 2019), fig. 9.1; **7.16** © T.Insoll; **7.17** © Marie-Lan Nguyen/Wikimedia Commons / CC-BY 4.0, https://commons.wikimedia.org/wiki/File:Stele_Almeria_Gao-Saney_MNM_R88-19-279.jpg; **7.18** © Sam Nixon; **7.19** After S. Nixon (ed.), *Essouk-Tadmekka: An Early Islamic Trans-Saharan Market Town* (Leiden, 2017), based on EOM aerial photos and adapted from Mauny 1961 and Moraes Farias 2003; **7.20** After A. Lagamma, *Sahel. Art and Empires on the shores of the Sahara* (Newhaven, 2020), fig.39, with additions; **7.21** From G. Connah, *African Civilizations. An Archaeological Perspective* (Cambridge, second edition 2001), fig.5.9; **7.22, 7.23** © Dirk Bakker/Bridgeman Images.

Chapter 8 opener and 8.20: BNF; **8.1** Wikipedia, Creative Commons Licence CC0, https://commons.wikimedia.org/wiki/File:SmrtLudvika91270.jpg; **8.2** Wikimedia https://commons.wikimedia.org/wiki/File:TabulaRogeriana_upside-down.jpg; **8.3** Author; **8.4** Luis Dafos/Getty Images; **8.5** Author; **8.6** ©British Library Board. All Rights Reserved/Bridgeman Images; **8.7** Eric Lafforgue/Art in All of Us /Getty Images; **8.8** After G. Connah, *African Civilizations. An Archaeological Perspective* (Cambridge, second edition 2001), figs. 6.1 and 6.2; **8.9** From M. Horton, *Shanga: the Archaeology of a Muslim Trading community on the Coast of East Africa* (London, 1996), fig. 5, by permission of Mark Horton; **8.10** Ulrich Doering/Alamy Stock Photo; **8.11** From P. S. Garlake, *The Early Islamic Architecture of the East African Coast* (Oxford, 1966), fig. 69, with the permission of the British Institute in Eastern Africa (BIEA); **8.12** Author, multiple sources including N. Levtzion, *Ancient Ghana and Mali* (London, 1973), map 1; **8.13** Institut de Recherches en Sciences Humaines, Université Abdou Moumouni de Niamey, Niger, © 2022. Image copyright The Metropolitan Museum of Art/Art Resource/Scala, Florence; **8.14** Jeff Overs/Getty Images; **8.15** from T. Insoll, *The Archaeology of Islam in Sub-Saharan Africa* (Cambridge, 2003), fig 5.8 © T.Insoll; **8.16** After P.F. De Moraes Farias, 'Islam in the West African Sahel' in A. Lagamma (Ed.) *Sahel. Art and Empires on the Shores of the Sahara* (Newhaven, 2020), fig 39; **8.17** After D. Gronenborn, 'Politics and trade in medieval Northern Nigeria', in K. B. Berzock (ed.), *Caravans of Gold, Fragments in Time* (Princeton, 2019), fig 11.1; **8.18** After T. Insoll, *The Archaeology of Islam in Sub-Saharan Africa* (Cambridge, 2003), fig. 6.11; **8.19** Gronenborn, Kassühlke /Römisch-Germanisches Zentralmuseum, after D. Gronenborn, *op. cit.*,fig 11.8.

Chapter 9 opener and 9.7: Wikimedia https://commons.wikimedia.org/wiki/File:L%C3%A1zaro_Luis_1563.jpg; **9.1** Joinmepic/Shutterstock; **9.2** Author, multiple sources; **9.3** US Geological Survey/Science Photo Library; **9.4** Antiqua Print Gallery/Alamy Stock Photo; **9.5** Album/Alamy Stock Photo; **9.6** Antiqua Print Gallery/Alamy Stock Photo; **9.8** Seth Lazar/Alamy Stock Photo; **9.9** After P. Ozanne, 'A new archaeological survey of Ife', *Odu 1* (1968); **9.10** © The Trustees of the British Museum; **9.11** After G. Connah, *African Civilizations. An Archaeological Perspective* (Cambridge, second edition 2001), fig. 6.6; **9.12** Harvard Art Museums/Fogg Museum, Gift of Mrs. John D. Rockefeller, Jr (Abby Aldrich Rockefeller), Photo ©President and Fellows of Harvard College, 1937.38; **9.13** Author, multiple sources; **9.14** Granger/ Alamy Stock Photo; **9.15** Author, multiple sources; **9.16** Ilona Kryzhanivska / Alamy Stock Photo; **9.17** After E. W. Bovill, *The Golden Trade of the Moors* (Princeton, 2009), map VII; **9.18** Michele Cattani/AFP/Getty Images; **9.19** Author, multiple sources; **9.20** Guido Alberto Rossi; **9.21** DEA/G. Dagli Orti/Getty Images; **9.22** Creative Commons CCo licence https://en.wikipedia.org/wiki/Capture_of_Tunis_(1569)#/media/File:The_Ottoman_Army_Marching_On_The_City_Of_Tunis_In_1569_Ce.jpg; **9.23** G. Dagli Orti/© NPL-DeA Picture Library/Bridgeman Images; **9.24** Author, multiple sources.

Chapter 10 opener and 10.3: Anna Serdyuk/Getty Images; **10.1** De Agostini Picture Library/Getty Images; **10.2** NASA/Goddard Space Flight Center; **10.4** Wikimedia/Zenodot Verlagsgesellschaft, https://commons.wikimedia.org/wiki/File:Yahy%C3%A2_ibn_Mahm%C3%BBd_al-W%C3%A2sit%C3%AE_005.jpg; **10.5** Historical Views/agefotostock; **10.6** Victor Englebert/Science Source Images; **10.7** Eric Feferberg/AFP/Getty Images; **10.8** DAWNING/Nick Parisse ; this picture is part of the project *On Whose Land?* by DAWNING.

The publisher apologizes for any errors or omissions in the above list. If contacted, they will be pleased to rectify these at the earliest opportunity.
Picture research by Sandra Assersohn.

INDEX

Note: the letter *f* refers to
illustrations, maps and diagrams

2 million years–6,000 BC the long
    beginning 37–61
  Arterian hunter-gatherers 43–4,
    44*f*
  ecozones and fauna 53–6, 55*f*
  greening the desert (10,000–6000
    BC) 52–6, 53*f*, 55*f*
  homo sapiens spread 41–2
  hunter-gatherers 38–9
  landscape changes 39–41, 40*f*
  later hunter-gatherers (42,000–
    10,000 BC) 45–52, 47*f*
  settlement of the desert (10,000–
    6000 BC) 56–61
  weather systems 52–3, 53*f*, 54*f*
6500–1000 BC domesticating the
    land 63–101
  African contribution 77–9
  Atlantic interface 83–6, 85*f*
  cereal crops, Near Eastern spread
    of 72–4, 72*f*
  climate stability and gradual
    change 79–83
  Indian Ocean interface 83, 84*f*
  Kerma, and the first kingdom of
    Kush 96–101

Mediterranean contribution
    76–7
Nile valley 86–8, 90*f*
pastoralism, beginnings of 64,
    65–70, 67*f*
Pharaonic Egypt, rise of 88–96
1000–140 BC creating connectivities
    103–43
  desert people 122–8
  Egypt (1069–30 BC) 131–5, 135*f*,
    139
  Ethiopia and the Red Sea 138–42,
    140*f*
  Garamantes 128–31, 129*f*
  lands to the north of the desert
    109–14
  Nubia and the kingdoms of Kush
    133–8, 136*f*, 139
  Sahel 115–20, 115*f*, 116*f*
  Sahel savannah 120–2
  travellers and explorers 104–9
140 BC–400 AD impact of empire
    145–81
  Africa within the Roman Empire
    156–63, 158*f*
  desert peoples and networks
    178–80
  exploring the desert fringes
    152–6

Garamantes, Classic period
    169–72, 169*f*, 171*f*, 175–7,
    176*f*, 181
Meroe, Aksum and beyond,
    Roman period 164–7, 165*f*,
    166*f*
Roman Africa, creation 146–52
Sahel, Roman period 172–3, 174*f*,
    175*f*
Sahel trading networks, Roman
    period 174–8, 175*f*, 176*f*
400–760: 183–211
  accommodation and revolt 200–1
  Arab Conquest of North Africa:
    first incursion 195–7, 196*f*
  Arab control 197–200
  Byzantine reconquest 191–4,
    192*f*, 193*f*
  changing elites 183–7
  desert communities 210–11
  Eastern front 194–5
  middle Nile polities 201–4
  Sahel, Western communities
    204–10
  Vandals in Africa 184, 185*f*,
    187–92, 189*f*
760–1150 emerging states 213–53
  Almoravid empire, rise of 228*f*,
    230–4

Fatimids, rise of 217–21
Fatimids in Egypt 221–3
forests of the south 249–52
Ghana, empire of 234–41, 236*f*
Indian Ocean coast 223–4
Maghrib under Berber control
 224–8
Northern polities in (700–900)
 214–17
Sahel, Central and Eastern
 communities 247–9, 248*f*
Sahel, Western neighbouring
 polities in 241–7
western arc 227–30
1150–1400 widening horizons 255–91
Almohad empire and thereafter
 259–64, 261*f*
Barbur, Zanj and Sofala lands
 269–74, 270*f*
crossing the desert 278–83, 280*f*
Egypt: the Ayyubids and the
 Mamluks 264–9
European interference 256–7
exploring the world 287–91
Mali empire 274–7, 275*f*, 278–83
new observers, new sources 257–8
Sudan kingdoms, central and
 eastern 283–7, 284*f*
1400–1600 Africa and the world
 293–335
Abyssinia, struggle for 325–7
al-Mansur's invasion of the Songhai
 Empire 329–32, 330*f*, 335
Chinese expeditions 294–6, 295*f*,
 298*f*
forest zone kingdoms 307–9, 311*f*
Gulf of Guinea explorations
 304–7, 305*f*, 306*f*
Morocco 327–8
Ottoman empire in the north 321,
 322*f*
Ottoman expansion, Maghrib and
 western Mediterranean 321–4,
 322*f*, 325*f*

Portuguese consolidation and
 exploration beyond the
 Guinea coast 311*f*, 312–16
Portuguese expeditions 296–304,
 298*f*, 300*f*, 301*f*, 302*f*, 303*f*,
 305*f*, 311*f*
Songhai empire 317–20, 318*f*, 320*f*
1600–present day: retrospect and
 prospect 337–54
climate 349–54
corridors of communication
 342–5
human contribution 338–41
innovation zones 341–2
the last four hundred years 346–9
population growth 349–54
Abalessa 124
Abbasid caliphate and dynasty 201,
 213, 215, 217, 226
Abd al-Malik, caliph 328
Abd al-Mumin 260
Abd al-Rahman al-Sa'di 333
Abd al-Rahman III 218
Abdullah al-Mahdi Billah 217–18
Abdullah ibn Yasin 231–2
Abu Abd Allah 217–18
Abu al-Abbas al-Saffah, caliph 213
Abu al-Fida 269
Abu al-Hassan Ali, caliph 264
Abu Bakr ibn Umar, caliph 186, 195,
 232
Abu Yazid rebellion 218
Abu Zakariyya 261
Abydos burial-grounds, Egypt 89–91,
 92, 93*f*
Abyssinia (1400–1600) 325–7
Acheulean assemblage 41–2
Actium battle of (31 BC), Ionian Sea
 149, 150
Adherbal, son of King Micipsa 146
Adrar Bous, Niger 32
Adulis, Red Sea port 27, 142, 164–6,
 168*f*
Aelius Gallus 162

Aezana, Aksumite king 164
Afar Triple Junction 18
Africa, circumnavigation of 104–5
Africa Proconsularis (Roman
 province) 148
African Humid Period 7–10, 14,
 56, 79
 and the Nile valley 87
African Late Stone Age 45–52
African Middle Stone Age 39, 41–2
African National Congress, South
 Africa 349
African rice (*Oryza glaberrima*) 77
African tectonic plates 2, 3*f*, 4
African Union 353
Afro-Asiatic language group 34, 34*f*
Aghlabid dynasty 213, 214*f*, 215–16,
 217
Ahaggar Mountains, Algeria 11, 13*f*
Ahmad al-Mansur, sultan 328, 329*f*
Ahmad ibn Ibrahim al-Ghazi, sultan
 326–7
Ahmose, pharaoh 95
Aïr Mountains, Niger 11
Akan goldfields 277, 307, 319–20
Aksum kingdom 139, 194, 195
 Roman period 164–7, 165*f*, 166*f*
Alans tribe 185*f*, 187
al-Bakri 229, 231, 232, 234, 235–6,
 237–9, 240, 244–5, 247, 258
Albertine Rift 4, 4*f*
Alcácer Quibir, battle of (1578),
 Morocco 328, 329*f*
Alcáçovas, treaty of (1479) 306
Alexander the Great 134
Alexandria 163, 196
 harbour 323*f*
al-Fazari 209
Alfonso V, king of Portugal 304
Alfonso VI, king of Castile 234
Alfonso VIII, king of Castile 256
Algeria, French occupation of 347
Ali ibn Yusuf, emir 259–60
al-Idrisi 229–30, 236, 239, 241, 269

al-Mahdiyya Great Mosque, Tunisia
218, 219f
al-Makkan family 344–5
al-Mansur, caliph 335
invasion of the Songhai empire
329–32, 330f, 335
al-Mansur, Zirid leader 225
Al-Masadi 215
al-Masudi 224, 258
Almeria marble, southern Spain 244,
244f
Almohad caliphate 255, 256, 260
Almoravid empire and dynasty
259–64, 261f, 344
in Christian Spain 234
rise of 228f, 230–4
al-Mu'azzam Turan Shah, Sultan 266
al-Muhullabi 248
al-Mu'izz, caliph 221, 224
al-Muwahhidun sect 260
Alodia, kingdom of 164, 201, 203–4
al-Qahira (Cairo) 220, 221
al-Sahil 287
al-Salih Ayyub, sultan 266
al-shidda al-uzma period (1063–
1072), Egypt 222
al-Umari 288
al-Yaqubi 229, 247
amazonite trade 177
American Colonization Society (est.
1816) 347–8
Ammon oracle, Siwa 123, 123f, 134
Ammonites tribe 123, 128
Antalas, Berber leader 190
Apadana relief, Persepolis 138f
Apuleius 157
aquifers 15–16
Arabian plate 3f, 4
Argaric culture 85
Arguin, Portuguese slave-trading
colony 299–300, 300f, 301f,
303–4
Asad al-Din Shirkuh 265
Asbystae people 106f, 109, 110

Askiya Dawud, Songhai ruler 319
Askiya Ishak, Songhai ruler 332–3
Askiya Muhammad I, Songhai ruler
317–19, 320, 320f
Askiya Nut, Songhai ruler 333, 334
Assyrians 136
invasion of Egypt (667 BC) 134
astronomical cycles and climate
change in the Sahara 7
Aswan, Egypt 19, 21
Atarantians tribe 124
Aterian hunter-gatherers 43–4, 44f
Aterian tools, African Middle Stone
Age 43–4, 43f
Atlantes tribe 124
Atlantic Multidecadal Oscillation
354
Atlantic ocean 25, 27–9, 28f
coast of Africa 23, 28–9, 104–6,
343–4
coastal zone 17, 18
interface 83–6, 85f
see also under Portugal
Atlas Mountains 16
Augila (Awjila) oasis 123–4
Augustus (Octavian), emperor 148,
149, 150–1
aurochs 66
Australopithecus 30
Austuriani tribe 181
Averroes, see Ibn Rushd
Awdaghust (modern Tegdaoust),
Mauritania 229–30, 232, 241
Ayyubid dynasty, Egypt 255, 265–6
Azores 297–9

Baal Hammon temple, Thugga 159
Badarian culture, Nile valley 74, 81
Bahariya oasis, Egypt 123
Balbus, Cornelius, expedition against
the Garamantes (20 BC) 152–3
Bamako, Mali 352
Bani Hasan people 282
Bantu language 34–5, 34f

Banu Hilal Bedouin nomads 214,
226–8
Banu Maqil nomadic Arabs 282
Banu Sulaym Berber nomads
226–8
Baqt, treaty between Muslim Egypt
and Christian Makuria 201–2,
204, 222
Baquates tribe 148, 151f, 152, 158
Barbarossa, Aruj 322–3
Barbarossa, Hayreddin 322–4, 324f
Barbary sheep 48, 56, 61
domestication 63, 64f, 68
barley 64, 65, 72f, 87
Barth, Heinrich 6
Bas Saharan Basin 15–16
Battimansa, Mandinka king 303
Bavares tribe, rebellion against Rome
(AD 253) 181
Bedouin migration to North Africa
226
tribal politics and movement
(c.1055) 223f
bedrock 2–5, 4f
Begho trading town, West Africa 307
Belisarius, Count 192
Bellin, Jacques Nicolas 303f
Benin, Nigeria 307–9, 308f, 310f
copper alloy head of oba (king)
310f
Berbers 214, 216, 345f
Arab invasion and occupation
197–201
elite 190–1
elite, under Byzantine rule 193–4
in Iberia 226
and Islam 200–1
revolt (from 740) 214–15
Roman rule 156
under the Vandals 188–91
see also individual tribes
Berenike, Red Sea port 27, 108f,
139–41, 140f, 162f, 163f, 164
Berghwata Berbers 232

Beta Giyorgis religious site, Ethiopia 139

Bilma salt mines, Niger 14

Bir el-Ater site, Algeria 43

Bir Kiseiba cattle bones, Nabta Playa 66, 68

Black Death (Damascus, 1348) 290

black slave soldiers 222

Blue Nile 19

boatbuilding:
 caravels 306, 344
 Neolithic 58–60, 60*f*
 Nile valley 87–8, 91*f*, 92*f*

Bocchus I, king of Mauretania 146, 147, 149

Bocchus II, king of Mauretania 148, 149

Bølling-Allerød Interstadial 52, 53*f*

Book of Routes and Realms (al-Bakri) 235, 245

brass 240–1

broomcorn millet (*Panicum miliaceum*) 83, 84*f*

Bubalus Period (10,000–4000 BC) rock art, Fazzan region 70, 71*f*

Bura-Asinda-Sikka horse-rider model, Niger 276*f*

Bure goldfields, Mali 275, 276

Butr/Barani divide 227

Byzantine empire 184–7
 defeat in Egypt by the Arabs 195–6
 reconquest of north Africa 191–4, 192*f*, 193*f*

Cabaon, nomad leader 190

Cadamosto, Alvise 300–1, 319

Cairo 19–20, 21, 124, 220*f*, 221, 268

Caligula, emperor 154

Cambyses, Persian king 137

camels (*Camelus dromedarius*) 178–9, 179*f*
 introduction to the Sahara 126–8, 127*f*

Canary Current 27, 28, 28*f*

Canary Islands 297

Cão, Diogo 312

Cap Dra'a 28, 29

Cape Bojador 29, 299

Cape of Good Hope (Cabo da Boa Esperança) 312–13

Capsian phase hunter-gatherers 46, 47*f*, 61

caravan routes, Saharan 108*f*, 123*f*, 128, 186, 195, 210, 282, 283, 320, 330, 342–3

caravans, desert 122–8

caravels 302, 302*f*, 306, 344

Cardial Ware (Impressed Ware) pottery 76

carnelian 177, 251

Carthage 111–14, 112*f*, 113*f*, 146, 163, 187, 199
 destruction (146 BC) 145, 146, 150
 mosaic floor, country estate 160*f*, 161
 refounded (Africa Proconsularis, 27 BC) 148
 traders 107, 142
 see also Punic Wars

Catalan Atlas (1375) 288, 289*f*

Catholic Church 192

cattle (*Bos Taurus*), African, domestication 66, 67*f*, 68–9

cattle sacrifice 81

cave painting, *see* rock art, Saharan

Central Rift valley, Kenya 41

Ceuta raid (1415), Morocco 293, 297

Chad conference on desertification (2002) 353

Chad mountains, Tibesti 12

Chapel of the Martyrs, Thabraca, Tunisia 189*f*

chariots, horse-drawn 124, 125–6, 127*f*

China, expeditions and exploration 294–6, 295*f*, 298*f*

Chott el-Djerid, Tunisia 14, 15*f*

Christianity:
 African branch 188
 kingdom of Aksum 166
 middle Nile 201–2, 202*f*, 203*f*

Cirta (Constantine), Algeria 114, 146–7, 148

Clark, J. G. D. 39

Cleopatra VII, queen of Egypt 149, 150

Cleopatra Selene II, queen of Egypt 149

climate change 349–54
 and desertification of the Sahara 339
 effects on the Sahel 350–4, 351*f*
 Holocene 6–10, 6*f*, 8*f*
 and human settlement 8–10, 9*f*

climatic zones, east–west 338

coastal zone, North Africa 16–17

Columbus, Christopher 313

Constantine, emperor 184

Constantinople 184, 193, 321, 341

copper smelting and working:
 Agadez, Niger 118
 Akjoujt, Mauritania 118
 Ghana 240
 Kerma, Egypt 118
 Nubia 118
 Red Sea Hills 89
 western Sahel 207

Coptic Church, middle Nile 201–2

Coptic Lustre Ware bowl, Egypt 222*f*

Cossus Cornelius Lentulus 153

councils of tribal elders (*seniores*) 158

cow-pea 77, 83, 120

Cresques, Abraham 289*f*

Cretaceous period 3*f*

Crusades 256, 257*f*, 265, 341
 Fifth Crusade (1217–21) 256
 Seventh Crusade (1248–54) 256, 266, 267*f*
 Eighth Crusade (1270) 256, 257*f*

Cutzinas, Berber leader 194

Cyrenaica 150, 151*f*
    coastline 25, 26
Cyrene, Greek colony 110, 125, 125*f*
Cyrus the Great 134

da Cintra, Pedro 303*f*
da Gama, Cristóvão 326, 327
da Gama, Estêvão 326
da Gama, Vasco 311*f*, 313–15, 314*f*, 343
Dabban phase hunter-gatherers 46
Daji Gwana Nok figurine, Nigeria 121*f*
Daju people 286–7
Darfur region 248, 248*f*, 249, 286–7
Darius I, king of Persia 137
Deir el-Bahri mortuary temple of Hatshepsut, Egypt 99, 136*f*
dental evulsion, Iberomaurusian cemeteries 48, 49*f*
Description of the Barbarians (Zhufan zhi) 269
desert nomads 172, 276, 282, 344–5, 345*f*
desertification of the Sahara 339, 352–4
Dia Shoma settlement, Mali 116
Dias, Bartholomeu 312–13
Dias, Dinís 299
Diocletian, emperor 184
Diodorus Siculus 163
Diogenes 167
djeddars (monumental tombs) 190–1, 191*f*
Djenné Great Mosque, Mali 278*f*
D'MT (pronounced Da'amat) culture 139
DNA analysis and evidence:
    African cattle 66
    D'MT populations 139
    early farmers, Morocco 76
    Homo sapiens 33, 35
    Taforalt populations 50
Dolabella, proconsul 154
Dom Duarte, king of Portugal 297

Dom Pedro 299
Dongola, Sudan 201, 202
donkeys 126
Down to Earth (Snigdha Das) 349
Dufuna dugout canoe, Nigeria 60, 60*f*
Dulcert, Angelino 287–8
Dunama Dabbalemi, king (*mai*) of Kanem 283
Durbi Takusheyi cemetery, Nigeria 285–6, 286*f*
Dutch colonization of Africa and the Indies 347

Eannes, Gil 299
East African coast exploration, Roman period 167, 168*f*
East African Garden of Eden 33–5
Egypt 88–96, 103
    4500–3000 BC, Predynastic period 89
    3000–2686 BC, Early Dynastic period 89
    2686–2160 BC, Old Kingdom 89, 92
    2160–2055 BC, First Intermediate period 89, 93–4
    2055–1650 BC, Middle Kingdom 89, 94
    1650–1550 BC, Second Intermediate period 89, 94
    1550–1069 BC, New Kingdom 89, 95–6, 97*f*
    1069–664 BC, Third Intermediate period 96, 131–5, 135*f*
    664–522 BC, Late period 131, 134
    332–30 BC, Ptolemaic period 131, 134–5, 139
    Arab invasion and occupation 195–6
    Ayyubids and the Mamluks 264–9
    Byzantine occupation 201
    Byzantine war with the Sasanians 185–6

    Fatimid attempts to occupy (AD 913/920) 218
    Fatimid caliphate (AD 969) 218, 220, 221–3, 226, 264–5
    grain supplies to Rome 161
    Libyan invasion of (1220 BC) 95–6
    Ottoman occupation 321
    Persian rule in 134, 138*f*
    Punt sea route 99–101
    Roman occupation 150–1, 156, 159–61, 162*f*
    Saite dynasty 134
    trading systems 89–91
    Tulunid occupation 216
Eighth Crusade (1270) 256, 257*f*
El-Badari figurine, Egypt 75*f*
El-Barga, Kerma, Sudan 68
elephants, *see* war elephants, from East Africa
El-Gebelein linen depiction of river craft and rowers, Upper Egypt 92*f*
El-Ghazali monastery, Sudan 203*f*
El-Kharga oasis, Egypt 128
Elmina, Ghana 312, 319, 320
El-Oualedji great tumulus, Mali 237
Ennedi plateau 13*f*
ensete (relative of the banana) 77
Erg Chebbi, Morocco 12*f*
Ethiopia 138–42, 140*f*, 342
    India trade 83
Ethiopian Dome 3*f*, 4, 18
Ethiopian Highlands 5, 18–19, 19*f*, 326, 339
    early farming 82
    as zone of innovation 342
Ethiopian Rift 4, 4*f*
European colonization of Africa 348–9
Euthymenes 107

Faiyum Oasis grain storage pits, Egypt 73, 73*f*
Fatima, daughter of the Prophet 217

Fatimid caliphate, Egypt (AD 969) 218, 220, 221–3, 226, 264–5
relations with the Zirids 226
rise of 217–21
Fifth Crusade (1217–21) 256
finger millet (*Eleusine coracana*) 77, 83
foggara system of irrigation 128, 129*f*, 131, 169*f*, 170
fonio cereals 77
frankincense 139, 166
Freetown, Sierra Leone 347, 348*f*
French occupation of Algeria 347
Frenda *djeddars*, Tahert, Algeria 191*f*
funerary monuments, western Sahel 208–9, 208*f*, 209*f*

Gadir (Cadiz), Spain 111
Gaetuli tribe 146, 147, 147*f*, 150, 151*f*, 152, 153
Gaia, king of Numidia 112
Gaius Petronius 152
Gajiganna region early pastoralists, Lake Chad 80–1
Gambia river 29, 105, 303*f*
Gao, Mali 22, 206, 206*f*, 209, 242*f*, 277, 279, 317, 318*f*, 320*f*
excavations 242–3, 242*f*
Saney excavations 242, 242*f*, 243–4, 244*f*
Umayyad Spain, links with 244
Garama (Jarma), Garamantian capital 129*f*, 131, 152, 156, 169, 170
Garamantes 124, 128–31, 129*f*, 143, 151*f*, 152, 153–4, 155–6, 210
arable crops and livestock 128–30
Cornelius Balbus expedition against (20 BC) 152–3
slave raids 125
underground aqueducts 128
Garamantes, Classic period 169–72, 169*f*, 171*f*, 175–7, 176*f*, 181
craft skills 170
farming 170

grave goods, elite tombs 170
Gauda, king of Numidia 147
Gaugamela, battle of (331 BC), Tigris 134
Geiseric, Vandal leader 187–8, 190
Georgios III of Makuria 222
Ghana (Wagadu), kingdom of 209, 229, 230, 235, 274, 275*f*
760–1150 234–41, 236*f*
and the Almoravids 228*f*
High Kings 235–6, 237
Ghana-Bénin Gap 16
Ghat oasis, Libya 124
gift exchange, Neolithic 58
Giralda, Seville 261
glass beads 125, 251, 252
globular *solidi* gold coins 247
Gnaeus Pompeius 148
Goa island, India 316
goats, domestication and introduction to Africa 66–8, 67*f*
Godala tribe 227
gold, West African 107, 124, 125*f*
Akan, Ghana 277, 307, 319–20
Bure, Mali 275, 276
kingdom of Ghana 236*f*, 237–9
panning, Kalsaka village, Yatenga province, Burkina Faso 239*f*
gold trade 229, 239–40
1400–1600 319–20
Roman period 177–8
Gomes, Fernão 304, 312
Grandes Chroniques de France (John the Good) 267*f*
Great Green Wall for the Sahara 353–4, 353*f*
Great Rift Valley 18
Gregory, exarch (governor) 197
Gregory Rift 4, 4*f*
Grotte aux Chauves-Souris, malachite mining 118
Grotte des Pigeons, Taforalt, Morocco 48, 49*f*

groundnut 77
Guinea, Gulf of, Portuguese exploration 304–7, 305*f*, 306*f*
Guinea Current 27–8, 28*f*
Guinea Highlands 22

hafirs (communal water tanks) 136–7
Hafsid dynasty and empire 255, 261, 263, 263*f*, 264, 324
Hagfet ed-Dabba site, Cyrenaica 46
hajj, pilgrimage to Mecca 253, 258, 287, 290
pilgrim caravans 345, 346*f*
Timbuktu to Cairo 124
Hammad, brother of al-Mansur 225
Hammadids, Berber dynasty 226
Hanno, voyage along the West African coast 23–4, 28–9, 104–6, 106*f*, 344
Harappa culture, Indus valley 83
harpoons, Neolithic 58, 59*f*
Hasan ibn al-Nu'man 199, 200
Hassan Mosque, Rabat 261
Hatshepsut, pharaoh 99, 100*f*
Hattab II cave, Morocco 46
Haua Fteah cave, Cyrenaica 43, 45–6, 45*f*, 61, 67, 76
Hausaland 284*f*, 285–6, 318, 318*f*, 320
Hawwa, ruler of Kanem 248
Hayir Bey 321
Henry the Navigator (Dom Henrique) 296–303, 304, 341
Herodotus 21, 22, 87, 104, 107–8, 109, 110, 122, 123–4, 125, 128, 131, 136, 137, 177, 240
Hiempsal, son of King Micipsa 146
Hiempsal II, king of Numidia 147, 148
Hiera Sykaminos (Maharraqa), Nile valley 152
Hierakonpolis, Egypt 89
Hilderic, Vandal king 190
Hippalus 142

Hippo Regius (Annaba), Algeria 187, 192

Hittites 95

Homo erectus 31*f*, 32

Homo ergaster 31*f*, 32

Homo georgicus 31*f*, 32

Homo habilis 31, 31*f*

Homo heidelbergensis 31*f*, 32

Homo neanderthalensis 31*f*, 32, 33

Homo rudolfensis 31, 31*f*

Homo sapiens 31*f*, 33
  DNA studies 33, 35
  spread of 41–2

Huelva, Spain 111

human diversity 33–5

human evolution 29–33, 31*f*, 32*f*

hunter-gatherers, later (42,000–10,000 BC) 45–52, 47*f*

Husuni Kubwa palace, Tanzania 271–2, 273*f*

hyacinth bean 77, 81

Hyksos elite, Egypt 94

Ibadis, Algeria 213, 214*f*, 215

Iberomaurusian phase 46–52, 47*f*
  tool kit 46, 47*f*

Ibn Abd al-Hakam 10, 199

Ibn Battuta 14, 258, 269–71, 272, 279–83, 288–90

Ibn Hawqal 229, 230, 241, 258

Ibn Khaldun 227, 258, 274–5, 277, 282

Ibn Rushd (known as Averroes) 260–1

Ibn Rustam 215

Ibn Salim al-Aswani 222

Ibn Tumart 260

Ibrahim ibn al-Aghlab, emir 215–16

Idris ibn Abd Allah, sultan 215

Idris II, sultan 215

Idrisids, Morocco 213, 214*f*, 215, 218

Ife, Nigeria 307, 308*f*
  bronze head 309*f*

Ifriqiya province, Tunisia and eastern Algeria 215

Ifriqiya uprising (1016) 226

Igbo Olokun, Nigeria 252

Igbo Ukwu burial, Nigeria 250*f*, 251, 252*f*, 253*f*

Impressed Ware (Cardial Ware) pottery 76

Indian Ocean:
  coastal maritime trading system 27, 223–4
  interface 83, 84*f*

Inner Niger Delta, *see under* Niger river

Intertropical Convergence Zone 14–15, 16, 22, 27, 52, 54*f*, 79

Iol Caesarea (Cherchel), Algeria 149

iron working and smelting 118, 119*f*
  Nok culture 119*f*, 121–2
  Sahel 119*f*, 120
  western Sahel 207

Isabella of Castile 304–6

Ishaq ibn al-Husayn 240

Islam 255, 287, 340
  modern radical groups 341, 350–2, 352*f*
  rise and spread of (760–1150) 186, 213–14, 252–3

Issos, battle of (333 BC), Syria 134

ivory trade 75*f*, 84–5, 85*f*, 88, 100, 137, 166

Iwo Eleru rock shelter skull, Nigeria 50, 51*f*

Izz al-Din Aybak, sultan 266

Jebel Barkal palace, Sudan 137

Jebel Gharbi site, Tripolitania 46

Jebel Irhoud cave, Morocco 42

Jebel Sahaba cemetery, Sudan 56

Jenné-jeno site, Inner Niger Delta, Mali 116–17, 117*f*, 204*f*, 205–6, 205*f*, 207, 208
  glass bead 125
  Roman period 173, 174*f*

Jerónimos church and monastery, Belém 315

John I, king of Portugal 293, 296, 297

John II, king of Portugal 312

Jolof empire, Senegal 277

Jos plateau, Nigeria 120

Juba I, king of Numidia 147, 148*f*, 149

Juba II, king of Numidia 149–50, 149*f*, 154

Judar, leader of the Moors 331–2

Jugurtha of Numidia 146–7

Jugurthine war (111 BC) 147

Julius Caesar 148, 149, 152

Julius Maternas 156, 173

Justinian, emperor 184, 192

Kahina, Berber leader 199, 200

Kairouan, Tunisia 197, 198*f*, 199, 201, 218, 225

Kanem empire 173, 283, 209, 210

Kanem region 247–9, 248*f*

Kano, Nigeria 284, 285*f*

Kaw Kaw kingdom 209–10, 241–2, 242*f*

Kenyan Dome 3*f*, 4, 18, 19

Kerma, and the First Kingdom of Kush 96–101, 99, 135
  copper melting 118

Kerné trading colony 24, 105

Kharijite sect and movement 200–1, 215, 218, 234

Khartoum 19

Khoisan language group 34, 34*f*

Kilwa Great Mosque, Tanzania 271, 273*f*

Kissi, Burkino Faso 206, 209
  fieldwork 173

Kitab al-'Ibar (Book of Lessons, Ibn Khaldun) 258

Knights Hospitaller, Malta 324

Knights of Rhodes expulsion (1522) 321

Knights of St John 324

Koï Gourrey (Killi) burial mound, Mali 237, 240

kola 77

Kolima Sud Est settlement, Méma
    region, Mali 116
Koran 186
Koubba pavilion, Marrakesh 233*f*
Koumbi Saleh, Mauritania 237
Ksar Lemsa Byzantine forts, Tunisia
    193*f*
Kusayla (Kasila), Berber king 197–8,
    199
Kush, Nubian kingdom of 103, 135*f*,
    132–8, 136*f*, 139, 164
    archers 136*f*, 136
    raid on Egypt (24 BC) 152, 153*f*
    tribute to Persian king 137, 138*f*
    see also Kerma, and the First
        Kingdom of Kush
Kutama, Berber tribe 217, 227
Kutubiyya Mosque, Marrakesh 261,
    262*f*

Laguatan tribe 194
Lake Chad 117, 156, 173, 247
Lamtuna, Berber tribe 227, 229, 231
language evolution 34–5, 34*f*
Las Navas de Tolosa, battle of (1212),
    Spain 256, 260, 261
Last Glacial Maximum 10, 41, 45,
    52, 53*f*
    and the Sahara desert 7
Late Glacial Interstadial 41
Leach, John 303*f*
Leo Africanus 319
Leo the Great, Pope 188
Leopold, king of Belgium 348
Lepanto, battle of (1571) 324
Leptis Magna, Libya 155, 163, 181
Leuathae/Laguatan tribe 190
Levallois-Mousterian assemblages 39
Libu tribe 132
Libyan tribes 106*f*, 109–10, 110*f*, 111
    in Egypt 132
    invasion of Egypt (1220 BC) 95–6
Libyco-Punic mausoleum, Dougga,
    Tunisia 158–9, 160*f*

Lipari quarries, Sicily 86
Lixos, Moroco 111
Lixos river 105
local messengers (*takhshif*) 281
lost wax casting 251
Louis IX, king of France 256, 257*f*,
    266, 267*f*
Luis, Lázaro nautical chart 305*f*

MacMillan, Harold 349
Mactar tombstone, Tunisia 157
Madagascar 4
Madeira 297
Maghrib 16, 76, 85–6, 85*f*, 109, 110,
    142
    1000–146 BC 110–14
    Arab conquest 197–200
    coastline 25–6, 315*f*, 316–17
    early ironworking 118–20, 119*f*
    hunter-gatherers 42, 46, 47*f*
    introduction of domesticated
        crops and animals 76
    Roman period 156–9, 158*f*
    southern Iberia contacts and trade
        84–6
Mahdi, messianic figure 217–18
Mahmud ibn Zarqun 333
Makuria, kingdom of 164, 201,
    202–3, 204, 265, 267
malachite mining, Akjoujt,
    Mauritania 118
Mali, empire of 278–83, 352
    1150–1400 274–7, 275*f*, 278–83
    1400–1600 317, 318*f*, 319
    burial mounds 237
Maliki Sunnism 231, 290
Malinke peoples 276
Mamluks 255, 321
    1400–1600 293
    control of Egypt 265–9
    Red Sea trade 268, 274
Mandela, Nelson 349
Mansa Musa, king of Mali vi, 258,
    277, 340

hajj pilgrimage 287–8, 289*f*, 345
Mansa Sulayman, king of Mali 277
Maqamat (al-Hairiri of Basra) 346*f*
Marine Isotope Stages (MIS) 39–41,
    40*f*, 42, 43
Marinids, Zenata Berbers 255, 262–4,
    263*f*, 297
Marinus of Tyre 167
Maritime Bell Beakers 85
Mark Anthony 149, 150
Marrakesh 232, 233*f*, 260, 264, 332
    Koubba pavilion 233*f*
    Kutubiyya Mosque 261, 262*f*
Masaesyli kingdom, Numidia 111,
    112–14, 146–8, 147*f*
Massyli kingdom, Numidia 111,
    112–14, 146–8, 147*f*
Masinissa, king of Numidia 114, 146
Masmuda Berbers 227
Masufa tribe 227
Mauretania (Mauri/Moors),
    kingdom of 103, 111, 145, 146,
    147*f*, 148–50, 151–2, 151*f*, 154,
    188, 190
    Roman provinces of Caesariensis
        and Tingitana 154
Maximian, emperor 184
Mazippa, Berber leader 154
Medinet Habu Great Temple relief,
    Egypt 95*f*, 96
Mediterranean 25–7, 26*f*
Medjerda river, Tunisia 24
Medracen, mausoleum of elite
    Numidian 150*f*
Mega-Chad lake 53, 55*f*
Méma region tell complexes 205–6
Memória das Armadas (1568) 314*f*
Merimde Beni Salama settlement,
    Egypt 73–4
    composite sickle 57*f*
Merneptah, pharaoh 95–6
Meroe, kingdom of 135–6, 155, 163,
    201
    relations with Rome 164

Meshwesh tribe 132

Micipsa, king of Numidia 114, 146, 158

Middle Awash valley, Ethiopia 41

Milanković, Milutin 6

Military Order of Christ 296

Ming dynasty, China 293, 294

Mogadishu 269–71

Mombasa 271

Mongol presence, Near East and Pontic steppe 268

Monleón, Rafael 302*f*

Monrovia, Liberia 347–8

Morocco:
  1400–1600 327–8
  early faming 84
  see also Almohads; Almoravids; Idrisids; Marinids; Wattasids

Mossi tribes 317, 318*f*

Muhammad, Prophet 186, 195, 217

Muhammad al-Idrisi 258

Muhammad Ali 346

Muhammad ibn Qu, Mali ruler 288

Musa ibn Nusayr 199

Muslim rebellion (Berber revolt, 740 AD) 213

Musulamii tribe 150, 151*f*, 152
  uprising (17 AD) 154

Myos Hormos (now Quseir el-Qadim), Red Sea port 27, 139–41, 140*f*, 162*f*, 163*f*, 164

myrrh 139, 166

Nabta Playa, Egypt:
  burial of oxen 69*f*
  pottery 59*f*

Napata, Egypt 135

Napoleon Bonaparte 346

Naqada, Egypt 89
  jar depicting river craft 91*f*

Narmer, pharaoh 94*f*

Narmer Palette, Hierakonpolis 91, 94*f*

Nasamones tribe 106*f*, 107–9, 123–4, 151*f*, 152, 153, 155

journey of exploration 124

Natufian hunter-gatherers, Levant 48–9

Naukratis trading colony, Nile Delta 134

Nebuchadnezzar, king 111

Nekau II, pharaoh 104

Nero, emperor 155

Niger river 22–4, 23*f*, 118, 338, 342
  Bend 124, 173
  Delta, agro-pastoralism 80
  Inner Delta 22, 24*f*, 115*f*, 116–18, 116*f*, 117*f*
  Inner Delta, Neolithic age 60–1

Niger-Congo languages 61

Nile delta 18–21
  early farming 73–4

Nile river 5, 19–24, 20*f*, 21*f*, 50, 338, 343*f*
  flood levels (935–1094) 221–2
  navigation and river craft 91*f*, 92*f*

Nile valley 10, 86–8, 90*f*
  beginnings of pastoralism 65
  hunter-gatherers 56
  timber and mineral deposits 88
  as zone of innovation 342

Nilo-Saharan language group 34, 34*f*, 61

Nin-Bèrè glass eye bead, Sèno Plain 125

Nineveh, battle of (627) 186

Nobadia kingdom, Nubia 164, 201

Nok culture, Nigeria 81, 115*f*, 120–1
  terracotta figurines 120–2, 120*f*, 121*f*

Normans:
  kingdom of Africa 256
  Sicily 260
  Tripoli 265

North African coast as zone of innovation 341

north-east trade winds 27, 28*f*

North Equatorial Current 27, 28*f*

Nubia 92–3, 94, 95*f*, 249

Christianity 203

Sandstone Aquifer System 15–16
  see also Kush, Nubian kingdom of

Nubian Swell 19

Numidia 103, 111, 157
  cavalry 126
  as client kingdom of Rome 146–50, 147*f*
  and the Punic Wars 112–14
  Thugga (Roman Dougga) mausoleum 158–9, 160*f*

Obelisk of Aksum 166, 166*f*

obsidian from Pantelleria 86

Oduduwa, Yaruba god 307

Oea (Tripoli) 112

oil palm 77, 78

oilseed noog (niger seed) 77

Old Dongola throne hall, Sudan 267, 268*f*

Oldowan tradition 30, 32
  Mode 1 tools 39

Olduvai Gorge, Tanzania 30, 31*f*
  hand axe 32*f*

Omanis of Arabia 347

Opone (modern Ras Hafun), Somalia 167, 168*f*

Oranian phase 46

Ormuz island, Persian Gulf 316

Ottoman empire:
  1400–1600 in the north 321, 322*f*
  attacks on Ethiopia 326–7
  expansion in the Maghrib and western Mediterranean 321–4, 322*f*, 325*f*, 334, 335, 347

Oued Dra'a river 105

Ounjougou pottery (9400 BC), Mali 58

Palmeda missile points 85

Pangaea 3*f*

Pangwari E Nok figurine, Nigeria 121*f*

Paranthropos 30

Pastoral Period (5200–1000 BC) rock art, Tassili-n-Ajjer, Algeria 70, 71*f*

pastoralism, beginnings 64, 65–70, 67*f*

pastoralist/farmer tensions 349–50

pearl millet (*Pennisetum glaucum*) 77, 79, 81, 83, 120, 130, 170

peas 77

Periplus of the Erythraean Sea 142, 343

Periplus of Hanno 28–9, 104–6, 106*f*

Permian period 2

Persian empire:
    control of Kush 136
    rule in Egypt 134, 138*f*

Philip II, king of Spain 328

Phoenician colonists and trade 103–4, 111–12, 112*f*, 142
    Atlantic coastal exploration 124
    sailors 25–6, 344

pilgrim caravans 345, 346*f*

pilgrimage to Mecca, *see* hajj pilgrimage to Mecca

plate tectonics 337–8

Pliny 150, 153, 155

population growth 349–54

Portugal:
    African expeditions 296–304, 298*f*, 300*f*, 301*f*, 302*f*, 303*f*, 305*f*, 311*f*
    consolidation and exploration beyond the Guinea coast 311*f*, 312–16
    maritime routes to India and the Far East 334–5
    Moroccan Atlantic coastline 315*f*, 316–17, 316*f*
    Moroccan enclaves 327–8, 329*f*
    sailors and ships 29

pottery 85, 86
    Cardial Ware (Impressed Ware) 76
    Nabta Playa, Egypt 59*f*
    Neolithic 58, 59*f*

Ounjougou (9400 BC), Mali 58

precession of the equinoxes and climate change in the Sahara 6–7

Procopius 187, 188, 190

Ptolemy of Mauritania 154

Ptolemy 167

Ptolemys, *see under* Egypt

Publius Sulpicius Quirinius 153

Punic Wars:
    First (264–241 BC) 112
    Second (218–201 BC) 112
    Third (149–146 BC) 112, 145

Punt, land of 99–101, 100*f*

Punt–Egypt sea route 99–101

Qadan site, Egypt 56

Qaitbay, Mamluk sultan 323*f*

Qal'a Bani Hammad, northern Algeria 225*f*

Qasr Ibrim site, Nubia 202*f*

Qattara Depression, Egypt 14

Rameses III, pharaoh 95*f*

Rao/Nguiguela burial site gold pectoral, Senegal 240*f*, 241, 243*f*

Red Sea 17–18, 25, 27, 138–42, 140*f*, 343*f*

Red Sea Hills copper 89

Red Sea trade:
    and Byzantium 186
    and the Fatimids 224
    Roman period 163*f*, 164–6, 165*f*, 167, 174

refugees and migrants 350

Rhapta, southeast African coast 167, 168*f*

rice growing, Sahel 117

rift valleys 4, 4*f*, 5*f*, 337

rock art, Saharan 6, 14, 69–70, 70*f*, 125, 126*f*, 127*f*
    Bubalus Period (10,000–4000 BC), Fazzan region 70, 71*f*

Pastoral Period (5200–1000 BC), Tassili-n-Ajjer, Algeria 70, 71*f*

Roger I of Sicily 256

Roger II of Sicily 258

Rome, republic and empire:
    Africa within the empire 156–63, 158*f*, 164–7, 165*f*, 166*f*
    African empire creation 146–52
    disintegration of empire 183–7
    and Egypt 150–1, 156, 159–61, 162*f*
    expedition up the Nile (AD 60s) 155
    grain supplies from Africa 156–7
    Kushites, Meroe and Aksum relations 164–7, 165*f*, 166*f*
    Sahel trading networks 174–8, 175*f*, 176*f*
    tetrarchy (rule of four) 184
    and the Vandals 187–8, 190

Royal Navy's West Africa Squadron, British 348

Saba kingdom, Yemen 139

Sa'di family in Morocco 327–8

Sahara desert 10–16, 11*f*, 12*f*
    astronomical cycles and climate change 7
    from space 2*f*
    trade routes (760–1150 AD) 227–30

Sahel 16, 22
    central and eastern communities (140 BC–AD 400) 247–9, 248*f*
    corridor as zone of innovation 342
    effects of contemporary climate change 350–4, 351*f*
    farming communities 79
    hierarchical social systems in western 207, 208
    rainfall cycles 354
    Roman period 172–3, 174*f*, 175*f*
    social unrest, present day 349–50

trading networks, Roman period
174–8, 175*f*, 176*f*

western communities (400–760)
204–10

western neighbouring polities
(140 BC–AD 400) 241–7

western trading networks 207–8

Sahel Initiative 353–4, 353*f*

Saite dynasty, Egypt 134

Salah al-Din (Saladin) 265

salt and gold trade, Saharan 14, 124,
229, 340*f*

salt lake sand marshes 14

salt production, Taghaza, western
Sahara 14, 335

Sanhaja Berbers 210–11, 227, 230, 231,
334, 344

São Jorge fort, Elmina 304, 305*f*,
306–7, 306*f*

Saqqara tombs, Egypt 92

Sasanian empire 183, 185–6, 194–5

Sataspes 107

Sayfawa dynasty, Kanem-Bornu 283

science and scholarship diffusion in
Andalusia 260–1

Scipio Africanus, Roman consul
114

'Scramble for Africa', European 347,
348–9

Sea People 65, 95, 95*f*, 96, 111, 132

seas and oceans of North Africa 25–9

Sebastian I, king of Portugal 328

Şehname-i Selim Han (Seyyid
Lokman) 325*f*

Sekhemkhet tomb, Egypt 91

Selim I, Ottoman sultan 321

Selim II, Ottoman sultan 324

Seneca 155

Senegal river 22–3, 29, 105, 107

Septimius Severus, emperor 172

Sergius, Byzantine commander 194

Seti I tomb, Egypt 110*f*

Seventh Crusade (1248–54) 256, 266,
267*f*

Shajar al-Durr, Bahri dynasty ruler,
Egypt 266

Shanga trading port 224, 271, 273*f*

sheep, domestication and
introduction to Africa 66–8,
67*f*; *see also* Barbary sheep

Shia Muslims 217, 218

Shihab al-Din al-Umari 258

Shimbra Kure, battle of (1529),
Ethiopia 326

Sicily 112
Norman regime 256

sickles, Neolithic stone 56, 57*f*

Sijilmasa trading centre, Morocco
215, 230, 232

silent trade 240

Sinan Pasha 324

Sittus 148

Siwa oasis, Western Desert 123, 123*f*,
128

slave trade 125, 131, 167, 170
Alodia 204
Nubia 222
outlawed by Britain (1807) 347
repatriation to West Africa
347–8, 348*f*
and the Roman world 177

Socota island, Indian Ocean 316

Sodmein Cave, Red Sea coast 67

Somali Muslims, war with Ethiopia
326–7

Songhai empire vi, 173, 274, 277, 279,
294, 344
1400–1600 317–20, 318*f*, 320*f*
invasion by the Moors 329–34,
330*f*, 335

Soninke kingdom of Ghana 229, 230,
232, 236, 241, 277

Sonni Ali, Songhai king 317

Sophonisba, Numidian queen 114

sorghum (*Sorghum bicolor*) 77, 78,
78*f*, 81, 83, 130, 170

South Equatorial Current 27, 28*f*

south-east trade winds 27, 28*f*

Spain, Arab invasion 199, 200, 201

Strabo 114, 146

Strait of Gibraltar 25

Sudan 349–50

Suebi tribe 185*f*, 187

Suellius Flaccus 155–6

Suetonius Paulinus 154

Sufriyya sect, Muslim 215

Suleiman the Magnificent, Ottoman
sultan 321, 322

Sundjata, Malinke war-leader 276

Sunni Muslims 217, 218

Susu tribe 241, 275–6

Swahili language 223

Syphax, king of Numidia 112, 114

Tabula Rogeriana 258, 259*f*

Tacfarinas 154

Tacitus 154

Tadmekka (modern Essouk), Mali
244–7, 245*f*, 246*f*, 277

Taforalt cave, Morocco 46

Taghaza salt mines, Mali 320, 330–1

Taghriba (March West, Abdel
Rahman el-Abnudi) 226

Takrur kingdom, Senegal 241

Tamar Hat site, Algeria 48

Tamashek language 210

Tangier (Tingis) 163, 199, 297

Tanit temple, Thugga, Tunisia 159

Tarikh al-Sudan chronicle (Abd
al-Sa'di) 317

Tariq, Berber commander 199, 200,
226

Tartessos, Spain 111

Tassili-n-Ajjer (Plateau of Rivers),
Algeria 11–12

Tébessa defensive walls, Algeria 192

t'ef (cereal grain) 77

Terrence 157

Tethys Sea (now the Mediterranean) 2

Thapsus, battle of (46 BC), Tunisia
152

Thebes 136

Theophilus 167

Thugga (Roman Dougga), Tunisia
158–9, 159*f*

Baal Hammon temple 159

Thutmose I, pharaoh 98

Tiberius, emperor 154

Tichitt-Walata-Néma escarpment,
early farmers 79–80, 80*f*, 81*f*,
115–16

Tilutan, Lamtuna leader 230

Timbuktu 22, 278–9, 279*f*, 317, 331, 333
and Islamic fundamentalists 352,
352*f*

Timgad (Colonia Marciana Ulpia
Traiana Thamugadi), Algeria
161*f*

Tin Hanan, queen 180, 210

Tin Hanan burial site, Ablessa, Algeria
179–80, 180*f*

Tingis, *see* Tangier

Ti-n-Torha huts, Libya 60

Tondibi, battle of (1591), Mali 332

Tondidarou megaliths, Mali 208,
208*f*, 209*f*

tools 39, 41–2
Aterian, African Middle Stone
Age 43–4, 43*f*
Dabban phase 46
earliest 30–1, 31*f*, 32
Iberomaurusian phase 46–52, 47*f*
tool kit 46, 47*f*
Mode 1 39
Mode 2 39
Mode 3 39, 41–2
Mode 4 39
Mode 5 39

Tordesillas, treaty of (1494) 313

tortoiseshell 166, 167

Travels (*The Rihla*, Ibn Battuta)
269–71, 272, 288

Tripolitania 150
Roman forts and outposts 172,
172*f*

Tristão, Nuno 299–300

Tritonis, Lake 109

trypanosomiasis (sleeping sickness)
79

tsetse fly (*Glossina* species) 79

Tuareg people 210, 282, 317, 331, 334,
344, 345*f*, 352

Tulunid dynasty, Egypt 213, 214*f*, 216

Tunis 324, 325*f*

Tunis, battle of (1270), Eighth
Crusade 256, 257*f*

Turan Shah, emir 265

Tyre, Lebanon 111

Uan Tabu rock shelter, Libya 43, 60

U-j tomb, Abydos, Upper Egypt 93*f*

Uli, Mali ruler 277

Uluç Ali, pasha of Algiers 325*f*

Umar ibn al-Khattab, caliph 186, 195,
196–7

Umayyad caliphate, Córdoba, Spain
197, 213, 214*f*, 220, 226

underground aqueducts 128

United Nations (UN) estimate of
climate change effects 350

Uqba ibn Nafi 197–8, 199, 200

Uthman, caliph 197

Utica, Tunisia 111

Valerius Festus 155, 156

Vandals in Africa 184, 185*f*, 187–92,
189*f*
Berber tribal relations 188–91
Rome relations 187–8, 190

Venice Peace treaty (1573) 324

Visigoth kingdom 199

Wad Ben Naqa storage jars, Sudan 137

Waganda people 235

Waggag ibn Zalwi 231

Walata, desert-edge town, Mauritania
278, 279, 282

War of the Castilian Succession
(1475–1479) 304

war elephants, East African 141*f*, 142

warfare as part of the social system
339

Wattasid dynasty (est. 1459), Morocco
293–4, 327

Wattasid-Portuguese alliance 327

Watwat mausoleum, Libya 171*f*

Wayna Daga, battle of (1543), Ethiopia
327

West African Monsoon system 354

wheat 87

White Nile 19

wild animals, trade in 170, 171*f*

Xerxes, king of Persia 107, 136

Yahya ibn Ibrahim 231

Yahya ibn Mahmud al-Wasiti 346*f*

Yahya ibn Umar 231, 232

yams 77

Yaqut al-Hamawi 258

Yeha temple, Ethiopia 139

Yemen 195

Yongle, Ming emperor 294

Yoruba mythology 307

Younger Dryas 7, 8, 41, 52, 53*f*, 54*f*

Yusuf ibn Tashfin, caliph 232, 234

Zaghawa people 247–9

Zama, battle of (202 BC), Tunisia 112,
114

Zarai customs tariff, Numidia 174–5

Zayyanid kingdom of Tlemcen 255,
261–2, 263, 263*f*, 264

zebu cattle (*Bos indicus*) 83, 84*f*

Zenata Berbers 225, 227, 230; *see also*
Marinids

Zhao Rukuo, Chinese official 269

Zheng He, admiral 293, 294–6, 295*f*,
298*f*

Zinkekra hill-fort, Garamantian 130*f*,
131

Zirids, Berber dynasty 224–8
relations with Fatimid caliphate,
Egypt 226

Zliten mosaic, Libya 171*f*

zones of vegetation 16–18, 17*f*